UNIVERSITY LIBRARY
U.W.-STEVENS POINT

W9-BEE-454

The Private Side of American History

READINGS IN EVERYDAY LIFE

UNIVERSITY LIBRARY
UW-STEVENS POINT

The Private Side of American History

READINGS IN EVERYDAY LIFE

I TO 1877

EDITED BY Gary B. Nash
UNIVERSITY OF CALIFORNIA, LOS ANGELES

UNDER THE GENERAL EDITORSHIP OF
John Morton Blum
YALE UNIVERSITY

Harcourt Brace Jovanovich, Inc.

NEW YORK   CHICAGO   SAN FRANCISCO   ATLANTA

© 1975 by Harcourt Brace Jovanovich, Inc.

All rights reserved. No part of this publication may be reproduced
or transmitted in any form or by any means, electronic or mechanical,
including photocopy, recording, or any information storage and retrieval
system, without permission in writing from the publisher.

ISBN: 0-15-571962-9

Library of Congress Catalog Card Number: 74-25578

Printed in the United States of America

PICTURE CREDITS

COVER Clockwise from top left: Library of Congress; Library of Congress; Culver Pictures;
Boston Athenaeum; Culver Pictures; Library of Congress.

7 Arents Collection, The New York Public Library (Astor, Lenox, and Tilden Foundations).
25 American Antiquarian Society. 42 Library of Congress. 59 Historical Pictures Service,
Chicago. 91 Courtesy Museum of Fine Arts, Boston. 103 Historical Pictures Service, Chicago.
123 American Antiquarian Society. 156 Culver Pictures. 179 The Bettmann Archive. 198
Flax Scutching Bee, Linton Park, National Gallery of Art, Washington, gift of Edgar William
and Bernice Chrysler Garbisch. 213 Courtesy New York Historical Society, New York City. 237
Courtesy Abby Aldrich Rockefeller Folk Art Collection. 269 Culver Pictures. 292 H. Armstrong
Roberts. 313 The Bettmann Archive. 330 Culver Pictures.

HN
57
.P74
v. 1
c.3

Preface

The Private Side of American History, Volume I, is designed to supplement traditional textbooks that emphasize the political and intellectual aspects of history.
This collection of readings draws on both primary and secondary sources to offer
a vivid description of everyday life in rural and urban America, from the colonial
period through the third quarter of the nineteenth century. The selections provide
a fresh perspective from which to view such vital but often neglected aspects
of American history as work; family life, child-rearing, and sex; education
and entertainment; religion; health, disease, and death; and conflicts created by
encounters between diverse population groups—Indians and colonists, blacks and
whites, and immigrants and established residents.

Arranged in roughly chronological order, the sixteen selections are grouped
into four sections, each of which concludes with an annotated bibliography. The
headnotes provided for the selections attempt to place the subject of each selection
in its historical context. A brief introduction to the volume describes the major
areas that should be considered in a historical study of everyday life.

For expert assistance and editorial criticism in preparing the manuscript for
this book I would like to thank Andrea Haight of Harcourt Brace Jovanovich. Thomas
A. Williamson and William J. Wisneski of Harcourt Brace Jovanovich originally sug-
gested the approach to American history reflected in this volume and offered
encouragement throughout. For scholarly assistance I would like to express my
appreciation to the following colleagues: Robert Bannister, Swarthmore College;
Carol Berkin, The Bernard M. Baruch College of the City University of New York;
John Morton Blum, Yale University; Paula S. Fass, University of California, Berkeley;
Thomas R. Frazier, The Bernard M. Baruch College of the City University of New
York; Alexander Saxton, University of California, Los Angeles; Robert Sklar, The
University of Michigan; Stephan Thernstrom, Harvard University; Laurence Veysey,
University of California, Santa Cruz; and Daniel J. Walkowitz, Rutgers University.

GARY B. NASH

253095

Contents

1790–1830
The Early Republic

1830–1877
The Expanding Nation

Topical Table of Contents

The Private Side of American History

READINGS IN EVERYDAY LIFE

Introduction

History has traditionally been written as a record of public rather than private events. The growth of institutions, the election of office-holders, the passage of laws, the conduct of diplomacy and war, the expansion of scientific knowledge, and the process of economic development—these are the major categories employed by historians to reveal the past, as the table of contents of most history textbooks will indicate. Of course any history that did not investigate these topics would be incomplete. But American historians are recognizing that the public aspects of our past reveal far less than we would like to know about how our society and culture developed. For example, though we may understand the forms of government under which the colonies were founded, or the commercial relations between England and her New World colonies, or the rise of schools and colleges in the eighteenth century, we will still comprehend little about the feelings, motivations, and behavior of the great mass of colonizers. In the nineteenth century we may profitably study the Bank War, the building of canals and railroads, the abolitionist crusade, or the evolution of the Whig Party. But the past will not have come alive because we will know virtually nothing about how people lived, felt, and interacted behind the curtain of public events.

For two reasons, then, the history of public events is lifeless and limited, unable to move us or recreate a feeling of the past. First, it deals for the most part with public figures—the important politicians, business leaders, intellectuals, and military commanders. As many critics have noted recently, this kind of historical writing is elitist. It concentrates on the few and ignores the many, assuming that it was the "dynamic," successful few who led the "passive," ordinary many. By narrowing our vision in this way, historians indulge in a dangerous assumption about how events and movements occur. They bury from sight the fascinating and important story of all those who lived, worked, and died without leaving a footprint on the public record. Secondly, the history of public events is as narrow in its understanding of human motivation and behavior as it is in its choice of subjects. It tells us little about the hidden sources of human action and the intimate experiences of life that play such a vital role in public action. Even the most powerful individuals in history could not separate their private and public lives. So to ignore the private side of American history is to cut ourselves off from sources rich with explanatory potential.

The historian-novelist Leo Tolstoy understood both of these failings of traditional history when he wrote *War and Peace*, his great epic of the

Russian people during the Napoleonic Wars. "To study the laws of history," he argued, "we must completely change the subject of our observation, must leave aside kings, ministers, and generals, and study the common infinitesimally small elements by which the masses are moved. No one can say how far it is possible for man to advance in this way toward an understanding of the laws of history; but it is evident that only along that path does the possibility of discovering the laws of history lie." Many would doubt that historical "laws" can be discovered at all. But Tolstoy had hit upon an understanding of how a people or a nation may better be studied. A century later we are beginning to follow his advice. His concern was not only to study "the masses" but also to find the "infinitesimally small elements" that moved all people, whether they numbered among the elite or among the peasantry.

It is primarily to this second question—by what small elements of life are people moved?—that this collection of readings is addressed. Many other books in American history direct our attention to the "forgotten" or "historically voiceless" people of our past—Native Americans, Afro-Americans, Chicanos, women, the poor, the deviant, and so forth. Some of these groups figure prominently in the selections that follow simply because they made up the vast majority of the population. But the readings have not been selected for this reason, but rather because they deal with the "private side" of American history. They are concerned with the experience of living and the daily aspects of life that mattered most to individual Americans of the past and, collectively, to American society at large.

What are the "infinitesimally small elements" that are so important to the experience of a society? Very roughly, they are those aspects of life that occupy most of our waking hours today, just as they did the daily rounds of people in the past: *work*—the performance of tasks, whether for pay or not, that consumes the greatest proportion of our time; *learning*—whether transmitted formally in schools or inculcated informally through everyday contact with family, peers, strangers around us, the media, or other sources; *family and sexual relations*—through which the most intimate desires and emotions are expressed and the most basic needs fulfilled; *reflection*—whether in the form of religious worship, political or social commitment, or merely daydreaming; *physical preservation*—the simple but vital concern for our health and the perpetual struggle against sickness and death; *social relations*—interaction with the world around us, which most often involves no more than conforming to the rules of the community but sometimes involves violence and war against our fellow beings; *protest and political action*—by which we express dissatisfaction with those around us, ourselves, and even forces beyond our ken or control. If studied with care, these areas of human experience, taken together, are profoundly revealing of the life of a society in the past. They apply to the rich and poor, the mighty and humble, male and female, black and white. And though they vary in importance depending upon the era under consideration, all have played important roles at every stage of human history.

It is well to keep in mind that the boundaries between the private dimensions of American life and the better known history of public events is usually blurred. For example, when epidemic disease broke out in our early cities public officials were obliged to take action. We read mostly of these public policies but comprehend little about how city dwellers experienced smallpox or yellow fever and how they were affected by it. When men and women took to the streets in pre-Revolutionary Boston they were expressing a private need to be heard in public matters. We can read much about the effects of their actions on English policy and colonial politics but still understand little about how their private lives were touched by participation in violent protest. Similarly, the private and public aspects of history overlapped in war. Historians have traditionally told us much about how wars began, how they were fought, and how diplomats drew up treaties to end conflict. But war involved personal trauma and changed the lives of its participants. Conversely, what individuals brought to war in terms of their private makeup had much to do with the outcome. Private and public life mingled everywhere, and only by adding studies of everyday life to the public record can we fully appreciate the richness and complexity of the past.

History is the record of change, so we must be attentive to how the private aspects of American life became transformed on the road from early Jamestown to Watergate. Careful comparison of articles that deal with the same aspect of everyday life in different eras should make this clear. Attitudes toward work among emigrating Englishmen in the seventeenth century, for example, played an important role in the way society evolved on the Chesapeake, as Edmund Morgan's essay demonstrates. By the early nineteenth century the work attitudes of urbanized, semi-industrial workers within a capitalist system were strikingly different, as David Montgomery's article reveals. Methods of child-rearing, to take another case, differed greatly between New Englanders and Iroquois in the seventeenth century, as is evident from the studies by John Demos and Anthony Wallace included in this collection. And neither culture transited the next two centuries without altering its modes of raising children. Those alterations are of no small importance. Indeed, many historians feel that without understanding changing attitudes toward children and modes of rearing them we can never obtain more than a clouded and incomplete picture of how societies have evolved over time. Methods and motives of protest also changed, as a comparison of the Stamp Act Riots of the 1760s in Boston with the conflict between weavers and artisans in Philadelphia in the 1840s will show. How the private side of life was changed by public events and, conversely, how changes in everyday life molded larger social and political movements are questions students will want to keep in mind as they ponder these essays.

One other reflection on the nature of social change is useful here. While the same aspect of everyday life can in many cases be studied in different eras, not every kind of experience is as inevitable a part of life as work or child-rearing. Dominant elements of everyday life were, in fact, replaced or modified, dramatically in some instances, as American society moved from the earliest colonial beginnings to the turbulent nineteenth century. For the first colonists, relations with native inhabitants of eastern

North America constituted a new and frightening experience. Invasion of an already inhabited land involved a fearsome contact with a "different" people; it produced violence on a massive scale; and it preoccupied the private thoughts of many men and women whose religiosity compelled them to seek a moral justification for this confrontation of cultures. But in the late eighteenth century, as Indian peoples withdrew to the west, this aspect of daily existence diminished except on the frontier. Another dominant theme in everyday life in the colonial period was illness and death. Infant mortality was high, the average lifespan was short, and epidemic diseases were common. Everyone had seen death and few were the families that had not buried several children before they reached adolescence. But intimacy with death waned in the nineteenth century. Medical science conquered many epidemic diseases, the average lifespan increased, and hospitals were created for the sick and dying. The sight and sound of mortal illness and death were gradually placed beyond the experience of most people. While these aspects of private life became less important, others rose in significance. Entertainment assumed far greater importance as working hours were reduced. Political involvement, only an occasional activity for the widely dispersed agricultural population of the eighteenth century, began to pervade the lives of an industrializing, urbanizing, nineteenth-century people. Other examples could be provided. But students will want to make their own calculations of when and how the "infinitesimally small elements" of American society changed, for taking part in the process of exploration is both the surest and most exciting way of gaining a fuller understanding of the past.

1600–1740
The Colonizers
and
the Colonized

The Labor Problem at
Jamestown, 1607–18

EDMUND S. MORGAN

In order to understand the everyday lives of the first European-Americans, we must understand their everyday lives as Englishmen, Irishmen, Scotsmen, Germans, Spaniards, Frenchmen, and so forth. Edmund Morgan whets that understanding in the selection that follows. By tracing attitudes toward labor and patterns of work in early seventeenth-century England, he is able to explain what has heretofore seemed hardly explicable—that men would starve to death and succumb to disease in an environment where Native Americans had lived satisfactorily for centuries, even without the aid of iron-age technology. Attitudes toward time, work, and disciplined behavior that we commonly accept in our own lives had little meaning in an earlier age.

Morgan also emphasizes that ideas about the natives of the New World reverberated in the heads of almost all who immigrated to early Virginia. Given the extensive experience of other Europeans in America for more than a century and the broad literature on the subject, it could hardly have been otherwise. Europeans approached North America as we might approach another planet—filled with anxieties about the reception they would meet, projecting onto the inhabitants of a strange land many of the fantasies they entertained about the least admissible aspects of their own experience. At the same time, the colonists expected the Indians to be an exploitable source of labor and were severely disappointed when their expectations proved ill founded.

Exploitation of labor did, however, become the central reality of life in early Virginia. Once the cultivation of tobacco as an export product was successfully established, the colony quickly became an extraordinarily oppressive society. While a few entrepreneurs and plantation owners reaped handsome profits, thousands of indentured servants, most of them men living without women, worked year after year without adequate food or shelter, debilitated by disease and malnutrition, and able to blot out their despair only with alcohol. The wretched lives of ordinary people in Virginia during and after the first tobacco boom were proof of how inherited ideas about work and social relationships could rapidly disintegrate under harsh and isolated conditions. In the absence of the restraining institutions of government and morality that applied in England, the exploiter was rebuked, if at all, only by his own inner murmurings.

Morgan suggests at the close of this selection that the methods of exploiting labor that were firmly established in early Virginia laid the foundation for the institution of Southern slavery. His exploration of attitudes toward work that were current in late sixteenth- and early seventeenth-century England helps us understand how those attitudes, transplanted to the Chesapeake, made the Virginia colony fertile ground for the exploitation of human lives.

The importance of Virginia far transcended the numbers who went there or the territory they occupied. In relations with the native inhabitants of the region, in patterns of exploiting labor, and in redefinitions of liberty and authority, Virginia left its mark on all that followed. The Virginians were the first English immigrants to set down permanent roots on the continent, and they provided both models and anti-models for all later colonists. Their imprint, of course, was strongest on the colonial South, but it was not limited to that area.

The story of Jamestown, the first permanent English settlement in America, has a familiar place in the history of the United States. We all know of the tribulations that kept the colony on the point of expiring: the shortage of supplies, the hostility of the Indians, the quarrels among the leaders, the reckless search for gold, the pathetic search for a passage to the Pacific, and the neglect of the crucial business of growing food to stay alive. Through the scene moves the figure of Captain John Smith, a little larger than life, trading for corn among the Indians and driving the feckless crew to work. His departure in October 1609 results in near disaster. The settlers fritter away their time and energy, squander their provisions, and starve. Sir Thomas Gates, arriving after the settlement's third winter, finds only sixty men out of six hundred still alive and those sixty scarcely able to walk.

In the summer of 1610 Gates and Lord La Warr get things moving again with a new supply of men and provisions, a new absolute form of government, and a new set of laws designed to keep everybody at work. But when Gates and La Warr leave for a time, the settlers fall to their old ways. Sir Thomas Dale, upon his arrival in May 1611, finds them at "their daily and usuall workes, bowling in the streetes." [1] But Dale brings order out of chaos. By enlarging and enforcing the colony's new law code (the famous Lawes Divine, Morall and Martiall) he starts the settlers working again and rescues them from starvation by making them plant corn. By 1618 the colony is getting on its feet and ready to carry on without the stern regimen of a Smith or a Dale. There are still evil days ahead, as the Virginia Company sends over men more rapidly than the infant colony can absorb them. But the settlers, having found in tobacco a valuable crop for export, have at last gone to work with a will, and Virginia's future is assured.

"The Labor Problem at Jamestown, 1607–18," by Edmund S. Morgan. From *American Historical Review* 76 (1971): 595–610. Reprinted by permission of the author.

[1] Ralph Hamor, *A True Discourse of the Present State of Virginia* (London, 1615; Richmond, 1957), 26.

The story probably fits the facts insofar as they can be known. But it does not quite explain them. The colony's long period of starvation and failure may well be attributed to the idleness of the first settlers, but idleness is more an accusation than an explanation. Why did men spend their time bowling in the streets when their lives depended on work? Were they lunatics, preferring to play games rather than clear and plow and plant the crops that could have kept them alive?

The mystery only deepens if we look more closely at the efforts of Smith, Gates, La Warr, and Dale to set things right. In 1612 John Smith described his work program of 1608: "the company [being] divided into tennes, fifteenes, or as the businesse required, 4 hours each day was spent in worke, the rest in pastimes and merry exercise." Twelve years later Smith rewrote this passage and changed the figure of four hours to six hours.[2] But even so, what are we to make of a six-hour day in a colony teetering on the verge of extinction?

The program of Gates and La Warr in the summer of 1610 was no more strenuous. William Strachey described it:

> it is to be understood that such as labor are not yet so taxed but that easily they perform the same and ever by ten of the clock have done their morning's work: at what time they have their allowances [of food] set out ready for them, and until it be three of the clock again they take their own pleasure, and afterward, with the sunset, their day's labor is finished.[3]

The Virginia Company offered much the same account of this period. According to a tract issued late in 1610, "the setled times of working (to effect all themselves, or the Adventurers neede desire) [requires] no more pains than from sixe of clocke in the morning untill ten, and from two of the clocke in the afternoone till foure." [4] The long lunch period described for 1610 was also a feature of the *Lawes Divine, Morall and Martiall* as enforced by Dale. The total working hours prescribed in the *Lawes* amounted to roughly five to eight hours a day in summer and three to six hours in winter.[5]

[2] John Smith, *Travels and Works,* ed. Edward Arber and A. G. Bradley (Edinburgh, 1910), 1: 149; 2: 466.

[3] L. B. Wright, ed., *A Voyage to Virginia in 1609* (Charlottesville, 1964), 69–70.

[4] *A True Declaration of the Estate of the Colonie in Virginia* (London, 1610), reprinted in Peter Force, ed., *Tracts and Other Papers* (Washington, 1844), 3, no. 1: 20; Smith, *Travels and Works,* 2: 502. Captain Daniel Tucker maintained a similar program in Bermuda in 1616: "according to the Virginia order, hee set every one [that] was with him at Saint Georges, to his taske, to cleere grounds, fell trees, set corne, square timber, plant vines and other fruits brought out of England. These by their taske—Masters by breake a day repaired to the wharfe, from thence to be imployed to the place of their imployment, till nine of the clocke, and then in the after-noone from three till Sunneset." *Ibid.,* 653.

[5] *For the Colony in Virginia Brittannia: Lawes Divine, Morall and Martiall* (London, 1612), 61–62.

It is difficult, then, to escape the conclusion that there was a great deal of unemployment or underemployment at Jamestown, whether it was the idleness of the undisciplined in the absence of strong government or the idleness of the disciplined in the presence of strong government. How are we to account for this fact? By our standards the situation at Jamestown demanded hard and continuous work. Why was the response so feeble?

One answer, given by the leaders of the colony, is that the settlers included too many ne'er-do-wells and too many gentlemen who "never did know what a dayes work was." [6] Hard work had to wait until harder men were sent. Another answer may be that the Jamestown settlers were debilitated by hunger and disease. The victims of scurvy, malaria, typhoid, and diphtheria may have been left without the will or the energy to work. Still another answer, which has echoed through the pages of our history books, attributed the difficulty to the fact that the settlement was conducted on a communal basis: everybody worked for the Virginia Company and everybody was fed (while supplies lasted) by the company, regardless of how much he worked or failed to work. Once land was distributed to individuals and men were allowed to work for themselves, they gained the familiar incentives of private enterprise and bent their shoulders to the wheel.[7] These explanations are surely all valid—they are all supported by the testimony of contemporaries—and they go far toward explaining the lazy pioneers of Jamestown. But they do not reach to a dimension of the problem that contemporaries would have overlooked because they would have taken it for granted. They do not tell us what ideas and attitudes about work, carried from England, would have led the first English settlers to expect so little of themselves in a situation that demanded so much. The Jamestown settlers did not leave us the kind of private papers that would enable us to examine directly their ideas and attitudes, as we can those of the Puritans who settled New England a few years later. But in the absence of direct evidence we may discover among the ideas current in late sixteenth- and early seventeenth-century England some clues to the probable state of mind of the first Virginians, clues to the way they felt about work, whether in the Old World or the New, clues to habits of thinking that may have conditioned their perceptions of what confronted them at Jamestown, clues even to the tangled web of motives that made later Virginians masters of slaves.

Englishmen's ideas about the New World at the opening of the seventeenth century were based on a century of European exploration and settlement. The Spanish, whose exploits surpassed all others, had not attempted to keep their success a secret, and by the middle of the sixteenth

[6] Smith, *Travels and Works*, 2: 487.
[7] A much more sophisticated version of this explanation is suggested by Professor Sigmund Diamond in his discussion of the development of social relationships in Virginia, "From Organization to Society: Virginia in the Seventeenth Century," *American Journal of Sociology*, 63 (1958): 457–75; see also his "Values as an Obstacle to Economic Growth: The American Colonies," *Journal of Economic History*, 27 (1967): 561–75.

century Englishmen interested in America had begun translating Spanish histories and memoirs in an effort to rouse their countrymen to emulation.[8] The land that emerged from these writings was, except in the Arctic regions, an Eden, teeming with gentle and generous people who, before the Spanish conquest, had lived without labor, or with very little, from the fruits of a bountiful nature.[9] There were admittedly some unfriendly exceptions who made a habit of eating their more attractive neighbors; but they were a minority, confined to a few localities, and in spite of their ferocity were scarcely a match for Europeans armed with guns.[10] Englishmen who visited the New World confirmed the reports of natural abundance. Arthur Barlowe, for example, reconnoitering the North Carolina coast for Walter Raleigh, observed that "the earth bringeth foorth all things in aboundance, as in the first creation, without toile or labour," while the people were "most gentle, loving, and faithfull, void of all guile, and treason, and such as lived after the manner of the golden age. . . ."[11]

English and European readers may have discounted the more extravagant reports of American abundance, for the same authors who praised the land often gave contradictory accounts of the hardships they had suffered in it. But anyone who doubted that riches were waiting to be plucked from Virginia's trees had reason to expect that a good deal might be plucked from the people of the land. Spanish experience had shown that Europeans could thrive in the New World without undue effort by exploiting the natives. With a mere handful of men the Spanish had conquered an enormous population of Indians in the Caribbean, Mexico, and Peru and had put them to work. In the chronicles of Peter Martyr Englishmen learned how it was done. Apart from the fact that the Indians were naturally gentle, their division into a multitude of kingdoms, frequently at odds with one another, made it easy to play off one against another. By aiding one group against its enemies the Spaniards had made themselves masters of both.[12]

The story of English plans to imitate and improve on the Spanish strategy is a long one. It begins at least as early as Francis Drake's foray in Panama in 1572–73, when he allied with a band of runaway slaves to rob

[8] See especially the translation of Peter Martyr, in Richard Eden, *The Decades of the new worlde or west India* (London, 1555); a useful bibliographical history is John Parker, *Books to Build an Empire* (Amsterdam, 1966).

[9] Gustav H. Blanke, *Amerika im Englishen Schrifttum Des 16. und 17. Jahrhunderts Beitrage Zur Englischen Philologie,* 46 (Bochum-Langendreer, 1962), 98–104.

[10] Since Peter Martyr, the principal Spanish chronicler, identified most Indians who resisted the Spaniards as cannibals, this became the familiar sixteenth-century epithet for unfriendly Indians. It is doubtful that many tribes actually practiced cannibalism, though some certainly did.

[11] D. B. Quinn, ed., *The Roanoke Voyages 1584–1590,* Works issued by the Hakluyt Society, 2d ser., 104, 105 (London, 1955), 1: 108.

[12] Eden, *Decades, passim.* For English awareness of the Spanish example, see Smith, *Travels and Works,* 2: 578–81, 600–03, 955–56, and Susan M. Kingsbury, ed., *The Records of the Virginia Company of London* (Washington, 1906–35), 3: 558, 560–62.

a Spanish mule train carrying treasure from Peru across the isthmus to Nombre de Dios on the Caribbean.[13] The idea of joining with dissident natives or slaves either against their Spanish masters or against their wicked cannibalistic neighbors became an important ingredient in English plans for colonizing the New World. Martin Frobisher's experiences with the Eskimos in Baffin Land and Ralph Lane's with the Indians at Roanoke[14] should perhaps have disabused the English of their expectations; but they found it difficult to believe that any group of natives, and especially the noble savages of North America, would fail to welcome what they called with honest pride (and some myopia) the "gentle government" of the English.[15] If the savages first encountered by a colonizing expedition proved unfriendly, the thing to do was to make contact with their milder neighbors and rescue them from the tyranny of the unfriendly tribe, who must be their enemies and were probably cannibals to boot.[16]

The settlers at Jamestown tried to follow the strategy, locating their settlement as the plan called for, near the mouth of a navigable river, so that they would have access to the interior tribes if the coastal ones were hostile. But as luck would have it, they picked an area with a more powerful, more extensive, and more effective Indian government than existed anywhere else on the Atlantic Coast. King Powhatan had his enemies, the Monacans of the interior, but he felt no great need of English assistance against them, and he rightly suspected that the English constituted a larger threat to his hegemony than the Monacans did. He submitted with ill grace and no evident comprehension to the coronation ceremony that the Virginia Company arranged for him, and he kept his distance from Jamestown. Those of his warriors who visited the settlement showed no disposition to work for the English. The Monacans, on the other hand, lived too far inland (beyond the falls) to serve as substitute allies, and the English were thus deprived of their anticipated native labor.[17]

[13] Irene A. Wright, ed., *Documents concerning English Voyages to the Spanish Main 1569–1580*, Works issued by the Hakluyt Society, 2d ser., 71 (London, 1932), gives the original sources, both English and Spanish.

[14] Richard Collinson, ed., *The Three Voyages of Martin Frobisher*, Works issued by the Hakluyt Society, 1st ser., 38 (London, 1867), 131, 141–42, 145–50, 269, 271, 280–89; Quinn, *Roanoke Voyages*, 1: 275–88.

[15] The phrase "gentle government" is the younger Hakluyt's, in a proposal to make use of Drake's Negro allies from Panama for a colony at the Straits of Magellan. E. G. R. Taylor, ed., *The Original Writings and Correspondence of the two Richard Hakluyts*, Works issued by the Hakluyt Society, 2d ser., 76, 77 (London, 1935), 1: 142.

[16] *Ibid.*, 121, 2: 241–42, 246–49, 257–65, 275, 318, 342.

[17] The secondary literature on the Indians of Virginia is voluminous, but see especially Nancy O. Lurie, "Indian Cultural Adjustment to European Civilization," in J. M. Smith, ed., *Seventeenth-Century America* (Chapel Hill, 1959), 33–60. The most helpful original sources, on which most of our information is necessarily based, are Smith, *Travels and Works*, and William Strachey, *The Historie of Travell into Virginia Britania* (composed 1612), ed. L. B. Wright and V. Freund, Works issued by the Hakluyt Society, 2d ser., 103 (London, 1953), 53–116.

They did not, however, give up their expectations of getting it eventually. In 1615 Ralph Hamor still thought the Indians would come around "as they are easily taught and may be lenitie and faire usage . . . be brought, being naturally though ingenious, yet idly given, to be no lesse industrious, nay to exceede our English." [18] Even after the massacre of 1622 Virginians continued to dream of an Indian labor supply, though there was no longer to be any gentleness in obtaining it. Captain John Martin thought it better to exploit than exterminate the Indians, if only because they could be made to work in the heat of the day, when Englishmen would not. And William Claiborne in 1626 invented a device (whether mechanical or political is not clear) that he claimed would make it possible to keep Indians safely in the settlements and put them to work. The governor and council gave him what looks like the first American patent or copyright, namely a three-year monopoly, to "have holde and enjoy all the benefitt use and profitt of this his project or inventione," and they also assigned him a recently captured Indian, "for his better experience and tryall of his inventione." [19]

English expectations of the New World and its inhabitants died hard. America was supposed to be a land of abundance, peopled by natives who would not only share that abundance with the English but increase it under English direction. Englishmen simply did not envisage a need to work for the mere purpose of staying alive. The problem of survival as they saw it was at best political and at worst military.

Although Englishmen long remained under the illusion that the Indians would eventually become useful English subjects, it became apparent fairly early that Indian labor was not going to sustain the founders of Jamestown. The company in England was convinced by 1609 that the settlers would have to grow at least part of their own food. [20] Yet the settlers themselves had to be driven to that life-saving task. To understand their ineffectiveness in coping with a situation that their pioneering descendants would take in stride, it may be helpful next to inquire into some of the attitudes toward work that these first English pioneers took for granted. How much work and what kind of work did Englishmen at the opening of the seventeenth century consider normal?

The laboring population of England, by law at least, was required to work much harder than the regimen at Jamestown might lead us to expect. The famous Statute of Artificers of 1563 (re-enacting similar provisions from the Statute of Laborers of 1495) required all laborers to work from five in the morning to seven or eight at night from mid-March to mid-September, and during the remaining months of the year from day break to night. Time out for eating, drinking, and rest was not to exceed two

[18] *True Discourse*, 2. See also Strachey, *Historie of Travell*, 91–94; Alexander Whitaker, *Good Newes from Virginia* (London, 1613), 40.
[19] Susan M. Kingsbury, ed., *The Records of the Virginia Company of London* (Washington, 1906–35), 3: 705–06; H. R. McIlwaine, ed., *Minutes of the Council and General Court of Colonial Virginia* (Richmond, 1924), 111.
[20] *Records of the Virginia Company*, 3: 17, 27.

and a half hours a day.[21] But these were injunctions not descriptions. The Statute of Laborers of 1495 is preceded by the complaint that laborers "waste much part of the day . . . in late coming unto their work, early departing therefrom, long sitting at their breakfast, at their dinner and noon-meat, and long time of sleeping after noon." [22] Whether this statute or that of 1563 (still in effect when Jamestown was founded) corrected the situation is doubtful.[23] The records of local courts show varying efforts to enforce other provisions of the statute of 1563, but they are almost wholly silent about this provision,[24] in spite of the often-expressed despair of masters over their lazy and negligent laborers.[25]

It may be said that complaints of the laziness and irresponsibility of workmen can be met with in any century. Were such complaints in fact justified in sixteenth- and early seventeenth-century England? There is some reason to believe that they were, that life during those years was characterized by a large amount of idleness or underemployment.[26] The outstanding economic fact of the sixteenth and early seventeenth century in England was a rapid and more or less steady rise in prices, followed at some distance by a much smaller rise in wages, both in industry and in agriculture. The price of provisions used by a laborer's family rose faster than wages during the whole period from 1500 to 1640.[27] The government

---

[21] R. H. Tawney and Eileen Power, eds., *Tudor Economic Documents* (London, 1924), 1: 342. For some seventeenth-century prescriptions of long working hours, see Gervase Markham, *A Way to get Wealth* (13th ed.; London, 1676), 115–17; Henry Best, *Rural Economy in Yorkshire in 1641*, Surtees Society, *Publications*, 33 (Durham, 1857), 44. See also L. F. Salzman, *Building in England down to 1540* (Oxford, 1952), 61–65.

[22] 11 Henry 7, cap. 22, sec. 4; Douglas Knoop and G. P. Jones, *The Medieval Mason* (Manchester, 1933), 117.

[23] Tawney and Power, *Tudor Economic Documents*, 1: 352–63.

[24] A minor exception is in J. H. E. Bennett and J. C. Dewhurst, eds., *Quarter Sessions Records . . . for the County Palatine of Chester, 1559–1760*, Publications of the Record Society for the Publication of Original Documents relating to Lancashire and Cheshire, 94 (Chester, 1940), 95–96, where a master alleged that his apprentice, John Dodd, "hath negligently behaved him selfe in his service in idleinge and sleepinge in severalle places where he hath been comanded to work." But sleeping (from eight in the morning till two in the afternoon and beyond) was only one of Dodd's offenses. On the enforcement of other provisions in the statute, see Margaret G. Davies, *The Enforcement of English Apprenticeship . . . 1563–1642* (Cambridge, Mass., 1956); R. K. Kelsall, *Wage Regulation under the Statute of Artificers* (London, 1938); and R. H. Tawney, "The Assessment of Wages in England by Justices of the Peace," *Vierteljahrschrift für Sozial- und Wirtschaftsgeschichte*, 11 (1913): 307–37, 533–64.

[25] E. S. Furniss, *The Position of the Laborer in a System of Nationalism* (Boston, 1920), 117–34; E. P. Thompson, "Time, Work-Discipline, and Industrial Capitalism," *Past and Present*, no. 38 (1967): 56–97.

[26] D. C. Coleman, "Labour in the English Economy of the Sixteenth Century," *Economic History Review*, 2d ser., 8 (1956), reprinted in E. M. Carus Wilson, ed., *Essays in Economic History* (London, 1954–62), 2: 291–308.

[27] E. H. Phelps Brown and Sheila V. Hopkins, "Seven Centuries of Building Wages," *Economica*, 2d ser., 22 (1955): 95–206; "Seven Centuries of the Prices of Consumables, compared with Builders' Wage-Rates," *ibid.*, 2d ser., 23 (1956): 296–314;

made an effort to narrow the gap by requiring the justices in each county to readjust maximum wages at regular intervals. But the wages established by the justices reflected their own nostalgic notions of what a day's work ought to be worth in money, rather than a realistic estimate of what a man could buy with his wages. In those counties, at least, where records survive, the level of wages set by the justices crept upward very slowly before 1630.[28]

Wages were so inadequate that productivity was probably impaired by malnutrition. From a quarter to a half of the population lived below the level recognized at the time to constitute poverty. Few of the poor could count on regular meals at home, and in years when the wheat crop failed, they were close to starvation.[29] It is not surprising that men living under these conditions showed no great energy for work and that much of the population was, by modern standards, idle much of the time. The health manuals of the day recognized that people normally slept after eating, and the laws even prescribed a siesta for laborers in the summer time.[30] If they slept longer and more often than the laws allowed or the physicians recommended, if they loafed on the job and took unauthorized holidays, if they worked slowly and ineffectively when they did work, it may have been due at least in part to undernourishment and to the variety of chronic diseases that undernourishment brings in its train.[31]

Thus low wages may have begot low productivity that in turn justified low wages.[32] The reaction of employers was to blame the trouble on deficiencies, not of diet or wages, but of character. A prosperous yeoman like Robert Loder, who kept close track of his expenses and profits, was

---

"Wage Rates and Prices: Evidence for Population Pressure in the Sixteenth Century," *ibid.*, 2d ser., 24 (1957): 289–306; H. P. R. Finberg, ed., *The Agrarian History of England and Wales*, 4, *1500–1640*, ed. Joan Thirsk (Cambridge, 1967), 435–57, 531, 583–695.

[28] Tawney, "Assessment of Wages," 555–64; Kelsall, *Wage Regulation*, 67–86. Tawney and Kelsall both argue that the enforcement of maximum wages according to the statute of 1563 demonstrates a shortage of labor; but except in a few isolated instances (there may well have been local temporary shortages) the evidence comes from the period after the middle of the seventeenth century.

[29] Coleman, "Labour in the English Economy," 295; Peter Laslett adduces figures to show that actual starvation was probably rare among English peasants (*The World We Have Lost* [London, 1965], 107–27), but there can be little doubt that they were frequently close to it and chronically undernourished. See Carl Bridenbaugh, *Vexed and Troubled Englishmen* (New York, 1968), 91–98.

[30] Thomas Elyot, *The Castel of Helthe* (London, 1541), fols. 45–46; Thomas Cogan, *The Haven of Health* (London, 1589), 231–39; *The Englishmans Doctor, or The School of Salerne* (orig. pub. London, 1608) (New York, 1920), 77.

[31] E. P. Thompson, "Time, Work Discipline, and Industrial Capitalism."

[32] On the prevalence of such a vicious circle in pre-industrial countries, see W. F. Moore, *Industrialization and Labor* (Ithaca, 1951), 106–13, 308. But see also E. J. Berg, "Backward-Sloping Labor Supply Functions in Dual Economies—The Africa Case," *Quarterly Journal of Economics*, 75 (1961): 468–92. For a comparison of Tudor and Stuart England with modern underdeveloped countries, see F. J. Fisher, "The Sixteenth and Seventeenth Centuries: The Dark Ages in English Economic History," *Economica*, 2d ser., 24 (1957): 2–18.

always bemoaning the indolence of his servants. Men who had large amounts of land that they could either rent out or work with hired labor generally preferred to rent because labor was so inefficient and irresponsible.[33]

Even the division of labor, which economists have customarily regarded as a means of increased productivity, could be a source of idleness. Plowing, for example, seems to have been a special skill—a plowman was paid at a higher rate than ordinary farm workers. But the ordinary laborer's work might have to be synchronized with the plowman's, and a whole crew of men might be kept idle by a plowman's failure to get his job done at the appropriate time. It is difficult to say whether this type of idleness, resulting from failure to synchronize the performance of related tasks, was rising or declining; but cheap, inefficient, irresponsible labor would be unlikely to generate pressures for the careful planning of time.

The government, while seeking to discourage idleness through laws requiring long hours of work, also passed laws that inadvertently discouraged industry. A policy that might be characterized as the conservation of employment frustrated those who wanted to do more work than others. English economic policy seems to have rested on the assumption that the total amount of work for which society could pay was strictly limited and must be rationed so that everyone could have a little,[34] and those with family responsibilities could have a little more. It was against the law for a man to practice more than one trade or one craft.[35] And although large numbers of farmers took up some handicraft on the side, this was to be discouraged, because "for one man to be both an husbandman and an Artificer is a gatheringe of divers mens livinges into one mans hand."[36] So as not to take work away from his elders, a man could not independently practice most trades until he had become a master through seven years of apprenticeship. Even then, until he was thirty years old or married, he was supposed to serve some other master of the trade. A typical example is the case of John Pikeman of Barking, Essex, a tailor who was presented by the grand jury because he "being a singleman and not above 25 years of age, does take in work of tailoring and works by himself to the hindrance of other poor occupiers, contrary to the law."[37]

---

[33] G. E. Fussell, ed., *Robert Loder's Farm Accounts 1610–1620*, Camden Society, 3d ser., 53 (London, 1936); Lawrence Stone, *The Crisis of the Aristocracy, 1558–1641* (New York, 1965), 295–97; Thirsk, *Agrarian History*, 198.

[34] Compare Bert F. Hoselitz, *Sociological Aspects of Economic Growth* (Glencoe, 1960), 33–34.

[35] [37] Edward 3, c.6. *A Collection in English of the Statutes now in Force* (London, 1594), fols. 22–23; Calendar of Essex Quarter Session Rolls (microfilm in the University of Wisconsin Library), 4: 228; 17: 124.

[36] Tawney and Power, *Tudor Economic Documents*, 1: 353.

[37] April 1594. Calendar of Essex Quarter Sessions Rolls, 16: 165. See also the indictment (1589) of four bachelors for taking up the trade of poulterer, which "hindreth other powre men." *Ibid.*, 15: 54. While the statute seems to allow single men and women under thirty to set up in trade unless their services are demanded by a master, the courts, in Essex County at least (where the earliest and most extensive records are preserved), required such persons to find themselves a master. More-

These measures doubtless helped to maintain social stability in the face of a rapid population increase, from under three million in 1500 to a probable four and a half million in 1640 (an increase reflected in the gap between wages and prices).[38] But in its efforts to spread employment so that every able-bodied person would have a means of support, the government in effect discouraged energetic labor and nurtured the workingman's low expectations of himself. By requiring masters to engage apprentices for seven-year terms and servants (in agriculture and in most trades) for the whole year rather than the day, it prevented employers from hiring labor only when there was work to be done and prevented the diligent and effective worker from replacing the ineffective. The intention to spread work is apparent in the observation of the Essex justices that labor by the day caused "the great depauperization of other labourers." [39] But labor by the year meant that work could be strung out to occupy an unnecessary amount of time, because whether or not a master had enough work to occupy his servants they had to stay and he had to keep them. The records show many instances of masters attempting to turn away a servant or apprentice before the stipulated term was up, only to have him sent back by the courts with orders that the master "entertain" him for the full period.[40] We even have the extraordinary spectacle of the runaway master, the man who illegally fled from his servants and thus evaded his responsibility to employ and support them.[41]

In pursuit of its policy of full employment in the face of an expanding population, the government often had to create jobs in cases where society offered none. Sometimes men were obliged to take on a poor boy as a servant whether they needed him or not. The parish might lighten the burden by paying a fee, but it might also fine a man who refused to take a boy assigned to him.[42] To provide for men and women who could not be foisted off on unwilling employers, the government established houses of correction in every county, where the inmates toiled at turning wool, flax, and hemp into thread or yarn, receiving nothing but their food and lodging for their efforts. By all these means the government probably did succeed in spreading employment. But in the long run its policy, insofar as it was effective, tended to depress wages and to diminish the amount of work expected from any one man.

---

over, the court was already issuing such orders before the statute of 1563. See *ibid.*, 1: 85, 116.

[38] See note 28.

[39] Calendar of Essex Quarter Sessions Rolls, 4: 128.

[40] For examples: William LeHardy, ed., *Hertfordshire County Records,* 5 (Hertford, 1928): 191–92, 451; E. H. Bates, ed., *Quarter Sessions Records for the County of Somerset,* 1, Somerset Record Society, 23 (London, 1907), 11–12, 21; B. C. Redwood, ed., *Quarter Sessions Order Book 1642–1649,* Sussex Record Society, 54 (1954), 34, 44, 46, 128, 145–46, 188, 190.

[41] For examples: *Hertfordshire County Records,* 5:376; *Quarter Sessions Records for Somerset,* 1: 97, 193, 258, 325.

[42] Bates, *Quarter Sessions . . . Somerset,* 114, 300; Redwood, *Order Book* (Sussex), 96, 146, 194; W. L. Sachse, ed., *Minutes of the Norwich Court of Mayoralty,* Norfolk Record Society, 15 (Norwich, 1942), 78, 216.

Above and beyond the idleness and underemployment that we may blame on the lethargy and irresponsibility of underpaid labor, on the failure to synchronize the performance of related tasks, and on the policy of spreading work as thinly as possible, the very nature of the jobs to be done prevented the systematic use of time that characterizes modern industrialized economies. Men could seldom work steadily, because they could work only at the tasks that could be done at the moment; and in sixteenth- and seventeenth-century England the tasks to be done often depended on forces beyond human control: on the weather and the seasons, on the winds, on the tides, on the maturing of crops. In the countryside work from dawn to dusk with scarcely an intermission might be normal at harvest time, but there were bound to be times when there was very little to do. When it rained or snowed, most farming operations had to be stopped altogether (and so did some of the stages of cloth manufacture). As late as 1705 John Law, imagining a typical economy established on a newly discovered island, assumed that the persons engaged in agriculture would necessarily be idle, for one reason or another, half the time.[43]

To be sure, side by side with idleness and inefficiency, England exhibited the first signs of a rationalized economy. Professor J. U. Nef has described the many large-scale industrial enterprises that were inaugurated in England in the late sixteenth and early seventeenth centuries.[44] And if the development of systematic agricultural production was advancing less rapidly than historians once supposed, the very existence of men like Robert Loder, the very complaints of the idleness and irresponsibility of laborers, the very laws prescribing hours of work all testify to the beginnings of a rationalized economy. But these were beginnings only and not widely felt. The laborer who seemed idle or irresponsible to a Robert Loder probably did not seem so to himself or to his peers. His England was not a machine for producing wool or corn. His England included activities and pleasures and relationships that systematic-minded employers would resent and that modern economists would classify as uneconomic. At the opening of the seventeenth century, England was giving him fewer economic benefits than she had given his grandfathers so that he was often ready to pull up stakes and look for a better life in another county or another country.[45] But a life devoted to more and harder work than he had known at home might not have been his idea of a better life.

Perhaps we may now view Jamestown with somewhat less surprise at the idle and hungry people occupying the place: idleness and hunger

---

[43] Coleman, "Labour in the English Economy"; E. P. Thompson, "Time, Work Discipline, and Industrial Capitalism"; Keith Thomas, "Work and Leisure in Pre-Industrial Society," *Past and Present*, no. 29 (1964): 50–66.

[44] J. U. Nef, *The Conquest of the Material World* (Chicago, 1964), 121–328.

[45] On the geographical mobility of the English population, see E. E. Rich, "The Population of Elizabethan England," *Economic History Review*, 2d ser., 2 (1949–56): 249–65; and Peter Laslett and John Harrison, "Clayworth and Cogenhoe," in H. E. Bell and R. L. Ollard, eds., *Historical Essays 1600–1750 Presented to David Ogg* (New York, 1963), 157–84.

were the rule in much of England much of the time; they were facts of life to be taken for granted. And if we next ask what the settlers thought they had come to America to do, what they thought they were up to in Virginia, we can find several English enterprises comparable to their own that may have served as models and that would not have led them to think of hard, continuous disciplined work as a necessary ingredient in their undertaking.

If they thought of themselves as settling a wilderness, they could look for guidance to what was going on in the northern and western parts of England and in the high parts of the south and east.[46] Here were the regions, mostly wooded, where wastelands still abounded, the goal of many in the large migrant population of England. Those who had settled down were scattered widely over the countryside in isolated hovels and hamlets and lived by pasture farming, that is, they cultivated only small plots of ground and ran a few sheep or cattle on the common land. Since the gardens required little attention and the cattle hardly any, they had most of their time to themselves. Some spent their spare hours on handicrafts. In fact, they supplied the labor for most of England's minor industries, which tended to locate in pasture-farming regions, where agriculture made fewer demands on the inhabitants, than in regions devoted to market crops. But the pasture farmers seem to have offered their labor sporadically and reluctantly.[47] They had the reputation of being both idle and independent. They might travel to the richer arable farming regions to pick up a few shillings in field work at harvest time, but their own harvests were small. They did not even grow the wheat or rye for their own bread and made shift to live in hard times from the nuts and berries and herbs that they gathered in the woods.

Jamestown was mostly wooded, like the pasture-farming areas of England and Wales; and since Englishmen used the greater part of their own country for pasture farming, that was the obvious way to use the wasteland of the New World. If this was the Virginians' idea of what they were about, we should expect them to be idle much of the time and to get grain for bread by trading rather than planting (in this case not wheat or rye but maize from the Indians); we should even expect them to get a good deal of their food, as they did, by scouring the woods for nuts and berries.

As the colony developed, a pasture-farming population would have been quite in keeping with the company's expectation of profit from a variety of products. The Spaniards' phenomenal success with raising cattle in the West Indies was well known. And the proposed employment of

---

[46] This paragraph and the one that follows are based on the excellent chapters by Joan Thirsk and by Alan Everitt, in Thirsk, *Agrarian History*.

[47] Thirsk, *Agrarian History*, 417–29; Joan Thirsk, "Industries in the Countryside," in F. J. Fisher, ed., *Essays in the Economic and Social History of Tudor and Stuart England* (London, 1961), 70–88. See also E. L. Jones, "Agricultural Origins of Industry," *Past and Present*, no. 40 (1968): 58–71. Lawrence Stone, "An Elizabethan Coalmine," *Economic History Review*, 2d ser., 3 (1950): 97–106, especially 101–02; Thirsk, *Agrarian History*, xxxv, 111.

the settlers of Virginia in a variety of industrial pursuits (iron works, silk works, glass works, shipbuilding) was entirely fitting for a pasture-farming community. The small gardens assigned for cultivation by Governor Dale in 1614 will also make sense: three acres would have been far too small a plot of land to occupy a farmer in the arable regions of England, where a single man could handle thirty acres without assistance.[48] But it would be not at all inappropriate as the garden of a pasture farmer. In Virginia three acres would produce more than enough corn to sustain a man for a year and still leave him with time to make a profit for the company or himself at some other job—if he could be persuaded to work.

Apart from the movement of migrant workers into wastelands, the most obvious English analogy to the Jamestown settlement was that of a military expedition. The settlers may have had in mind not only the expeditions that subdued the Irish[49] but also those dispatched to the European continent in England's wars. The Virginia Company itself seems at first to have envisaged the enterprise as partly military, and the *Lawes, Divine, Morall and Martiall* were mostly martial. But the conception carried unfortunate implications for the company's expectations of profit. Military expeditions were staffed from top to bottom with men unlikely to work. The nucleus of sixteenth-century English armies was the nobility and the gangs of genteel ruffians they kept in their service, in wartime to accompany them into the field (or to go in their stead), in peacetime to follow them about as living insignia of their rank.[50] Work was not for the nobility nor for those who wore their livery. According to the keenest student of the aristocracy in this period, "the rich and well-born were idle almost by definition." Moreover they kept "a huge labor force . . . absorbed in slothful and parasitic personal service." Aside from the gentlemen retainers of the nobility and their slothful servants the military

---

[48] Hamor, *True Discourse*, 16–17; Peter Bowden, in Thirsk, *Agrarian History*, 652. It is impossible to determine whether the settlers had had direct experience in pasture farming, but the likelihood that they were following familiar pasture-farming procedures and may have been expected to do so by the company is indicated by the kind of cattle they brought with them: swine, goats, neat cattle, and relatively few horses. When they proposed to set plows going, they were to be drawn by oxen as was the custom in pasture-farming areas. In arable farming areas it was more common to use horses. The company's concern to establish substantial herds is evident in the *Lawes Divine, Morall and Martiall* in the provisions forbidding slaughter without government permission.

[49] See Howard M. Jones, *O Strange New World* (New York, 1964), 167–79; David B. Quinn, "Ireland and Sixteenth Century European Expansion," in *Historical Studies*, ed. T. D. Williams, Papers Read at the Second Conference of Irish Historians (London, 1958); *The Elizabethans and the Irish* (Ithaca, 1966), 106–22. Professor Quinn and Professor Jones have both demonstrated how the subjugation of Ireland served as a model for the colonization of America. Ireland must have been in the minds of many of the settlers at Jamestown.

[50] W. H. Dunham, *Lord Hastings' Indentured Retainers 1461–1483*, Connecticut Academy of Arts and Sciences, *Transactions*, 39 (New Haven, 1955); Gladys S. Thompson, *Lords Lieutenants in the Sixteenth Century* (London, 1923); Stone, *Crisis of the Aristocracy*, 199–270.

expeditions that England sent abroad were filled out by misfits and thieves whom the local constables wished to be rid of. It was, in fact, government policy to keep the able-bodied and upright at home and to send the lame, the halt, the blind, and the criminal abroad.[51]

The combination of gentlemen and ne'er-do-wells of which the leaders at Jamestown complained may well have been the result of the company's using a military model for guidance. The Virginia Company was loaded with noblemen (32 present or future earls, 4 countesses, 3 viscounts, and 19 barons).[52] Is it possible that the large number of Jamestown settlers listed as gentlemen and captains came from among the retainers of these lordly stockholders and that the rest of the settlers included some of the gentlemen's personal servants as well as a group of hapless vagabonds or migratory farm laborers who had been either impressed or lured into the enterprise by tales of the New World's abundance? We are told, at least, that persons designated in the colony's roster as "laborers" were "for most part footmen, and such as they that were Adventurers brought to attend them, or such as they could perswade to goe with them, that never did know what a dayes work was."[53]

If these men thought they were engaged in a military expedition, military precedent pointed to idleness, hunger, and death, not to the effective organization of labor. Soldiers on campaign were not expected to grow their own food. On the other hand they *were* expected to go hungry often and to die like flies even if they never saw an enemy. The casualty rates on European expeditions resembled those at Jamestown and probably from the same causes: disease and undernourishment.[54]

But the highest conception of the enterprise, often expressed by the leaders, was that of a new commonwealth on the model of England itself. Yet this, too, while it touched the heart, was not likely to turn men toward hard, effective, and continuous work.[55] The England that Englishmen were saddled with as a model for new commonwealths abroad was a highly complex society in which the governing consideration in accomplishing a particular piece of work was not how to do it efficiently but who had the

---

[51] Stone, *Crisis of the Aristocracy*, 331; Lindsay Boynton, *The Elizabethan Militia 1558–1638* (Toronto, 1967); Thompson, *Lords Lieutenants*, 115.

[52] Stone, *Crisis of the Aristocracy*, 372. About fifty per cent of the other members were gentry. See Theodore K. Rabb, *Enterprise and Empire: Merchant and Gentry Investment in the Expansion of England 1575–1630* (Cambridge, Mass., 1967).

[53] Smith, *Travels and Works*, 2: 486–87.

[54] The expedition of the Earl of Essex in 1591 to assist Henry IV of France met with only a few skirmishes, but only 800 men out of 3,400 returned. Thompson, *Lords Lieutenants*, 111. Even the naval forces mustered to meet the Armada in 1588 suffered appalling losses from disease. In ten of the largest ships, in spite of heavy replacements, only 2,195 out of the original complement of 3,325 men were on the payroll by September. The total loss was probably equal to the entire original number. Lawrence Stone, "The Armada Campaign of 1588," *History*, 29 (1944): 120–43, especially 137–41.

[55] For typical statements implying that Virginia is a new commonwealth on the English model, see the *Lawes Divine, Morall and Martiall*, 47–48; Robert Johnson, *The New Life of Virginia*, in Force, *Tracts*, 1, no. 7: 17–18.

right or the duty to do it, by custom, law, or privilege. We know that the labor shortage in the New World quickly diminished considerations of custom, privilege, and specialization in the organization of labor. But the English model the settlers carried with them made them think initially of a society like the one at home, in which each of them would perform his own special task and not encroach on the rights of other men to do other tasks. We may grasp some of the assumptions about labor that went into the most intelligent planning of a new commonwealth by considering Richard Hakluyt's recommendation that settlers include both carpenters and joiners, tallow chandlers and wax chandlers, bowyers and fletchers, men to rough-hew pike staffs and other men to finish them.[56]

If Jamestown was not actually troubled by this great an excess of specialization, it was not the Virginia Company's fault. The company wanted to establish at once an economy more complex than England's, an economy that would include not only all the trades that catered to ordinary domestic needs of Englishmen but also industries that were unknown or uncommon in England: a list of artisans the company wanted for the colony in 1611 included such specialists as hemp planters and hemp dressers, gun makers and gunstock makers, spinners of pack thread and upholsterers of feathers.[57] Whatever idleness arose from the specialization of labor in English society was multiplied in the New World by the presence of unneeded skills and the absence or shortage of essential skills. Jamestown had an oversupply of glassmakers and not enough carpenters or blacksmiths, an oversupply of gentlemen and not enough plowmen. These were Englishmen temporarily baffled by missing links in the economic structure of their primitive community. The later jack-of-all-trades American frontiersman was as yet unthought of. As late as 1618 Governor Argall complained that they lacked the men "to set their Ploughs on worke." Although they had the oxen to pull them, "they wanted men to bring them to labour, and Irons for the Ploughs, and harnesse for the Cattell." And the next year John Rolfe noted that they still needed "Carpenters to build and make Carts and Ploughs, and skilfull men that know how to use them, and traine up our cattell to draw them; which though we indeavour to effect, yet our want of experience brings but little to perfection but planting Tobacco." [58]

Tobacco, as we know, was what they kept on planting. The first shipload of it, sent to England in 1617, brought such high prices that the Virginians stopped bowling in the streets and planted tobacco in them. They did it without benefit of plows, and somehow at the same time they managed to grow corn, probably also without plows. Seventeenth-century Englishmen, it turned out, could adapt themselves to hard and varied work if there was sufficient incentive.

But we may well ask whether the habits and attitudes we have been

[56] Taylor, *Writings of the two Richard Hakluyts*, 2: 323, 327–38.
[57] Alexander Brown, *The Genesis of the United States* (Boston, 1890), 1: 469–70.
[58] Smith, *Travels and Works*, 2: 538, 541.

examining had suddenly expired altogether. Did tobacco really solve the labor problem in Virginia? Did the economy that developed after 1618 represent a totally new set of social and economic attitudes? Did greater opportunities for profit completely erase the old attitudes and furnish the incentives to labor that were needed to make Virginia a success? The study of labor in modern underdeveloped countries should make us pause before we say yes. The mere opportunity to earn high wages has not always proved adequate to recruit labor in underdeveloped countries. Something more in the way of expanded needs or political authority or national consciousness or ethical imperatives has been required.[59] Surely Virginia, in some sense, became a success. But how did it succeed? What kind of success did it have? Without attempting to answer, I should like very diffidently to offer a suggestion, a way of looking ahead at what happened in the years after the settlement of Jamestown.

The founders of Virginia, having discovered in tobacco a substitute for the sugar of the West Indies and the silver of Peru, still felt the lack of a native labor force with which to exploit the new crop. At first they turned to their own overpopulated country for labor, but English indentured servants brought with them the same haphazard habits of work as their masters. Also like their masters, they were apt to be unruly if pressed. And when their terms of servitude expired—if they themselves had not expired in the "seasoning" that carried away most immigrants to Virginia —they could be persuaded to continue working for their betters only at exorbitant rates. Instead they struck out for themselves and joined the ranks of those demanding rather than supplying labor. But there was a way out. The Spanish and Portuguese had already demonstrated what could be done in the New World when a local labor force became inadequate: they brought in the natives of Africa.

[59] Moore, *Industrialization and Labor*, 14–47; Melville J. Herskovits, "The Problem of Adapting Societies to New Tasks," in Bert F. Hoselitz, *The Progress of Underdeveloped Areas* (Chicago, 1952), especially 91–92. See also William O. Jones, "Labor and Leisure in Traditional African Societies," Social Science Research Council, *Items*, 23 (1968): 1–6.

The Structure of the
Household

JOHN DEMOS

N   *Noah* did view
     The old World & new

O   Young *Obadias,*
     David, Josias,
     All were pious.

P   *Peter* deny'd
     His Lord, and cry'd.

Q   Queen *Esther* sues,
     And saves the *Jews.*

R   Young pious *Ruth,*
     Left all for Truth.

S   Young *Samuel* dear
     The Lord did fear.

For the Puritan settlers of New England family relationships were of the utmost importance. The nexus between wife and husband, child and parent, sister and brother, and master and servant was essential to the web of human experience. For all but a handful of settlers—trappers, Indian traders, or renegades from "civilization"—family ties provided the framework of life. Coming to a strange environment and confronting conditions that many colonists thought had the potential to drag them down into "a desert of wild beasts and wild men," early New Englanders saw the family as the basic building block in erecting a regenerated, godly community. That is why in early New England all single persons were required to live within a family; bachelor living was prohibited because no individual, it was thought, was safe from anarchic impulses if he or she lived outside a family fold. And all families were required to live within a specified distance of the meetinghouse, because it was the symbol of the larger family to which all individual households must necessarily be subordinate.

The Europeans who settled the New World stood at a point in time where the widespread abuse and abandonment of children was giving way to kindlier treatment and a desire to shape the personalities and mold the wills of children, while admitting them to the emotional circle of the family. Puritans, as it has been said, were nine-tenths Englishmen in their cultural traits, and thus the child-parent relationships in a New England community may not have been very different from those that prevailed in the society the Puritans fled. And Englishmen, whether Puritan or Anglican or Catholic, shared much with other western European societies in most of the ways they approached life. Thus the rules governing behavior between man and wife or parent and child in early Massachusetts were not markedly different from those that prevailed among Catholics in New France, Quakers in Pennsylvania, or Dutch Reformed in New Netherland. Everywhere "reciprocal obligations," as John Demos calls them in the following selection, were recognized between different members of the family. These basic elements of the "contract" among members of the family are carefully spelled out by the author.

It is especially important that we attain some precision in our understanding of family relationships in early America, because they form a baseline against which to measure change at later points in time. This change came most spectacularly in the twentieth century, but it occurred in other eras of American history as well. Why the change came slowly in some periods and rapidly in others is a question students will wish to ponder.

HUSBANDS AND WIVES

No aspect of the Puritan household was more vital than the relationship of husband and wife. But the study of this relationship raises at once certain larger questions of sex differentiation: What were the relative positions of men and women in Plymouth Colony? What attributes, and what overall valuation, were thought appropriate to each sex?

We know in a general way that male dominance was an accepted principle all over the Western World in the seventeenth century. The fundamental Puritan sentiment on this matter was expressed by Milton in a famous line in *Paradise Lost*: "he for God only, she for God in him;" and there is no reason to suspect that the people of Plymouth would have put it any differently. The world of public affairs was nowhere open to women —in Plymouth only males were eligible to become "freemen." Within the family the husband was always regarded as the "head"—and the Old Colony provided no exceptions to this pattern. Moreover, the culture at large maintained a deep and primitive kind of suspicion of women, solely on account of their sex. Some basic taint of corruption was thought to be inherent in the feminine constitution—a belief rationalized, of course, by the story of Eve's initial treachery in the Garden of Eden. It was no coincidence that in both the Old and the New World witches were mostly women. Only two allegations of witchcraft turn up in the official records of Plymouth,[1] but other bits of evidence point in the same general direction. There are, for example, the quoted words of a mother beginning an emotional plea to her son: "if you would beleive a woman beleive mee. . . ."[2] And why *not* believe a woman?

The views of the Pilgrim pastor John Robinson are also interesting in this connection. He opposed, in the first place, any tendency to regard women as "necessary evils" and greatly regretted the currency of such

"The Structure of the Household." From *A Little Commonwealth: Family Life in Plymouth Colony* by John Demos, pp. 82–106. Copyright © 1970 by Oxford University Press, Inc. Reprinted by permission.

[1] The first occurred in 1661, in Marshfield. A girl named Dinah Silvester accused the wife of William Holmes of being a witch, and of going about in the shape of a bear in order to do mischief. The upshot, however, was a suit for defamation against Dinah. The Court convicted her and obliged her to make a public apology to Goodwife Holmes. *Records of the Colony of New Plymouth, in New England*, ed. Nathaniel B. Shurtleff and David Pulsifer (Boston, 1855–61), III, 205, 207, 211. The second case (at Scituate, in 1677) resulted in the formal indictment of one Mary Ingham—who, it was said, had bewitched a girl named Mehitable Woodworth. But after suitable deliberations, the jury decided on an acquittal. *Plymouth Colony Records*, V, 223–24.

[2] From a series of depositions bearing on the estate of Samuel Ryder, published in *Mayflower Descendant*, XI, 52. The case is discussed in greater detail below, pp. 165–66.

opinions among "not only heathen poets . . . but also wanton Christians."
The Lord had created both man and woman of an equal perfection, and
"neither is she, since the creation more degenerated than he from the primitive goodness." [3] Still, in marriage some principles of authority were essential, since "differences will arise and be seen, and so the one must give
way, and apply unto the other; this, God and nature layeth upon the
woman, rather than upon the man." Hence the proper attitude of a wife
towards her husband was "a reverend subjection." [4]

However, in a later discussion of the same matter Robinson developed
a more complex line of argument which stressed certain attributes of inferiority assumed to be inherently feminine. Women, he wrote, were
under two different kinds of subjection. The first was framed "in in-
nocency" and implied no "grief" or "wrong" whatsoever. It reflected
simply the woman's character as "the weaker vessel"—weaker, most obviously, with respect to intelligence or "understanding." For this was a gift
"which God hath . . . afforded [the man], and means of obtaining it,
above the woman, that he might guide and go before her." [5] Robinson
also recognized that some men abused their position of authority and oppressed their wives most unfairly. But *even so*—and this was his central
point—resistance was not admissible. Here he affirmed the second kind of
subjection laid upon woman, a subjection undeniably "grievous" but justified by her "being first in transgression." In this way—by invoking the
specter of Eve corrupting Adam in paradise—Robinson arrived in the end
at a position which closely approximated the popular assumption of
woman's basic moral weakness.

Yet within this general framework of masculine superiority there
were a number of rather contrary indications. They seem especially evident in certain areas of the law. Richard B. Morris has written a most interesting essay on this matter, arguing the improved legal status of colonial
women by comparison to what still obtained in the mother country.[6]
Many of his conclusions seem to make a good fit with conditions in
Plymouth Colony. The baseline here is the common law tradition of England, which at this time accorded to women only the most marginal sort
of recognition. The married woman, indeed, was largely subsumed under
the legal personality of her husband; she was virtually without rights to
own property, make contracts, or sue for damages on her own account.
But in the New World this situation was perceptibly altered.

Consider, for example, the evidence bearing on the property rights
of Plymouth Colony wives. The law explicitly recognized their part in the
accumulation of a family's estate, by the procedures it established for the
treatment of widows. It was a basic principle of inheritance in this period
—on both sides of the Atlantic—that a widow should have the use or
profits of one-third of the land owned by her husband at the time of his
death and full title to one-third of his moveable property. But at least in

[3] *The Works of John Robinson,* ed. Robert Ashton (Boston, 1851), I, 236.
[4] *Ibid.,* 239–40.
[5] *Ibid.,* 240.
[6] Richard B. Morris, *Studies in the History of American Law* (New York, 1930),
Chapter III, "Women's Rights in Early American Law."

Plymouth, and perhaps in other colonies as well, this expressed more than the widow's need for an adequate living allowance. For the laws also prescribed that "if any man do make an irrational and unrighteous Will, whereby he deprives his Wife of her reasonable allowance for her subsistencey," the Court may "relieve her out of the estate, notwithstanding by Will it were otherwise disposed; especially in such case where the Wife brought with her good part of the Estate in Marriage, or hath by her diligence and industry done her part in the getting of the Estate, and was otherwise well deserving." [7] Occasionally the Court saw fit to alter the terms of a will on this acount. In 1663, for example, it awarded to widow Naomi Silvester a larger share of her late husband's estate than the "inconsiderable pte" he had left her, since she had been "a frugall and laborious woman in the procuring of the said estate." [8] In short, the widow's customary "thirds" was not a mere dole; it was her *due*.

But there is more still. In seventeenth-century England women were denied the right to make contracts, save in certain very exceptional instances. In Plymouth Colony, by contrast, one finds the Court sustaining certain kinds of contracts involving women on a fairly regular basis. The most common case of this type was the agreement of a widow and a new husband, made *before* marriage, about the future disposition of their respective properties. The contract drawn up by John Phillips of Marshfield and widow Faith Doty of Plymouth in 1667 was fairly standard. It stipulated that "the said Faith Dotey is to enjoy all her house and land, goods and cattles, that shee is now possessed of, to her owne proper use, to dispose of them att her owne free will from time to time, and att any time, as shee shall see cause." Moreover this principle of separate control extended beyond the realm of personal property. Phillips and widow Doty each had young children by their previous marriages, and their agreement was "that the children of both the said pties shall remaine att the free and proper and onely dispose of theire owne naturall parents, as they shall see good to dispose of them." [9] Any woman entering marriage on terms such as these would seem virtually an equal partner, at least from a legal standpoint. Much rarer, but no less significant, were contracts made by women *after* marriage. When Dorothy Clarke wished to be free of her husband Nathaniel in 1686, the Court refused a divorce but allowed a separation. Their estate was then carefully divided up by contract to which the wife was formally a party.[10] Once again, no clear precedents for this procedure can be found in contemporary English law.

7 William Brigham, *The Compact with the Charter and Laws of the Colony of New Plymouth* (Boston, 1836), 281.

8 *Plymouth Colony Records*, IV, 46.

9 *Ibid.*, 163–64. For another agreement of this type, see *Mayflower Descendant*, XVII, 49 (the marriage contract of Ephraim Morton and Mistress Mary Harlow). The same procedures can be viewed, retrospectively, in the wills of men who had been married to women previously widowed. Thus when Thomas Boardman of Yarmouth died in 1689 the following notation was placed near the end of his will: "the estate of my wife brought me upon marriage be at her dispose and not to be Invintoried with my estate." *Mayflower Descendant*, X, 102. See also the will of Dolar Davis, *Mayflower Descendant*, XXIV, 73.

10 *Mayflower Descendant*, VI, 191–92.

The specific terms of some wills also help to confirm the rights of women to a limited kind of ownership even within marriage. No husband ever included his wife's clothing, for example, among the property to be disposed of after his death. And consider, on the other side, a will like that of Mistress Sarah Jenny, drawn up at Plymouth in 1655. Her husband had died just a few months earlier, and she wished simply to "Despose of som smale thinges that is my owne proper goods leaveing my husbands will to take place according to the true Intent and meaning thereof." [11] The "smale thinges" included not only her wardrobe, but also a bed, some books, a mare, some cattle and sheep. Unfortunately, married women did not usually leave wills of their own (unless they had been previously widowed); and it is necessary to infer that in most cases there was some sort of informal arrangement for the transfer of their personal possessions. One final indication of these same patterns comes from wills which made bequests to a husband and wife separately. Thus, for example, Richard Sealis of Scituate conferred most of his personal possessions on the families of two married daughters, carefully specifying which items should go to the daughters themselves and which to their husbands.[12] Thomas Rickard, also of Scituate, had no family of his own and chose therefore to distribute his property among a variety of friends. Once again spouses were treated separately: "I give unto Thomas Pincin my bedd and Rugg one paire of sheets and pilloty . . . I give and bequeath unto Joane the wife of the aforsaid Thomas Pincin my bason and fouer sheets . . . I give and bequeath unto Joane Stanlacke my Chest . . . unto Richard Stanlacke my Chest . . . unto Richard Stanlacke my best briches and Dublit and ould Coate." [13]

The questions of property rights and of the overall distribution of authority within a marriage do not necessarily coincide; and modern sociologists interested in the latter subject usually emphasize the process of decision-making.[14] Of course, their use of live samples gives them a very great advantage; they can ask their informants, through questionnaires or interviews, which spouse decides where to go on vacation, what kind of car to buy, how to discipline the children, when to have company in, and so forth. The historian simply cannot draw out this kind of detail, nor can he contrive any substantial equivalent. But he is able sometimes to make a beginning in this direction; for example, the records of Plymouth do throw light on two sorts of family decisions of the very greatest importance. One of these involves the transfer of land, and illustrates further the whole trend toward an expansion of the rights of married women to hold property. The point finds tangible expression in a law passed by the General Court in 1646: "It is enacted &c. That the Assistants or any of them shall have full power to take the acknowledgment of a bargaine and sale of houses and lands . . . And that the wyfe hereafter come in & consent and

---

[11] *Mayflower Descendant*, VIII, 171.

[12] *Mayflower Descendant*, XIII, 94–96.

[13] *Mayflower Descendant*, IX, 155.

[14] See, for example, Robert O. Blood, Jr., and Donald M. Wolfe, *Husbands and Wives* (Glencoe, Ill., 1960), esp. ch. 2.

acknowledg the sale also; but that all bargaines and sales of houses and lands made before this day to remayne firm to the buyer notwithstanding the wife did not acknowledge the same." [15] The words "come in" merit special attention: the authorities wished to confront the wife personally (and even, perhaps, privately?) in order to minimize the possibility that her husband might exert undue pressure in securing her agreement to a sale.

The second area of decision-making in which both spouses shared an important *joint* responsibility was the "putting out" of children into foster families. For this there was no statute prescribing a set line of procedure, but the various written documents from specific cases make the point clearly enough. Thus in 1660 "An Agreement appointed to bee Recorded" affirmed that "Richard Berry of Yarmouth with his wifes Concent and other frinds; hath given unto Gorge Crispe of Eastham and his; wife theire son Samuell Berry; to bee att the ordering and Disposing of the said Gorge and his wife as if hee were theire owne Child." [16] The practice of formally declaring the wife's consent is evident in all such instances, when both parents were living. Another piece of legal evidence describes an actual deathbed scene in which the same issue had to be faced. It is the testimony of a mother confirming the adoption of her son, and it is worth quoting in some detail. "These prsents Witnesse that the 20th of march 1657–8 Judith the wife of William Peaks acknowlidged that her former husband Lawrence Lichfeild lying on his Death bedd sent for John Allin and Ann his wife and Desired to give and bequeath unto them his youngest son Josias Lichfeild if they would accept of him and take him as theire Child; then they Desired to know how long they should have him and the said Lawrence said for ever; but the mother of the child was not willing then; but in a short time after willingly Concented to her husbands will in the thinge." [17] That the wife finally agreed is less important here than the way in which her initial reluctance sufficed to block the child's adoption, in spite of the clear wishes of her husband.

Another reflection of this pattern of mutual responsibility appears in certain types of business activity—for instance, the management of inns and taverns ("ordinaries" in the language of the day). All such establishments were licensed by the General Court; hence their history can be followed, to a limited degree, in the official Colony Records. It is interesting to learn that one man's license was revoked because he had recently "buryed his wife, and in that respect not being soe capeable of keeping a publicke house." [18] In other cases the evidence is less explicit but still revealing. For many years James Cole ran the principal ordinary in the town of Plymouth, and from time to time the Court found it necessary to censure and punish certain violations of proper decorum that occurred there. In some of these cases Cole's wife Mary was directly implicated. In March

---

[15] Brigham, *The Compact with the Charter and Laws of the Colony of New Plymouth*, 86.

[16] *Mayflower Descendant*, XV, 34.

[17] *Mayflower Descendant*, XII, 134.

[18] *Plymouth Colony Records*, IV, 54.

1669 a substantial fine was imposed "for that the said Mary Cole suffered divers psons after named to stay drinking on the Lords day . . . in the time of publicke worshipp." [19] Indeed the role of women in all aspects of this episode is striking, since two of the four drinking customers, the "divers psons after named," turned out to be female. Perhaps, then, women had considerable freedom to move on roughly the same terms with men even into some of the darker byways of Old Colony life.

The Court occasionally granted liquor licenses directly to women. Husbands were not mentioned, though it is of course possible that all of the women involved were widows. In some cases the terms of these permits suggest retail houses rather than regular inns or taverns. Thus in 1663 "Mistris Lydia Garrett" of Scituate was licensed to "sell liquors, alwaies provided . . . that shee sell none but to house keepers, and not lesse than a gallon att a time;" [20] and the agreement with another Scituate lady, Margaret Muffee, twenty years later, was quite similar. [21] But meanwhile in Middlebury one "Mistress Mary Combe" seems to have operated an ordinary of the standard type. [22] Can we proceed from these specific data on liquor licensing to some more general conclusion about the participation of women in the whole field of economic production and exchange? Unfortunately there is little additional hard evidence on one side or the other. The Court Records do not often mention other types of business activity, with the single exception of milling; and no woman was ever named in connection with this particular enterprise. A few more wills could be cited—for instance, the one made by Elizabeth Poole, a wealthy spinster in Taunton, leaving "my pte in the Iron workes" to a favorite nephew. [23] But this does not add up to very much. The economy of Plymouth was, after all, essentially simple—indeed "underdeveloped"—in most important respects. Farming claimed the energies of all but a tiny portion of the populace; there was relatively little opportunity for anyone, man *or* woman, to develop a more commercial orientation. It is known that in the next century women played quite a significant role in the business life of many parts of New England, [24] and one can view this pattern as simply the full development of possibilities that were latent even among the first generations of settlers. But there is no way to fashion an extended chain of proof.

Much of what has been said so far belongs to the general category of the rights and privileges of the respective partners to a marriage. But what of their duties, their basic responsibilities to one another? Here, surely, is another area of major importance in any assessment of the character of married life. The writings of John Robinson help us to make a start with these questions, and especially to recover the framework of ideals within which most couples of Plymouth Colony must have tried to hammer out

[19] *Plymouth Colony Records,* V, 15.
[20] *Plymouth Colony Records,* IV, 44.
[21] *Plymouth Colony Records,* VI, 187.
[22] *Ibid.,* 141.
[23] *Mayflower Descendant,* XIV, 26.
[24] Elizabeth Anthony Dexter, *Colonial Women of Affairs* (Boston, 1911).

a meaningful day-to-day relationship. We have noted already that Robinson prescribed "subjection" as the basic duty of a wife to her husband. No woman deserved praise, "how well endowed soever otherwise, except she frame, and compose herself, what may be, unto her husband, in conformity of manners." [25] From the man, by contrast, two things were particularly required: "love . . . and wisdom." His love for his wife must be "like Christ's to his church: holy for quality, and great for quantity," and it must stand firm even where "her failings and faults be great." His wisdom was essential to the role of family "head"; without it neither spouse was likely to find the way to true piety, and eventually to salvation.

It is a long descent from the spiritual counsel of John Robinson to the details of domestic conflict as noted in the Colony Records. But the Records are really the only available source of information about the workings of actual marriages in this period. They are, to be sure, a negative type of source; that is, they reveal only those cases which seemed sufficiently deviant and sufficiently important to warrant the attention of the authorities. But it is possible by a kind of reverse inference to use them to reconstruct the norms which the community at large particularly wished to protect. This effort serves to isolate three basic obligations in which both husband and wife were thought to share.

There was, first and most simply, the obligation of regular and exclusive cohabitation. No married person was permitted to live apart from his spouse except in very unusual and temporary circumstances (as when a sailor was gone to sea). The Court stood ready as a last resort to force separated couples to come together again, though it was not often necessary to deal with the problem in such an official way. One of the few recorded cases of this type occurred in 1659. The defendant was a certain Goodwife Spring, married to a resident of Watertown in the Bay Colony and formerly the wife and widow of Thomas Hatch of Scituate. She had, it seems, returned to Scituate some three or four years earlier, and had been living "from her husband" ever since. The Court ordered that "shee either repaire to her husband with all convenient speed, . . . or . . . give a reason why shee doth not." [26] Exactly how this matter turned out cannot be determined, but it seems likely that the ultimate sanction was banishment from the Colony. The government of Massachusetts Bay is known to have imposed this penalty in a number of similar cases. None of the extant records describe such action being taken at Plymouth, but presumably the possibility was always there.

Moreover, the willful desertion of one spouse by the other over a period of several years was one of the few legitimate grounds for divorce. In 1670, for example, the Court granted the divorce plea of James Skiffe "having received sufficient testimony that the late wife of James Skiffe hath unlawfully forsaken her lawfull husband . . . and is gone to Roanoke, in or att Verginnia, and there hath taken another man for to be her husband." [27] Of course, bigamy was always sufficient reason in itself

25 *The Works of John Robinson*, I, 20.
26 *Plymouth Colony Records*, III, 174.
27 *Plymouth Colony Records*, V, 33.

for terminating a marriage. Thus in 1680 Elizabeth Stevens obtained a divorce from her husband when it was proved that he had three other wives already, one each in Boston, Barbadoes, and a town in England not specified.[28]

But it was not enough that married persons should simply live together on a regular basis; their relationship must be relatively peaceful and harmonious. Once again the Court reserved the right to interfere in cases where the situation had become especially difficult. Occasionally both husband and wife were judged to be at fault, as when George and Anna Barlow were "severely reproved for theire most ungodly liveing in contension one with the other, and admonished to live otherwise." [29] But much more often one or the other was singled out for the Court's particular attention. One man was punished for "abusing his wife by kiking her of from a stoole into the fier," [30] and another for "drawing his wife in uncivell manor on the snow." [31] A more serious case was that of John Dunham, convicted of "abusive carriage towards his wife in continuall tiranising over her, and in pticulare for his late abusive and uncivill carryage in endeavoring to beate her in a deboist manor." [32] The Court ordered a whipping as just punishment for these cruelties, but the sentence was then suspended at the request of Dunham's wife. Sometimes the situation was reversed and the woman was the guilty party. In 1655, for example, Joan Miller of Taunton was charged with "beating and reviling her husband, and egging her children to healp her, bidding them knock him in the head, and wishing his victuals might coak him." [33] A few years later the wife of Samuel Halloway (also of Taunton) was admonished for "carryage towards her husband . . . soe turbulend and wild, both in words and actions, as hee could not live with her but in danger of his life or limbs." [34]

It would serve no real purpose to cite more of these unhappy episodes —and it might indeed create an erroneous impression that marital conflict was particularly endemic among the people of the Old Colony. But two general observations are in order. First, the Court's chief aim in this type of case was to restore the couple in question to something approaching tranquility. The assumption was that a little force applied from the outside might be useful, whether it came in the form of an "admonition" or in some kind of actual punishment. Only once did the Court have to recognize that the situation might be so bad as to make a final reconciliation impossible. This happened in 1665 when John Williams, Jr., of Scituate, was charged with a long series of "abusive and harsh carriages" toward his wife Elizabeth, "in speciall his sequestration of himselfe from the marriage bed, and his accusation of her to bee a whore, and that especially in reference unto a child lately borne of his said wife by him denied to bee

[28] *Plymouth Colony Records*, VI, 44-45.
[29] *Plymouth Colony Records*, IV, 10.
[30] *Plymouth Colony Records*, V, 61.
[31] *Plymouth Colony Records*, IV, 47.
[32] *Ibid.*, 103-4.
[33] *Plymouth Colony Records*, III, 75.
[34] *Plymouth Colony Records*, V, 29.

legittimate." [35] The case was frequently before the Court during the next two years, and eventually all hope of a settlement was abandoned. When Williams persisted in his "abuses," and when too he had "himself . . . [declared] his insufficiency for converse with weomen," [36] a formal separation was allowed—though not a full divorce. In fact, it may be that his impotence, not his habitual cruelty, was the decisive factor in finally persuading the Court to go this far. For in another case, some years later, a separation was granted on the former grounds alone.[37]

The second noteworthy aspect of all these situations is the equality they seem to imply between the sexes. In some societies and indeed in many parts of Europe at this time, a wife was quite literally at the mercy of her husband—his prerogatives extended even to the random use of physical violence. But clearly this was not the situation at Plymouth. It is, for example, instructive to break down these charges of "abusive carriage" according to sex: one finds that wives were accused just about as often as husbands. Consider, too, those cases of conflict in which the chief parties were of opposite sex but not married to one another. Once again the women seem to have held their own. Thus we have, on the one side, Samuel Norman punished for "strikeing Lydia, the wife of Henery Taylor," [38] and John Dunham for "abusive speeches and carriages" [39] toward Sarah, wife of Benjamin Eaton; and, on the other side, the complaint of Abraham Jackson against "Rose, the wife of Thomas Morton, . . . that the said Rose, as hee came from worke, did abuse him by calling of him lying rascall and rogue." [40] In short, this does *not* seem to have been a society characterized by a really pervasive, and operational, norm of male dominance. There is no evidence at all of habitual patterns of deference in the relations between the sexes. John Robinson, and many others, too, may have assumed that woman was "the weaker vessel" and that "subjection" was her natural role. But as so often happens with respect to such matters, actual behavior was another story altogether.

The third of the major obligations incumbent on the married pair was a normal and exclusive sexual union. As previously indicated, impotence in the husband was one of the few circumstances that might warrant a divorce. The reasoning behind this is nowhere made explicit, but most likely it reflected the felt necessity that a marriage produce children. It is worth noting in this connection some of the words used in a divorce hearing of 1686 which centered on the issue of a man's impotence. He was, according to his wife, "always unable to perform the act of generation." [41] The latter phrase implies a particular view of the nature and significance of the sexual act, one which must have been widely held in this culture. Of course, there were other infertile marriages in the

[35] *Plymouth Colony Records*, IV, 93.
[36] *Ibid.*, 125.
[37] *Plymouth Colony Records*, VI, 191.
[38] *Plymouth Colony Records*, V, 39.
[39] *Ibid.*, 40.
[40] *Plymouth Colony Records*, IV, 11.
[41] *Plymouth Colony Records*, VI, 191.

same period which held together. But perhaps the cause of the problem had to be obvious—as with impotence—for the people involved to consider divorce. Where the sexual function appeared normal in both spouses, there was always the hope that the Lord might one day grant the blessing of children. Doubtless for some couples this way of thinking meant year after year of deep personal disappointment.

The problem of adultery was more common—and, in a general sense, more troublesome. For adultery loomed as the most serious possible distortion of the whole sexual and reproductive side of marriage. John Robinson called it "that most foul and filthy sin, . . . the disease of marriage," and concluded that divorce was its necessary "medicine." [42] In fact, most of the divorces granted in the Old Colony stemmed from this one cause alone. But adultery was not only a strong *prima facie* reason for divorce; it was also an act that would bring heavy punishment to the guilty parties. The law decreed that "whosoever shall Commit Adultery with a Married Woman or one Betrothed to another Man, both of them shall be severely punished, by whipping two several times . . . and likewise to wear two Capital Letters A.D. cut out in cloth and sewed on their uppermost Garments . . . and if at any time they shall be found without the said Letters so worne . . . to be forthwith taken and publickly whipt, and so from time to time as often as they are found not to wear them." [43]

But quite apart from the severity of the prescribed punishments, this statute is interesting for its definition of adultery by reference to a married (or bethrothed) *woman*. Here, for the first time, we find some indication of difference in the conduct expected of men and women. The picture can be filled out somewhat by examining the specific cases of adultery prosecuted before the General Court down through the years. To be sure, the man involved in any given instance was judged together with the woman, and when convicted their punishments were the same. But there is another point to consider as well. All of the adulterous couples mentioned in the records can be classified in one of two categories: a married woman and a married man, or a married woman and a single man. There was, on the other hand, no case involving a married man and a single woman. This pattern seems to imply that the chief concern, the essential element of sin, was the woman's infidelity to her husband. A married man would be punished for his part in this aspect of the affair—rather than for any wrong done to his own wife.

However, this does not mean that a man's infidelities were wholly beyond reproach. The records, for example, include one divorce plea in which the wife adduced as her chief complaint "an act of uncleanes" by her husband with another woman.[44] There was no move to prosecute and punish the husband—apparently since the other woman was unmarried. But the divorce was granted, and the wife received a most favorable settlement. We can, then, conclude the following. The adultery of a wife was

[42] *The Works of John Robinson,* I, 241.

[43] Brigham, *The Compact with the Charter and Laws of the Colony of New Plymouth,* 245–46.

[44] *Plymouth Colony Records,* III, 221.

treated as both a violation of her marriage (hence grounds for divorce) *and* an offense against the community (hence cause for legal prosecution). But for comparable behavior by husbands only the former consideration applied. In this somewhat limited sense the people of Plymouth Colony do seem to have maintained a "double standard" of sexual morality.

Before concluding this discussion of married life in the Old Colony and moving on to other matters, one important area of omission should at least be noted. Very little has been said here of love, affection, under-standing—a whole range of positive feelings and impulses—between hus-bands and wives. Indeed the need to rely so heavily on Court Records has tended to weight the balance quite conspicuously on the side of conflict and failure. The fact is that the sum total of actions of divorce, prosecu-tions for adultery, "admonitions" against habitual quarreling, does not seem terribly large. In order to make a proper assessment of their meaning several contingent factors must be recognized; the long span of time they cover, the steady growth of the Colony's population (to something like 10,000 by the end of the century),[45] the extensive jurisdiction of the Court over many areas of domestic life. Given this overall context, it is clear that the vast majority of Plymouth Colony families never once required the attention of the authorities. Elements of disharmony were, at the least, con-trolled and confined within certain limits.

But again, can the issue be approached in a more directly affirmative way? Just how, and how much, did feelings of warmth and love fit into the marriages of the Old Colony? Unfortunately our source materials have al-most nothing to say in response to such questions. But this is only to be expected in the case of legal documents, physical remains, and so forth. The wills often refer to "my loveing wife"—but it would be foolish to read anything into such obvious set phrases. The records of Court cases are completely mute on this score. Other studies of "Puritan" ideals about marriage and the family have drawn heavily on literary materials—and this, of course, is the biggest gap in the sources that have come down from Plymouth Colony. Perhaps, though, a certain degree of extrapolation is permissible here; and if so, we must imagine that love was quite central to these marriages. If, as Morgan has shown, this was the case in Massachu-setts Bay, surely it was also true for the people of Plymouth.[46]

There are, finally, just a few scraps of concrete evidence on this point. As previously noted, John Robinson wrote lavishly about the im-portance of love to a marriage—though he associated it chiefly with the role of the husband. And the wills should be drawn in once again, espe-cially those clauses in which a man left specific instructions regarding the care of his widow. Sometimes the curtain of legal terms and style seems to

45 There are three separate investigations dealing with this question: Richard L. Bowen, *Early Rehoboth* (3 vols.; Rehoboth, Mass., 1945), I, 15–24; Joseph B. Felt, "Population of Plymouth Colony," in American Statistical Association *Collections*, I, Pt. ii (Boston, 1845), 143–44; and William Bradford, *Of Plymouth Plantation*, ed. Samuel Eliot Morison (New York, 1952), xi.
46 See Edmund Morgan, *The Puritan Family* (New York, 1966), esp. 46 ff.

rise for a moment and behind it one glimpses a deep tenderness and concern. There is, for example, the will written by Walter Briggs in 1676. Briggs's instructions in this regard embraced all of the usual matters—rooms, bedding, cooking utensils, "lyberty to make use of ye two gardens." And he ended with a particular request that his executors "allow my said wife a gentle horse or mare to ride to meeting or any other occasion she may have, & that Jemy, ye neger, catch it for her." [47] Surely this kind of thoughtfulness reflected a larger instinct of love—one which, nourished in life, would not cease to be effective even in the face of death itself.

PARENTS AND CHILDREN

Egalitarianism formed no part of seventeenth-century assumptions about the proper relationship of parents and children. But at Plymouth this relationship involved a set of *reciprocal* obligations.

From the standpoint of the child, the Biblical commandment to "Honor thy father and mother" was fundamental—and the force of law stood behind it. The relevant statute directed that "If any Childe or Children above sixteen years old, and of competent Understanding, shall Curse or Smite their Natural Father or Mother; he or they shall be put to Death, unless it can be sufficiently testified that the Parents have been very Unchristianly negligent in the Education of such Children, or so provoked them by extreme and cruel Correction, that they have been forced thereunto, to preserve themselves from Death or Maiming." A corollary order prescribed similar punishment for behavior that was simply "Stubborn or Rebellious"—or indeed, for any sort of habitual disobedience. [48]

The rightful authority of the parents is clear enough here, but it should also be noted that this authority was limited in several ways. In the first place, a child less than sixteen years old was excluded from these prescriptions; he was not mature enough to be held finally responsible for his actions. Disobedience and disrespect on the part of younger children were surely punished, but on an informal basis and within the family itself. In such cases, presumably, the purpose of punishment was to form right habits; it was part of a whole pattern of learning. But for children of more than sixteen different assumptions applied. [49] Ultimate responsibility could now be imputed, and an offense against one's parents was also an offense against the basic values of the community. Hence the full retributive process of the laws might properly be invoked.

The clause relating to "extreme and cruel correction" implied a second limitation on parental power. The child did have the right to protect his own person from any action that threatened "Death or Maiming."

[47] *Plymouth Colony Records*, VI, 134-35.

[48] Brigham, *The Compact with the Charter and Laws of the Colony of New Plymouth*, 245.

[49] Sixteen was also the age at which children became fully liable in actions of lying and slander. See below, Chapter Ten, for a review of this and other evidence bearing on adolescence as a "developmental stage."

Finally, it seems significant that the arbiter of *all* such questions was not the parental couple directly involved but rather the constituted authorities of the Colony as a whole. The correct response to gross disobedience in a child was as follows: "his Father and Mother, . . . [shall] lay hold on him, and bring him before the Magistrates assembled in Court, and testifie unto them, that their Son is Stubborn and Rebellious, and will not obey their voice and chastisement." [50] This may sound rather menacing, but it did imply an important kind of negative. The parents shall *not* take matters completely into their own hands. The child shall also have *his* say in Court; and presumably he may try, if he wishes, to show that his behavior was provoked by some cruelty on the part of his parents.

It must be said that only a few cases of youthful disobedience to parents actually reached the Courts, and that these few are not very revealing. Certainly the death penalty was never invoked on such grounds; only once, in fact, was it even mentioned as a possibility. In 1679 "Edward Bumpus for stricking and abusing his parents, was whipt att the post; his punishment was alleviated in regard hee was crasey brained, otherwise hee had bine put to death or otherwise sharply punished." [51] In other instances the Court's function was to mediate between the affected parties or to ratify an agreement which had already been worked out on an informal basis. In 1669, for instance, it heard various testimonies about the "crewell, unnaturall, and extreame passionate carriages" of one Mary Morey toward her son Benjamin, and his own "unbeseeming" response. The situation was described as being so "turbulent . . . that severall of the naighbours feared murder would be in the issue of it." [52] Yet in the end the Court took no action beyond admonishing both principals and making them "promise reformation." Some years earlier Thomas Lumbert of Barnstable complained formally that "Jedediah, his sone, hath carryed stuburnly against his said father," and proposed that the boy be "freed, provided hee doe dispose himselfe in some honest family with his fathers consent." [53] The Court merely recorded this arrangement and decided not to interfere directly unless Jedediah neglected to find himself a good foster home. In sum, then, the role of the Court with regard to specific cases of this type, was quite limited. The laws on the matter should be viewed as expressing broad and basic values rather than an actual pattern of intervention in the day-to-day affairs of Old Colony households. In fact, most parents must have tried to define and enforce their authority very much on an individual basis. Quite likely an appeal to the Courts was a last resort, to be undertaken only with a keen sense of failure and personal humiliation.

The innermost dimensions of these vital intrafamily relationships cannot really be traced. But two particular matters seem noteworthy. Questions of inheritance were more closely intertwined with discipline

[50] Brigham, *The Compact with the Charter and Laws of the Colony of New Plymouth*, 245.
[51] *Plymouth Colony Records*, VI, 20.
[52] *Plymouth Colony Records*, V, 16.
[53] *Plymouth Colony Records*, III, 201.

in that period than is generally the case now. In some of the wills bequests to certain children were made contingent on their maintaining the proper sort of obedience. Thus, for example, Thomas Hicks of Scituate left most of his lands to "my two sonnes Daniell and Samuell upon this proviso that they bee Obedient unto theire mother and carrye themselves as they ought soe as they may live comfortably together but if the one or both live otherwise then they ought and undewtyfully and unquietly with theire Mother . . . then hee that soe carryeth himselfe shall Disinheritt himselte of his pte of this land." [54] The effectiveness of this kind of sanction among the settlers at large is difficult to assess. In many cases, of course, the point was never rendered so explicit as in the will of Thomas Hicks; but it must often have loomed in the background when conflict between parents and children reached a certain degree of intensity.

The same model of filial behavior seems to have obtained for grown as well as for young children, though perhaps in a somewhat attenuated form. In 1663, for example, the Court summoned Abraham Pierce, Jr. "to answare for his abusive speeches used to his father." [55] The younger Pierce was at this time twenty-five years old and married. Another Court case of a different sort involved a question of disputed paternity. Martha, wife of Thomas Hewitt, gave birth shortly—*too* shortly—after their marriage: her husband contended that he could not have been the child's father and so persuaded the Court. Instead suspicion pointed toward Martha's own father, Christopher Winter, raising thereby the awful specter of incest. Among the evidence presented was "Winters acknowlidgment, that after hee had had knowlidge of his said daughters being withchild,—being, as hee said, informed by Hewitt,—hee did not bring them together and enquire into it, nor reprove or beare witnes against her wickednes, as would have become a father that was innosent." [56] Apparently then, a parent would normally continue to concern himself directly in the personal affairs of his children, even when they had become adult and were involved with families of their own. And, by implication, the children should listen to his counsel and respond accordingly.

But if the child owed his parents an unceasing kind of obedience and respect, there were other obligations which applied in the reverse direction. The parent for his part must accept responsibility for certain basic needs of his children—for their physical health and welfare, for their education (understood in the broadest sense), and for the property they would require in order one day to "be for themselves." There were, moreover, legal provisions permitting the community to intervene in the case of parents who defaulted on these obligations. One statute affirmed that when "psons in this Gourment are not able to provide Competent and convenient food and raiment for theire Children," the latter might be taken in hand by local officials and placed in foster families where they would be more "comfortably provided for." [57] Another, more extended

[54] *Mayflower Descendant*, XI, 160.
[55] *Plymouth Colony Records*, IV, 47.
[56] *Plymouth Colony Records*, V, 13.
[57] *Plymouth Colony Records*, XI, 111.

set of enactments dealt with the whole educational side of the parental
role. Children should be taught to read, "at least to be able duely to read
the Scriptures." They should be made to understand "the Capital Laws"
and "the main Grounds and Principles of Christian Religion." And they
should be trained "in some honest lawful calling, labour or employment,
that may be profitable for themselves, or the Country." [58] Parents who
neglected any of this were subject to fines; and once again the ultimate
recourse of transferring children into new families might be applied if the
neglect were habitual. Unfortunately we cannot discover how often these
procedures were actually set in motion. The responsibility for specific
cases was assigned to local authorities in the various towns, and records
of their actions have not survived. But the basic intent behind the laws
which covered such matters is clear—and in itself significant.

The obligation to provide a "portion" of property for children when
they attained maturity was nowhere expressed in formal, legal terms. But
it can certainly be inferred from other types of evidence. Many wills
made specific mention of previous bequests to grown children—real or
personal property, or both. Deeds of apprenticeship and adoption sometimes included the promise of a portion as one of the essential terms. This
responsibility might, it seems, be transferred from a child's natural parents
to his new master, but it could not be overlooked altogether. Some men
gained the assistance of the government in arranging portions for their
young, witness the following type of Court Order: "Libertie is graunted
unto Mr. John Alden to looke out a portion of land to accomodate his
sons withall." [59] Indeed the fundamental laws of the Colony recognized
a special claim to such "accomodation" for "such children as heere born
and next unto them such as are heere brought up under their parents and
are come to the age of discretion." [60]

More often, however, portions were managed on a purely private
basis. One of the rare personal documents to survive from the Old Colony,
a letter written by Benjamin Brewster, describes the process as it operated
in a particular case: "Being at the hose of Gorge Geres upon the first of
may in the yere of our Lord: 1684 then and there was a discourse betwene
the aforesayd Geres and his son Jonathan he then being of age to be for
him selfe: upon som consederration mofeing the sayd Geres there to he
then declared what he would gefe his son Jonathan as the full of his
porshon except ypon his sons better behaver should desarve more which
was: 130: akers of Land that his father had of Owanneco up in the con-
tre: and: 2: best of 2 yere old: 1: stere of: 4: yer old and a cow." [61]

[58] Brigham, *The Compass with the Charter and Laws of the Colony of New Plymouth*, 270–71.
[59] *Plymouth Colony Records*, III, 120.
[60] Brigham, *The Compact with the Charter and Laws of the Colony of New Plymouth*, 46.
[61] *Mayflower Descendant*, II, 113.

The Seneca Nation of Indians

ANTHONY F. C. WALLACE

Most Americans have learned their colonial history as if it began with Sir Walter Raleigh at Roanoke Island, continued with the arrival of the Puritans in Massachusetts Bay, and proceeded through the seventeenth and eighteenth centuries with the establishment of thirteen colonies that finally joined hands in a common effort to protect freedom and other natural rights that were threatened by an autocratic mother country. This is mythological and ethnocentric history, primarily because it ignores the central fact of our early development —that for the first two centuries of European presence in North America the colonists were in constant and intimate contact with two other cultural groups, Native Americans and Africans. Our early history is the history of the convergence of three internally diverse peoples—each from a different continent but linked together by circumstances and design.

This alone requires that we understand the everyday lives of Native Americans, for there is no comprehension of "interaction" among three peoples when we know about the culture of only one of them. But for another reason also we must understand the everyday lives of "Indians"—the misnomer applied by Columbus to the people he met in the Caribbean in the late fifteenth century and the term used thereafter by European colonizers to describe all of the diverse native inhabitants of two continents. Colonizing Europeans drew upon Indian culture because their survival depended on it. They copied Indian forms of agriculture; incorporated Indian herbal cures into their pharmacology; absorbed Indian political concepts; and, ironically, employed Indian methods of warfare to defeat a people who could not be conquered by European military techniques. Europeans commonly spoke of Indians as "savages," described them as cannibalistic, and talked about raising up "the Heathen." Nonetheless, the colonizers borrowed extensively from the Indian cultures they disparaged, as they struggled for a foothold on the eastern edge of the continent.

Anthony Wallace gives us a vivid picture of Seneca culture. Nobody who reads his analysis should fail to understand that while Europeans and Iroquois were in different stages of technological development, each had a culture that served its purposes. That is why the Iroquois—and the point holds for each of the many Indian societies east of the Mississippi River—did not simply abandon their political organization, religious beliefs, kinship arrangements, and methods of child-rearing when confronted with invading Europeans who continually pronounced the superiority of their culture. Senecas took from the Europeans what they found useful in strengthening their

43

own society. They rejected the rest. So it was with the French, Dutch, and English who interacted with Senecas. Acculturation was a two-way process, with each society borrowing from the other as it deemed necessary.

By reading the selections by Demos and Wallace concurrently, students can compare cultural norms that conditioned everyday life in English and Iroquois communities. The concept of masculine domination was ingrained in European culture; the Iroquois matriarchate distributed power and status between the two sexes more evenly. European child-rearing was highly authoritarian; the Iroquois method was permissive. Europeans placed the private ownership of property at the center of their scheme of economic and social organization; Iroquois gave it a circumscribed role and emphasized communalism instead.

When Europeans acquired sufficient power to conquer a particular Indian society, they pointed to these cultural differences as proof of Indian "savagery" and thus justified their actions. But their proclamations of disdain cannot hide the fact that the colonizers often envied the Indian's ability to sustain himself in the North American environment, to live a life of simplicity, and to attain, almost without trying, the European goal of community, which the colonizers found so illusive.

Another common error is to assume that the history of Indian-white relations is simply the tale of white genocide and the cultural obliteration of Native American ways. It is true that European colonizers were the victors in several centuries of armed clashes, that the Indians were dispossessed of almost all their land, and that by the late nineteenth century the reservation had become the home of a majority of Indian peoples. But as Wallace shows elsewhere in his book, the Seneca survived through centuries of contact with European-Americans, continuously adapting their culture in a struggle for cultural as well as physical survival. Their culture is not dead today. It is different; and so is the culture of the Europeans who came to North America. The Senecas' ways of looking at the world around them still influence American culture, perhaps never so much as in the present day when their beliefs concerning the proper relationship between humans and their environment have captured the imagination of a growing number of people. And every reader will note the similarity of "modern" child-rearing practices to those of the Iroquois, which in the seventeenth century were termed "barbarous" by the first settlers.

The world in which Handsome Lake grew to manhood, and in which he took his place as an active hunter and warrior, was the world of an unvanquished Indian nation: the Seneca, the most populous and the most powerful of the confederated Iroquois tribes. They numbered about four thousand souls, and their tribal territory extended from the upper waters of the Allegheny and the Susquehanna rivers, on the south, to Lake Ontario, on the north. The western marches of the Seneca territory were the shores of Lake Erie. On the east, beyond Seneca Lake, were the Cayuga people. The other Iroquois tribes—Onondaga, Oneida (and Tuscarora), and Mohawk—lay successively eastward almost to the Hudson River. The whole area occupied by the Iroquoian confederacy between the Hudson River and Lake Erie was compared by the Iroquois themselves to a long-house compartmented by tribes; and in this longhouse the Seneca were "the keepers of the western door." They were guardians of that portal from which Iroquois warriors traditionally issued to attack the western and southern nations, through which Iroquois hunters passed to exploit the conquered lands along the Allegheny and Ohio, and on which other nations, in friendship or in war, must knock before entering the home country of the confederacy. Their warriors ranged from Hudson's Bay to the mountains of the Carolinas, and from the Atlantic to the Mississippi, fighting against members of alien tribes and, on occasion, against the French and the English; their chiefs and orators sat in council, year after year, with Europeans in the colonial capitals, working out a *modus vivendi* with the invaders. To be a Seneca was to be a member of one of the most feared, most courted, and most respected Indian tribes in North America.

VILLAGERS, WARRIORS, AND STATESMEN

A Seneca village in the eighteenth century was a few dozen houses scattered in a meadow. No plan of streets or central square defined a neat settlement pattern. The older men remembered days when towns were built between the forks of streams, protected by moats and palisades, and the dwellings within regularly spaced. But these fortified towns were no longer made, partly because of their earlier vulnerability to artillery and partly because times had become more peaceful anyway after the close of the fifty-odd years of war between 1649 and 1701. Now a village was simply an area within which individual families and kin groups built or abandoned their cabins at will; such focus as the area had for its several hundred inhabitants was provided by the council house (itself merely an enlarged dwelling), where the religious and political affairs of the com-

"The Seneca Nation of Indians." From *The Death and Rebirth of the Seneca* by Anthony F. C. Wallace, pp. 21–39. Copyright © 1969 by Anthony F. C. Wallace. Reprinted by permission of Alfred A. Knopf, Inc.

munity were transacted. Year by year the size of a village changed, depending on wars and rumors of war, the shifts of the fur trade, private feuds and family quarrels, the reputation of chiefs, the condition of the soil for corn culture, and the nearness of water and firewood. The same village might, over a hundred years' time, meander over a settlement area ten or fifteen miles square, increasing and decreasing in size, sometimes splitting up into several little settlements and sometimes coalescing into one, and even acquiring (and dropping) new names in addition to the generic name, which usually endured.

The traditional Iroquois dwelling unit was called a longhouse. It was a dark, noisy, smoke-filled family barracks; a rectangular, gable-roofed structure anywhere from fifty to seventy-five feet in length, constructed of sheets of elm bark lashed on stout poles, housing up to fifty or sixty people. The roof was slotted (sometimes with a sliding panel for rainy days) to let out some of the smoke that eddied about the ceiling. There was only one entrance, sometimes fitted with a wooden or bark door on wooden hinges, and sometimes merely curtained by a bearskin robe. Entering, one gazed in the half-light down a long, broad corridor or alleyway, in the center of which, every twelve or fifteen feet, smoldered a small fire. On opposite sides of each fire, facing one another, were doubledecker bunks, six feet wide and about twelve feet long. An entire family —mother, father, children, and various other relatives—might occupy one or two of these compartments. They slept on soft furs in the lower bunks. Guns, masks, moccasins, clothing, cosmetic paint, wampum, knives, hatchet, food, and the rest of a Seneca family's paraphernalia were slung on the walls and on the upper bunk. Kettles, braided corn, and other suspendable items hung from the joists, which also supported pots over the fire. Each family had about as much room for permanent quarters as might be needed for all of them to lie down and sleep, cook their meals, and stow their gear. Privacy was not easily secured because other families lived in the longhouse; people were always coming and going, and the fires glowed all night. In cold or wet weather or when the snow lay two or three feet deep outside, doors and roof vents had to be closed, and the longhouses became intolerably stuffy—acrid with smoke and the reeking odors of leftover food and sweating flesh. Eyes burned and throats choked. But the people were nonetheless tolerably warm, dry, and (so it is said) cheerful.

The inhabitants of a longhouse were usually kinfolk. A multifamily longhouse was, theoretically, the residence of a maternal lineage: an old woman and her female descendants, together with unmarried sons, and the husbands and children of her married daughters. The totem animal of the clan to which the lineage belonged—Deer, Bear, Wolf, Snipe, or whatever it might be—was carved above the door and painted red. In this way directions were easier to give, and the stranger knew where to seek hospitality or aid. But often—especially in the middle of the eighteenth century—individual families chose to live by themselves in smaller cabins, only eighteen by twenty feet or so in size, with just one fire. As time went on, the old longhouses disintegrated and were abandoned, and by the middle of the century the Iroquois were making their houses of logs.

Around and among the houses lay the cornfields. Corn was a main food. Dried and pounded into meal and then boiled into a hot mush, baked into dumplings, or cooked in whole kernels together with beans and squash and pieces of meat in the thick soups that always hung in kettles over the fires, it kept the people fed. In season, meats, fresh fruits, herb teas, fried grasshoppers, and other delicacies added spice and flavor to the diet. But the Iroquois were a cornfed people. They consumed corn when it was fresh and stored it underground for the lean winter months. The Seneca nation alone raised as much as a million bushels of corn each year; the cornfields around a large village might stretch for miles, and even scattered clearings in the woods were cultivated. Squash, beans, and tobacco were raised in quantity, too. Domesticated animals were few, even after the middle of the century: some pigs, a few chickens, not many horses or cattle. The responsibility for carrying on this extensive agricultural establishment rested almost entirely on the women. Armed with crude wooden hoes and digging-sticks, they swarmed over the fields in gay, chattering work bees, proceeding from field to field to hoe, to plant, to weed, and to harvest. An individual woman might, if she wished, "own" a patch of corn, or an apple or peach orchard, but there was little reason for insisting on private tenure: the work was more happily done communally, and in the absence of a regular market, a surplus was of little personal advantage, especially if the winter were hard and other families needed corn. In such circumstances hoarding led only to hard feelings and strained relations as well as the possibility of future difficulty in getting corn for oneself and one's family. All land was national land; an individual could occupy and use a portion of it and maintain as much privacy in the tenure as he wished, but this usufruct title reverted to the nation when the land was abandoned. There was little reason to bother about individual ownership of real estate anyway: there was plenty of land. Economic security for both men and women lay in a proper recognition of one's obligation to family, clan, community, and nation, and in efficient and cooperative performance on team activities, such as working bees, war parties, and diplomatic missions.

If the clearing with its cornfields bounded the world of women, the forest was the realm of men. Most of the men hunted extensively, not only for deer, elk, and small game to use for food and clothing and miscellaneous household items, but for beaver, mink, and otter, the prime trade furs. Pelts were the gold of the woods. With them a man could buy guns, powder, lead, knives, hatchets, axes, needles and awls, scissors, kettles, traps, cloth, ready-made shirts, blankets, paint (for cosmetic purposes), and various notions: steel springs to pluck out disfiguring beard, scalp, and body hair; silver bracelets and armbands and tubes for coiling hair; rings to hang from nose and ears; mirrors; tinkling bells. Sometimes a tipsy hunter would give away his peltries for a keg of rum, treat his friends to a debauch, and wake up with a scolding wife and hungry children calling him a fool; another might, with equal improvidence, invest in a violin, or a horse, or a gaudy military uniform. But by and large, the products of the commercial hunt—generally conducted in the winter and often hundreds of miles from the home village, in the Ohio country or down the Susquehanna River—were exchanged for a limited range of European consumer goods, which had become, after five generations of contact with beaver-hungry French, Dutch, and English traders, economic necessities. Many of these goods were, indeed, designed to Indian specifications and manufactured solely for the Indian trade. An Iroquois man dressed in a linen breechcloth and calico shirt, with a woolen blanket over his shoulders, bedaubed with trade paint and adorned with trade armbands and earrings, carrying a steel knife, a steel hatchet, a clay pipe, and a rifled gun felt himself in no wise contaminated nor less an Indian than his stone-equipped great-great-grandfather. Iroquois culture had reached out and incorporated these things that Iroquois Indians wanted while at the same time Iroquois warriors chased off European missionaries, battled European soldiers to a standstill, and made obscene gestures when anyone suggested that they should emulate white society (made up, according to their information and experience, of slaves, cheating lawyers with pen and paper and ink, verbose politicians, hypocritical Christians, stingy tavern keepers, and thieving peddlers).

Behavior was governed not by published laws enforced by police, courts, and jails, but by oral tradition supported by a sense of duty, a fear of gossip, and a dread of retaliatory witchcraft. Theft, vandalism, armed robbery, were almost unknown. Public opinion, gently exercised, was sufficient to deter most persons from property crimes, for public opinion went straight to the heart of the matter: the *weakness* of the criminal. A young warrior steals someone else's cow—probably captured during a raid on a white settlement—and slaughters it to feed his hungry family. He does this at a time when other men are out fighting. No prosecution follows, no investigation, no sentence: the unhappy man is nonetheless severely punished, for the nickname "Cow-killer" is pinned to him, and he must drag it rattling behind him wherever he goes. People call him a coward behind his back and snicker when they tell white men, in his presence, a story of an unnamed Indian who killed cows when he should have been killing men. Such a curse was not generalized to the point of ostracism, however. The celebrated Red Jacket, about whom the "Cow-killer" story was told, vindicated his courage in later wars, became the principal spokesman for his nation, and was widely respected and revered. But he never lost the nickname.[1]

Disputes between people rarely developed over property. Marital difficulties centering around infidelity, lack of support, or personal incompatibility were settled by mutual agreement. Commonly, in case of difficulty, the man left and the woman, with her children, remained with her mother. A few couples remained together for a lifetime; most had several marriages; a few changed mates almost with the season. Men might come to blows during drunken arguments over real or fancied slights to their masculine honor, over politics, or over the alleged mistreatment of their kinfolk. Such quarrels led at times to killings or to accusations of witchcraft. A murder (or its equivalent, the practice of witchcraft) was some-

[1] O'Reilly Collection, Vol. XV, d3 (recollections of Thomas Morris), New York Historical Society, New York.

thing to be settled by the victim's kinfolk; if they wished, they might kill the murderer or suspected witch without fear of retaliation from his family (provided that family agreed on his guilt). But usually a known killer would come to his senses, admit himself wrong, repent, and offer retribution in goods or services to the mourning family, who unless exceptionally embittered by an unprovoked and brutal killing were then expected to accept the blood money and end the matter.

Drunkenness was perhaps the most serious social problem. Two Moravian missionaries who visited the Iroquois country in 1750 had the misfortune to reach the Seneca towns at the end of June, when the men were just returning from Oswego, where they had sold their winter's furs, and were beginning to celebrate the start of summer leisure. Hard liquor was dissolving winter's inhibitions and regrets. At Canandaigua, the missionaries, who were guests at the house of a prominent warrior, had just explained the friendly nature of their errand when the rum arrived. "All the town was in a state of intoxication, and frequently rushed into our hut in this condition," complained the white men. "There was every reason to think that fighting might ensue, as there were many warriors among those who were perfectly mad with drink." After a sleepless night the missionaries traveled on, reaching the outskirts of Geneseo on the second of July. "The village," said the observers in surprise, "consisted of 40 or more large huts, and lies in a beautiful and pleasant region. A fine large plain, several miles in length and breadth, stretches out behind the village." But the kegs of rum had anticipated them. "When we caught sight of the town we heard a great noise of shouting and quarreling, from which we could infer that many of the inhabitants were intoxicated, and that we might expect to have an uncomfortable time. On entering the town we saw many drunken Indians, who looked mad with drink. . . ."

Alas, poor Christians! They had to hide in a stuffy garret, without food or water. David, their devoted Indian convert and servant, stole out toward evening with a kettle to fetch his masters some water and was seen. "A troop of drunken women came rushing madly toward him. Some of them were naked, and others nearly so. In order to drive them away he was obliged to use his fists, and deal blows to the right and left. He climbed up a ladder, but when he had scarcely reached the top they seized it and tore it from under his feet." David barely managed to escape "in safety" from these playful Amazons. The missionaries decided not to wait the two days until the liquor ran out to meet the chiefs in council; they bent their prayers to an early departure. They finally managed to escape at dawn by jumping down from an opening in the gable and tiptoeing away. "The Lord watched over us in such a manner that all the drunken savages were in their huts, not a creature to be seen. Even the dogs, numbering nearly 100 in the whole village, were all quiet, wonderful to relate, and not a sound was heard. A dense fog covered the town, so that we could not see 20 steps before us. A squaw stood at the door of the last hut, but she was sober and returned our greeting quietly." [2]

2 William M. Beauchamp, ed., *Moravian Journals Relating to Central New York, 1745–66* (Syracuse, 1916), 67–84.

But such drunken debauches were only occasional rents in a fabric of polite social behavior. Other missionaries were more favorably impressed than the Moravians. The Seneca, said a Quaker scribe, "appear to be naturally as well calculated for social and rational enjoyment, as any people. They frequently visit each other in their houses, and spend much of their time in friendly intercourse. They are also mild and hospitable, not only among themselves, but to strangers, and good natured in the extreme, except when their natures are perverted by the inflammatory influence of spirituous liquors. In their social interviews, as well as public councils, they are careful not to interrupt one another in conversation, and generally make short speeches. This truly laudable mark of good manners, enables them to transact all their public business with decorum and regularity, and more strongly impresses on their mind and memory, the result of their deliberations." [3]

THE IROQUOIS "MATRIARCHATE"

During the seventeenth and eighteenth centuries Iroquois men earned a reputation among the French and English colonists for being the most astute diplomatically and most dangerous militarily of all the Indians of the Northeast. Yet at the same time the Iroquois were famous for the "matriarchal" nature of their economic and social institutions. After the colonial era came to an end with the victory of the United States in the Revolutionary War, the traditional diplomatic and military role of the Iroquois men was sharply limited by the circumstances of reservation life. Simultaneously, the "matriarchal" character of certain of their economic, kinship, and political institutions was drastically diminished. These changes were codified by the prophet Handsome Lake. As we shall see later in more detail, the changes in kinship behavior that he recommended, and which to a considerable degree were carried out by his followers, amounted to a shift in dominance from the mother-daughter relationship to that of the husband-wife. Handsome Lake's reforms thus were a sentence of doom upon the traditional quasi-matriarchal system of the Iroquois.

The Iroquois were described as matriarchal because of the important role women played in the formal political organization. The men were responsible for hunting, for warfare, and for diplomacy, all of which kept them away from their households for long periods of time, and all of which were essential to the survival of Iroquois society. An expedition of any kind was apt to take months or even years, for the fifteen thousand or so Iroquois in the seventeenth and eighteenth centuries ranged over an area of about a million square miles. It is not an exaggeration to say that the full-time business of an Iroquois man was travel, in order to hunt, trade, fight, and talk in council. But the women stayed at home. Thus, an Iroquois village might be regarded as a collection of strings, hundreds of

---

[3] Halliday Jackson, *Sketch of the Manners, Customs, Religion and Government of the Seneca Indians in 1800* (Philadelphia, 1830), 19.

years old, of successive generations of women, always domiciled in their longhouses near their cornfields in a clearing while their sons and husbands traveled in.the forest on supportive errands of hunting and trapping, of trade, of war, and of diplomacy.

The women exercised political power in three main circumstances. First, whenever one of the forty-nine chiefs of the great intertribal League of the Iroquois died, the senior women of his lineage nominated his successor. Second, when tribal or village decisions had to be made, both men and women attended a kind of town meeting, and while men were the chiefs and normally did the public speaking, the women caucused behind the scenes and lobbied with the spokesmen. Third, a woman was entitled to demand publicly that a murdered kinsman or kinswoman be replaced by a captive from a non-Iroquois tribe, and her male relatives, particularly lineage kinsmen, were morally obligated to go out in a war party to secure captives, whom the bereaved woman might either adopt or consign to torture and death. Adoption was so frequent during the bloody centuries of the beaver wars and the colonial wars that some Iroquois villages were preponderantly composed of formally adopted war captives. In sum, Iroquois women were entitled formally to select chiefs, to participate in consensual politics, and to start wars.

Thus the Iroquois during the two centuries of the colonial period were a population divided, in effect, into two parts: sedentary females and nomadic males. The men were frequently absent in small or large groups for prolonged periods of time on hunting, trading, war, and diplomatic expeditions, simultaneously protecting the women from foreign attack and producing a cash crop of skins, furs, and scalps, which they exchanged for hardware and dry goods. These activities, peripheral in a geographical sense, were central to the economic and political welfare of the Six Nations. The preoccupation of Iroquois men with these tasks and the pride they took in their successful pursuit cannot be overestimated. But the system depended on a complementary role for women. They had to be economically self-sufficient through horticulture during the prolonged absences of men, and they maintained genealogical and political continuity in a matrilineal system in which the primary kin relationship (not necessarily the primary social relationship) was the one between mother and daughter.

Such a quasi-matriarchy, of course, had a certain validity in a situation where the division of labor between the sexes required that men be geographically peripheral to the households that they helped to support and did defend. Given the technological, economic, and military circumstances of the time, such an arrangement was a practical one. But it did have an incidental consequence: It made the relationship between husband and wife an extremely precarious one. Under these conditions it was convenient for the marital system to be based on virtually free sexual choice, the mutual satisfaction of spouses, and easy separation. Couples chose one another for personal reasons; free choice was limited, in effect, only by the prohibition of intraclan marriage. Marriages were apt to fray when a husband traveled too far, too frequently, for too long. On his return, drunken quarreling, spiteful gossip, parental irresponsibility, and flagrant infidelity might lead rapidly to the end of the relationship. The husband, away from the household for long periods of time, was apt in his travels to establish a liaison with a woman whose husband was also away. The wife, temporarily abandoned, might for the sake of comfort and economic convenience take up with a locally available man. Since such relationships were, in effect, in the interest of everyone in the longhouse, they readily tended to become recognized as marriages. The emotional complications introduced by these serial marriages were supposed to be resolved peacefully by the people concerned. The traveling husband who returned to find his wife living with someone else might try to recover her; if she preferred to remain with her new husband, however, he was not entitled to punish her or her new lover, but instead was encouraged to find another wife among the unmarried girls or wives with currently absent husbands.[4]

THE IDEAL OF AUTONOMOUS RESPONSIBILITY

The basic ideal of manhood was that of "the good hunter." Such a man was self-disciplined, autonomous, responsible. He was a patient and efficient huntsman, a generous provider to his family and nation, and a loyal and thoughtful friend and clansman. He was also a stern and ruthless warrior in avenging any injury done to those under his care. And he was always stoical and indifferent to privation, pain, and even death. Special prominence could be achieved by those who, while adequate in all respects, were outstanding in one or another dimension of this ideal. The patient and thoughtful man with a skin "seven thumbs thick" (to make him indifferent to spiteful gossip, barbed wit, and social pressures generally) might become a sachem or a "distinguished name"—a "Pine Tree" chief. An eloquent man with a good memory and indestructible poise might be a council speaker and represent clan, nation, even the confederacy in far-flung diplomatic ventures. And the stern and ruthless warrior (always fighting, at least according to the theory, to avenge the death or insult of a blood relative or publicly avowed friend) might become a noted war-captain or an official war-chief. The war-captain ideal, open as it was to all youths, irrespective of clan and lineage or of special intellectual qualifications, was perhaps the most emulated.

In the seventeenth century an Onondaga war-captain named Aharihon bore the reputation of being the greatest warrior of the country. He realized the ideal of autonomous responsibility to virtually pathological perfection. Let us note what is told of Aharihon in the *Jesuit Relations*.[5]

[4] This section is drawn from a paper entitled "Handsome Lake and the Decline of the Iroquois Matriarchate," which was read at the Wenner-Gren symposium at Burg Wartenstein, Austria, on Kinship and Behavior in the summer of 1966. The concept of dominant kin relationship is developed in Francis L. K. Hsu, "The Effect of Dominant Kinship Relationships on Kin- and Non-Kin Behavior: A Hypothesis," *American Anthropologist*, LXVII (1965), 638–61.

[5] Edna Kenton, ed., *The Indians of North America* (2 vols.; New York, 1927), II, 78–80.

Aharihon was a man of dignified appearance and imposing carriage, grave, polished in manner, and self-contained. His brother had been killed about 1654 in the wars with the Erie, a tribe westward of the Iroquois. As clansman and close relative, he was entitled—indeed obligated—either to avenge his brother's death by killing some Erie people or by adopting a war captive to take his place. Aharihon within a few years captured or had presented to him for adoption forty men. Each of them he burned to death over a slow fire, because, as he said, "he did not believe that there was any one worthy to occupy his [brother's] place." Father Lalemant was present when another young man, newly captured, was given to Aharihon as a substitute for the deceased brother. Aharihon let the young man believe that he was adopted and need have no further fear, and "presented to him four dogs, upon which to hold his feast of adoption. In the middle of the feast, while he was rejoicing and singing to entertain the guests, Aharihon arose, and told the company that this man too must die in atonement for his brother's death. The poor lad was astounded at this, and turned toward the door to make his escape, but was stopped by two men who had orders to burn him. On the fourteenth of February, in the evening, they began with his feet, intending to roast him, at a slow fire, as far up as the waist, during the greater part of the night. After midnight, they were to let him rally his strength and sleep a little until daybreak, when they were to finish this fatal tragedy. In his torture, the poor man made the whole village resound with his cries and groans. He shed great tears, contrary to the usual custom, the victim commonly glorying to be burned limb by limb, and opening his lips only to sing; but, as this one had not expected death, he wept and cried in a way that touched even these Barbarians. One of Aharihon's relatives was so moved with pity, that he advised ending the sufferer's torments by plunging a knife into his breast —which would have been a deed of mercy, had the stab been mortal. However, they were induced to continue the burning without interruption, so that before day he ended both his sufferings and his life." Aharihon's career of death continued without interruption, and by 1663 he was able to boast that he had killed sixty men with his own hand and had burned fully eighty men over slow fire. He kept count by tattooing a mark on his thigh for each successive victim. He was known then as the Captain General of the Iroquois and was nicknamed Nero by the Frenchmen at Montreal because of his cruelty.

The French finally captured him near Montreal, but even in captivity his manner was impressive. "This man," commented Father Lalemant, "commonly has nine slaves with him, five boys and four girls. He is a captain of dignified appearance and imposing carriage, and of such equanimity and presence of mind that, upon seeing himself surrounded by armed men, he showed no more surprise than if he had been alone; and when asked whether he would like to accompany us to Quebec, he deigned only to answer coldly that that was not a question to ask him, since he was in our power. Accordingly he was made to come aboard our Vessel, where I took pleasure in studying his disposition as well as that of an Algonquin in our company, who bore the scalp of an Iroquois but recently slain by him in war. These two men, although hostile enough to

eat each other, chatted and laughed on board that Vessel with great familiarity, it being very hard to decide which of the two was more skillful
in masking his feelings. I had Nero placed near me at table, where he bore
himself with a gravity, a self-control, and a propriety, which showed
nothing of his Barbarian origin; but during the rest of the time he was
constantly eating, so that he fasted only when he was at table."

But this voracious captain was not renowned among the Onondaga
as a killer only. He was, on the contrary, also a trusted ambassador, dispatched on occasion to Montreal on missions of peace. He was, in a word,
a noted man. He was a killer, but he was not an indiscriminate killer; he
killed only those whom it was his right to kill, tortured only those whom
he had the privilege of torturing, always as an expression of respect for
his dead brother. And although his kinfolk sometimes felt he was a little
extreme in his stern devotion to his brother's memory, they did not feel
that he was any the less a fine man, or that they had a right to interfere
with his impulses; they were willing to entrust the business of peace, as
well as war, to his hand. . . .

With this sort of man serving as an ego-ideal, held up by sanction
and by praise to youthful eyes, it is not remarkable that young men were
ambitious to begin the practice of war. All had seen captives tortured to
death; all had known relatives lost in war whose death demanded revenge
or replacement. The young men went out on practice missions as soon as
they were big enough to handle firearms; "infantile bands, armed with
hatchets and guns which they can hardly carry, do not fail to spread fear
and horror everywhere." [6] Even as late as the middle of the eighteenth
century, Handsome Lake and his brothers and nephews were still busy
at the old business of war for the sake of war. Cornplanter became a noted
war-captain; Blacksnake, his nephew, was one of the official war-chiefs of
the Seneca nation; and Handsome Lake himself took part in the scalping-
party pattern as a young man. But Handsome Lake became a sachem and
later a prophet, and he never gloried in the numbers of men he killed as
his brother Cornplanter (somewhat guiltily) did. "While I was in the use
of arms I killed seven persons and took three and saved their lives," said
Cornplanter. And Blacksnake, in later life, told with relish of his exploits
as a warrior. "We had a good fight there," he would say. "I have killed
how many I could not tell, for I pay no attention to or kept [no] account
of it, it was great many, for I never have it at all my Battles to think about
kepting account what I'd killed at one time. . . ." [7]

The cultivation of the ideal of autonomous responsibility—and the
suppression of its antinomy, dependency—began early in life. Iroquois
children were carefully trained to think for themselves but to act for
others. Parents were protective, permissive, and sparing of punishment;
they encouraged children to play at imitating adult behavior but did not
criticize or condemn fumbling early efforts; they maintained a cool de-
tachment, both physically and verbally, avoiding the intense confronta-

[6] Kenton, *Indians of North America*, II, 87–88.
[7] Draper Collection, 16 F 227 ("Cornplanter's Talk"), State Historical Society of
Wisconsin, Madison, Wis.

tions of love and anger between parent and child to which Europeans were accustomed. Children did not so much live in a child's world as grow up freely in the interstices of an adult culture. The gain was an early self-reliance and enjoyment of responsibility; the cost, perhaps, was a life-long difficulty in handling feelings of dependency.

The Seneca mother gave birth to her child in the privacy of the woods, where she retired for a few hours when her time came, either alone or in the company of an older woman who served as midwife and, if the weather was cold, built and tended a fire. She had prepared for this event by eating sparingly and exercising freely, which were believed (probably with good reason) to make the child stronger and the birth easier. The newborn infant was washed in cold water, or even in snow, immediately after parturition and then wrapped in skins or a blanket. If the birth were a normal one, the mother walked back to the village with her infant a few hours afterwards to take up the duties of housewife. The event was treated as the consummation of a healthful process rather than as an illness. The infant spent much of its first nine months swaddled from chin to toe and lashed to a cradleboard. The child's feet rested against a footboard; a block of wood was placed between the heels of a girl to mold her feet to an inward turn. Over its head stretched a hoop, which could be draped with a thin cloth to keep away flies or to protect the child from the cold. The board and its wrappings were often lavishly decorated with silver trinkets and beadwork embroidery. The mother was able to carry the child in the board, suspended against her back, by a tumpline around her forehead; the board could be hung from the limb of a tree while she hoed corn; and it could be converted into a crib by suspending it on a rack of poles laid horizontally on forks stuck in the ground. The mother was solicitous of the child's comfort, nursed it whenever it cried, and loosened it from the board several times a day to change the moss that served as a diaper and to give it a chance to romp. The children, however, tended to cry when released from the board, and their tranquility could often be restored only by putting them back. Babies were seldom heard crying.

The mother's feeling for her children was intense; indeed, to one early observer it appeared that "Parental Tenderness" was carried to a "dangerous Indulgence." [8] Another early writer remarked, "The mothers love their children with an extreme passion, and although they do not reveal this in caresses, it is nevertheless real." [9] Mothers were quick to express resentment of any restraint or injury or insult offered to the child by an outsider. During the first few years the child stayed almost constantly with the mother, in the house, in the fields, or on the trail, playing and performing small tasks under her direction. The mother's chief concern during this time was to provide for the child and to protect it, to "harden" it by baths in cold water, but not to punish. Weaning was not

[8] Draper Collection 16 F 32 ("Life of Governor Blacksnake"), State Hist. Soc. of Wis.

[9] Milton W. Hamilton, ed., "Guy Johnson's Opinions on the American Indian," *Pennsylvania Magazine of History and Biography*, LXXVII (1953), 320.

normally attempted until the age of three or four, and such control as the child obtained over its excretory functions was achieved voluntarily, not as a result of consistent punishment for mistakes. Early sexual curiosity and experimentation were regarded as a natural childish way of behaving, out of which it would, in due time, grow. Grandparents might complain that small children got into everything, but the small child was free to romp, to pry into things, to demand what it wanted, and to assault its parents, without more hazard of punishment than the exasperated mother's occasionally blowing water in its face or dunking it in a convenient river.

The years between about eight or nine and the onset of puberty were a time of easy and gradual learning. At the beginning of this period the beginnings of the differentiation of the roles of boys and girls were laid down. The girls were kept around the house, under the guidance of their mothers, and assigned to the lighter household duties and to helping in the fields. Boys were allowed to roam in gangs, playing at war, hunting with bows and arrows and toy hatchets, and competing at races, wrestling, and lacrosse. The first successes at hunting were greeted with praise and boasts of future greatness. Sometimes these roaming gangs spent days at a time away from the village, sleeping in the bush, eating wild roots and fruits, and hunting such small game as could be brought down by bow and arrow, blowgun, or snare. These gangs developed into war parties after the boys reached puberty. Among themselves, both in gangs and among siblings of the same family, the children's playgroups were not constantly supervised by parents and teachers, and the children governed themselves in good harmony. Said one close observer, "Children of the same family show strong attachments to each other, and are less liable to quarrel in their youthful days than is generally the case with white children." [10]

The parents usually tried to maintain a calm moderation of behavior in dealing with their children, a lofty indifference alike to childish tantrums and seductive appeals for love. Hardihood, self-reliance, and independence of spirit were sedulously inculcated. When occasion presented itself, fathers, uncles, or other elder kinfolk instructed their sons in the techniques of travel, firemaking, the chase, war, and other essential arts of manhood, and the mothers correspondingly taught their daughters the way to hoe and plant the cornfields, how to butcher the meat, cook, braid corn, and other household tasks. But this instruction was presented, rather than enforced, as an opportunity rather than as a duty. On occasion the parent or other responsible adult talked to the child at length, "endeavoring," as a Quaker scribe gently put it, "to impress on its mind what it ought to do, and what to leave undone." [11] If exhortation seemed inadequate in its effect, the mentor might ridicule the child for doing wrong, or gravely point out the folly of a certain course of action, or even warn him that he courted the rage of offended supernatural beings. Obedience as such was no virtue, however, and blows, whippings, or restraints of any kind, such as restriction to quarters, were rarely imposed, the faults of the child being left to his own reason and conscience to correct as he

[10] Joseph Lafitau, *Moeurs des sauvages Americains* (2 vols., Paris, 1724), I, 393.
[11] Jackson, *Sketch of the Manners*, p. 20.

grew mature. With delicate perception the adults noted that childish faults "cannot be very great, before reason arrives at some degree of maturity." [12]

Direct confrontation with the child was avoided, but when things got seriously out of hand, parents sometimes turned older children over to the gods for punishment. A troublesome child might be sent out into the dusk to meet Longnose, the legendary Seneca bogeyman. Longnose might even be impersonated in the flesh by a distraught parent. Longnose was a hungry cannibal who chased bad children when their parents were sleeping. He mimicked the child, crying loudly as he ran, but the parents would not wake up because Longnose had bewitched them. A child might be chased all night until he submitted and promised to behave. Theoretically, if a child remained stubborn, Longnose finally caught him and took him away in a huge pack-basket for a leisurely meal. And—although parents were not supposed to do this—an unusually stubborn infant *could* be threatened with punishment by the great False Faces themselves, who, when invoked for this purpose, might "poison" a child or "spoil his face." "I remember," recalled a Cayuga woman of her childhood, "how scared I was of the False-faces; I didn't know what they were. They are to scare away disease. They used to come into the house and up the stairs and I used to hide away under the covers. They even crawled under the bed and they made that awful sound. When I was bad my mother used to say the False-faces would get me. Once, I must have been only 4 or 5, because I was very little when I left Canada, but I remember it so well that when I think of it I can hear that cry now, and I was going along a road from my grandfather's; it was a straight road and I couldn't lose my way, but it was almost dark, and I had to pass through some timber and I heard that cry and that rattle. I ran like a flash of lightening and I can hear it yet." [13]

At puberty some of the boys retired to the woods under the stewardship of an old man, where they fasted, abstained from any sort of sexual activity (which they had been free to indulge, to the limit of their powers, before), covered themselves with dirt, and mortified the flesh in various ways, such as bathing in ice water and bruising and gashing the shinbones with rocks. Dreams experienced during such periods of self-trial were apt to be regarded as visitations from supernatural spirits who might grant *orenda*, or magical power, to the dreamer, and who would maintain a special sort of guardianship over him. The person's connection with this supernatural being was maintained through a charm—such as a knife, a queerly shaped stone, or a bit of bone—which was connected with the dream through some association significant to the dreamer. Unlike many other tribes, however, the Iroquois apparently did not require these guardian-spirit visions for pubescent youths. Many youths were said not to have had their first vision until just before their first war party. Furthermore, any man could have a significant dream or vision at any time. Girls too went through a mild puberty ritual, retiring into the woods at first menstruation and paying particular attention to their dreams. With

[12] *Ibid.*
[13] *Ibid.*

the termination of the menstrual period the girl returned to the household; but hereafter, whenever she menstruated, she would have to live
apart in a hut, avoiding people, and being careful not to step on a path, or
to cook and serve anyone's food, or (especially) to touch medicines,
which would immediately lose their potency if she handled them.[14]

The Europeans who observed this pattern of child experience were
by no means unfavorably impressed although they were sometimes
amazed. They commented, however, almost to a man, from early Jesuit
to latter-day Quaker, on a consequence that stood out dramatically as
they compared this "savage" maturation with "civilized." "There is nothing," wrote the Jesuit chronicler of the Iroquois mission in 1657, "for
which these peoples have a greater horror than restraint. The very children
cannot endure it, and live as they please in the houses of their parents,
without fear of reprimand or chastisement." [15] One hundred and fifty
years later, the Quaker Halliday Jackson observed that "being indulged
in most of their wishes, as they grow up, liberty, in its fullest extent, becomes their ruling passion." [16] The Iroquois themselves recognized the intensity of their children's resentment at parental interference. "Some Savages," reported Le Mercier of the Huron, "told us that one of the principal reasons why they showed so much indulgence toward their children,
was that when the children saw themselves treated by their parents with
some severity, they usually resorted to extreme measures and hanged
themselves, or ate of a certain root they call *Audachienrra*, which is a very
quick poison." [17] The same fear was recorded among the Iroquois, including the Seneca, in 1657. And while suicides by frustrated children were
not actually frequent, there are nevertheless a number of recorded cases
of suicide where parental interference was the avowed cause. And *mutatis
mutandis*, there was another rationalization for a policy of permissiveness:
that the child who was harshly disciplined might grow up, some day, to
mistreat his parents in revenge.

This theory of child raising was not taken for granted by the Seneca;
on the contrary, it was very explicitly recognized, discussed, and pon-
dered. Handsome Lake himself, in later years, insisted that parents love
and indulge their children.

[14] William N. Fenton, "Problems Arising from the Historic Northeastern Position
of the Iroquois," *Smithsonian Miscellaneous Collections*, C (1940), 429.
[15] Kenton, *Indians of North America*, II, 90.
[16] Jackson, *Sketch of the Manners*, p. 19.
[17] Kenton, *Indians of North America*, p. 90n.

Indians and Colonists at War

Violence, or the threat of violence, was a primary fact of life for almost every colonist. That is why in most colonies almost every free white male between sixteen and sixty was required to serve in the militia. Eternal readiness to ward off hostile forces was everybody's responsibility, and therefore military service became a key element of everyday life.

It is a mistake, however, to accept the notion that the ever-present threat of violence originated in hostile Indians. For most European colonizers violence was a state of mind before it was a physical reality. Even before they arrived in North America, Englishmen carried in their minds a split image of the Native American. On the one hand the native people were seen as brutish, even cannibalistic, inhabitants of "a savage wilderness" that threatened chaos on every side and might drag "civilized" men down to the level of beasts. On the other hand the Indians were pictured as winsome, if ignorant, creatures living in an Arcadia of which Europeans had long dreamed.

It was the negative side of this split image that quickly prevailed in most minds. Land was the key to English settlement in North America, and it was logical to assume that the native occupiers of the land would not willingly give it up. The stereotype of a hostile, heathen "savage" that quickly dominated colonial thinking about Native Americans was linked to the problem of land. Seeing Indians in this way helped assuage the guilt that arose inevitably when Europeans, whose culture was based on the concept of private property, embarked on a campaign to dispossess another people of the ground that sustained them. To type-cast the Indian as a "savage" was to justify European seizure of the land. Moreover, as the American historian Richard Slotkin has recently shown, colonizing Englishmen, especially Puritans, developed the belief that through heroic but violent conquest of the New World "wilderness" and its inhabitants corrupt Europeans could experience renewal and purification.

It was this cast of mind that brought Massachusetts to war with neighboring Indians before the colony was seven years in existence. The charter of the colony pronounced that the "principall ende of this plantacion" was to "wynn and incite the natives of [the] country, to the knowledge and obedience of the onlie true God and Savior of mankinde." But violence, not preaching, became the instrument most frequently employed in Puritan relations with the Indians. The destruction rather than the conversion of the indigenous people, who came to be thought of as Satan's disciples, became the dominant fact of seventeenth-century Indian-European relations. From the extermination of the Pequots in 1637, which served the economic purpose of

opening up rich new lands for the growing population of Massachusetts and the psychological purpose of establishing Puritan "order" over Indian "chaos," armed conflict with Native Americans was
an integral part of the colonial experience. "The Indian wars," writes
Slotkin, in his book **Regeneration Through Violence: The Mythology
of the American Frontier,** "became the distinctive event of American
history, the unique national experience."

The following account of the Pequot War, written by a participant, gives vivid insights into this mental framework of Puritan colonizers. It also yields clues to the process by which colonists borrowed
from Indian culture in their everyday struggle against their enemies.
This adaptation took place in every colony where colonial land hunger
was met with Indian resistance and war was the result. From Maine
to Georgia, Indian wars punctuated the colonial period. In these wars,
the colonists usually prevailed only insofar as they were able to borrow
the tactics of their antagonists, as is shown in Douglas Leach's description of the long and discouraging attempts of the populous New
England colonies to defeat Metacom (whom they called King Philip)
and his followers, whose numbers were comparatively insignificant.
In reading Leach, students should carefully compare the vocabulary
employed to describe Indian motives and actions, on the one hand,
and Puritan motives and behavior on the other.

After 1675–76, when two long Indian wars were fought in New
England and Virginia, these conflicts became even more threatening
because Indian societies were frequently allied with the Spanish and
French, England's rivals for supremacy on the continent. From 1688,
when King William's War began, until 1814, the Americans would
be intermittently engaged in bloody conflicts against dozens of eastern tribes allied with France or Spain. Nobody living in Anglo-America
for the first two centuries of its existence was very far from at least
several of these wars at some point in his life. Thus violence became
ingrained in everyday experience.

The History of the Pequot War

JOHN UNDERHILL

The cause of our war against the Block Islanders, was for taking away
the life of one Master John Oldham, who made it his common course to
trade amongst the Indians. He coming to Block Island to drive trade with
them, the islanders came into his boat, and having got a full view of

"The History of the Pequot War," by John Underhill. From *Newes from America:
Or, A New and Experimentall Discoverie of New England* . . . (London, 1638),
reprinted in *Collections of the Massachusetts Historical Society*, 3d ser., 6 (1837),
3–13, 15–19, 23–28.

commodities which gave them good content, consulted how they might destroy him and his company, to the end they might clothe their bloody flesh with his lawful garments. The Indians having laid the plot, into the boat they came to trade, as they pretended; watching their opportunities, knocked him in the head, and martyred him most barbarously, to the great grief of his poor distressed servants, which by the providence of God were saved. This island lying in the road way to Lord Sey and the Lord Brooke's plantation, a certain seaman called to John Gallop, master of the small navigation standing along to the Mathethusis Bay, and seeing a boat under sail close aboard the island, and perceiving the sails to be unskilfully managed, bred in him a jealousy, whether that the island Indians had not bloodily taken the life of our countrymen, and made themselves master of their goods. Suspecting this, he bore up to them, and approaching near them was confirmed that his jealousy was just. Seeing Indians in the boat, and knowing her to be the vessel of Master Oldham, and not seeing him there, gave fire upon them and slew some; others leaped overboard, besides two of the number which he preserved alive and brought to the Bay. The blood of the innocent called for vengeance. God stirred up the heart of the honored Governor, Master Henry Vane, and the rest of the worthy Magistrates, to send forth a hundred well appointed soldiers, under the conduct of Captain John Hendicot, and in company with him that had command, Captain John Underhill, Captain Nathan Turner, Captain William Jenningson, besides other inferior officers. I would not have the world wonder at the great number of commanders to so few men, but know that the Indians' fight far differs from the Christian practice; for they most commonly divide themselves into small bodies, so that we are forced to neglect our usual way, and to subdivide our divisions to answer theirs, and not thinking it any disparagement to any captain to go forth against an enemy with a squadron of men, taking the ground from the old and ancient practice, when they chose captains of hundreds and captains of thousands, captains of fifties and captains of tens. We conceive a captain signifieth the chief in way of command of any body committed to his charge for the time being, whether of more or less, it makes no matter in power, though in honor it does. Coming to an anchor before the island, we espied an Indian walking by the shore in a desolate manner, as though he had received intelligence of our coming. Which Indian gave just ground to some to conclude that the body of the people had deserted the island.

But some knowing them for the generality to be a warlike nation, a people that spend most of their time in the study of warlike policy, were not persuaded that they would upon so slender terms forsake the island, but rather suspected they might lie behind a bank, much like the form of a barricado. Myself with others rode with a shallop, made towards the shore, having in the boat a dozen armed soldiers. Drawing near to the place of landing, the number that rose from behind the barricado were between fifty or sixty able fighting men, men as straight as arrows, very tall, and of active bodies, having their arrows notched. They drew near to the water side, and let fly at the soldiers, as though they had meant to have made an end of us all in a moment. They shot a young gentleman in the neck through a collar, for stiffness as if it had been an oaken board, and entered his flesh a good depth. Myself received an arrow through my coat sleeve, a second against my helmet on the forehead; so as if God in his providence had not moved the heart of my wife to persuade me to carry it along with me, (which I was unwilling to do), I had been slain. Give me leave to observe two things from hence; first, when the hour of death is not yet come, you see God useth weak means to keep his purpose unviolated; secondly, let no man despise advice and counsel of his wife, though she be a woman. It were strange to nature to think a man should be bound to fulfil the humor of a woman, what arms he should carry; but you see God will have it so, that a woman should overcome a man. What with Delilah's flattery, and with her mournful tears, they must and will have their desire, when the hand of God goes along in the matter; and this is to accomplish his own will. Therefore let the clamor be quenched I daily hear in my ears, that New England men usurp over their wives, and keep them in servile subjection. The country is wronged in this matter, as in many things else. Let this precedent satisfy the doubtful, for that comes from the example of a rude soldier. If they be so courteous to their wives, as to take their advice in warlike matters, how much more kind is the tender, affectionate husband to honor his wife as the weaker vessel? Yet mistake not. I say not that they are bound to call their wives in council, though they are bound to take their private advice (so far as they see it make for their advantage and their good); instance Abraham. But to the matter. The arrows flying thick about us, we made haste to the shore; but the surf of the sea being great, hindered us, so we could scarce discharge a musket, but were forced to make haste to land. Drawing near the shore through the strength of wind, and the hollowness of the sea, we durst not adventure to run ashore, but were forced to wade up to the middle; but once having got up off our legs, we gave fire upon them. They finding our bullets to outreach their arrows, they fled before us. In the meanwhile Colonel Hindecot made to the shore, and some of this number also repulsed him at his landing, but hurt none. We thought they would stand it out with us, but they perceiving we were in earnest, fled; and left their wigwams, or houses, and provision to the use of our soldiers. Having set forth our sentinels, and laid out our pardues, we betook ourselves to the guard, expecting hourly they would fall upon us; but they observed the old rule, 'Tis good sleeping in a whole skin, and left us free from an alarm.

The next day we set upon our march, the Indians being retired into swamps, so as we could not find them. We burnt and spoiled both houses and corn in great abundance; but they kept themselves in obscurity. Captain Turner stepping aside to a swamp, met with some few Indians, and charged upon them, changing some few bullets for arrows. Himself received a shot upon the breast of his corselet, as if it had been pushed with a pike, and if he had not had it on, he had lost his life.

A pretty passage worthy observation. We had an Indian with us that was an interpreter; being in English clothes, and a gun in his hand, was spied by the islanders, which called out to him, What are you, an Indian or an Englishman? Come hither, saith he, and I will tell you. He pulls up his cock and let fly at one of them, and without question was the death of him. Having spent that day in burning and spoiling the island, we took up the quarter for that night. About midnight myself went out with ten men about two miles from our quarter, and discovered the most eminent plantation they had in the island, where was much corn, many wigwams, and great heaps of mats; but fearing less we should make an alarm by setting fire on them, we left them as we found them, and peaceably departed to our quarter; and the next morning with forty men marched up to the same plantation, burnt their houses, cut down their corn, destroyed some of their dogs instead of men, which they left in their wigwams.

Passing on toward the water side to embark our soldiers, we met with several famous wigwams, with great heaps of pleasant corn ready shelled; but not able to bring it away, we did throw their mats upon it, and set fire and burnt it. Many well-wrought mats our soldiers brought from thence, and several delightful baskets. We being divided into two parts, the rest of the body met with no less, I suppose, than ourselves did. The Indians playing least in sight, we spent our time, and could no more advantage ourselves than we had already done, and having slain some fourteen, and maimed others, we embarked ourselves, and set sail for Seasbrooke fort, where we lay through distress of weather four days; then we departed.

The Pequeats having slain one Captain Norton, and Captain Stone, with seven more of their company, order was given us to visit them, sailing along the Nahanticot shore with five vessels. The Indians spying of us came running in multitudes along the water side, crying, What cheer, Englishmen, what cheer, what do you come for? They not thinking we intended war, went on cheerfully until they come to Pequeat river. We thinking it the best way, did forbear to answer them; first, that we might the better be able to run through the work; secondly, that by delaying of them, we might drive them in security, to the end we might have the more advantage of them. But they seeing we would make no answer, kept on their course, and cried, What, Englishmen, what cheer, what cheer, are you hoggery, will you cram us? That is, are you angry, will you kill us, and do you come to fight? That night the Nahanticot Indians, and the Pequeats, made fire on both sides of the river, fearing we would land in the night. They made most doleful and woful cries all the night, (so that we could scarce rest) hallooing one to another, and giving the word from place to place, to gather their forces together, fearing the English were come to war against them.

The next morning they sent early aboard an ambassador, a grave senior, a man of good understanding, portly carriage, grave and majestical in his expressions. He demanded of us what the end of our coming was. To which we answered, that the governors of the Bay sent us to demand the heads of those persons that had slain Captain Norton and Captain Stone, and the rest of their company, and that it was not the custom of the English to suffer murderers to live; and therefore, if they desired their own peace and welfare, they will peaceably answer our expectation, and give us the heads of the murderers.

They being a witty and ingenious nation, their ambassador labored to excuse the matter, and answered, We know not that any of ours have slain any English. True it is, saith he, we have slain such a number of men; but consider the ground of it. Not long before the coming of these English into the river, there was a certain vessel that came to us in way of trade. We used them well, and traded with them, and took them to be such as would not wrong us in the least matter. But our sachem or prince coming aboard, they laid a plot how they might destroy him; which plot discovereth itself by the event, as followeth. They keeping their boat aboard, and not desirous of our company, gave us leave to stand hallooing ashore, that they might work their mischievous plot. But as we stood they called to us, and demanded of us a bushel of wampam-peke, which is their money. This they demanded for his ransom. This peal did ring terribly in our ears, to demand so much for the life of our prince, whom we thought was in the hands of honest men, and we had never wronged them. But we saw there was no remedy; their expectation must be granted, or else they would not send him ashore, which they promised they would do, if we would answer their desires. We sent them so much aboard, according to demand, and they, according to their promise, sent him ashore,* but first slew him. This much exasperated our spirits, and made us vow a revenge. Suddenly after came these captains with a vessel into the river, and pretended to trade with us, as the former did. We did not discountenance them for the present, but took our opportunity and came aboard. The sachem's son succeeding his father, was the man that came into the cabin of Captain Stone, and Captain Stone having drunk more than did him good, fell backwards on the bed asleep. The sagamore took his opportunity, and having a little hatchet under his garment, therewith knocked him in the head. Some being upon the deck and others under, suspected some such thing; for the rest of the Indians that were aboard, had order to proceed against the rest at one time; but the English spying treachery, run immediately into the cook-room, and, with a fire-brand, had thought to have blown up the Indians by setting fire to the powder. These devil's instruments spying this plot of the English, leaped overboard as the powder was a firing, and saved themselves; but all the English were blown up. This was the manner of their bloody action. Saith the ambassador to us, Could ye blame us for revenging so cruel a murder? for we distinguish not between the Dutch and English, but took them to be one nation, and therefore we do not conceive that we wronged you, for they slew our king; and thinking these captains to be of the same nation and people as those that slew him, made us set upon this course of revenge.

Our answer was, They were able to distinguish between Dutch and English, having had sufficient experience of both nations; and therefore, seeing you have slain the king of England's subjects, we come to demand an account of their blood, for we ourselves are liable to account for them. The answer of the ambassador was, We know no difference between the Dutch and the English; they are both strangers to us, we took them to be all one; therefore we crave pardon; we have not wilfully wronged the English.—This excuse will not serve our turns, for we have sufficient testimony that you know the English from the Dutch. We must have the heads of those persons that have slain ours, or else we will fight with you. He

* This was noways true of the English, but a devised excuse.

answered, Understanding the ground of your coming, I will entreat you to give me liberty to go ashore, and I shall inform the body of the people what your intent and resolution is; and if you will stay aboard, I will bring you a sudden answer.

We did grant him liberty to get ashore, and ourselves followed suddenly after before the war was proclaimed. He seeing us land our forces, came with a message to entreat us to come no nearer, but stand in a valley, which had between us and them an ascent, that took our sight from them; but they might see us to hurt us, to our prejudice. Thus from the first beginning to the end of the action, they carried themselves very subtilely; but we, not willing to be at their direction, marched up to the ascent, having set our men in battalia. He came and told us he had inquired for the sachem, that we might come to a parley; but neither of both of the princes were at home; they were gone to Long Island.

Our reply was, We must not be put off thus, we know the sachem is in the plantation, and therefore bring him to us, that we may speak with him, or else we will beat up the drum, and march through the country, and spoil your corn. His answer, If you will but stay a little while, I will step to the plantation and seek for them. We gave them leave to take their own course, and used as much patience as ever men might, considering the gross abuse they offered us, holding us above an hour in vain hopes. They sent an Indian to tell us that Mommenoteck was found, and would appear before us suddenly. This brought us to a new stand the space of an hour more. There came a third Indian persuading us to have a little further patience, and he would not tarry, for he had assembled the body of the Pequeats together, to know who the parties were that had slain these Englishmen. But seeing that they did in this interim convey away their wives and children, and bury their chiefest goods, we perceived at length they would fly from us; but we were patient and bore with them, in expectation to have the greater blow upon them. The last messenger brought us this intelligence from the sachem, that if we would but lay down our arms, and approach about thirty paces from them, and meet the heathen prince, he would cause his men to do the like, and then we shall come to a parley.

But we seeing their drift was to get our arms, we rather chose to beat up the drum and bid them battle. Marching into a champaign field we displayed our colors; but none would come near us, but standing remotely off did laugh at us for our patience. We suddenly set upon our march, and gave fire to as many as we could come near, firing their wigwams, spoiling their corn, and many other necessaries that they had buried in the ground we raked up, which the soldiers had for booty. Thus we spent the day burning and spoiling the country. Towards night embarked ourselves. The next morning, landing on the Nahanticot shore, where we were served in like nature, no Indians would come near us, but run from us, as the deer from the dogs. But having burnt and spoiled what we could light on, we embarked our men, and set sail for the Bay. Having ended this exploit, came off, having one man wounded in the leg; but certain numbers of theirs slain, and many wounded. This was the substance of the first year's service. Now followeth the service performed in the second year.

This insolent nation, seeing we had used much lenity towards them, and themselves not able to make good use of our patience, set upon a course of greater insolence than before, and slew all they found in their way. They came near Seabrooke fort, and made many proud challenges, and dared them out to fight.

The lieutenant went out with ten armed men, and starting three Indians they changed some few shot for arrows. Pursuing them, a hundred more started out of the ambushments, and almost surrounded him and his company; and some they slew, others they maimed, and forced them to retreat to their fort, so that it was a special providence of God that they were not all slain. Some of their arms they got from them, others put on the English clothes, and came to the fort jeering of them, and calling, Come and fetch your Englishmen's clothes again; come out and fight, if you dare; you dare not fight; you are all one like women. We have one amongst us that if he could kill but one of you more, he would be equal with God, and as the Englishman's God is, so would he be. This blasphemous speech troubled the hearts of the soldiers, but they knew not how to remedy it, in respect of their weakness.

The Conetticot plantation, understanding the insolence of the enemy to be so great, sent down a certain number of soldiers, under the conduct of Captain John Mason, for to strengthen the fort. The enemy lying hovering about the fort, continually took notice of the supplies that were come, and forbore drawing near it as before; and letters were immediately sent to the Bay, to that right worshipful gentleman, Master Henry Vane, for a speedy supply to strengthen the fort. For assuredly without supply suddenly came, in reason all would be lost, and fall into the hands of the enemy. This was the trouble and perplexity that lay upon the spirits of the poor garrison. Upon serious consideration, the governor and council sent forth myself, with twenty armed soldiers, to supply the necessity of those distressed persons, and to take the government of that place for the space of three months. Relief being come, Captain John Mason, with the rest of his company, returned to the plantation again. We sometimes fell out, with a matter of twenty soldiers, to see whether we could discover the enemy or no. They seeing us (lying in ambush) gave us leave to pass by them, considering we were too hot for them to meddle with us. Our men being completely armed, with corselets, muskets, bandoleers, rests, and swords, (as they themselves related afterward), did much daunt them. Thus we spent a matter of six weeks before we could have anything to do with them, persuading ourselves that all things had been well. But they seeing there was no advantage more to be had against the fort, they enterprised a new action, and fell upon Watertowne, now called Wethersfield, with two hundred Indians. Before they came to attempt the place, they put into a certain river, an obscure small river running into the main, where they encamped, and refreshed themselves, and fitted themselves for their service, and by break of day attempted their enterprise, and slew nine men, women and children. Having finished their action, they suddenly returned again, bringing with them two maids captives, having put poles in their canoes, as we put masts in our boats, and upon them hung our English men's and women's shirts and smocks, instead of sails, and in way of bravado came along in sight of us as we stood upon Seybrooke fort [at the mouth of the

Connecticut River]. And seeing them pass along in such a triumphant manner, we much fearing they had enterprised some desperate action upon the English, we gave fire with a piece of ordnance, and shot among their canoes. And though they were a mile from us, yet the bullet grazed not above twenty yards over the canoe, where the poor maids were. It was a special providence of God it did not hit them, for then should we have been deprived of the sweet observation of God's providence in their deliverance. We were not able to make out after them, being destitute of means, boats, and the like. . . .

I told you before, that when the Pequeats heard and saw Seabrooke fort was supplied, they forbore to visit us. But the old serpent, according to his first malice, stirred them up against the church of Christ, and in such a furious manner, as our people were so far disturbed and affrighted with their boldness that they scarce durst rest in their beds; threatening persons and cattle to take them, as indeed they did. So insolent were these wicked imps grown, that like the devil, their commander, they run up and down as roaring lions, compassing all corners of the country for a prey, seeking whom they might devour. It being death to them for to rest without some wicked employment or other, they still plotted how they might wickedly attempt some bloody enterprise upon our poor native countrymen.

One Master Tilly, master of a vessel, being brought to an anchor in Conetticot river, went ashore, not suspecting the bloody-mindedness of those persons, who fell upon him and a man with him, whom they wickedly and barbarously slew; and, by relation, brought him home, tied him to a stake, flayed his skin off, put hot embers between the flesh and the skin, cut off his fingers and toes, and made hatbands of them; thus barbarous was their cruelty! Would not this have moved the hearts of men to hazard blood, and life, and all they had, to overcome such a wicked, insolent nation? But letters coming into the Bay, that this attempt was made upon Wethersfield in Conetticot river, and that they had slain nine men, women and children, and taken two maids captives, the council gave order to send supply. In the mean while the Conetticot plantations sent down one hundred armed soldiers, under the conduct of Captain John Mason, and Lieutenant Seily, with other inferior officers, who by commission were bound for to come to rendezvous at Seabrooke fort, and there to consult with those that had command there, to enterprise some stratagem upon these bloody Indians. The Conetticot company having with them threescore Mohiggeners, whom the Pequeats had drove out of their lawful posessions, these Indians were earnest to join with the English, or at least to be under their conduct, that they might revenge themselves of those bloody enemies of theirs. The English, perceiving their earnest desire that way, gave them liberty to follow the company, but not to join in confederation with them; the Indians promising to be faithful, and to do them what service lay in their power. But having embarked their men, and coming down the river, there arose great jealousy in the hearts of those that had chief oversight of the company, fearing that the Indians in time of greatest trial might revolt, and turn their backs against those they professed to be their friends, and join with the Pequeats. This perplexed the hearts of many very much, because they had had no experience of their fidelity. But Captain Mason having sent down a shallop to Seybrooke fort, and sent the Indians over land to meet and rendezvous at Seabrooke fort, themselves came down in a great massy vessel, which was slow in coming, and very long detained by cross winds. The Indians coming to Seabrooke, were desirous to fall out on the Lord's day, to see whether they could find any Pequeats near the fort; persuading themselves that the place was not destitute of some of their enemies. But it being the Lord's day, order was given to the contrary, and wished them to forbear until the next day. Giving them liberty, they fell out early in the morning, and brought home five Pequeats' heads, one prisoner, and mortally wounded the seventh. This mightily encouraged the hearts of all, and we took this as a pledge of their further fidelity. Myself taking boat, rowed up to meet the rest of the forces. Lying aboard the vessel with my boat, the minister, one Master Stone, that was sent to instruct the company, was then in prayer solemnly before God, in the midst of the soldiers; and this passage worthy observation I set down, because the providence of God might be taken notice of, and his name glorified, that is so ready for to honor his own ordinance. The hearts of all in general being much perplexed, fearing the infidelity of these Indians, having not heard what an exploit they had wrought, it pleased God to put into the heart of Master Stone this passage in prayer, while myself lay under the vessel and heard it, himself not knowing that God had sent him a messenger to tell him his prayer was granted. O Lord God, if it be thy blessed will, vouchsafe so much favor to thy poor distressed servants, as to manifest one pledge of thy love, that may confirm us of the fidelity of these Indians towards us, that now pretend friendship and service to us, that our hearts may be encouraged the more in this work of thine. Immediately myself stepping up, told him that God had answered his desire, and that I had brought him this news, that those Indians had brought in five Pequeats' heads, one prisoner, and wounded one mortally; which did much encourage the hearts of all, and replenished them exceedingly, and gave them all occasion to rejoice and be thankful to God. A little before we set forth, came a certain ship from the Dutch plantation. Casting an anchor under the command of our ordnance, we desired the master to come ashore. The master and merchant, willing to answer our expectation, came forth, and sitting with us awhile unexpectedly revealed their intent, that they were bound for Pequeat river to trade. Ourselves knowing the custom of war, that it was not the practice, in a case of this nature, to suffer others to go and trade with them our enemies, with such commodities as might be prejudicial unto us, and advantageous to them, as kettles, or the like, which make them arrow-heads, we gave command to them not to stir, alleging that our forces were intended daily to fall upon them. This being unkindly taken, it bred some agitations between their several commanders; but God was pleased, out of his love, to carry things in such a sweet, moderate way, as all turned to his glory, and his people's good.

These men, seeing they could not have liberty to go upon their design, gave us a note under their hands, that if we would give them liberty to depart, they would endeavor, to the utmost of their ability, to release those two captive maids, and this should be the chief scope and drift of their design. Having these promises, depending upon their faithfulness, we gave them liberty. They set sail and went to Pequeat river, and sent to shore the master of the vessel to Sasacoose, their prince, for to crave liberty to trade; and what would they trade for but the English maids? which he much disliked. Suddenly withdrawing himself he returned back to the vessel, and by way of policy allured seven Indians into the bark, some of them being their prime men. Having them aboard, acquainted them with their intent, and told them without they might have the two captives delivered safely aboard, they must keep them as prisoners and pledges, and therefore must resolve not to go ashore, until such time they had treated with the sagamore. One of the Dutch called to them on the shore, and told them they must bring the two captive maids, if they would have the seven Indians; and therefore, briefly, if you will bring them, tell us; if not, we set sail, and will turn all your Indians overboard in the main ocean, so soon as ever we come out. They taking this to be a jest, slighted what was said unto them. They weighing anchor set sail, and drew near the mouth of the river. The Pequeats then discerned they were in earnest, and earnestly desired them to return and come to an anchor, and they would answer their expectation. So they brought the two maids, and delivered them safely aboard, and they returned to them the seven Indians. Then they set sail and came to Seabrooke fort. Bringing them to Seabrooke fort, request was made to have them ashore. But in regard of the Dutch governor's desire, who had heard that there was two English maids taken captives of the Pequeats, and thinking his own vessel to be there a trading with them, he had managed out a pinnace purposely, to give strict order and command to the former vessel to get these captives, what charge soever they were at, nay, though they did hazard their peace with them, and to gratify him with the first sight of them after their deliverance. So they earnestly entreated us that they might not be brought ashore so as to stay there, or to be sent home until they had followed the governor's order; which willingly was granted to them, though it were thirty leagues from us; yet were they safely returned again, and brought home to their friends. Now for the examination of the two maids after they arrived at Seabrooke fort. The eldest of them was about sixteen years of age. Demanding of her how they had used her, she told us that they did solicit her to uncleanness; but her heart being much broken, and afflicted under that bondage she was cast in, had brought to her consideration these thoughts—How shall I commit this great evil and sin against my God? Their hearts were much taken up with the consideration of God's just displeasure to them, that had lived under so prudent means of grace as they did, and had been so ungrateful toward God, and slighted that means, so that God's hand was justly upon them for their remissness in all their ways. Thus was their hearts taken up with these thoughts. The Indians carried them from place to place, and showed them their forts and curious wigwams and houses, and encouraged them to be merry. But the poor souls, as Israel, could not frame themselves to any delight or mirth under so strange a king. They hanging their harps upon the willow trees, gave their minds to sorrow; hope was their chiefest food, and tears their constant drink. Behind the rocks, and under the trees, the eldest spent her breath in supplication to her God; and though the eldest was but young, yet must I confess the sweet affection to God for his great

kindness and fatherly love she daily received from the Lord, which sweet-
ened all her sorrows, and gave her constant hope that God would not nor
could not forget her poor distressed soul and body; because, saith she, his
loving kindness appeareth to me in an unspeakable manner. And though
sometimes, saith she, I cried out, David-like, I shall one day perish by the
hands of Saul, I shall one day die by the hands of these barbarous Indians;
and specially if our people should come forth to war against them. Then
is there no hope of deliverance. Then must I perish. Then will they cut
me off in malice. But suddenly the poor soul was ready to quarrel with
itself. Why should I distrust God? Do not I daily see the love of God
unspeakably to my poor distressed soul? And he hath said he will never
leave me nor forsake me. Therefore I will not fear what man can do unto
me, knowing God to be above man, and man can do nothing without
God's permission. These were the words that fell from her mouth when
she was examined in Seabrooke fort. I having command of Seabrooke fort,
she spake these things upon examination, in my hearing. . . .

Having embarked our soldiers, we weighed anchor at Seabrooke fort,
and set sail for the Narraganset Bay, deluding the Pequeats thereby, for
they expected us to fall into the Pequeat river; but crossing their expectation, bred in them a security. We landed our men in the Narraganset Bay,
and marched over land above two days' journey before we came to
Pequeat. Quartering the last night's march within two miles of the place,
we set forth about one of the clock in the morning, having sufficient intelligence that they knew nothing of our coming. Drawing near to the
fort, yielded up ourselves to God, and entreated his assistance in so weighty
an enterprise. We set on our march to surround the fort;* Captain John
Mason, approaching to the west end, where it had an entrance to pass into
it; myself marching to the south side, surrounding the fort; placing the
Indians, for we had about three hundred of them, without side of our
soldiers in a ring battalia, giving a volley of shot upon the fort. So remarkable it appeared to us, as we could not but admire at the providence of
God in it, that soldiers so unexpert in the use of their arms, should give so
complete a volley, as though the finger of God had touched both match
and flint. Which volley being given at break of day, and themselves fast
asleep for the most part, bred in them such a terror, that they brake forth
into a most doleful cry; so as if God had not fitted the hearts of men for
the service, it would have bred in them a commiseration towards them. But
every man being bereaved of pity, fell upon the work without compassion,
considering the blood they had shed of our native countrymen, and how
barbarously they had dealt with them, and slain, first and last, about thirty
persons. Having given fire, we approached near to the entrance, which
they had stopped full with arms of trees, or brakes. Myself approaching to
the entrance, found the work too heavy for me, to draw out all those
which were strongly forced in. We gave order to one Master Hedge, and
some other soldiers, to pull out those brakes. Having this done, and laid

* This fort, or palisado, was well nigh an acre of ground, which was surrounded
with trees and half trees, set into the ground three feet deep, and fastened close one
to another.

them between me and the entrance, and without order themselves, proceeded first on the south end of the fort. But remarkable it was to many of us. Men that run before they are sent, most commonly have an ill reward. Worthy reader, let me entreat you to have a more charitable opinion of me (though unworthy to be better thought of) than is reported in the other book.* You may remember there is a passage unjustly laid upon me, that when we should come to the entrance, I should put forth this question, Shall we enter? Others should answer again, What came we hither for else? It is well known to many, it was never my practice, in time of my command, when we are in garrison, much to consult with a private soldier, or to ask his advice in point of war; much less in a matter of so great a moment as that was, which experience had often taught me was not a time to put forth such a question; and therefore pardon him that hath given the wrong information. Having our swords in our right hand, our carbines or muskets in our left hand, we approached the fort, Master Hedge being shot through both arms, and more wounded. Though it be not commendable for a man to make mention of anything that might tend to his own honor, yet because I would have the providence of God observed, and his name magnified, as well for myself as others, I dare not omit, but let the world know, that deliverance was given to us that command, as well as to private soldiers. Captain Mason and myself entering into the wigwams, he was shot, and received many arrows against his head-piece. God preserved him from many wounds. Myself received a shot in the left hip, through a sufficient buff coat, that if I had not been supplied with such a garment, the arrow would have pierced through me. Another I received between neck and shoulders, hanging in the linen of my head-piece. Others of our soldiers were shot, some through the shoulders, some in the face, some in the head, some in the legs, Captain Mason and myself losing each of us a man, and had near twenty wounded. Most courageously these Pequeats behaved themselves. But seeing the fort was too hot for us, we devised a way how we might save ourselves and prejudice them. Captain Mason entering into a wigwam, brought out a firebrand, after he had wounded many in the house. Then he set fire on the west side, where he entered; myself set fire on the south end with a train of powder. The fires of both meeting in the centre of the fort, blazed most terribly, and burnt all in the space of half an hour. Many courageous fellows were unwilling to come out, and fought most desperately through the palisadoes, so as they were scorched and burnt with the very flame, and were deprived of their arms—in regard the fire burnt their very bowstrings—and so perished valiantly. Mercy they did deserve for their valor, could we have had opportunity to have bestowed it. Many were burnt in the fort, both men, women, and children. Others forced out, and came in troops to the Indians, twenty and thirty at a time, which our soldiers received and entertained with the point of the sword. Down fell men, women, and children; those that scaped us, fell into the hands of the Indians that were in the rear of us. It is reported by them-

* [The "other book" is *Vincent's Relation of the Pequot War*, which appears immediately after Underhill's account in *Collections of the Massachusetts Historical Society*, 3d ser., 6 (1837).]

selves, that there were about four hundred souls in this fort, and not above five of them escaped out of our hands. Great and doleful was the bloody sight to the view of young soldiers that never had been in war, to see so many souls lie gasping on the ground, so thick, in some places, that you could hardly pass along. It may be demanded, Why should you be so furious? (as some have said). Should not Christians have more mercy and compassion? But I would refer you to David's war. When a people is grown to such a height of blood, and sin against God and man, and all confederates in the action, there he hath no respect to persons, but harrows them, and saws them, and puts them to the sword, and the most terriblest death that may be. Sometimes the Scripture declareth women and children must perish with their parents. Sometimes the case alters; but we will not dispute it now. We had sufficient light from the word of God for our proceedings.

Having ended this service, we drew our forces together to battalia. Being ordered, the Pequeats came upon us with their prime men, and let fly at us; myself fell on scarce with twelve or fourteen men to encounter with them; but they finding our bullets to outreach their arrows, forced themselves often to retreat. When we saw we could have no advantage against them in the open field, we requested our Indians for to entertain fight with them. Our end was that we might see the nature of the Indian war; which they granted us, and fell out, the Pequeats, Narragansets, and Mohigeners changing a few arrows together after such a manner, as I dare boldly affirm, they might fight seven years and not kill seven men. They came not near one another, but shot remote, and not point-blank, as we often do with our bullets, but at rovers, and then they gaze up in the sky to see where the arrow falls, and not until it is fallen do they shoot again. This fight is more for pastime, than to conquer and subdue enemies. But spending a little time this way, we were forced to cast our eyes upon our poor maimed soldiers, many of them lying upon the ground, wanting food and such nourishable things as might refresh them in this faint state. But we were not supplied with any such things whereby we might relieve them, but only were constrained to look up to God, and to entreat him for mercy towards them. Most were thirsty, but could find no water. The provision we had for food was very little. Many distractions seized upon us at the present. A chirurgeon we wanted; our chirurgeon, not accustomed to war, durst not hazard himself where we ventured our lives, but, like a fresh water soldier, kept aboard, and by this means our poor maimed soldiers were brought to a great strait and faintness, some of them swounding away for want of speedy help; but yet God was pleased to preserve the lives of them, though not without great misery and pain to themselves for the present. Distractions multiplying, strength and courage began to fail with many. Our Indians, that had stood close to us hitherto, were fallen into consultation, and were resolved for to leave us in a land we knew not which way to get out. Suddenly after their resolution, fifty of the Narraganset Indians fell off from the rest, returning home. The Pequeats spying them, pursued after them. Then came the Narragansets to Captain Mason and myself, crying, Oh, help us now, or our men will be all slain. We answered, How dare you crave aid of us, when you are leaving of us in this distressed condition, not knowing which way to march out of the country? But yet you shall see it is not the nature of Englishmen to deal like heathens, to requite evil for evil, but we will succor you. Myself falling on with thirty men, in the space of an hour rescued their men, and in our retreat to the body, slew and wounded above a hundred Pequeats, all fighting men, that charged us both in rear and flanks. Having overtaken the body, we were resolved to march to a certain neck of land that lay by the sea-side, where we intended to quarter that night, because we knew not how to get our maimed men to Pequeat river. As yet we saw not our pinnaces sail along, but feared the Lord had crossed them, which also the master of the barque much feared. We gave them order to set sail on the Narraganset Bay, about midnight, as we were to fall upon the fort in the morning, so that they might meet us in Pequeat river in the afternoon; but the wind being cross, bred in them a great perplexity what would become of us, knowing that we were but slenderly provided, both with munition and provision. But they being in a distracted condition, lifted up their hearts to God for help. About twelve of the clock the wind turned about and became fair; it brought them along in sight of us, and about ten o'clock in the morning carried them into Pequeat river. Coming to an anchor at the place appointed, the wind turned as full against them as ever it could blow. How remarkable this providence of God was, I leave to a Christian eye to judge. Our Indians came to us, and much rejoiced at our victories, and greatly admired the manner of Englishmen's fight, but cried Mach it, mach it; that is, It is naught, it is naught, because it is too furious, and slays too many men. Having received their desires, they freely promised, and gave up themselves to march along with us, wherever we would go. God having eased us from that oppression that lay upon us, thinking we should have been left in great misery for want of our vessels, we diverted our thoughts from going to that neck of land, and faced about, marching to the river where our vessels lay at anchor. One remarkable passage. The Pequeats playing upon our flanks, one Sergeant Davis, a pretty courageous soldier, spying something black upon the top of a rock, stepped forth from the body with a carbine of three feet long, and, at a venture, gave fire, supposing it to be an Indian's head, turning him over with his heels upward. The Indians observed this, and greatly admired that a man should shoot so directly. The Pequeats were much daunted at the shot, and forbore approaching so near upon us. Being come to the Pequeat river we met with Captain Patrick, who under his command had forty able soldiers, who was ready to begin a second attempt. But many of our men being maimed and much wearied, we forbore that night, and embarked ourselves, myself setting sail for Seabrooke fort. Captain Mason and Captain Patrick marching over land, burned and spoiled the country between the Pequeat and Conetticot river, where we received them. The Pequeats having received so terrible a blow, and being much affrighted with the destruction of so many, the next day fell into consultation. Assembling their most ablest men together, propounded these three things. First, whether they would set upon a sudden revenge upon the Narragansets, or attempt an enterprise upon the English, or fly. They were in great dispute one amongst another. Sasachus, their chief commander, was all for blood; the rest for flight, Alleging these arguments: We are a people bereaved of courage, our hearts are sadded with the death of so many of our dear friends; we see upon what advantage the English lie; what sudden and deadly blows they strike; what advantage they have of their pieces to us, which are not able to reach them with our arrows at distance. They are supplied with everything necessary; they are flote and heartened in their victory. To what end shall we stand it out with them? We are not able; therefore let us rather save some than lose all. This prevailed. Suddenly after, they spoiled all those goods they could not carry with them, broke up their tents and wigwams, and betook themselves to flight. Sasachus, flying towards Conetticot plantation, quartered by the river side; there he met with a shallop sent down to Seabrooke fort, which had in it three men; they let fly upon them, shot many arrows into them. Courageous were the English, and died in their hands, but with a great deal of valor. The forces which were prepared in the Bay were ready for to set forth. Myself being taken on but for three months, and the soldiers willing to return to the Bay, we embarked ourselves, and set to sail. In our journey we met with certain pinnaces, in them a hundred able and well appointed soldiers, under the conduct of one Captain Stoughton, and other inferior officers; and in company with them one Mr. John Wilson, who was sent to instruct the company. These falling into Pequeat river, met with many of the distressed Indians. Some they slew, others they took prisoners.

A Time of Troubles

DOUGLAS EDWARD LEACH

During the month of January [1676], following the Great Swamp Fight, there seemed to be a lull in the war, for the only major activity which occurred was the futile northward pursuit of the beaten Narragansetts by Winslow's haggard army. Then when the army gave up the chase and disbanded early in February, for a few days virtually nothing happened, and the gods of war seemed to be pausing to catch their breath. During this interval all of New England, like a great wounded beast, lay trembling in the snow, while the icy winds of winter sobbed over the land as though in mourning. Among the settlers the prevailing mood was one of apprehension. As the people went about their affairs, heavily muffled against the cold, they cast frequent nervous glances toward the surrounding forest, being careful not to get too far away from the fortified garrison houses which would be their refuge in case of attack. New England in those cold gray days of early February might be likened to a man who finds himself trapped in a locked and darkened room, realizing that he has just disturbed and infuriated a nest of hornets.

"A Time of Troubles." From *Flintlock and Tomahawk: New England in King Philip's War* by Douglas Edward Leach, pp. 155–61, 164–68, 182–89. Reprinted by permission of W. W. Norton & Company, Inc. Copyright © 1958 by Douglas Edward Leach.

The Indians, meanwhile, were passing the winter in the wild reaches of the Nipmuck country and beyond the Connecticut River. Some of the river Indians were encamped in the neighborhood of Squakeag, while other groups were located near Mount Wachusett, some twelve miles west of Lancaster. Most of the Nipmucks were concentrated in the vicinity of Menameset on the Ware River, and the Narragansetts, greatly reduced in strength but still dangerous, were trekking northward into the same area. Thus the bulk of the enemy was located at various points in the region bounded by Squakeag, Mount Wachusett, Quabaug, and the Connecticut River. This was the hornets' nest.

During the long weeks of midwinter, the Indians lived on whatever supplies of meat and corn they were able to accumulate. They had obtained some of their food from abandoned English settlements whose only function now was to be a gleaning ground for the savages. Huddled around their campfires, the warriors nursed their weapons, and laid their plans for the coming months when they hoped to drive the English out of the land.

As early as the 24th of January the English had received the first distinct hint of what was in store for them. Two Christian Indians, James Quannapohit and Job Kattenanit, had previously been sent into the Nipmuck country as spies, and now James, traveling hard on snowshoes, returned from his adventure bearing ominous news. He and Job had actually gone among the enemy Indians at Menameset under the pretext of being hostile to the English. One of the sachems had talked rather freely to these spies, boasting that within three weeks the Indians would attack the town of Lancaster. The bridge leading to the settlement was to be destroyed, so that the inhabitants would be unable to retreat and help would be unable to reach them. Following the destruction of Lancaster, there would be a series of attacks upon the exposed frontier towns of Groton, Marlborough, Sudbury, and Medfield. Despite this clear warning, however, the government of Massachusetts seems to have felt that the enemy's boasting did not call for any drastic countermeasures.[1] Some additional emphasis was given to James' testimony when, on the first of February, the enemy fell upon an isolated farm several miles from Sudbury, burning the farmhouse, and killing or carrying away the inhabitants. News of this event stimulated the authorities to order two mounted patrols to cover the frontier line from Groton down to Medfield.[2] Even yet, however, the government seems to have been unaware of the immediate danger.

Captain Daniel Gookin had already retired to bed in his Cambridge home on the evening of February 9th when there came a pounding at the door. It was the second Indian spy, Job Kattenanit, just arrived from the Nipmuck country with additional information. The news brought by this

---

[1] Daniel Gookin, *An Historical Account of the . . . Christian Indians of New England* (*Transactions and Collections of the American Antiquarian Society*, II), 486–89; Connecticut State Archives (hereafter CA), War I, 35c; *Collections of the Massachusetts Historical Society* (hereafter MHC), 1st ser. VI, 205–08; Cotton Papers, Part VII, 4 (Boston Public Library).

[2] Massachusetts State Archives (hereafter MA), XXX, 210a, 211, LXVIX, 105.

weary messenger was such as to bring Gookin bounding out of his warm
bed. A party of the enemy, four hundred strong, was even now on its
way to attack Lancaster, just as James had warned a fortnight earlier. The
assault was due the next morning, and so whatever action should be taken
must be started at once. After discussing the situation briefly with Thomas
Danforth, his near neighbor and fellow magistrate, Gookin dispatched
messengers to Concord, Marlborough, and Lancaster with orders for a
hasty converging of troops upon the threatened town.[3] Had Gookin acted
with less speed and determination, the ensuing event might have had a
far different ending.

At daybreak of the 10th Captain Samuel Wadsworth, commander
of a small military force which had been stationed at Marlborough when
Winslow's army was demobilized, learned of the impending attack on
Lancaster. Quickly assembling his men, Wadsworth led about forty of
them northward to the scene of action. As he neared Lancaster, he knew
that the enemy was there before him. The climbing columns of gray
smoke, the hideous din of Indian yelling, and the sporadic crack of musket
fire prepared him and his men for the scene ahead. Reaching the bridge
leading across the Nashua River and into the main part of town, Wadsworth's company found it partially destroyed by the enemy, just as James
Quannapohit had warned it would be. Nevertheless, the soldiers forced
their away across the bridge and into the town.[4]

The arrival of Wadsworth helped turn the tide, and the Indians ultimately withdrew, but not until they had destroyed most of the deserted
homes and outbuildings in the town. Fortunately, the inhabitants of Lancaster had taken shelter in six garrison houses, five of which had managed
to hold out successfully against the enemy's onslaught. Only at one of the
houses, that of the town's minister, Mr. Joseph Rowlandson, did the Indians
have their way. As it happened, because Mr. Rowlandson had gone to
Boston to plead with the Council for more adequate protection for his
town, he escaped the disaster at his own home. Returning from his mission shortly after the attack, the horrified pastor found his home in ruins.
Sadly the neighbors told him how his wife and children and other relatives
had been seized and taken away by the enemy. "In such a Junction of Affairs a Man had need have a God to go to for Support, and an Interest in
Christ to yield him Consolation," was the solemn comment of one contemporary writer.[5] Altogether about a dozen inhabitants had been killed at
this one house, and perhaps twenty or more taken prisoner. Total casualties
for the entire community were probably more than fifty. Six weeks later
the town was abandoned.

After the attack on Lancaster, in all the frontier towns as well as many

[3] Gookin, *op. cit.*, pp. 489–90; 4 MHC, V, 1–2.
[4] *Calendar of State Papers, Colonial Series, America and West Indies* (London),
1675–76, pp. 350–51; Gookin, *op. cit.*, p. 490.
[5] Charles H. Lincoln, ed., *Narratives of the Indian Wars* (New York, 1913), pp. 83–84,
113, 116, 118–22; Henry S. Nourse, ed., *The Early Records of Lancaster, Massachusetts* (Lancaster, 1884), pp. 104–06; *The New England Historical and Genealogical Register* (NEHGR), L, 483–85.

less exposed communities there was a renewed flurry of excitement and tension as the inhabitants sought to increase their meager security against the ruthless foe. People stayed closer to the designated garrison houses; guards were more alert. Some towns such as Wrentham and Medfield apprised the government of their weak condition, and begged for military aid or advice; others busied themselves about their fortifications in an attempt to strengthen the town defenses. Chelmsford reported hostile Indians in the vicinity, and told of travelers being waylaid on the road from Groton.[6] Five days after the attack on Lancaster the government of Massachusetts ordered Captain Moseley to Sudbury for the purpose of strengthening the endangered frontier area.[7] It began to look as though the outer ring of towns from Chelmsford and Groton down to Medfield and Wrentham might be like a giant string of firecrackers, with Lancaster being only the first to be lit by the enemy.

The next blow fell upon Medfield, a settlement less than twenty miles southwest of Boston. The inhabitants had gone to bed on the evening of February 20th feeling reasonably secure, for within the town there were now quartered about a hundred colony soldiers in addition to the local trainband of approximately the same number. These troops, except for a small force of some thirty men on duty at the principal fortification near the meetinghouse, were quartered at various houses throughout the town rather than at one place. Sometime before daybreak on the 21st, while the townspeople slept in their beds and the guard force doubtless grumbled about the length of the night, several hundred Indians crept silently into the town, and dispersed to various hiding places under fences and behind barns. If a dog sniffed the cold night air and growled at the coming of the intruders, no-one seemed to pay much attention.

The silent enemy, well-equipped with guns, ammunition, and combustible material, waited patiently in their various coverts until the first gray light of dawn began to steal across the fields. Then as sleepy farmers and soldiers stepped out of their doors they were met by deadly musket fire. At Goodman Dwight's house the Indians bounced missiles against the building, and when the wondering Dwight peered out to learn what was going on, they shot him through the shoulder. At another place Lieutenant Henry Adams, hearing the alarm, hastened out to do his duty, but as he stepped over the threshold he was struck in the neck by a bullet, and fell down dead. While the startled community was trying to organize its defenses and bring the scattered troops into some kind of order, the savages hastened to set fire to as many of the buildings as possible. Altogether some forty or fifty houses and barns were put to the torch. As one contemporary later remarked, "The sight of this poor people was very astonishing in the morning, fires being kindled round about them, the enemy numerous and

---

[6] The Committee of Militia of Chelmsford to the Governor and Council, Feb. 15, 1675/6, Shattuck Papers; MA, LXVIII, 133b, 134a; William T. Davis, ed., *Records of the Town of Plymouth* (Plymouth, 1889), I, 146–47; Haverhill Town Records, II and III, 235.

[7] MA, LXVIII, 135.

shouting so as the earth seemed to tremble, and the cry of terrifyed persons very dreadful. . . . Few when they Lay downe thought of such a dolefull morning." [8]

Meanwhile, the soldiers stationed at the main fortification had fired cannon to warn Dedham, the nearest town toward Boston. The loud reports of this weapon, plus the awareness that there were an unexpectedly large number of soldiers in Medfield, seemed to persuade the savages that the time for retreat had come. Loaded with plunder, they withdrew across the Charles River by way of the bridge leading to Sherborn, and then set the bridge on fire to prevent pursuit. As a consequence, the English attempt to follow after them was completely foiled, and the exulting savages were able to stand on the far side of the stream, hurling taunts and insults at the settlers. Later, after the warriors had gone, someone found attached to the ruined bridge a note which read as follows:

> Know by this paper, that the Indians that thou hast provoked to wrath and anger, will war this twenty one years if you will; there are many Indians yet, we come three hundred at this time. You must consider the Indians lost nothing but their life; you must lose your fair houses and cattle.[9]

Four nights after the burning of Medfield some marauding Indians fired a number of buildings at Weymouth, thereby carrying the offensive to the very coast of Massachusetts.

The latest depredations only served to emphasize once more that the war was entering a new and terrible phase. Men spoke solemnly of God's wrath, while at the same time public suspicion and hatred of all Indians, even those who professed to be loyal to the English, mounted to new heights. The General Court hastened to tighten up the regulations governing scouting and other defensive activity along the frontier, ordered that brush be cleared away along the roads, and offered a substantial reward for enemy Indians killed or captured by English scouts.[10] On February 23rd, while a solemn Day of Humiliation was being observed in the meeting-house at Boston, the people were startled by an alarm caused by rumors that the Indians were less than ten miles away. Within the next few days the land along the southern shore of Boston Bay from Milton to Hingham was said to be infested with the enemy, and a small military force under Captains Wadsworth and John Jacob was ordered to the area. Plymouth Colony, fearing that the raiding parties would cross the line into its territory, ordered the establishment of a garrison at Scituate, directed that a

---

[8] Curwin Papers (American Antiquarian Society, Worcester, Mass.), III, 9; *A True Account of the Most Considerable Occurrences; Narratives*, pp. 80–81, 127; MA, LXVIII, 139; Gookin, *op. cit.*, pp. 493–94.

[9] Gookin, *op. cit.*, p. 494.

[10] Nathaniel B. Shurtleff, ed., *Records of the Governor and Company of the Massachusetts Bay in New England* (Boston, 1854), V, 71–72 (hereafter MCR).

group of local Indians be transferred to Clark's Island, and tightened the rules for watching and warding in the towns.[11]

.   .   .

Under the severe strains of wartime conditions, public morale in New England showed alarming signs of deterioration. If we were to plot the morale line on a graph, it would begin at an arbitrarily chosen point of normality, and would drop almost constantly for the first five months of the war. Then there would be perhaps a slight upswing during December [1775] when the armies were making their drive against the Narragansetts. This temporary improvement, however, would quickly reverse itself, and the downward trend would continue for another four months before showing any substantial signs of a change. The low state of civilian morale during the first ten or eleven months of the struggle can be directly attributed to the astounding successes of the enemy, together with the attendant suffering experienced by the colonists.

Conditions in the fortified garrison houses were difficult, to say the least. Imagine fifty or sixty men, women, and children living together in a house designed for ten or twelve. Not only the people themselves but also their most prized possessions, and probably some of their food supply as well, were squeezed into the garrison house to preserve them from the torches of the enemy. In the daytime the inhabitants might be so bold as to attempt some work outside the house, but at night they were crowded together inside, sleeping on straw or blankets strewn over the floor. The sleepers were frequently awakened by the crying of small children and the changing of the guards at shuttered windows and doors. The sudden sharp barking of a dog out in the darkness would startle everyone into scalp-prickled wakefulness. Were the bloodthirsty savages upon them? Thanks be to God, a false alarm, and so back once more to a troubled sleep. Under these conditions it is no wonder that tempers sometimes grew short, and the days and nights seemed interminably long.

In the army also, morale was the victim of Indian successes and tactics. The men were dismayed by the enemy's ability to strike without warning, and evade pursuit by hiding in snake-infested swamps. As ambush followed ambush, the English soldiers, with their heavy, cumbersome equipment, began to doubt their own ability to stand up to the Indians, man for man. Their earlier enthusiasm for going after the renegade redskins was now rapidly waning. The silent arrow, the sudden deadly volley from the brush, were playing havoc with the fighting spirit of men trained in the traditions of civilized warfare.

For long periods of time military units were kept on garrison duty in the frontier towns, a situation which further added to the problem of public morale. In theory all military matters on the local level were supposed to be under the control of the selectmen and militia officers of the

---

[11] Increase Mather, *A Brief History of the War* (Boston, 1676), p. 23; MA, LXVIII, 145a, 151; Nathaniel B. Shurtleff and David Pulsifer, eds., *Records of the Colony of New Plymouth in New England* (Boston, 1855–61), V, 185–87 (hereafter PCR).

town, who together constituted the town's own council of war. Now with colony troops brought into the local community, there was danger that the real control would fall into the hands of the "strangers." It must be remembered that in any well-laid plan for defending a typical frontier town, a few strong houses, strategically located, would be selected to serve as the nuclei of the town's defensive works, while many other homes would have to be written off as undefendable. Naturally, if such a bitter decision had to be made, the townsmen preferred to have it made by their own chosen representatives, not some outsider. On the other hand it seems likely that the colony soldiers, in turn, would feel some resentment at being placed under the command of men whose interests and vision were limited to the boundaries of their own towns. In this way mutual resentment grew.[12]

Many of the soldiers, bored and irritated by garrison duty on the frontier, did little to endear themselves to the townspeople. Doubtless they complained frequently about their quarters and food, blaming all of their woes upon the unhappy inhabitants. Some of the troops were indentured servants who were finding in garrison life an unaccustomed chance to swagger as they had never been able to do at home. Their roughness and arrogance must have contributed to the irritation felt by the local people.

In general the colony governments felt that the towns which were given the added protection of garrison soldiers ought to be willing to feed them. As the Council of Massachusetts remarked, "It is enough for the country to pay wages and find ammunition." [13] Yet oftentimes the towns resented the imposition of this additional burden at a time when they were having trouble feeding their own people. However, the authorities insisted on the point. In September, 1675, when Massachusetts was allotting garrison soldiers to the newly threatened towns of Dunstable, Groton, and Lancaster, the officers in charge of the operation were ordered to leave no soldiers in any town which refused to furnish their provisions.[14]

Before the depredations of the war became widespread, the towns made little attempt to conceal their resentment of the garrison forces quartered upon them, but this attitude tended to change in remarkable fashion as the enemy drew near. The burning of Springfield on October 5, 1675, did much to produce a new appreciation of the garrison forces in the towns of the upper Connecticut Valley. Whereas formerly the people had groaned whenever the numbers of troops in the towns were increased, now they hated to see the soldiers called out on an expedition, for fear the Indians would come in their absence. The townsmen of Northampton actually wrote to Boston, begging that a garrison of forty men be left in the town, and promising to feed them. Later the same town requested

---

12 MA, LXVII, 252, LXVIII, 151; MCR, V, 50; R.I. Historical Society Manuscripts (Providence, R.I.), X, 152.

13 MA, LXVIII, 59; George M. Bodge, *Soldiers in King Philip's War*, 3d ed. (Boston, 1906), p. 328.

14 MA, LXVII, 252; MCR, V, 54. The difficulties experienced by Lieutenant John Ruddock, commander of the garrison at Marlborough, furnish a good example of the tensions that existed. See MA, LXVII, 279, LXVIII, 4, 31; Bodge, pp. 211–12.

additional men, even offering to pay their wages.[15] The garrison soldier in King Philip's War—unwanted when the enemy was far away, grudgingly accepted as danger mounted, eagerly sought after when the war-whoops began to sound—would have read Kipling's *Tommy* with real appreciation. . . .

Efforts to recruit additional men for military service encountered increasing resistance as the war dragged on. Towns which believed themselves to be in danger of attack tried to retain their own men for local defense, a tactic which became increasingly serious as the enemy expanded his operations. As early as September, 1675, Woburn requested blanket exemption from the draft.[16] Eastham, when presented with a new quota, judged that some mistake had been made, and resolved "to send our full Complement of men and no more." [17] A petition of February 26, 1675/6, informed Governor Leverett that the towns of Milton, Braintree, Weymouth, and Hingham were now infested with the enemy, and asked to be freed from the press. Weymouth even requested that its ten men then in garrison on the Connecticut River be allowed to come home to defend their own town.[18]

Cases of resistance to the draft occurred from the very beginning of the war, but not until morale began to tumble appreciably did the problem assume serious proportions. In September Secretary Rawson, in a letter to Major Pynchon, confided that enemy successes were having an adverse effect upon recruiting. "Some escape away from the press and others hide away after they are impressed," Rawson complained.[19] In one town a warrant of impressment came open, so that its contents became generally known. As a result, when the constable made his rounds he was unable to find any of the men wanted. Other cases simply confirm the situation.[20]

The appalling hardships of the winter campaign in the Narragansett country brought military morale to a new low, making even more difficult the raising of sorely needed reinforcements. Men sought to dodge the draft by "sculking from one Toune to Another," which caused the government of Massachusetts to announce that any town apprehending such fly-by-nights could apply them against its own quota. Some towns apparently placed a broad interpretation on this decree, for one Joshua Ray complained that he had been snapped up in the press while visiting another town on business. Similar complaints were heard from Connecticut, where inhabitants of some of the inland towns were drafted by the seaside towns when they arrived there to carry on necessary affairs.[21]

By February, coincidental with the start of the enemy's new offen-

---

[15] MA, LXVII, 288, LXVIII, 48, 51, 168, 182.

[16] MA, LXVII, 259.

[17] Eastham Records, 1650–1705.

[18] MA, LXVIII, 179a.

[19] MA, LXVII, 270.

[20] MA, LXVIII, 21, 71; NEHGR, XXIII, 327; J. Hammond Trumbull, ed., *The Public Records of the Colony of Connecticut* (Hartford, 1850–59), II, 272–73 (hereafter CCR).

[21] MA, LXVIII, 106, 117; CA, War I, 115.

sive, the recruiting program of the United Colonies was entering its period of greatest difficulty. Increasingly the towns were falling far short of their quotas, and all too often the men actually sent were physically unfit for combat duty. April was the blackest month of all. People in eastern Massachusetts, Plymouth, and the Rhode Island mainland were in a state of near panic because of the successful Indian assaults on Providence, Rehoboth, Clark's garrison, and many other settlements. When five men were impressed in Boston, one of them said he was going home to get some clothes, but never came back. Of the others, three could not be found. John Pittam and Robert Miller, when ordered to report for military service, defiantly replied that they would be "hanged drawne and quartered rather than goe." [22]

. . . Late in April the government of Plymouth Colony was forced to admit its inability to place any large body of soldiers in the field, and so could do little more than conduct scouting operations around the various settlements. Massachusetts soon yielded to the clamor of its own exposed frontier communities by ordering that all soldiers from Medfield, Sudbury, Concord, Chelmsford, Andover, Haverhill, and Exeter be released from the army to go home and defend those towns. The released men were granted immunity from further impressment so long as they remained active in local defense. To all appearances the whole war effort of the United Colonies was being undermined by men's reluctance to leave their own concerns and unite for offensive action against the savages. [23]

All during the war, increased enemy activity usually sent droves of frightened settlers straggling along the trails toward the safer towns. These unfortunate refugees often were not welcome in the places to which they fled. Generally speaking, New England towns were closed corporations which tended to view outsiders with suspicion. Under ordinary conditions, such strangers would not be allowed to remain long in town without an affirmative vote of the inhabitants assembled in town meeting. The war, of course, tended to break down the rigidity of these standards, but the influx of refugees was still viewed with a certain amount of apprehension by the local people. The reason for this apparently selfish attitude was that the arrival of considerable numbers of destitute strangers threatened to unsettle the closely knit moral and economic life of the town, creating a host of new problems for the already heavily burdened community. [24]

In Massachusetts the major responsibility for providing financial aid for needy refugees was assumed by the colony treasury, thereby relieving the towns of one great worry. Later the Council issued a special proclamation designed to assure a proper disciplinary control over the incomers. The selectmen of each town containing such people were ordered to make

[22] MA, LXVIII, 203, 216a, 234a.
[23] MA, LXVIII, 179, 227, 234; MCR, V, 79–80; NEHGR, XXIII, 328; Bodge, pp. 214, 216; Billerica Records (Transcript), 1653–1685, p. 187. It was almost as hard to conscript a horse as a man. See MA, LXVII, 245, LXIX, 1; Connecticut Colonial Probate Records, III, County Court, 1663–1667, p. 151.
[24] Marshfield Records (Transcript), I, 137; *Town Records of Salem, Massachusetts* (Salem, Mass., 1913), II, 204–205; Billerica Records (Transcript), 1653–1685, p. 186.

a special survey or census of refugees, in order that they might be known and closely observed. Moreover, the local officials were authorized to see that these refugees were kept busy at some suitable work for their own support, with particular attention being paid to young unmarried people who might otherwise get into trouble.[25]

The official attitude of the colonial governments toward the people who fled the frontier towns was conditioned by two opposite interests. Naturally, the authorities were concerned for the safety of individuals, but they were also concerned for the preservation of established townships and the maintenance of the frontier lines of defense. If the increasing tendency of the people in outlying districts to abandon their homes should become a stampede, there was real danger that the area of English settlement would be pushed back to the seacoast. When Massachusetts ordered the smaller frontier towns to evacuate all women and children not actually needed there, she also declared that persons who abandoned their homes without authorization were to lose their property and right in those places. In Plymouth Colony the government took a similar stand. Rhode Island, on the contrary, admitted her inability to protect the mainland people living at Providence and Warwick, and consequently urged them to take refuge on Aquidneck Island.[26]

. . . The acute scarcity of food in some towns unfortunately led to profiteering. In Andover, people who had corn to sell insisted on cash in return, an impossible condition for many hungry purchasers at that time. John Kingsley of Rehoboth begged his friends in Connecticut to send some meal, "for if wee send . . . [to] road island there is won wolf in the way, and hee wil have money, which won of 40 hath not it to pay, tho thay starve; yea 1 sh for 1 bushel, caring and Bringing. There is unother, that is the miller, and hee takes an 8 part." [27]

The flail of war created a multitude of other human problems as well. What should be done with the aging widows of men killed in the country's service? Who would take care of the little girls and boys deprived of their parents by Indian tomahawks? For the most part such cases were quietly handled, often by relatives and friends, without recourse to the government. It was always possible to put homeless children, even as young as six years old, into articled service to learn a trade and earn their keep. The records of the county court at Northampton describe a case in which both the mother and the father of three small children had been slain by the Indians. The court appointed two uncles to take care of the children and

[25] MCR, V, 64; *Proceedings of the Massachusetts Historical Society*, 2d ser., XII, 402.
[26] MA, LXVIII, 12; MCR, V, 48, 51; NEHGR, XXII, 462; PCR, V, 185–86; *The Early Records of the Town of Providence* (Providence, 1892–1915), XV, 160; John R. Bartlett, ed., *Records of the Colony of Rhode Island and Providence Plantations, in New England* (10 vols.; Providence, 1856–65), II, 533.
[27] CA, War I, 68; CCR, II, 445–47; Richard LeBaron Bowen, *Early Rehoboth* (3 vols.; Rehoboth, Mass., 1945), III, 20–23; MA, LXVIII, 202a. Roger Williams testified that Governor Coddington himself was a wartime profiteer. See "An Answer to a Letter Sent From Mr. Coddington," *Proceedings of the Rhode Island Historical Society*, 1875–1876.

look after the estate.[28] Tragedies such as this were a bitter everyday reality in King Philip's War.

In viewing the whole tragic picture of the suffering and distress caused by the conflict, we cannot fail to be impressed by the tremendous scope of the problem. A sizable proportion of New England's relatively small population had been demoralized and cut adrift in a world of confusion, danger, and want. There was no adequate organization ready and able to channel the efforts of all who wanted to help. The colonial governments were chiefly occupied with other affairs which seemed to be more important. Moreover, the colonies were far from wealthy, and the expense of military operations was a very heavy burden for the people, without adding to it the costs of relief for unfortunate victims of the conflict. For all of these reasons the relief afforded was, to say the least, inadequate. Administration of the relief program, if indeed there was any such effort worthy of the name, was haphazard. Private charity did its best to fill in the gaps left by official inadequacies.[29] The sacrificial giving of Christian people both here and abroad deserves all due honor, but these efforts were simply swamped by the tremendous size of the disaster. New England's inability to take care of herself adequately in such a crisis was a humbling experience, and a somber warning that the price of this land had not been fully paid by the labor and suffering of the first generation.

[28] Hampshire County Court Record, I, 172.
[29] CA, War I, 92; CCR, II, 445, 454–55, 457; Curwin Papers, III, 7, 77; Cotton Papers (Boston Public Library), Part VII, 10; *Narratives,* pp. 36, 38, 41.

Suggestions for Further Reading

The everyday lives of colonizing Europeans in the seventeenth century are disclosed in a variety of recent work in American history. For ideas about the New World and what immigrants might expect to find, see Howard Mumford Jones, *O Strange New World: American Culture, The Formative Years** (New York, 1964); Richard Slotkin, *Regeneration Through Violence: The Mythology of the American Frontier, 1600–1860** (Middletown, Conn., 1973); Louis B. Wright, *The Colonial Search for a Southern Eden* (University, Ala., 1953); and Henri Baudet, *Paradise on Earth: Thoughts on European Images of Non-European Man*, trans. Elizabeth Wentholt (New Haven, Conn., 1965).

Attitudes toward work are discussed in Keith Thomas, "Work and Leisure in Pre-Industrial Society," *Past and Present*, no. 29 (1964), pp. 50–66, and David Bertelson, *The Lazy South* (New York, 1967).

Family relations—including attitudes toward sex, love, marriage, and familial rights and responsibilities—are discussed in Edmund S. Morgan, *The Puritan Family: Religion and Domestic Relations in Seventeenth-Century New England** (New York, 1966) and *Virginians at Home; Family Life in the Eighteenth Century** (Williamsburg, Va., 1952); Philip J. Greven, Jr., *Four Generations: Population, Land, and Family in Colonial Andover, Massachusetts** (Ithaca, N.Y., 1970); and John Demos, "Families in Colonial Bristol, Rhode Island: An Exercise in Historical Demography," *William and Mary Quarterly* 25 (1968):40–57. For attitudes toward child-rearing, see Joseph Illick, "Child-rearing in 17th-Century England"; and John F. Walzer, "A Period of Ambivalence: Eighteenth-Century Childhood," in Lloyd deMause, *The History of Childhood* (New York, 1974).

The special case of Anne Hutchinson is perceptively approached in Emery Battis, *Saints and Sectaries: Anne Hutchinson and the Antinomian Controversy in Massachusetts Bay Colony* (Chapel Hill, N.C., 1962), and Lyle Koehler, "The Case of the American Jezebels: Anne Hutchinson and Female Agitation During the Years of Antinomian Turmoil, 1636–1640," *William and Mary Quarterly* 31 (1974):55–78.

For Indian cultures of the Northeast Woodlands at the time of European arrival, the literature is vast. For a general introduction the student may consult Gary B. Nash, *Red, White, and Black: the Peoples of Early America** (Englewood Cliffs, N.J., 1974), and Francis Jennings, *The Invasion of America: Indians, Colonialism,*

* Available in paperback edition.

and the Cant of Conquest (Chapel Hill, N.C., 1975). Also valuable are Harold Fey and D'Arcy McNickle, *Indians and Other Americans: Two Ways of Life Meet** (New York, 1959), and Kenneth Macgowan and Joseph A. Hester, Jr., *Early Man in the New World** (Garden City, N.Y., 1962).

In studying early attitudes toward the Indians and the conflict that resulted, Richard Slotkin, *Regeneration through Violence*, is indispensable. Also of great value are Roy Harvey Pearce, *Savagism and Civilization: A Study of the Indian and the Idea of Civilization** (Baltimore, 1953), and Wilcomb E. Washburn, *The Governor and the Rebel: A History of Bacon's Rebellion in Virginia** (Chapel Hill, N.C., 1957).

Other insights into the daily lives of the earliest colonists can be gleaned from David H. Flaherty, *Privacy in Colonial New England* (Charlottesville, Va., 1972); Darrett B. Rutman, *Husbandmen of Plymouth: Farms and Villages of the Old Colony, 1620–1692* (Boston, 1967); and from John Barth's marvelously revealing novel about early life on the Chesapeake, *The Sotweed Factor** (Garden City, N.Y., 1960).

1740–1790

Revolutionary America

The Religious Experience

In the age of exploration, when Europeans reached out to conquer and colonize other parts of the world, human control over the natural environment was slight. With their power to master the awesome forces of nature severely limited by the meagre extent of scientific and technological knowledge, people of all societies tended to attribute to supernatural forces what could not be understood or controlled. Religious faith, not scientific reason, governed life. This was true for Native Americans as well as Europeans, although most Indian cultures were polytheistic—worshipping many Gods to whom they attributed natural forces—while the Europeans were monotheistic—worshipping one God.

Religion, then, whether polytheistic or monotheistic, can be understood as a formula for living, a way of making sense out of the uncontrollable forces and events surrounding human experience, a way of giving order and meaning to one's world and one's place in it. It was not tangential but central to both the colonizers and the colonized in the New World of the seventeenth and eighteenth centuries. Rather than being a ritual observed once a week, religion pervaded life on every day.

Given the centrality of religion, it is not surprising that people fought so passionately in defense of what each called "true" religion and against all other "false" religions. In Europe, Christians battled Moslems for centuries before the discovery of the New World. Within the Christian fold, Catholics and Protestants slaughtered each other in countless wars, and both looked upon the occupation of the New World as an opportunity to claim millions of "Indians" for their system of Christian belief. Even within the Protestant camp, bitter dispute raged throughout the colonial era as to which variant interpretation of Christianity was "orthodox" and which was "blasphemous." The magistrates of the Massachusetts Bay Colony banished Roger Williams and Anne Hutchinson in the early years of the settlement because they preached variant forms of Puritanism, which itself had been driven underground in England by Anglicanism—another variation of Protestant belief. When Quakers came to Massachusetts in the 1650s, advocating what they regarded as a purer form of Protestant worship, they were ordered to leave. The magistrates regarded them as so heretical that when they refused, they were jailed, whipped, mutilated, and finally, in several cases, hanged on Boston Common.

Such theological factionalism, and such resorts to violence, tell us much about the importance of religion in the lives of these seventeenth-century colonists. But only by understanding that men and women still regarded life as a preparation for afterlife can we begin to comprehend this hostility between religious groups.

One of the major themes of colonial history is the gradual secularization of society. While piety and self-denial were still central values in the lives of New Englanders in the late seventeenth century, the ideas of the European Enlightenment, emphasizing "reason" over "faith," tended in the eighteenth century to dilute the importance of religion. Material success in the New World and a preoccupation with accumulating worldly goods began to overtake the obsession with life after death. But as the following three selections on religious experience in the eighteenth century indicate, religion was still a vital force in the lives of most people. In Puritan New England, the Great Awakening of the 1740s sent tremors coursing through the towns. Revivalistic religion, stressing personal participation and emotional involvement of great intensity, swept into the churches many who had lost the religious impulse. One colonial historian, Richard L. Bushman, sees the religious passion of the 1740s as a subconscious attempt to assuage the guilt produced by the pursuit of economic goals in the face of opposition from religious leaders. In an environment where the Puritan standards of piety and simplicity were still acknowledged, even if they had been widely breached in practice since the days of John Winthrop and William Bradford, the revivalist message of "sinners in the hands of an angry God" struck with great force.

Secularization by no means extinguished the fires of religious contention and intolerance. By the eighteenth century it was generally agreed that individuals should be free to practice their own faith, though Protestants were not yet prepared to offer civil rights to Catholics and Jews. But this did not mean that intolerance was dead, as the passages from the diary of Charles Woodmason, an itinerant Anglican missionary in the Carolina backcountry, indicate. For Woodmason, carrying the Anglican message to thousands of Scotch-Irish Presbyterians, who were flooding into the backcountry from Pennsylvania to Georgia, was little different from proselytizing among Indian "savages."

Students may also wish to consider the role of religion as a social institution that reflects secular as well as religious needs and values. In the frontier areas of the Carolinas, the Puritan preoccupation with the afterlife was rarely found. To the dismay of the Anglican Woodmason, the Presbyterian revellers were more interested in a sensuous celebration of life and an erotic release from work and boredom. In sharp contrast was the quiet devotion of the urbane Quakers of Philadelphia described by the Swedish botanist Peter Kalm in the 1750s. Why, we must ask, did religious worship assume such radically different forms from area to area?

Report of the Great Awakening
in New London, Connecticut

New-London, March 14th 1742/3

To the Publisher of the *Boston Post-Boy.*

SIR,

 The Conduct of some of the People call'd N Lights, or Christians, as they please to call themselves, has been so extraordinary here the last Week, that 'tis desired by some that an Account of their wild, frantick and extravagant Management may be inserted in one of your next Prints; and therefore send you the following Sketch of some of their Transactions;

 At the Beginning of the present Month came to this Place the famous Mr *Davenport,* accompanied with Three Armour-Bearers, and some others; upon his Arrival, the Christians, or dear Children, gather'd round about him in Crouds, who paid him such profound Respect, Reverence and Homage, that his well-known great Modesty and Humility oblig'd him to check their Devotion, by telling them, he was not a God, but a Man. However this did not abate their Veneration for him so much, but that even the Chief of them ('tis credibly said) made auricular Confessions to him; and this being over, (and it may be reasonably suppos'd ample Absolution, and proper Indulgences were given thereupon,) they might judge themselves to be in a good Condition to do some memorable Exploits, to the lasting Honour of their Sect, and the Establishment of their Religion; and having by Fasting and Prayer sought for Direction to do something, one of them declar'd, he had a Revelation; which was, that they should root out Heresy and pull down Idolatry: The Motion was well approved by the Assembly, who soon resolv'd to make a bold and vigorous Attempt to effect it; and accordingly on the 6th Instant, it being the Lord's Day, just before the Conclusion of the Publick Worship, and also as the People were returning from the House of GOD, they were surpriz'd with a great Noise and Outcry; Multitudes hasten'd toward the Place of Rendezvous, directing themselves by the Clamor and Shouting, which together, with the ascending Smoak bro't them to one of the most public Places in the Town, and there found these good People encompassing a Fire which they had built up in the Street, into which they were casting Numbers of Books, principally on Divinity, and those that were well-approved by *Protestant* Divines, *viz.* Bp. *Beveridge's* Thoughts, Mr. *Russel's* Seven Sermons, one of Dr. *Colman's,* and one of *Dr. Chauncy's* Books, and many others. Nothing can be more astonishing than their insolent Behaviour was during the Time

"Report of the Great Awakening in New London, Connecticut" (editor's title). From *Boston Weekly Post-Boy,* March 28, 1743.

of their Sacrifice, as 'tis said they call'd it; whilst the Books were in the Flames they cry'd out, *Thus the Souls of the Authors of those Books, those of them that are dead, are roasting in the Flames of Hell;* and that *the Fate of those surviving, would be the same, unless speedy Repentance prevented:* On the next Day they had at the same Place a second Bonfire of the like Materials, and manag'd in the same manner. Having given this fatal Stroke to *Heresy*, they made ready to attack *Idolatry*, and sought for Direction, as in the Case before; and then Mr. *D—p—t* told them to look at Home first, and that they themselves were guilty of idolizing their Apparel, and should therefore divest themselves of those Things especially which were for Ornament, and let them be burnt: Some of them in the heighth of their Zeal, conferred not with Flesh and Blood, but fell to stripping and cast their Cloaths down at their Apostle's Feet; one or two hesitated about the Matter, and were so bold as to tell him they had nothing on which they idoliz'd: He reply'd, that such and such a Thing was an Offence to him; and they must down with them: One of these being a Gentleman of Learning and Parts ventur'd to tell Mr. *D—p—t*, that he could scarce see how his disliking the Night-Gown that he had on his Back, should render him, guilty of Idolatry. However, This carnal Reasoning avail'd nothing; strip he must, and strip he did: By this Time the Pile had grown to a large Bulk, and almost ripe for Sacrifice; and that they might be clear and well-warranted in the Enterprize, Mr. *D—p—t* order'd one of his Armour-Bearers to pray for a full Discovery of the Mind—in the Affair; he did accordingly, but had no Answer: Another also at his Direction pray'd, but no Answer yet: Next Mr. *D—p—t* pray'd himself; and now the Oracle spake clear to the Point, without Ambiguity, and utter'd that *the Things must be burnt;* and to confirm the Truth of the Revelation, took his wearing Breeches, and hove them with Violence into the Pile, saying, *Go you with the Rest.* A young Sister, whose Modesty could not bear to see the Mixture of Cloaks, Petty Coats and Breeches, snatch'd up his Breeches, and sent them at him, with as much Indignation, as tho' they had been the Hire of a Wh—— or the Price of a Dog: At this Juncture came in a Brother from a neighbouring Town; a Man of more Sense than most of them have; and apply'd warmly to Mr. *D—p—t*, told him, He was *making a Calf*, and that he thot', *the D——l was in him:* Mr. *D—p—t* said, He *tho't so too;* and added, That he *was under the Influence of an* evil Spirit, *and that God had left Him.* His most famous Armour Bearer has had bitter Reflections on their late odd Transactions; and declar'd, That *altho' he had for three Years* past believ'd (and why not *known) himself to be a Child of God,* he now tho't *he was a Child of the D——l, and a* Judas; *and thought he should be hang'd between Heaven and Earth, and have his Bowels gush out.* Another poor young Man of *Boston,* (whom I wish with his Friends) said the same Things (save that he did not foresee the same dismal Fate) at that Time, in the same Company, and all in the Presence of Mr. *D—p—t*, who is now indispos'd in Body, but better compos'd in Mind: I wish him nothing worse than, *Mens sane, in Corpore sano.*

Who am, Sir,

Your humble Servant.

Description of a Philadelphia
Quaker Meeting

PETER KALM

To-day I attended service in a Quaker meeting-house. I was once present at such a service in London, and once in this city, where there are two meeting-houses or churches. It is known that the Quakers are a religious sect that arose in England during the last century, of whom the majority is found in Pennsylvania, since this province was granted to Penn, who was a Quaker and who brought his religious followers to this territory. But I should like first to describe the service that took place in their church to-day, and then speak about their faith and customs.

The Quakers in this town attend meeting three times on Sunday—from ten to twelve in the morning, at two, and finally, at six in the evening. Besides, they attend service twice during the week, namely on Tuesdays from ten to twelve and on Thursdays at the same time. Then also a religious service is held in the church the last Friday of each month, not to mention their general gatherings, which I shall discuss presently.— To-day we appeared at ten, as the bells of the English church were ringing. We sat down on benches made like those in our academies on which the students sit. The front benches, however, were provided with a long, horizontal pole in the back, against which one could lean for support. Men and women sit apart. (In London they sat together). The early comers sit on the front seats, and so on down. Nearest the front by the walls are two benches, one on either side of the aisle, made of boards like our ordinary pews, and placed a little higher up than the other seats in the church. On one of them, on the men's side, sat to-day two old men; on the other, in the women's section, were four women. In these pews sit those of both sexes who either are already accustomed to preach or who expect on that particular day to be inspired by the Holy Ghost to expound the Word. All men and women are dressed in the usual English manner. When a man comes into the meeting-house he does not remove or raise his hat but goes and sits down with his hat on.—Here we sat and waited very quietly from ten o'clock to a quarter after eleven, during which the people gathered and then waited for inspiration of the Spirit to speak. Finally, one of the two old men in the front pew rose, removed his hat, turned hither and yon, and began to speak, but so softly that even in the middle of the church, which was not very large, it was impossible to hear anything except the confused murmur of the words. Later he began to talk a little louder, but so slowly that four or five minutes elapsed between the sentences; the words came both louder and faster. In their preaching the Quakers have a peculiar mode of expression, which is half singing,

"Description of a Philadelphia Quaker Meeting" (editor's title), by Peter Kalm. From Adolph B. Benson, ed., *The America of 1750: Peter Kalm's Travels in North America* (2 vols.; New York: Dover Publications, 1966), vol. 2, pp. 648–51. Reprinted by permission of the publisher.

with a strange cadence and accent, and ending each cadence, as it were, with a full or partial sob. Each cadence consists of from two to four syllables, but sometimes more, according to the demand of the words and meaning; i.e. my friends//put in your mind//we can//do nothing//good of our self//without God's//help and assistance//etc. In the beginning the sobbing is not heard so plainly, but the deeper and farther the reader or preacher gets into his sermon the more violent is the sobbing between the cadences. The speaker to-day had no gestures, but turned in various directions; sometimes he placed a hand on his chin; and during most of the sermon kept buttoning and unbuttoning his vest. The gist of his sermon was that we can do nothing of ourselves without the help of our Savior. When he had stood for a while using his sing-song method he changed his manner of delivery and spoke in a more natural way, or as ministers do when they read a prayer. Shortly afterwards, however, he reverted to his former practice, and at the end, just as he seemed to have attained a certain momentum he stopped abruptly, sat down and put on his hat. After that we sat quietly for a while looking at each other until one of the old women in the front pew arose, when the whole congregation stood up and the men removed their hats. The woman turned from the people to the wall and began to read extemporaneously a few prayers with a loud but fearfully sobbing voice. When she was through she sat down, and the whole congregation with her, when the clock struck twelve, whereupon after a short pause each one got up and went home. The man's sermon lasted half an hour. During the sermon a man would get up now and then, but in order to show that he did not do so to speak he would turn his back to the front of the church—a sign that he did not arise from any spiritual inspiration. There were some present who kept their hats off; but these sheep were not of this flock, only strangers who had come from curiosity and not because of any special prompting by the Spirit.

The meeting-house was whitewashed inside and had a gallery almost all the way around. The tin candle-holders on the pillars supporting the gallery constituted the only ornaments of the church. There was no pulpit, altar, baptismal font, or bridal pew, no prie-dieu or collection bag, no clergyman, cantor or church beadle, and no announcements were read after the sermon, nor were any prayers said for the sick.—This was the way the service was conducted today.

But otherwise there are often infinite variations. Many times after a long silence a man rises first, and when he gets through a woman rises and preaches; after her comes another man or woman; occasionally only the women speak; then again a woman might start, and so on alternately; sometimes only men rise to talk; now and then either a man or woman gets up, begins to puff and sigh, and endeavors to speak, but is unable to squeeze out a word and so sits down again. Then it happens, also, that the whole congregation gathers in the meeting-house and sits there silently for two hours, waiting for someone to preach; but since none has prepared himself or feels moved by the Spirit, the whole audience rises again at the end of the period and goes home without the members having accomplished anything in the church except sitting and looking at each other. The women who hope to preach and therefore sit in a special pew generally keep their heads bowed, or hold a handkerchief with both hands over their eyes. The others, however, sit upright and look up, and do not cover their eyes. The men and women have separate doors, through which they enter and leave the church.

Religion in the Carolina Backcountry
CHARLES WOODMASON

December 1767. . . . The Church Warden below came up, and with some other Serious Christians accompanied me to Little Lynch's Creek, where had a very religious Congregation of 70 persons—had 15 or 16 Communicants—In afternoon rode 5 Miles to another Congregation and gave Service to them—Spending the Evening in singing Psalms and Hymns.

This Day we had another Specimen of the Envy Malice and Temper of the Presbyterians—They gave away 2 Barrels of Whisky to the Populace to make drink, and for to disturb the Service—for this being the 1st time that the Communion was ever celebrated in this Wild remote Part of the World, it gave a Great Alarm, and caus'd them much Pain and Vexation. The Company got drunk by 10 oth Clock and we could hear them firing, hooping, and hallowing like Indians. Some few came before the Communion was finish'd and were very Noisy—and could I have found out the Individuals, would have punish'd them.

They took another Step to interrupt the Service of the Day. The Captain of the Corps of Militia on this Creek being a Presbyterian, order'd the Company to appear as this day under Arms to Muster—The Church People refus'd. He threatn'd to fine—They defy'd Him: And had he attempted it, a Battle would certainly have ensu'd in the Muster field between the Church folks and Presbyterians, and Blood been spilt—His Apprehension of Danger to his person made him defer it till the 26th. . . .

Not long after, they hir'd a Band of rude fellows to come to Service who brought with them 57 Dogs (for I counted them) which in Time of Service they set fighting, and I was obliged to stop—In Time of Sermon they repeated it—and I was oblig'd to desist and dismiss the People. It is in vain to take up or commit these lawless Ruffians—for they have nothing, and the Charge of sending of them to Charlestown, would take me a Years Salary—We are without any Law, or Order—And as all the Magistrates are Presbyterians, I could not get a Warrant—If I got Warrants as the Constables are Presbyterians likewise, I could not get them serv'd—If serv'd, the Guard would let them escape—Both my Self and other Episcopals have made this Experiment—They have granted me Writs thro' fear

From Richard J. Hooker, ed., *The Carolina Backcountry on the Eve of the Revolution: The Journal and Other Writings of Charles Woodmason, Anglican Itinerant* (Chapel Hill: University of North Carolina Press, 1953), pp. 30–31, 45, 56, 61, 101–04. Originally published for the Institute of Early American History and Culture. Reprinted by permission of the University of North Carolina Press.

of being complain'd off, but took Care not to have them serv'd—I took up
one fellow for a Riot at a Wedding, and creating disturbance—The people
took up two others for entering the House where I was when in Bed—
stealing my Gown—putting it on—and then visiting a Woman in Bed, and
getting to Bed to her, and making her give out next day, that the Parson
came to Bed to her—This was a Scheme laid by the Baptists—and Man and
Woman prepared for the Purpose. The People likewise took up some
others for calling of me Jesuit, and railing against the Service—The Constable let them all loose—No bringing of them to Justice—I enter'd In-
formations against some Magistrates for marrying—but cannot get them
out of the other Justices Hands till too late to send to Town for a Judges
Warrant. . . .

Tuesday August 16. In Consequence of a Promise made, set off this
Morning with a Guide for Flatt Creek—Here I found a vast Body of
People assembled—Such a Medley! such a mixed Multitude of all Classes
and Complexions I never saw. I baptized about 20 Children and Married
4 Couple—Most of these People had never before seen a Minister, or heard
the Lords Prayer, Service or Sermon in their Days. I was a Great Curiosity
to them—And they were as great Oddities to me. After Service they went
to Revelling Drinking Singing Dancing and Whoring—and most of the
Company were drunk before I quitted the Spot—They were as rude in
their Manners as the Common Savages, and hardly a degree removed from
them. Their Dresses almost as loose and Naked as the Indians, and differing
in Nothing save Complexion—I could not conceive from whence this vast
Body could swarm—But this Country contains ten times the Number of
Persons beyond my Apprehension. . . .

It would be (as I once observ'd before) a Great Novelty to a Lon-
doner to see one of these Congregations—The Men with only a thin Shirt
and pair of Breeches or Trousers on—barelegged and barefooted—The
Women bareheaded, barelegged and barefoot with only a thin Shift and
under Petticoat—Yet I cannot break [them?] of this—for the heat of the
Weather admits not of any [but] thin Cloathing—I can hardly bear the
Weight of my Whig and Gown, during Service. The Young Women have
a most uncommon Practise, which I cannot break them off. They draw
their Shift as tight as possible to the Body, and pin it close, to shew the
roundness of their Breasts, and slender Waists (for they are generally
finely shaped) and draw their Petticoat close to their Hips to shew the
fineness of their Limbs—so that they might as well be in Puri Naturalibus
—Indeed Nakedness is not censurable or indecent here, and they expose
themselves often quite Naked, without Ceremony—Rubbing themselves
and their Hair with Bears Oil and tying it up behind in a Bunch like the
Indians—being hardly one degree removed from them—In few Years, I
hope to bring about a Reformation, as I already have done in several Parts
of the Country. . . .

For only draw a Comparison between them [the Presbyterians] and
Us [the Anglicans], and let an Impartial Judge determine where *Offence*
may chiefly be taken, At our Solemn, Grave, and Serious Sett Forms, or
their Wild Extempore Jargon, nauseaus to any Chaste or refin'd Ear. There
are so many Absurdities committed by them, as wou'd shock one of our

Cherokee Savages; And was a Sensible Turk or Indian to view some of
their Extravagancies it would quickly determine them against Christianity.
Had any such been in their Assembly as last Sunday when they communicated, the Honest Heathens would have imagin'd themselves rather amidst
a Gang of frantic Lunatics broke out of Bedlam, rather than among a
Society of religious Christians, met to celebrate the most sacred and Solemn
Ordinance of their Religion. Here, one Fellow mounted on a Bench with
the Bread, and bawling, *See the Body of Christ,* Another with the Cup
running around, and bellowing—*Who cleanses his Soul with the Blood of
Christ,* and a thousand other Extravagancies—One on his knees in a Posture
of Prayer—Others singing—some howling—These Ranting—Those Crying—Others dancing, Skipping, Laughing and rejoycing. Here two or 3
Women falling on their Backs, kicking up their Heels, exposing their
Nakedness to all Bystanders and others sitting Pensive, in deep Melancholy
lost in Abstraction, like Statues, quite insensible—and when rous'd by the
Spectators from their pretended Reveries Transports, and indecent Pos-
tures and Actions declaring they knew nought of the Matter. That their
Souls had taken flight to Heav'n, and they knew nothing of what they said
or did. Spect[at]ors were highly shocked at such vile Abuse of sacred
Ordinances! And indeed such a Scene was sufficient to make the vilest
Sinner shudder. Their Teacher, so far from condemning, or reproving,
them, call'd it, the Work of God, and returned Thanks for Actions deserving of the Pillory and Whipping Post. But that would not have been *New*
to some of them. And if they can thus transgress all bounds of Decency
Modesty, and Morality, in such an Open Public Manner, it is not hard to
conceive what may pass at their Nocturnal Meetings, and Private Assemblies. Is there any thing like this in the Church of England to give Offence?
      But another vile Matter that does and must give Offence to all Sober
Minds Is, what they call their *Experiences;* It seems, that before a Person
be dipp'd, He must give an Account of his Secret Calls, Conviction, Conversion, Repentance &c &c. Some of these Experiences have been so ludicrous and ridiculous that *Democritus* in Spite of himself must have burst
with Laughter. Others, altogether as blasphemous Such as their Visions,
Dreams, Revelations—and the like; Too many, and too horrid to be mention'd. Nothing in the *Alcoran* Nothing that can be found in all the
Miracles of the Church of Rome, and all the Reveries of her Saints can be
so absurd, or so Enthusiastic, as what has gravely been recited in that
Tabernacle Yonder—To the Scandal of Religion and Insult of Common
Sense. And to heighten the Farce, To see two or three fellows with fix'd
Countenances and grave Looks, hearing all this Nonsense for Hours together, and making particular Enquiries, when, How, Where, in what
Manner, these Miraculous Events happen'd—To see, I say, a Sett of Mon-
grels under Pretext of Religion, Sit, and hear for Hours together a String
of Vile, cook'd up, Silly and Senseless Lyes, What they know to be Such,
What they are Sensible has not the least foundation in Truth or Reason,
and to encourage Persons in such Gross Inventions must grieve, must give
great Offence to ev'ry one that has the Honour of Christianity at Heart.
      Then again to see them Divide and Sub divide, Split into Parties—Rail

at and excommunicate one another—Turn out of Meeting, and receive into another—And a Gang of them getting together and gabbling one after the other (and sometimes disputing against each other) on Abstruse Theological Question—Speculative Points—Abstracted Notions, and Scholastic Subtelties, such as the greatest Metaph[ys]icians and Learned Scholars never yet could define, or agree on—To hear Ignorant Wretches, who can not write—Who never read ten Pages in any Book, and can hardly read the Alphabett discussing such Knotty Points for the Edification of their Auditors, is a Scene so farcical, so highly humoursome as excels any Exhibition of Folly that has ever yet appear'd in the World, and consequently must give High offence to all Inteligent and rational Minds.

If any Thing offensive beyond all This to greive the Hearts and Minds of serious Christians presents it Self to view among them, it is their Mode of Baptism, to which Lascivous Persons of both Sexes resort, as to a Public Bath. I know not whether it would not be less offensive to Modesty for them to strip wholly into Buff at once, than to be dipp'd with those very thin Linen Drawers they are equipp'd in—Which when wet, so closely adheres to the Limbs, as exposes the Nudities equally as if none at All. If this be not Offensive and a greivous Insult on all Modesty and Decency among Civiliz'd People I know not what can be term'd so. Certainly a few chosen Witnesses of the Sex of the Party, and performance of the Ceremony in a Tent, or Cover'd Place, would be equally as *Edifying*, as Persons being stript and their Privities expos'd before a gaping Multitude who resort to these Big Meetings (as they are term'd) as they would to a Bear or Bullbaiting.

It must give Great Scandal and Offence to all Serious Minds thus to see the Solemn Ordinances of God become the Sport, Pastime and Derision of Men—and to view them marching in Procession singing Hymns before the poor wet half naked Creature—Very edifying this! Just as much as I saw lately practis'd at Marriage of one of their Notable She Saints around whom (the Ceremony ended) they march'd in Circles singing Hymns, and chanting Orisons, with a vast Parade of Prayer Thanks givings and Religious Foppery; Which had such marvellous Effect on the virtuous Devotee as to cause her to bring a Child in five Months after, as a Proof that their Prayers for her being fruitful was answer'd.

This Devotee was highly celebrated for her extraordinary Illuminations, Visions and Communications. It is the same who in her Experience told a long Story of an Angel coming to visit her in the Night thro' the Roof of her Cabbin—In flames of Fire too! It was very true that she was visited in the Night, and that the Apparation did jump down upon her Bed thro' the Shingles by an opening she had made for the Purpose—and that it came to her all on Fire. Yes! But it was in the Fire of Lust; And this Angel was no other than her Ghostly Teacher, to whom she communicated a Revelation that it was ordain'd He should caress Her; And He Good Man, was not disobedient to this Heav'nly Call—He afterward had a Revelation That it was the Will of God such a Man was to take her to Wife Which the Poor unthinking Booby did, in Conformity to the Divine Will express'd by his prophet—Little dreaming that He was to Father the Prophets Bastard. All this (and much more) the Woman has confess'd to Me. But You see hereby that Revelations now a days, are not strictly to be depended On—and that those who have such extraordinary Gifts of the Spirit given, are apt to fall into Mistakes, as did a Neighbouring Teacher lately in the Night Poor Man Mistaking another Woman for his Wife— and the Spirit in her making no resistance. . . .

White Servitude

RICHARD HOFSTADTER

This Indenture MADE the *Thirteenth* Day of *May* in the Year of our Lord one thousand, seven hundred and *eighty four* BETWEEN *Alexr. Beard of Broughshane in the County of Antrim Taylor by Consent of his Father* of the one Part, and *John Duhey of Cullybackey in the said County* —Gentleman— of the other Part, WITNESSETH, that the said *Alexandr. Beard* doth hereby covenant, promise and grant, to and with the said *John Duhey* —— *his* ——Executors, Administrators and Affigns, from the Day of the Date hereof until the first and next Arrival at *Philadelphia* —in America, and after for and during the Term of *three* —— Years to ferve in fuch Service and Employment as the said *John Duhey* —— or *his* Affigns fhall there employ *him* according to the Cuftom of the Country in the like Kind. In Confideration whereof the said *John Duhey* —— doth hereby covenant and grant to and with the said *Alexr. Beard* to pay for *his* Paffage, and to find allow *him* Meat, Drink, Apparel and Lodging, with other Neceffaries, during the faid Term; and at the End of the faid Term to pay unto *him* the ufual Allowance, according to the Cuftom of the Country in the like Kind. IN WITNESS whereof the Parties above-mentioned to thefe Indentures have interchangeably put their Hands and Seals, the Day and Year firft above written.

Signed, Sealed, and Delivered,
in the Prefence of

Peter Dillon

John Weir

Alexr. Beard

John Duhey

Land and labor are indispensable ingredients in the development of all new societies. In North America it was the land of Native Americans and the unfree labor performed by indentured servants and slaves upon which most colonial wealth was built. As many as half of the Europeans who arrived in North America in the seventeenth and eighteenth centuries may have come as indentured servants. As such, they were not free to move where they wanted, marry, or work for themselves. They had "bound out" their labor and their lives for four to seven years to somebody in the colonies whom they had never seen before.

In this essay, Richard Hofstadter paints a portrait of the life of indentured servants who came to the English colonies in the eighteenth century. Primarily they were Scotch-Irish, Irish, and Germans. Because they were so numerous and important to the developing economy, we cannot ignore them in any consideration of everyday life in America.

One of the most important comparisons the student may wish to make while reading this and the following selection is between the quality of life for the white indentured servant and that for the black slave. Both servant and slave endured a debilitating and disorienting Atlantic passage; both faced not only physical acclimatization in North America but psychological adjustment to a new condition; and both were locked into an intimate and oppressive contact with a hitherto unknown master. Of course there were major differences between servitude and slavery. The slave was bound for life and the servant for a limited period of time. The children of slaves inherited their parents' status, whereas children of servants were born free. And the slave, if freed, faced many more obstacles than the indentured servant who had served his or her time. But the large number of servants who ran away or committed suicide suggests that the conditions of life during the period of bondage may not have been so different for the servant and the slave.

Because so much of our history is centered on the idea that the settlement of America by Europeans was an epic exercise in the enlargement of individual rights and the pursuit of opportunity, we tend to pay little attention to the ordinary experiences and feelings of the people who made the settlement possible—especially those who did not achieve success. Richard Hofstadter attempts to correct this distortion by giving the reader a feeling for what life was like for most indentured servants. Also, rather than focusing on the fact that all servants attained their freedom, assuming they survived the years of servitude, he directs our attention to the prospects that lay before servants at the moment of freedom. The great goal of every servant was to obtain a place on the ladder of opportunity—or what, from villages in Scotland, Ireland, and Germany, seemed to be such a ladder. But as Hofstadter notes, the chief beneficiaries of the system of servitude were not the laborers themselves but those for whom they labored. Although the survival rate among servants was undoubtedly higher in the eighteenth century than it had been earlier in Virginia's history, the opportunities for the recently freed servant to attain a secure niche in society as a landowner or independent artisan were considerably less, according to recent studies. The likelihood of physical survival for indentured servants in the eighteenth century increased, but among survivors the probability of economic success decreased.

1

The transportation to the English colonies of human labor, a very profitable but also a very perishable form of merchandise, was one of the big businesses of the eighteenth century. Most of this labor was unfree. There was, of course, a sizable corps of free hired laborers in the colonies, often enjoying wages two or three times those prevalent in the mother country. But never at any time in the colonial period was there a sufficient supply of voluntary labor, paying its own transportation and arriving masterless and free of debt, to meet the insatiable demands of the colonial economy. The solution, found long before the massive influx of black slaves, was a combined force of merchants, ship captains, immigrant brokers, and a variety of hard-boiled recruiting agents who joined in bringing substantial cargoes of whites who voluntarily or involuntarily paid for their passage by undergoing a terminable period of bondage. This quest for labor, touched off early in the seventeenth century by the circulars of the London Company of Virginia, continued by William Penn in the 1680's and after, and climaxed by the blandishments of various English and continental recruiting agents of the eighteenth century, marked one of the first concerted and sustained advertising campaigns in the history of the modern world.

If we leave out of account the substantial Puritan migration of 1630–40, not less than half, and perhaps considerably more, of all the white immigrants to the colonies were indentured servants, redemptioners, or convicts. Certainly a good many more than half of all persons who went to the colonies south of New England were servants in bondage to plant-

"White Servitude." From *America at 1750: A Social Portrait* by Richard Hofstadter, pp. 33–65. Copyright © 1971 by Beatrice K. Hofstadter, Executrix of the Estate of Richard Hofstadter. Reprinted by permission of Alfred A. Knopf, Inc.

ers, farmers, speculators, and proprietors.[1] The tobacco economy of Virginia and Maryland was founded upon the labor of gangs of indentured servants, who were substantially replaced by slaves only during the course of the eighteenth century. "The planters' fortunes here," wrote the governor of Maryland in 1755, "consist in the number of their servants (who are purchased at high rates) much as the estates of an English farmer do in the multitude of cattle." Everywhere indentured servants were used, and almost everywhere outside New England they were vital to the economy. The labor of the colonies, said Benjamin Franklin in 1759, "is performed chiefly by indentured servants brought from Great Britain, Ireland, and Germany, because the high price it bears cannot be performed in any other way." [2]

Indentured servitude had its roots in the widespread poverty and human dislocation of seventeenth-century England. Still a largely backward economy with a great part of its population permanently unemployed, England was moving toward more modern methods in industry and agriculture; yet in the short run some of the improvements greatly added to the unemployed. Drifting men and women gathered in the cities, notably London, where they constituted a large mass of casual workers, lumpenproletarians, and criminals. The mass of the poverty-stricken was so large that Gregory King, the pioneer statistician, estimated in 1696 that more than half the population—cottagers and paupers, laborers and out-servants—were earning less than they spent. They diminished the wealth of the realm, he argued, since their annual expenses exceeded income and had to be made up by the poor rates, which ate up one-half of the revenue of the Crown.[3] In the early seventeenth century, this situation made people believe the country was overpopulated and emigration to the colonies was welcomed; but in the latter part of the century, and in the next, the over-population theory gave way to the desire to hoard a satisfactory labor surplus. Yet the strong outflow of population did not by any means cease. From the large body of poor drifters, many of them diseased, feckless, or given to crime, came a great part of the labor supply of the rich sugar islands and the American mainland. From the London of Pepys and then of Hogarth, as well as from many lesser ports and inland towns, the English poor, lured, seduced, or forced into the emigrant stream, kept coming to America for the better part of two centuries. It is safe to guess that few of them, and indeed few persons from the other sources of emigration, knew very much about what they were doing when they committed themselves to life in America.

Yet the poor were well aware that they lived in a heartless world. One of the horrendous figures in the folklore of lower-class London in the seventeenth and eighteenth centuries was the "spirit"—the recruiting agent

[1] Abbott E. Smith, *Colonists in Bondage* (1947), 3–4; Richard B. Morris, *Government and Labor in Colonial America* (1946), 315–16.

[2] Smith, 27; M. W. Jernegan, *Laboring and Dependent Classes in Colonial America* (1931), 55; see also K. F. Geiser, *Redemptioners and Indentured Servants in . . . Pennsylvania* (1901), 24–5.

[3] Christopher Hill, *The Century of Revolution* (1961), 206.

who waylaid, kidnapped, or induced adults to get aboard ship for America. The spirits, who worked for respectable merchants, were known to lure children with sweets, to seize upon the weak or the gin-sodden and take them aboard ship, and to bedazzle the credulous or weak-minded by fabulous promises of an easy life in the New World. Often their victims were taken roughly in hand and, pending departure, held in imprisonment either on shipboard or in low-grade hostels or brothels. To escaped criminals and other fugitives who wanted help in getting out of the country, the spirits could appear as ministering angels. Although efforts were made to regulate or check their activities, and they diminished in importance in the eighteenth century, it remains true that a certain small part of the white colonial population of America was brought by force, and a much larger portion came in response to deceit and misrepresentation on the part of the spirits.

With the beginnings of substantial emigration from the Continent in the eighteenth century the same sort of concerted business of recruitment arose in Holland, the Rhenish provinces of Germany, and Switzerland. In Rotterdam and Amsterdam the lucrative business of gathering and trans-shipping emigrants was soon concentrated in the hands of a dozen prominent English and Dutch firms. As competition mounted, the shippers began to employ agents to greet the prospective emigrants at the harbor and vie in talking up the comforts of their ships. Hence the recruiting agents known as *Neülander*—newlanders—emerged. These newlanders, who were paid by the head for the passengers they recruited, soon branched out of the Dutch ports and the surrounding countryside and moved up the Rhine and the Neckar, traveling from one province to another, from town to town and tavern to tavern, all the way to the Swiss cantons, often passing themselves off as rich men returned from the easy and prosperous life of America in order to persuade others to try to repeat their good fortune. These confidence men—"soul sellers" as they were sometimes called— became the continental counterparts of the English spirits, profiteers in the fate of the peasantry and townspeople of the Rhineland. Many of the potential emigrants stirred up by the promises of the newlanders were people of small property who expected, by selling some part of their land or stock or furnishings, to be able to pay in full for their passage to America and to arrive as freemen. What the passage would take out of them in blood and tears, not to speak of cash, was carefully hidden from them. They gathered in patient numbers at Amsterdam and Rotterdam often quite innocent of the reality of what had already become for thousands of Englishmen one of the terrors of the age—the Atlantic crossing.

2

In 1750 Gottlieb Mittelberger, a simple organist and music master in the Duchy of Württemberg, was commissioned to bring an organ to a German congregation in New Providence, Pennsylvania, and his journey inspired him to write a memorable account of an Atlantic crossing. From Heilbronn, where he picked up his organ, Mittelberger went the well-traveled route along the Neckar and the Rhine to Rotterdam, whence he sailed to a stopover at Cowes in England, and then to Philadelphia. About four hundred passengers were crowded onto the ship, mainly German and Swiss redemptioners, men pledged to work off their passage charges. The trip from his home district to Rotterdam took seven weeks, the voyage from Rotterdam to Philadelphia fifteen weeks, the entire journey from May to October.

What moved Mittelberger, no literary man, to write of his experiences was first his indignation against the lies and misrepresentations used by the newlanders to lure his fellow Germans to America, and then the hideous shock of the crossing. The voyage proved excruciating and there is no reason to think it particularly unusual. The long trip down the Rhine, with constant stops at the three dozen customs houses between Heilbronn and Holland, began to consume the limited funds of the travelers, and it was followed by an expensive stop of several weeks in Holland. Then there was the voyage at sea, with the passengers packed like herring and cramped in the standard bedsteads measuring two feet by six. "During the journey," wrote Mittelberger, "the ship is full of pitiful signs of distress—smells, fumes, horrors, vomiting, various kinds of sea sickness, fever, dysentery, headaches, heat, constipation, boils, scurvy, cancer, mouth-rot, and similar afflictions, all of them caused by the age and the highly-salted state of the food, especially of the meat, as well as by the very bad and filthy water, which brings about the miserable destruction and death of many. Add to all that shortage of food, hunger, thirst, frost, heat, dampness, fear, misery, vexation, and lamentation as well as other troubles. Thus, for example, there are so many lice, especially on the sick people, that they have to be scraped off the bodies. All this misery reached its climax when in addition to everything else one must suffer through two or three days and nights of storm, with everyone convinced that the ship with all aboard is bound to sink. In such misery all the people on board pray and cry pitifully together." [4]

Even those who endured the voyage in good health, Mittelberger reported, fell out of temper and turned on each other with reproaches. They cheated and stole. "But most of all they cry out against the thieves of human beings! Many groan and exclaim: 'Oh! If only I were back at home, even lying in my pig-sty!' Or they call out: 'Ah, dear God, if I only once again had a piece of good bread or a good fresh drop of water.'" It went hardest with women in childbirth and their offspring: "Very few escape with their lives; and mother and child, as soon as they have died, are thrown into the water. On board our ship, on a day on which we had a great storm, a woman about to give birth and unable to deliver under the circumstances, was pushed through one of the portholes into the sea because her corpse was far back in the stern and could not be brought forward to the deck." Children under seven, he thought (though the port records show him wrong here), seldom survived, especially those who had not already had measles and smallpox, and their parents were condemned to watch them die and be tossed overboard. The sick members of families

[4] For the voyage, Mittelberger, *Journey to Pennsylvania* (edn. 1960), ed. and trans. by Oscar Handlin and John Clive, 10–13.

infected the healthy, and in the end all might be lying moribund. He believed disease was so prevalent because warm food was served only three times a week, and of that very little, very bad, very dirty, and supplemented by water that was often "very black, thick with dirt, and full of worms . . . towards the end of the voyage we had to eat the ship's biscuit, which had already been spoiled for a long time, even though no single piece was there more than the size of a thaler that was not full of red worms and spiders' nests."

The first sight of land gave heart to the passengers, who came crawling out of the hatches to get a glimpse of it. But then for many a final disappointment lay in wait: only those who could complete the payment of their fare could disembark. The others were kept on board until they were bought, some of them sickening within sight of land and, as they sickened, losing the chance of being bought on good terms. On landing some families were broken, when despairing parents indentured their children to masters other than their own.

Not even passengers of means who paid their way, moved more or less freely about ship, occupied cabins or small dormitories, and had superior rations could take an Atlantic crossing lightly. In addition to the hazards of winds too feeble or too violent, of pirates, shipwrecks, or hostile navies, there were under the best of circumstances the dangers of sickness. Travelers in either direction frequently died of smallpox or other diseases on board or soon after arrival. Anglican colonials often complained of the high mortality rate among their young would-be clergymen crossing to England to be ordained. The Dutch Reformed preacher Theodorus Frelinghuysen lost three of his five sons on their way to be ordained in Amsterdam. The evangelist George Whitefield on his first crossing to the colonies in 1738 saw a majority of the soldiers on board afflicted with fever and spent much of his time "for many days and nights, visiting between twenty and thirty sick persons, crawling between decks upon his knees, administering medicines and cordials" and giving comfort. On this voyage the captain's Negro servant died, was wrapped in a hammock and tossed into the sea. In the end all but a handful of the passengers took the fever, including Whitefield, who survived treatment by bleeding and emetics. The ship on which he returned a few months later was afflicted by a "contrary wind," drifted for over a week to the point at which crew and passengers were uncertain where they were, and took so long to arrive at Ireland that water rations, which had been cut to a pint a day, were just about to run out.[5]

When paying passengers were exposed to such afflictions, how much worse must have been the sufferings of the servants and redemptioners packed into the holds, frequently at a density that violated the laws, and without adequate ventilation. Food provisions were calculated to last fourteen weeks, which was normally sufficient, but the rations deteriorated rapidly, especially in summer. Water turned stale, butter turned rancid, and beef rotted. If Mittelberger's voyage ranked among the worst, Atlantic

[5] Quoted in Luke Tyerman, *The Life of the Rev. George Whitefield* (1876), I, 124–5, 144–5.

crossings were frequently at or near the worst, and many more disastrous ventures were recorded.[6] With bad luck, provisions could give out. The *Love and Unity* left Rotterdam for Philadelphia in May 1731 with more than 150 Palatines and a year later landed with 34, after having put in toward the end at Martha's Vineyard for water and food. On the way rations became so low that water, rats, and mice were being *sold*, and the storage chests of the dead and dying were broken open and plundered by the captain and crew. A ship called the *Good Intent*—the names of eighteenth-century vessels often reek with irony—arrived off the American coast in the winter of 1751 but found herself unable to make port because of the weather; she was able to put in to harbor in the West Indies only after twenty-four weeks at sea. Nearly all of the passengers had died long before. The *Sea Flower*, which left Belfast with 106 passengers in 1741, was at sea sixteen weeks, and lost 46 passengers from starvation. When help arrived, six of the corpses had been cannibalized.

It is true that given adequate ventilation, a stock of lemon juice and vegetables, and good luck with the winds, decent sanitary arrangements were possible. The philanthropic Georgia Trustees, who were concerned about the health of their colonists, "put on board turnips, carrots, potatoes, and onions, which were given out with the salt meat, and contributed greatly to prevent the scurvy." Out of some fifteen hundred people who had gone to Georgia at the public expense, it was claimed in 1741, not more than six had died in transit. A traveler to Jamaica in 1739 reported that the servants on his ship "had lived so easily and well during the voyage, that they looked healthful, clean and fresh, and for this reason were soon sold," yet he saw another vessel arrive not long afterward with "a multitude of poor starved creatures, that seemed so many skeletons: misery appeared in their looks, and one might read the effects of sea-tyranny by their wild and dejected countenances." [7]

3

The situation in which the indentured servant or the redemptioner found himself upon his arrival depended in large measure upon his physical condition. There would be a last-minute effort to clean up and appear presentable, and in some ports the healthy were separated from the sick, once colonial officials adopted quarantine measures. Boston, the most vigilant of the ports, had long kept a pesthouse on an island in the harbor and fined captains who disregarded the regulations. "As Christians and men," the governor of Pennsylvania urged in 1738, "we are obliged to make a charitable provision for the sick stranger, and not by confining him to a ship, inhumanly expose him to fresh miseries when he hopes that his sufferings are soon to be mitigated." [8] Pennsylvania then designated Province

---

[6] See Geiser, chapter 1; F. R. Diffenderfer, *German Immigration into Pennsylvania* . . . (1900), chapter v, esp. 63–7.
[7] Smith, 217–18.
[8] Diffenderfer, 82.

Island for quarantine and built a pesthouse to harbor sick immigrants. In 1750 and again in 1765 it passed laws to bar overcrowding on ships. Laws passed by Virginia and Maryland in the 1760's providing for the quarantine on convict ships were frowned upon in London, and Virginia's law was disallowed.

Buyers came on shipboard to take their pick of the salably healthy immigrants, beginning a long process of examination and inspection with the muscles and the teeth, and ending with a conversational search for the required qualities of intelligence, civility, and docility. At Philadelphia buyers might be trying to find Germans and eschew the Scotch-Irish, who were reputed to be contumacious and work resistant and disposed to run away. Some buyers were "soul drivers" who bought packs of immigrants and brutally herded them on foot into the interior where they were offered along the way to ready purchasers. On the ships and at the docks there were final scenes of despair and frenzy as servants searched for lost articles of indenture, or lamented the disappearance of baggage, unexpected overcharges, the necessity of accepting indentures longer than their debts fairly required, the separation of families.

The final crisis of arrival was the process we would call acclimatization, in the eighteenth century known as "seasoning." Particularly difficult in the tropical islands, seasoning also took a heavy toll in the Southern colonies of the mainland. People from cities and from the mild English climate found the summer hard going in any colony from Maryland southward, especially on plantations where indentured servants were put to arduous field labor by owners whose goal it was to get a maximum yield of labor in the four or five years contracted for. Fevers, malaria, and dysentery carried many off, especially in their first years of service. Seasoning was thought to be more or less at an end after one year in the new climate, and servants who had been wholly or partly seasoned were at a premium.

During the voyage, thoughtful servants might have recalled, quite a number of persons had battened on their needs—the spirit or the newlander, the toll collectors and the parasites of the seaports, the ship captain or merchant; now there was the master. Any traffic that gave sustenance to so many profiteers might well rest on a rather intense system of exploitation. A merchant who would spend from six to ten pounds to transport and provision an indentured servant might sell him on arrival—the price varied with age, skill, and physical condition—for fifteen to twenty pounds, although the profits also had to cover losses from sickness and death en route. The typical servant had, in effect, sold his total working powers for four or five years or more in return for his passage plus a promise of minimal maintenance. After the initially small capital outlay, the master simply had to support him from day to day as his services were rendered, support which was reckoned to cost about thirteen or fourteen pounds a year. In Maryland, where exploitation was as intense as anywhere, the annual net yield, even from unskilled labor, was reckoned at around fifty pounds sterling.[9] The chief temptation to the master was to

[9] Raphael Semmes, *Crime and Punishment in Early Maryland* (1938), 80, 278; *cf.* Samuel McKee, Jr., *Labor in Colonial New York* (1935), 111.

drive the servant beyond his powers in the effort to get as much as possible out of him during limited years of service. The chief risk was that the servant might die early in service before his purchase price had been redeemed by his work. That he might run away was a secondary risk, though one against which the master had considerable protection. Still, hard as white servitude bore on servants, it was nevertheless not always a happy arrangement for owners, especially for those with little capital and little margin for error: shiftless and disagreeable servants, as well as successful runaways, were common enough to introduce a significant element of risk into this form of labor.

Indentured servants lived under a wide variety of conditions, which appear to have softened somewhat during the eighteenth century. Good or bad luck, the disposition of the master, the length of the term of work, the size of the plantation or farm, the robustness or frailty of the worker— all these had a part in determining the fate of each individual. Servants in households or on small farms might be in the not uncomfortable situation of familiar domestic laborers. Tradesmen who were trying to teach special skills to their workers, or householders who wanted satisfactory domestic service, might be tolerable masters. The most unenviable situation was that of servants on Southern plantations, living alongside—but never with— Negro slaves, both groups doing much the same work, often under the supervision of a relentless overseer. One has to imagine the situation of a member of the English urban pauper class, unaccustomed to rural or to to any sustained labor, thrust into a hot climate in which heavy field labor—including, worst of all, the backbreaking task of clearing new land of rocks, trees, and shrubs—was his daily lot. Even as late as 1770 William Eddis, the English surveyor of customs at Annapolis, thought that the Maryland Negroes were better off than "the Europeans, over whom the rigid planter exercises an inflexible severity." The Negroes, Eddis thought, were a lifelong property so were treated with a certain care, but the whites were "strained to the utmost to perform their allotted labour; and, from a prepossession in many cases too justly founded, they were supposed to be receiving only the just reward which is due to repeated offenses. There are doubtless many exceptions to this observation, yet, generally speaking, they groan beneath a worse than Egyptian bondage." Yet in Virginia, as the blacks arrived in greater numbers, white laborers seemed to have become a privileged stratum, assigned to lighter work and more skilled tasks.[10]

The status and reputation of Southern indentured laborers were no doubt kept lower than elsewhere because there were a considerable number of transported convicts among them. Colonies to the north were not completely free of convict transportees, but the plantation system regularly put honest unfortunates alongside hardened criminals and lumped all together as rogues who deserved no better than what was meted out to them. Among the by-products of English social change of the seventeenth and eighteenth centuries was a very substantial pool of criminal talents. The

[10] William Eddis, *Letters from America* (1777), 69–70; J. C. Ballagh, *White Servitude in the Colony of Virginia* (1895), 89–92.

laws devised to suppress the criminal population were so harsh—scores of crimes were defined as felonies and hanging was a standard punishment for many trivial offenses—that England would have been launched upon mass hangings far beyond the point of acceptability had it not been for two devices that let many accused off the penalties prescribed for felons. One was the benefit of clergy—a practice inherited from the Middle Ages and continued until the early nineteenth century—which permitted a convicted felon to "call for the book" and prove his literacy. On the ancient assumption that those who could read were clerics and thus exempt from severe punishments by the secular state, the relatively privileged class of literate felons could be permitted to escape with the conventional branding of the thumb.

A second practice, the predecessor of convict transportation, was to secure royal pardons for ordinary offenders deemed by the judges to be worthy of some indulgence. Until the end of the French wars in 1713 it was customary to send them into the army, but in peacetime England did not know what to do with felons and drifters. In 1717 Parliament passed an act which in effect made royal clemency contingent upon transportation to the colonies for a term of labor; in consequence the large-scale shipping of convicts began which continued to the time of the American Revolution. To America at large, including the island colonies, around thirty thousand felons were transported in the eighteenth century, of whom probably more than two-thirds reached Virginia and Maryland, where they were readily snapped up by the poorer planters.[11]

The whole procedure, though clearly intended to be a humane and useful alternative to wholesale hangings, was dreadfully feared by convicts, who may have guessed, quite rightly, that whoever bought their services would try to get the most out of them during their seven-year terms (fourteen years in the case of transmuted death penalties) of hard labor. In transit felons probably were fed somewhat better than they were used to, but usually they were kept below deck and in chains during the entire voyage, and on the average perhaps one in six or seven would die on the way. "All the states of horror I ever had an idea of," wrote a visitor to a convict ship, "are much short of what I saw this poor man in; chained to a board in a hole not above sixteen feet long, more than fifty with him; a collar and padlock about his neck, and chained to five of the most dreadful creatures I ever looked on." [12] Mortality could run very high: on one ship, the *Honour*, which arrived in Annapolis in 1720, twenty of the sixty-one convicts had died. Merchants transporting felons on government contracts pleaded for subsidies to cover losses that hit them so hard.

While some planters rushed to the seaports to find convicts for their field labor supply, others were disturbed by the effect they expected criminals would have on the character of the population. These hazardous importations caused most anxiety in the colonies that received masses of transported felons. Pennsylvania subjected the importation of convicts to

---

[11] See Smith, 116–19; *cf.* Lawrence H. Gipson, *The British Empire before the American Revolution*, II (1936), 69, 79.

[12] Smith, 125.

constant statutory harassment after 1722. Virginia at mid-century seems
to have thought herself in the midst of a crime wave. The Virginia *Ga-*
zette complained in 1751: "When we see our papers fill'd continually with
accounts of the most audacious robberies, the most cruel murders, and infinite other villainies perpetrated by convicts transported from Europe,
what melancholy, what terrible reflections it must occasion! What will become of our posterity? These are some of thy favours Britain. Thou art
called our Mother Country; but what good mother ever sent thieves and
villains to accompany her children; to corrupt some with their infectious
vices and murder the rest? What father ever endeavour'd to spread a
plague in his family? . . . In what can Britain show a more sovereign con-
tempt for us than by emptying their jails into our settlements; unless they
would likewise empty their jakes [privies] on our tables!" [13] The concluding metaphor seems to have come quite naturally to the colonials: Franklin
also used it, although he is better remembered for his suggestion that the
Americans trade their rattlesnakes for the convicts.[14] But all laws rejecting
transported convicts were disallowed in England by the Board of Trade
and the Privy Council, while subterfuge measures designed to impede or
harass the trade were looked at with suspicion.

4

The system of indenture was an adaptation, with some distinctively
harsh features, of the old institution of apprenticeship. In fact, a few
native-born colonials, usually to discharge a debt or answer for a crime
but sometimes to learn a trade, entered into indentures not altogether
unlike those undertaken by immigrants. In law an indenture was a contract in which the servant promised faithful service for a specified period
of time in return for his housing and keep and, at the end of his term of
work, that small sum of things, known as "freedom dues," which his master
promised him upon their parting. The typical term was four or five years,
although it might run anywhere from one or two years to seven. Longer
terms were commonly specified for children, and were calculated to bring
them to freedom at or just past the time they reached majority. Most indentures followed a standard pattern: as early as 1636 printed forms were
available, needing only a few details to be filled out by the contracting
parties. Often an emigrant's original indenture was made out to a merchant or a ship's captain and was sold with its holder to an employer on
arrival. Indentures became negotiable instruments in the colonies, servants
bound under their terms being used to settle debts, even gambling debts.
In theory the contract protected the servant from indefinite exploitation,
but in practice it had quite limited powers. It was a document vulnerable
to loss, theft, or destruction, and when one considers both the fecklessness
and inexperience of most indentured servants and the lack of privacy un-

[13] Ibid., 130.
[14] Cheesman A. Herrick, *White Servitude in Pennsylvania* (1926), 131-2.

der which they lived, it is little wonder that their contracts often disappeared.

During the eighteenth century, however, circumstances began to alter the prevailing system of indentures and to lessen its severities, particularly when a special class of bonded servants, the redemptioners, became numerous. The redemptioner appeared at the beginning of the century, coming largely from the Continent, often emigrating with a family and with a supply of tools and furnishings. The passengers who traveled with Mittelberger were mostly redemptioners. Indentured servants were simply a part of a ship's cargo, but redemptioners were low-grade, partially paid-up passengers. The redemptioner embarked without an indenture, sometimes having paid part of the money for his own and his family's passage, and arranged with the shipping merchant to complete payment within a short time after landing. Once here, he might try to find relatives or friends to make up his deficit; failure to pay in full meant he would be sold to the highest bidder to redeem whatever part of his fare was unpaid. The length of his servitude would depend upon the amount to be redeemed. It could be as short as one or two years, although four years seems to have been much more common. Redemptioners would try to go into service as a whole family group. Although redemptioners were often swindled because of their lack of English and were overcharged for interest, insurance, and the transportation of their baggage, it was less profitable to carry them than indentured servants. Still, merchants were eager to fill their ships as full as possible with a ballast of redemptioners.[15]

All bonded servants, indentured and redemptionist, were chattels of their masters, but the terminability of their contracts and the presence of certain legal rights stood between them and slavery. A servant could be freely bought and sold, except in Pennsylvania and New York where laws required the consent of a court before assigning a servant for a year or more. His labor could be rented out; he could be inherited on the terms laid down in his master's will. Yet he could own property, although he was forbidden to engage in trade. He could also sue and be sued, but he could not vote. It was expected that he would be subject to corporal punishment by his master for various offenses, and whipping was common; but a master risked losing his servant on the order of a court for a merciless or disfiguring beating. The right of a servant to petition the courts against abuse was more than a negligible protection. Penniless servants were, of course, at a disadvantage in courts manned by representatives of the master class: in effect they were appealing to the community pride, compassion, or decency of the magistrates, and the sense that there were certain things that ought not be done to a white Christian. Yet the frequency of complaints by servants makes it clear that the prerogative of appeal was widely used, and the frequency of judgments rendered for servants shows that it was not used in vain. No colony recognized the validity of agreements between master and servant made *during* servitude unless both parties appeared before a magistrate and registered their consent. Statutes regulated the terms of servitude in cases in which no papers of indenture existed.

[15] Smith, 41.

For many thousands of servants their term of indentured servitude was a period of enforced celibacy. Marriage without the consent of the master was illegal, and the crimes of fornication and bastardy figure importantly in the records of bound servitude—not surprisingly, when we realize how many of the servant population were between the ages of eighteen and thirty. The sexuality of redemptioners, since they commonly came in families, was a much less serious problem for them and their masters. Among indentured servants as a whole, however, there were many more men than women. The situation of maidservants was full of both opportunities and hazards. Their services were considerably prized, and a clever or comely woman, as mistress or wife, might escape from the dreariest exactions of servitude. Still, women were also vulnerable to sexual abuse, and the penalties for simply following their own inclinations were high. Masters were unwilling to undergo the loss of time, the expense of rearing a child, or the impairment of health or risk of death in childbirth, and thus were unlikely to give consent to marriage. But the laws contrived to give masters the chance to turn such events to their own account. For fornication and bastardy there were ceremonial whippings, usually of twenty-one lashes; more to the point, sentences of from one to two or three years of extra service were exacted, an overgenerous compensation for the loss of perhaps no more than a few weeks of work. From Pennsylvania southward, Richard B. Morris has concluded, the master was often enriched far beyond his actual losses. Where a manservant fathered a child, he could be required to do whatever extra service was necessary to provide for its maintenance. Merely for contracting unsanctioned marriages, servants could be put to a year's extra service. If a maidservant identified her master as the father of her child, he could be punished for adultery, and she removed from him and resold. A keen disrelish for miscegenation provided an additional term of punishment: for bearing a mulatto bastard a woman might get heavy whipping and seven years of extra service. Despite such restraints, there were a substantial number of illegitimate births, mulatto and otherwise.

However, the commonest crime committed by servants, not surprisingly, was running away—not an easy thing to get away with, since in the colonies everyone had to carry a pass, in effect an identity card, and stiff penalties ranging from fines and personal damages to corporal punishment were imposed upon persons harboring fugitives. Runaways were regularly advertised in the newspapers, rewards were offered, and both sheriffs and the general public were enlisted to secure their return. Returned they often were, and subjected to what were regarded as suitable penalties; captured servants who were unclaimed were resold at public auction. On the whole, and especially in Pennsylvania and colonies to the south, the laws turned the punishment of the recovered runaway into an advantage for the master. The standard penalty in the North, not always rigorously enforced, was extra service of twice the time the master had lost, though whipping was also common. In Pennsylvania, a five-to-one penalty was fixed and commonly enforced, while in Maryland, the harshest of all the colonies, a ten-to-one penalty was authorized by a law of 1661 and very often enforced to the letter. A habitual runaway, or one who succeeded in getting away for weeks, could win himself a dreary extension of servitude. There was one horrendous case of a maidservant in Anne Arundel County, Maryland, who ran off habitually for short terms, and whose master quietly kept a record, true or false, of her absences. Finally taking her to court, the master rendered an account of 133 accumulated days of absence. Since it was impossible for her to deny her frequent absences, she had no shadow of an answer, and was booked for 1,330 days of extra service.[16] Hers was an unusual but not a singular case: there are recorded penalties of 1,530 days, 2,000 days, and even one of 12,130 days, which the master handsomely commuted to an even five years.[17] Virginia assessed double time, or more if "proportionable to the damages" which could be high in tobacco-harvesting time, plus an additional punishment, more commonly inflicted in the seventeenth than the eighteenth century, of corporal punishment. On the eve of the Revolution, Negro slavery had largely replaced indentures in the tidewater plantations but indentures were still important on the accessible and inviting edges of settlement, and there runaways became a critical problem. In South Carolina, where fear of insurrection had been a dominant motive, a law of 1691 had authorized a week's extra service for a day of absence, and for absences that ran as long as a week, a year for a week—a fifty-two-to-one ratio that made Maryland seem relaxed. In 1744 the week-for-a-day ratio was still kept, but the maximum penalty was set at a year's service. Whipping was also routine.

The problem of preventing and punishing runaways was complicated by what was held to be the "pirating" of labor by competing employers— and it became necessary to establish a whole series of penalties for enticing or distracting indentured labor. Plainly, if neighbors could entice bound laborers from their owners for occasional or even permanent service by offering money or promising better treatment, a rudimentary subterranean labor market would begin to replace servitude, and property in servants would become increasingly hazardous. Pirating was not taken lightly in the law, and enticers of labor were subject to personal damage suits as well as to criminal prosecution, with sentences ranging from whipping or sitting in the stocks to fines. The penalties were so heavy in the tobacco colonies that law-abiding planters might even hesitate to feed or shelter a servant who had apparently been deserted by his master. Indeed, inn-keepers in these colonies were often fined simply for entertaining or selling liquor to servants. Suits for damages for brief enticements were hardly worth the trouble in the case of servants whose work was valued at a few pence a day. But in New York a skilled cabinetmaker and chair carver indentured in 1761 was lured away by a competitor at frequent intervals, and a few years later his master won a smashing judgment of £128.[18]

Plots hatched by several servants to run away together occurred mostly in the plantation colonies, and the few recorded servant uprisings were entirely limited to those colonies. Virginia had been forced from its very earliest years to take stringent steps against mutinous plots, and severe

16 Ibid., 268–9.
17 Morris, 452.
18 Ibid., 416–29, esp. 421–3.

punishments for such behavior were recorded. Most servant plots occurred in the seventeenth century: a contemplated uprising was nipped in the bud in York County in 1661; apparently led by some left-wing offshoots of the Great Rebellion, servants plotted an insurrection in Gloucester County in 1663, and four leaders were condemned and executed; some discontented servants apparently joined Bacon's Rebellion in the 1670's. In the 1680's the planters became newly apprehensive of discontent among the servants "owing to their great necessities and want of clothes," and it was feared they would rise up and plunder the storehouses and ships; in 1682 there were plant-cutting riots in which servants and laborers, as well as some planters, took part.

By the eighteenth century, either because of the relaxed security of the indenture system or the increasing effectiveness of the authorities, disturbances were infrequent, although in 1707 a gang of runaways planned to seize military stores, burn Annapolis, steal a ship, and set up as pirates, but were stopped. Again in 1721 a band of convict servants conspired unsuccessfully to seize military stores at Annapolis. An insurrection of some consequence did actually break out among white servants under the British regime in East Florida during the summer of 1768, when three hundred Italians and Greeks in that very heterogeneous colony revolted against hard work and stern treatment, seized the arms and ammunition in the storehouse, and prepared to set sail from a ship at anchor in the river at New Smyrna. They were intercepted by a government vessel and promptly surrendered. Three leaders were convicted of piracy, one of whom was pardoned on condition that he execute his two comrades. Discontent and dissension, reaching into the local elite, were still rife in Florida at the time of the Revolution.[19]

A serious threat to the interests of masters, one which gives testimony to the onerousness of servitude, was the possibility of military enlistment. In New England, where there were not many servants, military service was obligatory and seems to have posed no major temptation to escape servitude, but in Pennsylvania and the tobacco colonies, where servants were numerous and essential, the competing demand by the army for manpower in the intercolonial war of the 1740's, and, even more, in the French and Indian War of the 1750's, aroused great anxiety among the masters. In the 1740's, more than a third of the Pennsylvania enlistments were from men in the servant class whose masters were compensated at the colony's expense; in Maryland, during the French and Indian War, Governor Horatio Sharpe reported not only that "servants immediately flocked in to enlist, convicts not excepted," but also that recruits among freemen were extremely scarce, and in Virginia George Washington urged that servants be allowed to enlist in the Virginia volunteers lest they seize the alternative and join the regular army.[20] The resistance of the Pennsylvania Assembly to enlistments during the 1750's became provocatively stubborn and in Maryland there was armed resistance and rioting against recruitment. Parliament, whose interest it was to increase the army, passed

[19] On insurrections, see ibid., 169–81.
[20] Ibid., 284n, 286; E. I. McCormac, *White Servitude in Maryland* (1904), 90.

a measure in 1756 authorizing officers to enlist indentured servants regardless of restraining colonial laws or practices. The best that masters could hope for was compensation from their colony's legislature, a practice that was repeated in Pennsylvania in 1763, or suing the recruiting officer for civil damages. During the Revolution, the Continental Congress and some of the states encouraged the enlistment of servants, but Pennsylvania and Maryland exempted them from military service. When despite this recruiting officers in Pennsylvania continued to enlist servants, a group of Cumberland County masters complained with magnificent gall that apprentices and servants "are the property of their masters and mistresses, and every mode of depriving such masters and mistresses of their property is a violation of the rights of mankind. . . ." [21] A good number of servants ran off to the British forces, especially in Virginia, but neither the wars nor the Revolution ended the practice of servitude, which declined but did not die until the nineteenth century.

5

Numerous as are the court records of penalties which lengthened service, most servants did not run afoul of the law; their periods of servitude did at last come to an end, entitling them to collect "freedom dues" if they could, and to start in life for themselves. Freedom dues were usually specified by law, but little seems to be known about their payment. Virginia and North Carolina laws of the 1740's required £3 in money, and North Carolina added an adequate suit of clothes. The Crown provided 50 acres of land, free of quitrent for ten years, in South Carolina. A Pennsylvania law of 1700 specified two complete suits of clothes, one of which was to be new, one new ax, one grubbing hoe, and one weeding hoe. Massachusetts long before in the seventeenth century had provided in biblical fashion that servants after seven years' labor should "not be sent away empty," but what this maxim was actually worth to servants is difficult to say. Like the dues of ordinary apprentices, freedom dues may have functioned most importantly as a kind of inducement to servants to carry out in good faith the concluding months and weeks of servitude. Where the labor of a servant was particularly valuable, his master might strengthen that inducement by a cash payment considerably beyond what had been promised.[22]

What was the economic situation of the servant after completing his servitude? It varied, no doubt, from colony to colony, and with the availability of lands. In the mainland colonies, it appears to have been assumed that an ex-servant was to be equipped for work as a free hired man with enough clothes and tools or money to give him a small start. It was assumed that wages for a freeman were high enough to enable him to earn an adequate competence or to provide himself with a plot of land within a

21 Morris, 292; on the enlistment problem generally, see ibid., 278–94; Geiser, 94–101; Smith, 278–84; McCormac, 82–91.
22 McKee, 95–6.

fairly short time. Some ex-servants no doubt went westward and took up new lands. "The inhabitants of our frontiers," wrote Governor Alexander Spotswood of Virginia in 1717, "are composed generally of such as have been transported hither as servants, and being out of their time, settle themselves where land is to be taken up that will produce the necessaries of life with little labour." [23] But it is quite likely that Spotswood erred considerably on the side of optimism. For example, in Maryland, where a freed servant in the seventeenth century was entitled to 50 acres of land upon showing his certificate of freedom at the office of the land office secretary, the records show that relatively few became farmers, though many assumed their land rights and sold them for cash. Abbott E. Smith, in one of the most authoritative studies of colonial servitude, estimates that only one out of ten indentured servants (not including redemptioners) became a substantial farmer and another became an artisan or an overseer in reasonably comfortable circumstances. The other eight, he suggests, either died during servitude, returned to England when it was over, or drifted off to become the "poor whites" of the villages and rural areas. There is reason to think that in most places servants who had completed a term of bondage and had a history of local residence met the prevailing parochial, almost tribal qualifications for poor relief, and were accepted as public charges.[24] Redemptioners, Smith remarks, did a good deal better, but the scrappy evidence that has thus far been found does not yet allow much precision. Sir Henry Moore, governor of New York, thought them so anxious to own land that they made great sacrifices to do so: "As soon as the time stipulated in their indentures is expired, they immediately quit their masters, and get a small tract of land, in settling which for the first three or four years they lead miserable lives, and in the most abject poverty; but all this is patiently borne and submitted to with the greatest cheerfulness, the satisfaction of being land holders smooths every difficulty, and makes them prefer this manner of living to that comfortable subsistence which they could procure for themselves and their families by working at the trades in which they were brought up." [25] An Englishman who traveled in America in the opening years of the nineteenth century noticed "many families, particularly in Pennsylvania, of great respectability both in our society and amongst others, who had themselves come over to this country as redemptioners; or were children of such." [26]

As for the indentured servants, the dismal estimate that only two out of ten may have reached positions of moderate comfort is an attempt to generalize the whole two centuries of the experience of English servitude, taking the seventeenth century when the system was brutal and opportunities were few with the eighteenth, when it became less severe.[27] In the early years more servants returned to England, and mortality was also higher. But it will not do simply to assume that freed servants, especially

[23] Smith, 297.
[24] See ibid., 251–2.
[25] McKee, 112–13.
[26] Geiser, 108–9.
[27] See Smith, 288–9, on later conditions.

those from the tobacco fields, were in any mental or physical condition to start vigorous new lives, or that long and ripe years of productivity lay ahead for them. If we consider the whole span of time over which English indentured servitude prevailed, its heavy toll in work and death is the reality that stands out.

The Horatio Alger mythology has long since been torn to bits by students of American social mobility, and it will surprise no one to learn that the chance of emergence from indentured servitude to a position of wealth or renown was statistically negligible. A few cases to the contrary are treasured by historians, handed down from one to another like heirlooms—but most of them deal with Northern servants who came with education or skills. The two most illustrious colonial names with servitude in their family histories are Benjamin Franklin and the eminent Maryland lawyer Daniel Dulany. Franklin's maternal grandfather, Peter Folger of Nantucket, a man of many trades from teacher and surveyor to town and court clerk and interpreter between whites and Indians, had bought a maidservant for £20 and later married her. Dulany, who came from a substantial Irish family, arrived in 1703 with two older brothers; the brothers melted into the anonymity that usually awaited indentured arrivals, but Daniel was picked up by a lawyer who was pleased to buy a literate servant with some university training to act as his clerk and help with his plantation accounts. The closest thing to a modest, American-scale family dynasty to come out of servitude was that of the New England Sullivans. John Sullivan and Margery Browne both came to Maine as indentured servants in the 1720's. After Sullivan earned his freedom he became a teacher, bought Margery out of servitude, and married her. Their son John became a lawyer, a Revolutionary patriot, one of Washington's leading generals, and governor of New Hampshire. His younger brother, James, also a lawyer, became a congressman from Massachusetts and in time governor of the state. In the third generation, John's son, George, became a Federalist congressman and the attorney general of New Hampshire; James's son, William, pursued a successful legal career in Boston, played a prominent role in state politics, and was chosen to be one of the three delegates to take the manifesto of the Hartford Convention to Washington. John Lamb, a leader of the Sons of Liberty and later an officer in the Revolution, was the son of Anthony Lamb who had followed an improbable career: an apprentice instrument maker in London, Anthony became involved with a notorious burglar who ended on the gallows at Tyburn; as a first offender, Lamb was sentenced to be transported, served out an indenture in Virginia, moved to New York, and became a reputable instrument maker and a teacher of mathematics, surveying, and navigation. Charles Thomson, one of six children orphaned by the death of their father on shipboard in 1739, began his American life as an indentured servant and became a teacher in Philadelphia, a merchant, a Revolutionary patriot, and Secretary of the Continental Congress. Matthew Thornton, whose parents came to Maine in the Scotch-Irish emigration of 1718, began life under indenture, became a physician, a patriot leader in New Hampshire, and a signer of the Declaration of Independence. Matthew Lyon, who won notoriety as a peppery Republi-

can congressman from Vermont and as a victim of the Sedition Act, emi-
grated from Ireland in 1765 and paid off his passage by three years of
indentured service on farms in Connecticut before he bought his own
farm in Vermont. And there were others, brands snatched from the burning, triumphs of good fortune or strong character over the probabilities.

6

Thoreau, brooding over the human condition in the relatively idyllic
precincts of Concord and Walden Pond, was convinced that the mass of
men lead lives of quiet desperation. His conviction quickens to life again
when we contemplate the human costs of what historians sometimes
lightly refer to as the American experiment. It is true that thousands came
to the colonies in search of freedom or plenty and with a reasonably good
chance of finding them, and that the colonies harbored a force of free
white workers whose wages and conditions might well have been the envy
of their European counterparts. Yet these fortunate men were considerably outnumbered by persons, white or black, who came to America in
one kind of servitude or another. It is also true that for some servants,
especially for those who already had a skill, a little cash, or some intelligence or education or gentility, servitude in America might prove not
a great deal worse than an ordinary apprenticeship, despite the special
tribulations and hazards it inflicted. But when one thinks of the great
majority of those who came during the long span of time between the
first settlements and the disappearance of white servitude in the early
nineteenth century—bearing in mind the poverty and the ravaged lives
which they left in Europe, the cruel filter of the Atlantic crossing, the
high mortality of the crossing and the seasoning, and the many years of
arduous toil that lay between the beginning of servitude and the final
realization of tolerable comfort—one is deeply impressed by the measure
to which the sadness that is natural to life was overwhelmed in the condition of servitude by the stark miseries that seem all too natural to the
history of the poor. For a great many the journey across the Atlantic
proved in the end to have been only an epitome of their journey through
life. And yet there must have seemed to be little at risk because there was
so little at stake. They had so often left a scene of turbulence, crime, exploitation, and misery that there could not have been much hope in most
of them; and as they lay in their narrow bedsteads listening to the wash
of the rank bilge water below them, sometimes racked with fever or lying in their own vomit, few could have expected very much from American life, and those who did were too often disappointed. But with white
servants we have only begun to taste the anguish of the early American
experience.

Africans Become New Negroes

GERALD W. MULLIN

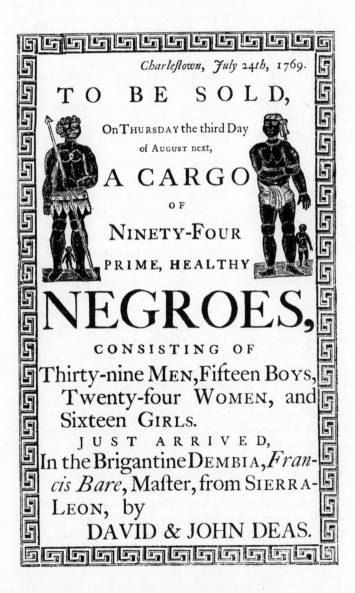

It is commonly assumed that African slaves, brought to European colonies in North and South America, were simply fitted into a closed system of forced labor where they lived out their lives—cowed, brutalized, and de-Africanized. The historical focus has been on the slave system fashioned by slave owners: the black codes they enacted, their treatment of slaves, and the economic development they directed. But the slaves themselves are often forgotten as active participants in a cultural process. How did they experience life in an environment vastly different from their native one? To what degree did they adopt the norms of white colonial society? How did they respond to the loss of freedom and to the separation from all that was familiar in their own society? To what extent did they fashion a new Afro-American culture that blended their traditional mores with those of their European masters? Only by posing questions of this kind can we study the lives of slaves rather than the lives of the masters who held the power of life and death over their human property.

Over the last few decades many historical analyses of slavery have been written in response to the thesis of Stanley Elkins that plantation slavery was a uniquely brutal and closed system of forced labor in North America. In the English colonies, Elkins argues, masters were unrestrained by the institutions of church, law, and government that mediated between slave and master in the Spanish and Portuguese colonies. Ironically, a far more repressive and dehumanizing system of slavery developed in the more "enlightened" and "modern" environment of English North America than in the more "feudalistic" and "authoritarian" milieu of Latin America. Racial lines were more strictly drawn in the English colonies, manumission of slaves was less frequent, and freed slaves had less opportunity to attain any worthy status than in New Spain or Brazil.

The effect upon slaves in the two regions, Elkins argues, was strikingly different. In the Spanish and Portuguese colonies, slaves developed a sense of autonomy and self-respect, for freedom was always a possibility. And once freed, former slaves could regard themselves as full-fledged citizens of the society that had enslaved them. But in the English colonies, the chances of freedom were so improbable and the slave system was so brutal that slaves, in order to survive at all, had to adapt their personalities to the conditions of bondage. They became compliant, docile, and dependent. According to Elkins, slaves who were trapped in such a system, where authority was exercised with brutal finality, could only revert to childlike posturing. They never acted conspicuously or independently and rarely asserted the full range of human emotions. The typical plantation slave, writes Elkins, "was docile but irresponsible, loyal but lazy, humble but chronically given to lying and stealing; his behavior was full of infantile silliness and his talk inflated with childish exaggeration. His relationship with his master was one of utter dependence and childish attachment."

Developed at length in Elkins's book **Slavery: A Problem in American Institutional and Intellectual Life,** this postulation of comparative slave behavior has generated almost two decades of sharp debate and in this sense has greatly furthered slave studies. But only in the last few years have historians begun to probe the daily lives of slaves in eighteenth-century America. Gerald Mullin's study of Virginia slavery gives us far more particular insights into the daily life of slaves than we have heretofore had available. His analysis of the stages of African adaptation to English slavery quite obviously challenges Elkins at every major point. The slaves portrayed in Mullin's account are far from passive; they are not stripped of their identities or their African culture; they are rarely childishly attached to their masters. Instead they are locked into a dynamic relationship with their owners in which, despite the grotesquely uneven distribution of power, they are extraordinarily ingenious at setting limits on the master's ability to coerce them. However brutal the power held over them, slaves are actively and continuously involved in carving out psychological "space" for themselves. Survival is their great goal. But they struggle for survival in far different ways than Elkins posits. And if recent demographic studies of slavery are correct, they survived in the English colonies as nowhere else in the Europeanized regions of the hemisphere.

Mullin's picture of Chesapeake slavery in the eighteenth century also allows us insights into the lives of slaveowners. As has often been noted, the masters of slaves were as chained to the institution of slavery as the slaves themselves. Slavery pervaded their lives, for the "peculiar institution" had social and psychological as well as economic dimensions. This becomes clear in Mullin's investigation of the attempts of Virginia plantation owners to mold a community of black and white in which whites functioned, ideally, as benevolent patriarchs.

T he available sources on slavery in eighteenth-century Virginia—plantation and county records, the newspaper advertisements for runaways —describe rebellious slaves and few others. The slaves described were lazy and thieving; they feigned illnesses, destroyed crops, stores, tools,

"Africans Become New Negroes." From *Flight and Rebellion: Slave Resistance in Eighteenth-Century Virginia* by Gerald W. Mullin, pp. 34–52, 54–70, 78, 81–82. Copyright © 1972 by Oxford University Press, Inc. Reprinted by permission.

and sometimes attacked or killed overseers. They operated blackmarkets in stolen goods. Runaways were defined as various types, they were truants (who usually returned voluntarily), "outlaws" (a legal term for "outlying" slaves who refused to give themselves up), and slaves who were actually fugitives: men who visited relatives, went to town to pass as free, or tried to escape slavery completely, either by boarding ships and leaving the colony, or banding together in cooperative efforts to establish villages or hide-outs on the frontier. The commitment of another type of rebellious slave was total: these men became killers, arsonists, and insurrectionists.

Patterns based on the slave's origin (birthplace) and position in the work hierarchy emerge from this wealth of detail. The sources themselves can be divided this way: plantation records deal primarily with field slaves and house servants, while most skilled slaves are described in newspaper advertisements for runaways. Native Africans and American-born slaves, plantation slaves (field and house slaves), and artisans reacted differently to slavery. Only native Africans who were new arrivals and referred to as "outlandish," ran off in groups or attempted to establish villages of runaways on the frontier. Most plantation slaves (generally Africans who had been introduced into slavery and from then on known as "new Negroes") were merely truants, if they ran off at all. And American-born skilled slaves nearly always ran off alone into the most settled areas of the colony to pass as free men.

In assessing these observable differences in slave behavior, scholars usually ask whether a particular rebellious style represented resistance to slavery's abuses or real resistance to slavery itself. When slave behavior is examined in light of its political content, the most menial workers, the field slaves, fare badly. Speaking generally, their "laziness," boondoggling, and pilferage represented a limited, perhaps self-indulgent type of rebelliousness. Their reactions to unexpected abuses, or to sudden changes in plantation routine were at most only token acts against slavery. But the plantation slaves' organized and systematic schemes to obstruct the plantation's workings—their persistent acts of attrition against crops and stores, and cooperative night-time robberies that sustained the blackmarkets—were more "political" in their consequences, and represented resistance to slavery itself.

Yet arguments about the political aspect of slave resistance have only been part of a larger, and more misleading, scholarly controversy: the extent to which slaves "accommodated" to a "system" characterized as a type of "total" institution. This conceptualization is anachronistic; it views rebellious slaves out of their historical context, and in concentrating on the whites and the structural features of the institution they created, it does not account well for: the insurrectionists, who resisted slavery totally; field slaves, who cooperated in acts of sabotage; and skilled fugitives, solitary, self-centered rebels who often ran away to hire themselves out, to become someone else's slave while enjoying a modicum of freedom, and at the same time, denying their former owners their highly valued services.

Focusing on the political dimension of resistance, nonetheless, may greatly expand our understanding of slave behavior, if we employ a method that shifts attention to the slaves themselves, and seeks to uncover the psychological implications of the rebellious slave's goals, and the significance of those goals for the slave and his society. A useful way of evaluating these issues is to distinguish between inward and outward goals. This typology is based on an evaluation of the direction or thrust of a particular rebellious action. That is, each style had direction in two ways: on the one hand, in a psychological sense of inward, internalized rebelliousness, or violence, that for the slave was self-defeating or even self-destructive, or an outward, self-enhancing, rebellious action; and on the other hand, direction in the sense of the setting and objectives for a style of resistance channeled either inward toward the plantation world, or outward toward a town, or out of the society altogether.

Plantation slaves most often directed their limited, sometimes self-defeating, acts against the plantation itself. Scarcely knowledgeable of the society beyond their world, too limited in such acculturative resources as conversational English to pass as free men in town, they reacted to their only "home," the plantation or quarter. Outlaws are an especially good example of inward-directed rebelliousness. Making little effort to save themselves by actually running away, they turned their rage back on its source; and before they were recaptured (or killed outright) they burned and pillaged their masters' property. Skilled fugitives, on the other hand, resisted outwardly in the sense of setting and goals: they were determined to get as far as possible from their masters and the plantation. Their flight from and repulsion of the plantation, moreover, were a fitting corollary to the psychological consequences of their training and work routines.

Styles of rebelliousness may be distinguished as inward and outward in a more subjective sense, one that focuses on the psychological implications of a pattern of resistance for the slave as an individual. The plantation slave's actions were typically short-range, direct attempts to deal immediately with his material environment: to fill his hunger, ease his fatigue, or to get revenge on an overseer or master. His punitive, sporadic, and sometimes desperate inward activities usually worsened his situation. He committed his transgression and then could do little more than wait to be discovered and punished. The skilled slave who frequently worked on and off the plantation, was usually better off. He rebelled to ameliorate his situation, and occasionally, to reject it outright. His resistance, which was seldom violent and directed inward on himself or the plantation, was aimed toward such long-range and intangible goals as more freedom of movement and leisure time than he normally enjoyed. As a runaway passing as a free man, hired by townsmen who asked few questions about his former owner, he often achieved these objectives. But it should be emphasized that many field slaves who resisted were especially successful because they did so cooperatively (Africans who were new arrivals also saw slavery as a collective problem). However, until the last years of the century, the skilled slaves cut off from the community of plantation slaves by their challenging and varied routines viewed resistance as an individual problem. Thus this typology, which examines rebelliousness from the slave's point of view, also illuminates the relationship between rebellion and adjustments to slavery by uncovering the fundamental determinants of slave behavior in the colonial period: the acculturative experience and task allotment.

Whether a slave resisted in an inward or outward way was chiefly attributable to these two interdependent variables. The slave's origin and degree of familiarity with English determined where he was placed in the work hierarchy. Conversely, job placement governed the rate and extent of acculturation (used interchangeably with the term assimilation). Resistance, the most thoroughly documented aspect of slave behavior, stemmed from the interaction of the two variables, the nature of acculturation and of the work routine.

The experience of acculturation[1] means that as slaves came to know varieties of whites and their ways, they acquired occupational skills, fluent English, and a distinctive, "sensible" manner in speaking situations. This acculturative process—usually accelerated when a man once exclusively a plantation slave acquired a work routine allowing him to travel outside the plantation "family"—also transformed slaves in a more basic, dynamic way. Relatively assimilated slaves (often referred to as artisans or skilled slaves), for example, were imbued with a pride and confidence that enhanced their ability to cope resourcefully with whites when they became fugitives.

Work was the second variable determining adjustments to slavery. So much of a slave's life was expressed in his job, that it is more appropriate to speak of his world of work, one that provided him with a particular outlook and self-view, and to recognize that a slave's task influenced the quality of his relations with other slaves and determined the frequency and intensity of his encounters with his master (a decisive factor in the adjustments of house servants). In the eighteenth century there were three types of task assignments: in the fields, household, and workshops. The actual location or setting of a slave's job was as important as his routine, or "bundle of tasks," because it controlled his degree of access to colonial values and ways requisite for outward types of resistance. Slaves assigned to the fields and household were confined and cut-off from the acculturative experiences that made slavery less oppressive and more manageable for those whose jobs permitted travel beyond the plantation boundaries. So important was the correlation between acculturation and the mobility factor, that two types of semi-skilled slaves —watermen and waitingmen—whose tasks required them to travel frequently, reacted outwardly to slavery. More fugitives capable of passing as free men, in fact, came from these occupations than from any others.

While the nature of the slave's work is the most apparent explanation for different adjustments, it is not a sufficient one. It does not account for the actions of the "outlandish" African who was recently enslaved. The new arrival was a slave without a job. His unique behavior as a fugitive and a hesitant learner of English (the most important measures of level of acculturation) indicates that such facets of his African

[1] See fn. 27 on acculturation.

upbringing as communalism provided norms for his initial reaction to slavery. Only after the African became a "new Negro" did his job replace aspects of his heritage as a basic reference point for his reaction to slavery. Jobs for all slaves were so fundamentally important that the very few Africans who acquired skilled positions acted like American-born slaves: they too were assimilated, mobile, individualistic, and outwardly rebellious.

The hypotheses are: that slavery in eighteenth-century Virginia may also be construed as an encounter between two cultures, African and English colonial; that one dimension of slave behavior in the colonial period was the slave's participation in an on-going process of cultural change; and that as slaves acculturated they became outwardly rebellious and more difficult for whites to control. Given the correlation between assimilation and outward forms of resistance, the Virginia colonists' goals for their plantation communities and their slaves were indeed contradictory. The desire to assimilate Africans as quickly as possible in order to increase occupational specialization while maintaining stable, self-sufficient plantation communities, created a cruel dilemma. Community and acculturation—the first a static design, the latter a process—were not compatible. Assimilation into colonial society made a few Africans and many of their descendants outwardly rebellious and so, more difficult to control.

Slaves Without Jobs: The "Outlandish" African's Reactions to Enslavement

The acculturative process whereby Africans came to be "new Negroes," and a much smaller number assimilated slaves, was marked by three stages. First, the "outlandish" Africans reacted to slavery on the basis of the communal lives they had been living when enslaved. As their prior cultural directives proved unworkable, they began as best they could to bend such elements of the new culture as the English language, and in rare instances, technical skills to their advantage. Nearly all Africans became field laborers, "new Negroes," who represented the second level of assimilation. Since there seemed to be a "fit," or degree of congruence, between their cultural background and the plantation's communal norms, few Africans ever became more than "new Negroes." But those who did, the more educable and thoroughly assimilated Africans, were representative of the third level of acculturation. The latter were usually artisans, whose imaginative exploits as fugitives dramatized the reciprocal relationship between the acquisition of skills and more advanced assimilation. Artisanship and acculturation made blacks individuals while enhancing their ability to cope creatively with slavery. And individualism, already a basic ideal in colonial American society, was not, as we shall see, a very highly developed phenomenon in African tribes. Thus for the planter the acculturated slave's altered perception of himself and slavery had some unforeseen and undesirable consequences.

Newspaper advertisements for fugitive slaves are the most useful and reliable source for demonstrating the effectiveness of the acculturation argument.[2] The advertisements are fairly objective, unlike such narrative sources as Hugh Jones's. Slaveowners who used them were neither explaining nor defending slavery, they simply—in sparse, graphic phrases —listed their runaway's most noticeable physical and psychological characteristics, while commenting on his origin, work, and use of English. Since the notices also lend themselves well to a quantitative analysis of such characteristics as height, posture, skin color, habits of grooming and dress, and emotional peculiarities—for example, speech defects and uncontrollable movements of hands and face—they are indispensable for studying the change of physical norms, demographic make-up, and acculturation levels in the colonial slave population. For example:[3]

> RUN AWAY about the First Day of *June* last from the Subscriber, living on *Chickahominy* River, *James City* County. A Negroe Man, short and well-set, aged between 30 and 40 Years, but looks younger, having no Beard, is smooth-fac'd, and has some Scars on his Temples, being the Marks of his Country; talks pretty good *English;* is a cunning, subtile Fellow, and pretends to be a Doctor. It is likely, as he has a great Acquaintance, he may have procur'd a false Pass. Whoever brings him to me at my House aforesaid, shall have two Pistoles Reward, besides what the Law allows.
>
>   Michael Sherman

Approximately 1,500 notices in newspapers published from 1736 to 1801 in Williamsburg, Richmond, and Fredericksburg were analyzed, including all notices in all of the various editions of the *Virginia Gazette* that are extant. These described 1,138 men and 142 women. Another 400 people were advertised as runaways taken up by constables or jailers. In this period only 138 fugitives, about 1 in 8, were advertised as born in Africa. These exceptions were usually two kinds: "outlandish" Africans, and the relatively acculturated slaves who were long-time residents in Virginia. "New Negroes," isolated on the quarters and in a phase of acculturation between the new arrivals and the assimilated slaves, are conspicuously absent from the notices.

Since the new arrivals and their masters had talked informally about

---

[2] Eighteenth-century Virginia newspapers that were used were all those available on microfilm in the University of California library. The films were comprised of all of the newspapers printed in the colonial period as well as the major newspaper published in the new state from 1776 to 1801. About seven-eighths of the advertisements were published in various extant editions of the *Virginia Gazette*, the colony's only newspaper before Independence. Only a small number of notices were printed during the first years of publication; for example, there were 20 notices for 30 runaways in the late 1740's. By 1770, about 65 advertisements were published yearly for approximately 70 fugitives.

[3] *VaG*, Nov. 21, 1745, Michael Sherman.

Africa—an intriguing insight into the nature of procurement for both sides—the notices are filled with information about what Africans chose to tell whites about their lives before enslavement. Bonnaund told his master that he was from "the Ibo Country," where he "served in the Capacity of a Canoe Man." [4] Charles and Frank were also Ibo runaways, whose identities were conspicuous even though they were unable to tell their jailer whether or not they were Africans: their teeth were filed and chipped and their foreheads carved with ritual scars. While Frank's filed teeth were described as "sharp," Charles, who had "lost or broke off one or two of his fore Teeth," presumably tried to explain his ritual mutilations in what he already perceived to be a socially acceptable manner, said it was "done by a Cow in his country." [5]

Ritual scars were dramatic testimony to the West Africans' life before slavery. To see how these men may have stood out among all others in colonial America, compare reproductions of an Ife brass head and an eighteenth-century portrait painted, say, by Benjamin West or John Durand. On the one side, blacks have faces marked from ear to ear, hairline to throat, by deep striations proclaiming a heritage that was based on a fully ritualized cultural existence, and which sustained a society that functioned on a corporate and traditional basis. On the other side, whites are without scars or with "scars" outside themselves of velvet and lace at cuff and throat, feather fans and open books—symbols of a European culture which centuries earlier had reduced its ceremonies of human and social renewal to compartmentalized activities as neat as the sitting rooms in which they posed. Symbols too of a society—at least beyond the plantation—that functioned on an impersonal, civil, and individual basis.[6]

Many slaveowners had closely observed the Africans' scars and could describe them in minute detail. "He is marked in the manner of his country with dots under both eyes, and on the right side of his neck with something resembling a ladder." "He has a very noted mark carved on his forehead resembling a diamond, and some marks of his country on his temples"; or this variation: "he has a Flower in his Forehead made in the Form of a Diamond with Specks down to the End of his Nose." And "he has six rings of his country marks round his neck, his ears full of holes." [7]

These slaves had received their marks in ceremonies of pain, mys-

---

[4] *VaG* (Purdie and Dixon; and Rind, see both editions), Dec. 24, 1772, Richard Booker.

[5] *VaG* (Purdie and Dixon), Oct. 7, 1773, Joseph Hilliard.

[6] For a provocative model of man in primitive society complementary to man in maximally politicized civilizations, such as our own, see Stanley Diamond, "Primitive Society in Its Many Dimensions," in Kurth Wolff and Barrington Moore, Jr., eds., *The Critical Spirit, Essays in Honor of Herbert Marcuse* (Boston, 1967), 21–30.

[7] *VaG* (Rind), Oct. 8, 1772, Westmoreland jailor; (Dixon and Nicolson), Dec. 18, 1779, Samuel Calland; (Purdie and Dixon), Nov. 5, 1772, James Ball. For additional descriptions of "country marks" and filed teeth see (Purdie and Dixon), Dec. 12, 1771, Peter Pelham; (Purdie), Dec. 5, 1777, Michael Grate; March 1745, Alice Needle; Nov. 14, 1751, Archibald Cary; (Rind), Aug. 8, 1776, T. Poindexter; Aug. 10, 1769, Alexander Spark.

tery, and celebration, which inculcated a distinctive sense of history (e.g. of reckoning time) and a sense of community, and made their initial adjustments unique among slaves.[8] On the personal level the rite was an unforgettable ordeal in which the emotional ties of a group of young adults were reoriented from their families to their village society. The ceremonies, calculated to burn the lesson of companionship and community into the very souls of the young participants, also left indelible scars that were visible. These "country-marks" announced: "I am because we are, and since we are, I am." [9] The West African scholar, John Mbiti, further explains that the rites united the celebrants with the rest of the community both living and dead, and "humanly speaking nothing can separate him from this corporate society." [10]

Thus, on the community level, the rites were a matter of survival. Most colonial slaves came from small-scale, technologically simple societies that lived in a precarious relationship with their environment. The facts of individual differences, of varied and uneven rates of growth among their young men of the same age, constituted a grave threat to the basic ordering of society, particularly during the grim and perilous days of the international slave trade. Individual preference and initiative, unnatural thoughts of self-improvement at the community's expense, all had to be redirected; thus the schema of the rites of passage. "The individual person or [age] group is cut off, isolated and then restored," writes the anthropologist David F. Pocock, "but never again to be the same; in this restoration individual distinctions and differences are translated into social ones." [11]

Philosophically, the coming of age ceremony was an integral part of the tribesman's conception of time. And the way the African slave marked time was at the core of how he made the world intelligible. Time in western technological society is a predictable and uniform movement; it is a commodity, too, that is utilized, measured in units, and so often bought and sold. For the African, however, time was created: it was based either on the major events of his life, such as coming of age, or at another level, on certain repetitive cyclic natural events, such as phases of the moon and the harvest seasons.[12]

The essentials of this non-western folk ethos, man-in-community and discontinuous time-reckoning, survived enslavement and became an inte-

---

[8] The following interpretations of rites of passage were especially useful in writing this section, John S. Mbiti, *African Religions and Philosophy* (New York, 1969); Yehudi A. Cohen, *The Transition from Childhood to Adolescence: Cross-Cultural Studies of Initiation Ceremonies, Legal Systems and Incest Taboos* (Chicago, 1964); David F. Pocock, "The Anthropology of Time Reckoning," in John Middleton, ed., *Myth and Cosmos* (New York, 1967), 301–15; and Paul Bohannan, *The Tiv of Central Nigeria* (London, 1953), 66–67.

[9] Mbiti, *African Religions and Philosophy*, 117.

[10] *Ibid.*

[11] Pocock, "The Anthropology of Time Reckoning," 308–9.

[12] In addition to Mbiti and Pocock, see E. E. Evans-Pritchard, "Neur Time-Reckoning," *Africa*, 12 (April 1939), 189–216; Paul Bohannan, "Concepts of Time Among the Tiv of Nigeria," in Middleton, ed., *Myth and Cosmos*, 315–30.

gral part of the African's behavior as a slave. But only for a while. When his heritage proved unworkable, his job and other factors became reference points for his adjustment. Those Africans who initially reacted to slavery as runaways, and their later activities as learners of English, provide an opportunity to evaluate both their adjustment and the usefulness of the acculturation model itself for future studies of American Negro slavery.

"Outlandish" slaves, still to become "new Negroes," were unique among runaways in the colonial period. Whatever the precise meaning of procurement for the African as a person, his fellowship or affectivity, a core area of human behavior, remained intact as a slave. Africans, assuming that resistance was a group activity, ran off with their own countrymen, and American-born slaves including mulattoes. In all of the advertisements there were only a very few groups of American-born slaves and these were made up of not more than three men. But there were five larger groups, all composed of Africans. A sixth group included two African men and their American-born wives, and another pair, an African and a white indentured servant. Africans were also the only fugitives in eighteenth-century Virginia reported to be in even larger groups, pursuing cooperative ventures (usually in their determination to return "home," as they said) or to be in the more remote areas of the colony. Step, for example, left Petersburg with a twelve-year-old girl. "He went off with several others," his master wrote, "being persuaded that they could find the Way back to their own Country." Six weeks later this group was discovered in Mecklenburg County on the colony's frontier.[13]

. . . The majority of Virginia slaves advertised as "taken up" had evidently fled soon after their enslavement. Fugitive Africans who were recaptured—often cold and frost-bitten, nearly naked after long treks and weeks in the wilds of the colonial South—could at most usually only speak a few words of English: they are "all in rags"; he has "nothing on but a blanket"; they are "entirely naked . . . and by lying in the cold, their feet and legs have swelled very much, so that they are not able to be sent to the [Charleston] work house." "He speaks very bad English, but says his master's name is *William Cook,* as plain as he can." [14]

The jailers listened carefully to the Africans' replies, and were sometimes sufficiently interested to record and print literally what they were told. Consequently this data provides invaluable insights into how Africans thought in their own languages while conversing in English. Their responses also suggest that they looked upon slavery as a temporary misfortune, that perhaps the jailer might help them return "across grandy-

13 *VaG* (Purdie and Dixon), Sept. 12, 1771, George Robertson; see also, Nov. 2, 1739, John Shelton; May 16, 1745, William Hunter; (Purdie and Dixon), Dec. 13, 1770, James Buchanan; (Purdie and Dixon), Oct. 28, 1773, John Burnley's notice for the largest group of runaways advertised in an eighteenth-century Virginia newspaper. "Hanover Town, ranaway, FOURTEEN NEW NEGROES: about 2 months ago."

14 *VaG* (Purdie and Dixon), Jan. 28, 1773, John Taylor; (Purdie), Dec. 27, 1776, John Berryman; (Purdie), Nov. 21, 1777, Mary Wills; *S.C. Gaz.,* Feb. [12], 1771, John Brown; Jan. 1, 1771, William Heatley.

water" to their real homes in Africa. For example, when asked where they came from they took this to mean Africa, not the colonies. He "only calls himself Peter [and] says he is of the Bumbarozo Country." [15] Or, he "calls his Country Mundingo," [16] part of the Western Sudan. Most of the Africans who responded in this way, in fact, were from this area. Sarah, for example (one of the very few African women who ran away in eighteenth-century Virginia and was later described in a newspaper advertisement), was a 14-year-old with severe "choaking fits." She spoke English so poorly that she could not tell her master's name. She did, however, identify herself as a Mundingo.[17] But Africans who were long time residents in slavery soon learned the proper cues. Dick, a small fellow about 50 years of age, had roamed about the Stafford County seat for months before he was taken up, and was described this way: "by what little English he talks and by signs he makes, he belongs to one *William Helm*, as he expressed it, in *Maryland*." [18]

The Africans' efforts to talk about what their new masters meant to them are perhaps also more understandable when seen in connection with their upbringing. In going from old to new authorities, Africans obviously made various adjustments; but one type of authority relationship which the African considered no longer valid when his master died is persistently alluded to in the advertisements. For example: the jailer of a South Carolina runaway advertised: he "says master dead";[19] an Angolan, also taken up in South Carolina, made the revealing statement that his master was one William Anderson, "but [he] being dead, he cannot live with the family";[20] James, with filed teeth and the slave of a Richard Adams, said that his master was dead "and his widow ha[d] gone out of the country";[21] and a notice for two fugitives, who spoke "little English," said "their father's name is Davis but he is now dead." [22]

These two runaways had traveled a great distance for a considerable time. But their jailer had to estimate where they were from (he said either the Carolinas or Georgia), because he had to superimpose his reckoning of time on theirs. The Africans knew the proper words but still reacted to their old cultural directives. They had been, they said, "ten Moons from home." [23]

Occasionally in such conversations the two cultures' mythic paradigms for explaining location in time and space were set side by side. Sandy with filed teeth was asked how long he had been in the colony. He had, he replied, "made two crops for his master," and had been "absent from his service [for] two moons." [24] "All I can learn from her,"

[15] *VaG* (Purdie and Dixon), Sept. 12, 1771, Robert Owen.
[16] *VaG* (Dixon and Hunter), May 16, 1777, Josiah Daly.
[17] *VaG* (Purdie and Dixon), July 28, 1775, Samuel Wallace.
[18] *VaG* (Rind), Oct. 19, 1769, Supplement, William Garrand.
[19] *S.C. Gaz.*, Feb. 25, 1764, M. T. Savage.
[20] *Ibid.*, Sept. 10, 1771, John Brown.
[21] *VaG* (Dixon and Nicolson), Sept. 18, 1779, Joseph Hightower.
[22] *VaG*, July 19, 1754, William Clinch.
[23] *Ibid.*
[24] *VaG* (Rind), Sept. 22, 1768, John Daniel.

wrote another jailer, "is that she belongs to one Mr. Ruff, who lives in a great town, by a grandywater." [25] Another African, who spoke "much broken," said he lived near "one Mr. Burley's where long leaf pine grows." [26] Although data of this type is fragmentary—as is so often the case with historical reality for the "inarticulate"—it suggests that even though the African had partially adopted a new set of language symbols, his frame of reference had not changed. The "outlandish" slave's initial reaction to slavery as a runaway and his reluctance or inability to learn English demonstrate that at the dynamic level of his behavior, the level of philosophical orientation, he had remained an African. [27]

But in a year or so the "outlandish" African changed. As he became a "new Negro" he acquired English and new work routines which transformed his communal and outward style of rebelliousness. For the African, learning English was the key to this process of cultural change, for the norms of the slave society were mediated through his captor's language. In acquiring English the "new Negro" learned about slavery, and how whites expected field hands to act.

A record of runaway notices that included comments on the slave's proficiency in English indicates that the African's acquisition of his second language fell into two periods. [28] During the first few months after

25 *VaG* (Rind), Sept. 5, 1771, Edward Hurst; see also (Purdie and Dixon), Jan. 28, 1773, John Taylor.

26 *VaG* (Purdie), Oct. 16, 1778, Hampshire County jailer.

27 Melville J. Herskovits's argument for concrete African "survivals," "Africanisms" (*The Myth of the Negro Past*, Boston, 1941) cannot be applied successfully in North America because, among other problems, there is almost no data on tribal origins. Nor can his methodology, without serious modifications, be applied to the Americas generally if one accepts the conclusions of scholars who have seriously challenged Herskovits's most essential assumption; namely, the West African "cultural (or "focal") area" concept: see M. G. Smith, "The African Heritage in the Caribbean" (and George E. Simpson's reply) in Vera Rubin, ed., *Caribbean Studies: A Symposium* (Seattle, 1960), 34ff; Paul Bohannan, *Africa and Africans* (New York, 1964), 126–28 is particularly devastating in his criticism of the concept. See also G. J. Jones's review of Robin Horton's *Kalabari Sculpture* in *Africa*, 37 (Jan. 1967), 109. "The author's conclusions will shatter many of the fond illusions held by those who postulate a Pan-African cultural unity in the field," Jones writes, "as he shows that Kalabari ideas and practices in this field, differ completely from those of the Yoruba and Bini or for that matter of other Southern Nigerian peoples."

Consequently, it is preferable to talk about a less rigorous but more flexible African "background" (rather than "survivals"), and concentrate on ways of thinking rather than artifacts and other "Africanisms." This is a position Herskovits discussed in one of his last papers, "Ethnophilosophy," in Melford E. Spiro, ed., *Context and Meaning in Cultural Anthropology, in Honor of A. Irving Hallowell* (New York, 1965). At this more general and manageable, level of analysis the aforementioned paradigm by Stanley Diamond (see fn. 6) is particularly useful, as is Robert A. LeVine, "Africa," in Francis L. K. Hsu, ed., *Psychological Anthropology: Approaches to Culture and Personality* (Homewood, Ill., 1961), 48–92.

28 There were 657 fugitive men advertised between 1736–75; 118 (16 per cent) or about 1 in 6 were Africans. One-half of the native Africans (64) were recently

procurement, while some were trying to form settlements or return "home," Africans were unable to learn even a word of English. But after about six months, knowledge of the language increased sharply; and within another two or two and a half years most Africans were conversant in English. There are few notices of this type, however, because most runaways were not Africans and those who were represented either end of the acculturation scale: they were either new arrivals who spoke no English whatsoever, or assimilated Africans who spoke English fluently. For example, an October 1752 notice stated matter-of-factly, "they were imported in August and can't speak any English." [29] Another mentioned that five months after Charles's arrival he could only "call himself Charles which is every word of English he can speak." [30] Three runaways from an ironworks were "all new Negroes who had not been above 8 Months in the Country." Nonetheless one of them, Sambo, a small, thin, 30-year-old man, could speak English "so as to be understood." [31] Tom, a Mundingo, had been "in this Country about eighteen Months," his master reported. "He lived this Year under the direction of Mr. *Edward Giles*, and if he should be strictly questioned can tell either Mr. *Gile's* name or my Name." [32] Proficiency came after about three years of residence.

Age at time of importation, location (in or outside the plantation world), and job, in that order, were the most important variables with regard to the rate at which the African learned English. If the slave had been imported as a youth or had worked in an urban setting, for example, it was expected that he would speak "sensibly." A Fredericksburg merchant wrote a slave trader in surprise, that "although [Dobbo] has been constantly in Town [he] cannot yet speak a word of English," and was therefore an exceptional case.[33] Another master noted that his 30-year-old "*Angola* fellow" spoke "very good *English*, as he was imported young." [34]

The Field Slaves' Adjustment to Slavery

Dobbo was an exceptional African; virtually all new arrivals were forced into field labor on the up-country quarters. These small, specialized plantations were a world of their own. Large planters divided their lands into small tracts called quarters. Usually from 500 to 1,500 acres in size, the quarters were economically specialized and isolated—separated

imported "outlandish" slaves who did not learn any English in the first weeks of captivity. During this period about 50 subscribers commented on the slaves' use of English; but only about a dozen included an additional note on the date of importation.

29 *VaG*, Oct. 20, 1752, William Randolph.
30 *VaG* (Rind), Feb. 7, 1771, John Jacob.
31 *VaG*, May 16, 1745, William Hunter.
32 *VaG* (Purdie and Dixon), Nov. 4, 1773, Josiah Daly.
33 Charles Yates to Captain John Duncan, Fredericksburg, April 25, 1775, Yates Letterbook, 1773–83, Univ. of Virginia (hereafter UVA) microfilm collection.
34 *VaG*, Dec. 12, 1755, Daniel Parke Custis.

from the activity and diversity of the home plantation, and surrounded by woods, swamps, rivers, and reserve land. There was a subtle compatibility among the quarter's essential components: the field slaves and overseer, the small flocks of fowl, herds of cattle and pigs, the coarse, makeshift slave huts and crude outbuildings amidst fields of tobacco, corn, small grain, and sometimes hemp.

Newspaper advertisements, plantation accounts (inventories and overseers' contracts), and wills portray the small-scale, economically limited, and sequestered quarter as environment, the setting in which the Africans as "new Negroes" began to assimilate slowly, and seldom very completely, into the society beyond their world. Advertisements and estate inventories often mentioned the number of slaves per quarter, and occasionally the land-man ratio. A 1777 notice read:

> A tract of good tobacco land in the county of Orange, about 8 miles above the courthouse . . . containing by estimation 1000 acres, with a plantation thereon sufficient to work 8 hands. A large swamp runs through the whole of this tract, where is a great quantity of limestone, also a great deal of fine meadow land on both sides of the swamp.[35]

The land-man ratio was high. Another notice described a "good" plantation of 1,400 acres on the Finnywood River and the branches of Bluestone Creek in Mecklenburg County. It had land cleared for 10 to 12 hands. Another advertisement described a 1,000-acre tract in Halifax County on the Dan River, which included 250 acres of low ground "in good order for cropping, sufficient to work ten or twelve hands to high advantage." [36] These figures are representative of notices in the *Virginia Gazette* (all extant issues 1736–79). All of the advertisements offering plantations for sale were tabulated, and the mean number of hands per quarter was about eight.[37]

[35] *VaG* (Purdie), Aug. 8, 1777, T. Barbour. Advertisements are an invaluable source for understanding how a planter worked his land and distributed slaves, crops, orchards, and outbuildings. The following notices are especially detailed and informative: *Md.G.*, Aug. 22, 1799, John Francis Mercer; *VaG*, Oct. 3, 1751, Thomas Eldridge; (Purdie), Aug. 22, 1777, Nat. Jones; (Pinkney), June 22, 1775; (Purdie), May 16, 1777, "Supplement," for a description of Augustine Smith's "Shooter's Hill"; (Dixon and Hunter), March 14, 1777, for Adam Fleming's estate near Cabin Point on the lower James River.

[36] *VaG* (Purdie), May 16, 1777, William Murray; and Nov. 7, 1777, "Supplement," James Le Grand. For other notices that give an indication of the quarter's isolation and land-slave ratio, see (Purdie), April 18, 1772, "Supplement," Phil. Johnson; Nov. 17, 1775, "Supplement," Anne Burwell; (Dixon and Hunter), Sept. 14, 1776, Robert Walton, Jr.

[37] For notices offering to sell plantations worked by fewer than 10 "hands," see (Purdie), Oct. 31, 1777, Robert C. Nicholas; Sept. 5, 1777, John Timberlake; (Dixon and Hunter), Nov. 27, 1778, William Whitlock's executors; (Dixon and Nicolson), March 12, 1779, Otway Byrd.

Occasionally plantation records yielded a detailed letter from a planter to

Although it is not possible to determine precisely the number of slaves per quarter, probably the majority of plantations were worked by about 10 hands or "shares," who represented about a third of the full complement of slaves. The remainder were women and children, who since they were not full time field workers, did not receive a full "share" of the provisions. On the quarters, however, nearly all of the women and children over about 12 or 13 years of age worked in the field. Inventories for John Parke Custis's estate (1771 and 1774) are among the most complete available, and particularly useful because they list the workers' ages. On 9 quarters in York, New Kent, King William counties, and on the Eastern Shore, nearly 45 per cent of the slaves per quarter were 14 years of age or younger. Although 27 slaves were 50 or older (including an 85-year-old man), only John and Arlington were listed without their ages, because they were "very old & past Labour." There was no consistent ratio of men to women per quarter: on 2 plantations there were twice as many men as women (10 men and 4 women; 7 and 3)—excluding the young and old slaves listed above; but on the Mill quarter there were 3 men and 8 women; and on 2 others there were nearly equal numbers of men and women (4 men and 5 women, and 7 each). Characteristically, Custis's craftsmen, such as carpenters and shoemakers, were only included in the inventory for his "Great House." [38] This division of the work force into small groups on the quarters was fairly representative. "King" Carter, who used no less than 45 quarters in 1732, owned at least 6 that had fewer than 8 hands each.[39] Landon Carter employed 4 men at one quarter. His nephew, "Councillor" Carter, worked 5 Richmond County quarters from 1782 to 1791; one had 37 slaves, but he had 2 quarters with 3 slaves each, and 5 more with fewer than 10 workers.[40]

---

his steward regarding the establishment of a new quarter or home plantation. More than any other type of plantation record, these plans most satisfactorily convey the mood of the up-country quarter. See Hugh Nelson to Battaile Muse, York County, Feb. 10, March 28, and April 12, 1779; and Warner Lewis, Jr., to Muse, Gloucester County, Feb. 25, 1784, Muse Papers, Duke Univ. Library (hereafter DUL).

For account- and day-books kept by stewards and overseers that are illustrative of life on the quarter, see the Carter's Grove Account Book, 1738–55, Burwell Family Papers, Colonial Williamsburg Inc. Research Center (hereafter CW) microfilm; Nomini [Nomony] Hall Waste Book, 1773–83, CW microfilm, original at UVA; ["Councillor" Carter] Memo Book ("Book of Miscellanies"), 1788–89, Library of Congress (hereafter LC). This is one of the most informative of its kind; it contains detailed descriptions of Carter's many quarters in Westmoreland and Richmond counties. Carter abandoned these plantations after the Revolutionary War, and leased them to tenants. These descriptions were part of the contracts with the lessees. See also Dudley Digges's reports to Charles W. Dabney, Dabney Papers, Southern Historical Collection, Chapel Hill, N.C. (hereafter SHC), CW microfilm; and James Semple's reports in the Richard Corbin Letterbook, CW microfilm.

[38] Custis Papers, Virginia Historical Society, Richmond (hereafter VHS).

[39] *Virginia Magazine of History and Biography*, VII (1899), 64–68.

[40] Louis Morton, *Robert Carter of Nomini Hall* (Charlottesville, 1945), Table 9 following 276.

These small allotments of land and slaves were probably related to problems of supervision on the planter's absence. At least one slave-owner noted that his overseer could only manage about 10 slaves. Slave gangs (or even concentrations of slaves in excess of 25 or 30 per quarter) are virtually non-existent in the records of eighteenth-century Virginia plantations. . . .[41]

The field slave "is called up in the morning at daybreak, scarcely allowed time to swallow three mouthfuls of homminy," wrote the English traveler J. F. D. Smyth. Brief notations like this in travelers' and plantation accounts and record books must suffice for data on the field slave's material condition. Although the records are sketchy, his diet, although probably adequate in bulk, was scarcely nourishing. "Homminy," Indian corn, was the slaves' staple food.

Random accounts of quantities of corn allotted suggest that provisions were sometimes based on the worker's productivity. During the Revolutionary War, "Councillor" Carter asked that "the stronger Shears [shares] men & women" be given one peck of corn per week, "the Remainder of the Black People they to have ¼ Peck per Week each." By 1787 Carter, who was one of the least oppressive slave masters, increased this slightly. He ordered 44 pecks of shelled Indian corn as two weeks' allowance for 26 slaves, less than a full peck per week per laborer. (One peck equals 14 lbs. of Indian corn.)[42]

Meat was seldom given to slaves. Smyth said slaves ate hoecakes and little else; unless their master "be a man of humanity the slave eats a little fat, skimmed milk, and rusty bacon." La Rochefoucauld-Liancourt said that on large plantations the slave subsisted on corn and sometimes on buttermilk. They were given meat 6 times a year. Robert "Councillor" Carter estimated that the common allowance for wheat per hand per year was 15 bushels for those "negroes, who are not fed with animal food" (e.g. meat). These slaves only received meat on special occasions. Joseph Ball wrote his steward that slaves were to "have ffresh meat when they are sick, if the time of the year will allow it." The cuts were to be the least desirable, although not necessarily the least nutritious. When calves were slaughtered, Ball ordered him to give the field hands the "head and Pluck"; the "ffat backs, necks, and other Coarse pieces" of hogs were also to be reserved for the slaves. James Mercer directed his steward to give the slaves the innards of chickens unless he sold them to the local Negro chicken merchants.[43]

[41] Battaile Muse to John Hatley Norton, July 26, 1789, Norton Papers, CW; also Herbert C. Bradshaw, *History of Prince Edward County, Virginia* (Richmond, 1955), 95.

[42] John Ferdinand D. Smyth, *A Tour of the United States of America* . . . (2 vols., London, 1784), I, 44; "Councillor" Carter to William Brickey, Jan. 6, 1779, Letterbook III, pt. 2, 86; Carter to Thomas Muse, March 2, 1784, V, 182. See also Carter to [William] Taylor, Dec. 14 [1773], I, 168–69, DUL.

[43] La Rochefoucauld-Liancourt, *Travels through the United States of North America* (2 vols., London, 1799), II, 69; Carter to Battaile Muse, March 2, 1784, Letterbook V, 182, DUL; Ball to Joseph Chinn, Stratford-by-Bow, England, Feb. 18, 1774. See also Ball to Chinn, Oct. 22, 1756, Ball Letterbook, CW microfilm; J[ame]s Mercer to Muse, April 3, 1779, Muse Papers, DUL.

Plantation slaves wore clothing usually cut from a heavy, coarse cloth of flax and tow originally manufactured in Osnabrük, Germany. Following the non-importation agreements of the late 1760's, coarse-textured cotton wool weave, "Virginia plains," "country linen," replaced "Osnabrugs." Unlike the colorful variety of many of the artisan's clothing, the notices for runaways after 1770 indicate that field laborers wore uniform pants and trousers. "They are well clothed in the usual manner for Negroes"; "clothed as usual" and "the usual winter clothing for corn field negroes" are representative descriptions from advertisements of that period.[44]

Black women who worked on the quarter wore clothing of the same weight and texture as the men. They usually dressed in a loose-fitting smock or shift, often tied at the waist; a short waistcoat was fitted over this dress. A Dutch blanket used for a sleeping robe and shoes and stockings completed the plantation Negroes' clothing allowance.[45]

Housing for slaves varied widely. But there are frequent references in travelers' accounts to clusters of slave cabins that looked like small villages, and, in plantation records, numerous directions from masters indicating a concern for warm, dry houses with floors, lofted roofs, and on occasion, fireplaces. Slave quarters, however, may have been a late development. Subscribers who used advertisements to sell plantations frequently mentioned "negro quarters," but usually only in those notices published in the last quarter of the century. The plantation's size, location, and wealth were not factors; nearly all had slave quarters. It is likely that the smaller planter's field hands may have slept in the lofts of barns, in tobacco houses, and other outbuildings before the war. Joseph Ball told his nephew that the slaves "must ly in the Tobacco house" while their quarters, 15 by 20 feet with fireplace and chimney, were "lathed & fitted." However, several planters, including George Washington, used a less substantial, pre-fab arrangement. These shacks were small, temporary, and were moved from quarter to quarter following the seasonal crop.[46]

---

44 *VaG* (Purdie and Dixon), Nov. 22, 1770, James Henderson; June 7, 1770 (Purdie and Dixon), Joseph Pleasants; (Rind), July 12, 1770, William Dudley. For a field slave who was described as "well-clothed," see *VaG* (Dixon and Hunter), March 7, 1777. Berryman Simon ran away with shoes, stockings, two coats, a checked linen shirt, a pair of brown sheeting breeches.

45 For example, Martha Massie's Moll, *VaG*, Nov. 3, 1752. See also the following plantation records: "Councillor" Carter, Nomini Hall Waste Book 1773–83, entries for Nov.–Dec. 1773, CW microfilm collection; Carter to J[ame]s Harrison, March 22, 1785, Letterbook VI, 119–20; Carter to [?], Dec. 18, 1790, IX, 197, DUL; "King" Carter to Thomas Colmore, Feb. 15, 1723/4; and Carter to Robert Jones, Oct. 22, 1729, Carter Letterbook, VHS.

46 *VaG* (Purdie), Sept. 5, 1777, Mordecai Throckmorton; (Dixon and Nicolson), Sept. 25, 1779, John Powell; Dec. 25, 1779, John Potts; *Virginia Herald and Fredericksburg Advertiser* (hereafter *VaH & FA*), June 28, 1792, Job Cart[er]; Ball to Chinn, Feb. 18, 1744, April 23, 1754, Ball Letterbook.

Also Ball to Chinn, Nov. 13, 1746: "I will have no New Quarters built in the forest [one of his quarters]: but you may pull off the Covering; weather boards, studes, & Rafters; and then New Post, Cill, Stud, and Rafter them; and let them

J. F. D. Smyth was forced to take shelter one evening in a "miserable shell" inhabited by six slaves and their overseer. Unlike many slaves' houses "it was not lathed nor plaistered, neither ceiled nor lofted above . . . one window, but no glass in it, not even a brick chimney, and, as it stood on blocks about a foot above the ground, the hogs lay constantly under the floor, which made it swarm with flies." [47]

On the home plantations, "servants," like the crop hands, usually slept in their own quarters. A planter who moved to the valley in 1781 asked his steward to place the "house Servants for they have been more indulged than the rest" with the overseer and his family, "till Such Time as Warehouses can be provided for them." Slaves evidently rarely slept in the great house. A letter dated 1823 written to Dr. A. D. Galt of Williamsburg, mentioned that the writer's father could not find a house, "and the ones he has seen have not had separate quarters for the servants." They would then "have to stay in the basement or the garret rooms." This, she concluded, "[as] you know cannot be very agreeable to Virginians." . . .

The lean, spare character of the field slave's material condition was a function of his place in the servile work hierarchy. Most plantation slaves worked in the fields where their tasks were tedious, sometimes strenuous, and usually uninspiring. Although tobacco is a difficult and challenging crop, field laborers—especially the "new Negroes"—were forced into the most routine tasks of transplanting seedlings, weeding, suckering, and worming. Following the harvest their work days extended into the night, when they sorted, bundled, and pressed the tobacco into hogsheads for shipment. . . .[48]

Lazy, wasteful, and indifferent work was a chronic problem on eighteenth-century plantations. Slaves understood that there was a great deal of time to waste, and little hope of improving their lot. "It will be better to have more eyes than one over such gangs," Landon Carter noted. Following another inspection he complained, "the old trade, take one hour from any Job and it makes a day loss in work." Most plantation slaves desired challenging tasks, but once they had them, they dragged out the job as long as possible. Herdsman Johnny, charged with breaking

---

be well Cover'd weather boarded, and Lath'd & filled, and the floor rais'd higher within than without, and a Good plank Door, with Iron hinges, & a Good Lock & key; and let there be good Substantial Cills, of which Oak or Chesnut, laid a little way in the Ground."

[47] Smyth, *A Tour of the United States*, II, 75.

[48] See William Tatham, *Historical and Practical Essay on the Culture and Commerce of Tobacco* (London, 1800), which is still the most knowledgeable source. See also Melvin Herndon, "The Sovereign Remedy," *Tobacco in Colonial Virginia* (Williamsburg, 1957); David J. Mays, *Edmund Pendleton, 1721–1803: A Biography* (2 vols., Cambridge, Mass., 1952), I, 9–10, 99ff. Useful primary sources are the Reverend Robert Rose, Account Book and Diary (*ca.* 1727–50) entries for June–July 1748, CW microfilm; Richard Corbin to J. Semple, Jan. 1, 1759, Corbin Letterbook, CW microfilm; *Landon Carter's Diary*, I, 414–15, 426–27, 480, 482; and there is a detailed account on tobacco cultivation in the Wellford Papers (Landon Carter), n.d. [early 1770's], "Rough to [John] Boughton," UVA.

up the quarter patch at Sabine Hall, "does not intend to finish," Carter wrote, "by contriving that all his lambs should get out of the yard that he may be trifling about after them." [49]

Careful planters habitually spot-checked their slaves' productivity. Planters like Landon Carter and George Washington who demanded from their slaves punctiliousness, order, and a high output, were convenient and effective targets for the slaves' piddling laziness and wasteful procedures. A 1760 entry in Washington's diary noted that four of his sawyers hewed about 120 feet of timber in a day. Dissatisfied with this rate of production, and determined to apply gentle pressure, Washington stood and watched his men. They subsequently fell to work with such energy and enthusiasm that he concluded that one man could do in one day what four had previously accomplished in the same length of time.[50]

How many seemingly routine plantation practices were actually concessions to the unreliability of slave labor? For years Landon Carter refused to introduce plows and carts onto his quarters since he felt that these technological innovations would only serve "to make Overseers and people extremely lazy . . . wherever they are in great abundance there is the least plantation work done." [51]

Feigned illness was another remarkably simple but effective ruse. When a slave asked to "lay-in," his master often suspected he was faking, but could never be certain. Too many had stood helplessly by while a strange and lethal "distemper," or "ague," suddenly swept through their slave quarters and carried off numbers of workers. Plantation records are filled with notes on these epidemics: "The mortalities in ties in my families are increased. . . . The number of my dead is now fifteen working slaves. I thank God I can bear these things with a great deal of resignation," or "a grevious mortality of my familys hath swept away an abundance of my people"; and, "we kept the plantations on James River to try to make Crops, but there broke out a malignant fever amongst the Negroes & swept off most of the able Hands; this threw all into Confusion & there has been little or no thing made since." [52]

Women who feigned illness were usually more effective than men. "As to Sall," James Mercer wrote his steward, "I believe her old complaint is mere deceit, if it is not attended with a fever it must be so unless it is owing to her monthly disorder & then can only last two days, and exercise is a necessary remedy." Washington complained of women who "will lay up a month, at the end of which no visible change in their countenance, nor the loss of an ounce of flesh, is discoverable; and their allow-

[49] *Landon Carter's Diary,* I, 301, 358, 534; also 303, 369.

[50] Haworth, *George Washington: Farmer,* 198; see also George Washington to William Pearce, Philadelphia, Feb. 22, 1794, *Mount Vernon,* 166.

[51] *Landon Carter's Diary,* I, 386; see also 445.

[52] "King" Carter to [?], Corotoman, March 3, 1720/21; Carter to Mr. Edward Tucker, May 11, 1727, Carter Letterbooks, 1720–21, 1727–28, UVA microfilm. Louis B. Wright, ed., *Letters of Robert Carter, 1720–1727: The Commercial Interests of a Virginia Gentleman* (San Marino, Cal., 1940), 85–87. Robert Carter Nicholas to John H. Norton, Oct. 14, 1771, Norton Papers, CW.

ance of provision is going on as if nothing ailed them." Exasperated and uncertain about the health of a black woman, Betty Davis, he explained that "she has a disposition to be one of the most idle creatures on earth, and besides one of the most deceitful." When two of his slave women approached clutching their sides, Landon Carter told them to work or be whipped. He observed that they had no fever (the test of whether or not slaves were ill). "They worked very well with no grunting about pain." But Sarah, one of the women who had pretended to be pregnant for eleven months earlier in the year, soon ran off. When Wilmot used the same stratagem, Carter noted: "it cost me 12 months, before I broke her." This lesson was not satisfactory; for a third woman "fell into the same scheme," and "really carried it to a great length." So Carter whipped her severely; and she was "a good slave ever since only a cursed thief in making her Children milk Cows in the night." [53]

Plantation slaves who "hid out" in the woods and fields as runaways represented a more serious breach of plantation security. They often returned to the quarter in the evening for food and shelter, and were an invitation to others to follow their example. But truancy was also inward rebelliousness: it was sporadic, and it was directed toward the plantation or quarter. Unlike the real fugitives, truants had no intention of leaving the immediate neighborhood and attempting to permanently change their status. Truancy was so common that most planters either did not make it a matter of record, or simply referred to it in a random manner in their correspondence. "King" Carter actually viewed it as part of his "outlandish" slaves' learning process: "Now that my new negro woman has tasted the hardships of the woods," he observed to an overseer, "she'll stay nearer to home where she can have her belly full." [54] Planters accepted the fact that absenteeism, particularly in the evening hours, was scarcely controllable. In response to Landon Carter's complaint that his pet deer were straying in the Sabine Hall fields, John Tayloe wrote:

> Dear Col
>   . . . Now give me leave to complain to you, That your Patroll do not do their duty, my people are rambleing about every night, . . . my man Billie was out, he says he rode no horse of Master & that he only was at Col. Carter's, by particular invitation, so that the Entertainment was last night at Sabine Hall, & may probably be at Mt Airy this night, if my discoverys do not disconcert the Plan, these things would not be so I think, if the Patrollers did the duty they are paid for.[55]

53 J[ame]s Mercer to Muse, June 13, 1778, Muse Papers, DUL; Washington to Pearce, Philadelphia, March 8, 22, 1795, *Mount Vernon*, 175, 179, see also 94, 194. Washington required frequent "sick reports" from his steward Pearce. See Pearce to Washington, Mount Vernon, Feb. 1, 8, 1794, Washington Papers, Ser. 4, LC; *Landon Carter's Diary*, I, 371, 373.
54 "King" Carter to Mr. Robert Jones, Corotoman, Oct. 10, 1727, Letterbook 1727–28, UVA microfilm.
55 John Tayloe to Landon Carter, Mount Airy, "Easter Sunday," March 21, 1771, Wellford Papers, UVA.

Plantation slaves probably "rambled" to the "entertainment" in the neighborhood several nights of the week; as long as they reported for work the following day few efforts were made, or could be made, to curtail this practice.[56]

Truants habitually remained very close to the quarter or plantation; but this did not make it much easier for the planter to recapture them. Evidently they were sufficiently clever (and the other plantation slaves were sufficiently secretive) to keep themselves in hiding until they decided to return on their own. Sarah ran off because Carter refused to let her "lie-in" as ill. She spent a week in the woods and ate during the evening hours while visiting the slave quarters. Simon, an ox-carter, also hid beneath the vigilant Carter's very nose. He "lurked" in Johnny's "inner room," and in the "Kitchen Vault." [57]

The outlaw, a far more dangerous type of runaway, used his temporary freedom to inflict punishment on his tormentors. Outlawing a slave was a legal action, placing the runaway beyond the law, making him a public liability, and encouraging his destruction by any citizen. Those who killed outlaws did so without fear of legal prosecution; they also collected a fee from the public treasury and a reward from the slave's owner. The master's advertisements usually did not encourage the slave's preservation: George America was worth forty shillings if taken alive; five pounds if destroyed. . . .[58]

Some potentially explosive outlaws stayed on the quarters and physically assaulted their overseers. One of Landon Carter's supervisors, Billy Beale, chastised a slave who was weeding a corn patch. Told that his work was "slovenly," the slave replied "a little impudently" and Beale was "obliged to give him a few licks with a switch across his Shoulders"; but the slave fought back, and he and Beale "had a fair box." Subsequently, the laborer was brought before his master; and Carter noted that "it seems nothing scared him." Direct confrontations such as these, between comparatively unassimilated slaves and whites, seem to have been rare; a few, however, are described in detail in the advertisements for runaways. Two fugitives, for example, a husband and wife, were recaptured by an overseer while crossing a field, and were "violently" taken from the overseer and set free by field workers. Another runaway, also a field hand, escaped by "cutting his Overseer in Several Pieces [places?] with a Knife." John Greenhow of Williamsburg lost a slave who "laid violent hands" on him: this man ran off with another field slave who had also beaten his overseer.[59]

[56] "Councillor" Carter Daybook, June 15, 1784, XVI, 11–12 DUL; see Acting Governor Edmund Jenings's Proclamation (March 1709) warning overseers and planters who were too lenient in allowing slaves to "go abroad and remaining absent longer time than the Law allows." March 12, 1709, Colonial Office Papers, ser. 5/1316, 166, 167 (Public Record Office, London, Colonial Office Papers; microfilmed by Virginia Colonial Records Project, CW).

[57] *Landon Carter's Diary*, I, 291, 371, 389.

[58] *VaG* (Rind), April 11, 1766, Thomas Watkins.

[59] *Landon Carter's Diary*, II, 754. *VaG* (Rind), May 23, 1771, Joseph Calland; (Purdie and Dixon), April 18, 1771, George Narthsworthy; (Purdie), Jan. 17, 1777, John Greenhow.

Murders, small and unplanned uprisings, and suicides are instances of rebelliousness that was clearly inward-directed in a psychological sense as well as directed against the confines of the plantation. A September 1800 newspaper story graphically illustrates how even the most calculating, courageous, and murderously violent action could be, in a fashion, internalized violence: for after this slave methodically stalked and killed his master he simply "went home."

Captain John Patteson, a tobacco inspector at Horsley's warehouse in Buckingham County, punished his slave for "some misdemeanor"; and from that time, the slave told the court, "he ever after meditated [Patteson's] destruction."

> On the evening to which it was effected, my master directed me to set off home . . . and carry a hoe which we used at the place. . . . I concluded to way-lay him . . . after waiting a considerable time, I heard the trampling of horses' feet . . . I got up and walked forwards—my master soon overtook me, and asked me (it being then dark) who I was: I answered Abram; he said he thought I had gone from town long enough to have been further advanced on the road; I said, I thought not; I spoke short to him, and did not care to irritate him—I walked on however; sometimes by the side of his horse, and sometimes before him.—In the course of our traveling an altercation ensued; I raised my hoe two different times to strike him, as the circumstance of the places suited my purpose, but was intimidated. . . . [W]hen I came to the fatal place, I turned to the side of the road; my master observed it, and stopped; I then turn'd suddenly round, lifted my hoe, and struck him across the breast; the stroke broke the handle of the hoe—he fell—I repeated my blows; the handle of the hoe broke a second time—I heard dogs bark, at a house which we passed, at a small distance; I was alarmed, and ran a little way, and stood behind a tree, 'till the barking ceased; in running, I stumbled and fell—I returned to finish the scene I began, and on my way picked up a stone, which I hurl'd at his head, face, &c. again and again and again, until I thought he was certainly dead—and then I went home.[60]

The most violent reactions to slavery were small, unorganized uprisings. A newspaper account written in 1770 reported a battle between slaves and free men, which suddenly erupted during the Christmas holidays on a small plantation quarter in New Wales, Hanover County. The reporter's explanation for the uprising was a familiar one. "Treated with too much lenity," the plantation slaves became "insolent and unruly." When a young and inexperienced overseer tried to "chastise" one of them

---

[60] *Va. Argus*, Sept. 5, 1800; also *ValC*, Aug. 16, 1786, Francis Alison; *VaH & FA*, Aug. 16, 1792; *VMHB*, VII (Jan. 1900), 444; and James Hugo Johnston, *Race Relations and Miscegenation in the South, 1776–1860* (Amherst, Mass., 1970), 24, 26, 317ff.

by beating him to the ground and whipping him the man picked himself up and "slash[ed] at the overseer with an axe." He missed, but a group of slaves jumped on the white and administered such a severe beating that the "ringleader," the slave whom the overseer had whipped, intervened and saved his life. The overseer ran off in search of reinforcements; and instead of fleeing or arming themselves, the slaves tied up two other whites and "whipped [them] till they were raw from neck to waistband." Twelve armed whites arrived, and the slaves retreated into a barn where they were soon joined by a large body of slaves, "some say forty, some fifty." The whites "tried to prevail by persuasion," but the slaves, "deaf to all, rushed upon them with a desperate fury, armed solely with clubs and staves." Two slaves were shot and killed, five others were wounded, and the remainder fled.[61]

Some slaves took their own lives. The journals of the House of Burgesses contain 55 petitions from slaveowners who sought reimbursement from public funds for slaves who committed suicide. Most of these men were outlawed runaways who, since they feared trial and conviction for capital crimes, hanged or drowned themselves.[62] Since few petitioners reported the circumstances of a slave's death, the journals are not too informative. But one suicide, William Lightfoot's Jasper, was also described in a runaway notice:

> [A] well set Negro Man Slave, much pitted with the Small-pox; he was lately brought from *New-York*, but was either born or lived in the *West-Indies*, by which he has acquired their peculiar Way of speaking, and, seems to frown when he talks; he carried with him different Sorts of Apparel.[63]

If indeed Jasper was a suicide his decision to "dash his brains out against a rock" must have been sudden, for he took a change of clothing with him.[64]

But the field slaves' rebelliousness was not typically violent, self-destructive, or even individualistic. In fact they were much more inclined to attack the plantation in a quietly cooperative and effective way than were the slave artisans. Pilferage was a particularly rewarding and often organized action. "I laughed at the care we experienced in Milk, butter, fat, sugar, plumbs, soap, Candles, etc.," wrote Landon Carter. "Not one

---

[61] *VaG* (Rind), Jan. 25, 1770. The small and sporadic eighteenth-century conspiracies before Gabriel's insurrection (1800), analyzed by Herbert Aptheker, *American Negro Slave Revolts* (New York, 1943), Ch. VIII, can be compared to the rebellious styles discussed in this chapter.

[62] For example, J. P. Kennedy and Henry R. McIlwaine, eds., *Journals of the House of Burgesses, 1619–1776* (13 vols., Richmond, 1905–15), 1726–40, 254, 262, 263. Three suicides were reported in all issues of the *VaG*, July 10, 1752; March 17 and Sept. 17, 1775.

[63] *VaG*, Aug. 14, 1752, William Lightfoot.

[64] *JHB*, 1752–55, 258.

of these ennumerations lasted my family half the year. All gone, no body knows how . . . thievish servants . . . Butter merely vanishing." Washington estimated that his servants stole two glasses of wine to every one consumed by the planter's visitors. His slaves made a practice of stealing nearly everything they could lay their hands on. Washington had to keep his corn and meat houses locked; apples were picked early, and sheep and pigs carefully watched. . . .[65]

Many slaves were fences for stolen goods; they had licenses from "over-tender" masters to sell produce. Whites, too, cooperated with the plantation slaves; they were referred to in the newspapers as "common proprietors of orchards," "liquor fellers," and "idle scatter lopping people." One writer made the interesting observation that some slaveowners, with "a modest blush," were so ashamed to sell certain farm products that they gave them to their slaves to dispose of. "Pray why is a fowl more disgraceful," he asked, "in the sale of it at market, than a pig, lamb, a mutton, a veal, a cow or an ox?" . . .[66]

The plantation slaves' organized burglaries were similar to the rebellious styles of the mobile, comparatively assimilated slaves. These crimes required planning; they took the slaves outside the plantation, and evidently compensated them with money and goods which could be exchanged for articles they needed.

Most field slaves, however, never acquired sufficient literate and occupational skills to move away from the quarter and into the society beyond it. Most were Africans and they remained "new Negroes" all of their lives. There are, then, two possible aspects to the personal dimension of slave life on the quarter. First, from an outsider's point of view, the quarter was a stultifying experience which slowed and restricted the slave's rate of acculturation. Second, from the slave's point of view, life on the quarter was perhaps preferable to daily contact with his captors, because it allowed him to preserve some of his ways.

[65] *Landon Carter's Diary*, I, 359. Washington to Pearce, Philadelphia, Nov. 23, 1794, *Mount Vernon*, 35–36, 129–30, 189–90.

[66] *VaG* (Rind), March 17, 1768, B——E——; March 29, 1770. On Feb. 3, 1772, Landon Carter noted that he was dissatisfied with the House of Burgesses; they had not passed a law prohibiting "those night shops," nor had they listened to his "repeated letters in Public against allowing these night shops." Professor Greene's note to the above (*Landon Carter's Diary*, II, 649n) reads: "a search of copies of the *Gazette* failed to reveal any of these letters." But the tone of the letters cited above, and fact that Carter, a staunch patriot or anti-court man, would not publish in Purdie and Dixon's edition of the *VaG*, suggests that the letters are his.

On several occasions, slaves gave to their masters money and jewelry they found along the roads and river banks; the masters, in turn, advertised the lost article in the *Gazette*. One of Landon Carter's "servants" found a money bag with £204 near Littlepage's Bridge, see *VaG* (Dixon and Nicolson), Feb. 19, 1779; also (Dixon and Hunter), Sept. 21, 1776, Gabriel Jones; April 13, 1776, James Cocke; June 8, 1776, Thomas Fenner; (Pinkney), Nov. 2, 1775, James Bray Johnson. There are several more.

Plantation Slaves Who Were "Privileged"
House Servants

Household slavery entwined the lives of whites and blacks. In the household more than anywhere else, there were direct and personal encounters that intensified the meaning of slavery for slaves and free alike. For the black servant these situations were often harrowing experiences which threatened to expose a nature sharply divided between enervating fear and aggressive hostility. His inward styles of rebelliousness and such related neurotic symptoms as speech defects were often manifestations of a profound ambiguity about whites and his own "privileged" status. For the white master the intimate presence of so many blacks subtly influenced domestic affairs, particularly his behavior toward his wife and children. The roles developed in household slavery restricted the master's actions toward his servants too. Once a style of discipline and correct order had been established, the master's reactions were often determined by what the slaves had come to expect of him. Highly sensitive to the patriarch's role, servants were quick to exploit any weakness in his performance. If the master was insecure, so were his dependents; but they also kept him that way by their persistent and petty rebelliousness. Household slavery then was the epitome of Professor Tannenbaum's dynamic view of human relationships in slave societies in which slavery was "not merely for blacks, but for the whites [and] . . . Nothing escaped, nothing, and no one." [67]

The greatly enlarged situational (or interpersonal) dimension of slavery in the household is fundamentally important for another reason. Our limited understanding of slave behavior is based almost exclusively on interpretations of these personal encounters. These interpretations, which argue that slaves became the characters they played for whites, that their masters' view of them as infants or Sambos became their self-view, must be used with extreme caution. The interpersonal encounter was only a fragment of slavery's reality for both whites and blacks. When slaves were among their own and using their own resources as fugitives and insurrectionists, it is abundantly clear that much of their true character was concealed or intentionally portrayed in a dissembling manner in the presence of whites.

The reciprocal—and often harmful—nature of human relations in the great mansions of his society was discussed by Thomas Jefferson in Query XVIII in *Notes on Virginia:*

> The whole commerce between master and slave is a perpetual exercise of the most boisterous passions, the most unremitting despotism on the one part, and degrading submissions on the other. Our children see this, and learn to imitate it. . . . The parent storms, the child looks on, catches the lineaments of wrath, puts on the same airs in the circle of smaller slaves, gives loose to the worst of pas-

[67] Frank Tannenbaum, *Slave and Citizen: The Negro in the Americas* (New York, 1946), 115.

sions, and thus nursed, educated and daily exercised in tyranny, cannot but be stamped by it with odious peculiarities. The man must be a prodigy who can retain his manners and morals undepraved by such circumstances.[68]

In placing slavery in the context of "family" relations Jefferson uncovered its essential nature: an intensely private affair for both servant and master. But other parts of his statement warrant critical examination. Servants did not typically participate in "degrading submissions," nor were masters usually blustering despots. Their roles were more intricate than that, and varied greatly in the patriarchal households of William Byrd II [and] Landon Carter. . . .[69]

William Byrd II was a well-educated, urbane man whose lordly disdain for those dependent upon him was sometimes tempered by a lusty but keen sense of humor.[70] He has left two Virginia diaries. The first one, 1709–12, was written by a proud man in his mid-thirties, married to passionate and shrewish Lucy Parke Custis. Byrd contributed significantly to his wife's unhappiness, often handling the proud young girl in an offhand and belittling manner. When the servants were drawn into these domestic quarrels, they were sometimes cruelly punished by the defeated party. In the second diary, 1739–41, his blood had cooled. Married for fifteen years to Maria Taylor, a quiet, efficient, and unassuming woman,

[68] Adrienne Koch and William Peden, eds., *The Life and Selected Writings of Thomas Jefferson* (New York, 1944), 278.

[69] The paternalistic aspect of American Negro slavery, an essential feature of Stanley Elkins's interpretation (*Slavery*, 103–4), is an especially controversial issue; for it involves the now familiar problem of whether or not accommodationist behavior was a prominent feature of the slave's adjustment. Ulrich B. Phillips wrote most fully on this subject—at times as a scholar, at other times as an apologist. See his *American Negro Slavery* (Gloucester, Mass., 1959) *passim*, but esp. 512, 513; and *Life and Labor in the Old South* (Boston, 1963), ch. XI, "Life in Thraldom," in which he makes the following statement which he unfortunately does not follow up: "The simplicity of the social structure on the plantations facilitated Negro adjustment, the master taking the place of the accustomed chief." Professor Genovese, like Elkins, also emphasizes Southern paternalism as a key factor in slavery; see his introduction to a new paperback edition of the 1918 *American Negro Slavery* (Baton Rouge, 1967); "The Legacy of Slavery and the Roots of Black Nationalism," *Studies on the Left*, VI (Nov.–Dec. 1966), 6f, 9, 11, 14; and most recently, *The World the Slaveholders Made* (New York, 1969).

[70] For biographical information on William Byrd II, see John Spencer Bassett's useful introduction to *The Writings of "Colonel William Byrd of Westover in Virginia Esqr"* (New York, 1901); Louis B. Wright, *The First Gentlemen of Virginia* (Charlottesville, 1940), Ch. XI; and Wright's introduction to the most recent edition of Byrd's writings, *The Prose Works of William Byrd of Westover* (Cambridge, Mass., 1966), as well as the introductions to Byrd's two Virginia diaries: L. B. Wright and Marion Tinling, eds., *The Secret Diary of William Byrd of Westover, 1709–1712* (Richmond, 1941); and M. Tinling and Maude H. Woodfin, eds., *Another Secret Diary of William Byrd of Westover, 1739–1741* (Richmond, 1942).

Byrd was more secure about his position in the family. Certain phrases recur in each diary. These concern slaves and morning or evening salutations to God. In the earlier diary the young planter usually closed an entry with a version of, "I neglected to say my prayers, but had good health, good thoughts, and good humor, thanks be to God Almighty"; or, "I rose at 5 o'clock, danced my dance, read a chapter in Hebrew, and said my prayers." Another recurring notation was a version of "Jenny and Eugene were whipped"; or "Molly [Jenny, Eugene, Anaka, little Lucy] was whipped for a hundred faults." In the later diary there are very few reported whippings; most entries end simply: "I walked about the plantation, talked with the people and prayed." [71]

In the first diary, Byrd's relationship with his servants was intimate. There was a play element in many of their encounters. The slaves seldom won; they were repeatedly whipped; and on one occasion, Byrd's wife scarred "little Lucy" with a hot branding iron.[72] Since Byrd humiliated his wife as well as his servants, the interpersonal situations were often ludicrous, confused, and sad. "In the evening my wife and little Jenny had a great quarrel in which my wife got the worse but at last by the help of the family Jenny was overcome and soundly whipped." [73]

The encounters in the Westover household were intricate and game-like. This picture of a 16-year-old girl presented with an opportunity to defeat her mistress in an argument that terminated only when other family members extricated Lucy Parke and thrashed the slave, dramatizes the complicated texture of lives in slave-society households, and the difficulties of stereotyping those lives.

Unlike most great planters, Byrd did not spend a great deal of time surveying his plantations. But while he was home time passed quickly because his favorite servants, who took liberties in the privacy of Westover that would have been inconceivable elsewhere, engaged in rounds of entertaining games. The slaves were clever; and Byrd, an able and vigilant opponent, was determined to curtail their devious and childish pranks: "Anaka was whipped yesterday for stealing the rum and filling the bottles with water." "Eugene was whipped for cheating in his work and so was little Jenny." At times it seemed the mischievous servants craved physical correction: "In the afternoon I beat Jenny for throwing water on the couch." [74]

Byrd's tempestuous marriage and his enjoyment of women, the excitement of their pursuit as well as love-making itself, enlivened activities in his household. One way he re-created the chase at Westover was to occasionally resolve his spats with Lucy Parke by "flourishing" her on the couch or pool table. Byrd however did not "roger" the servant women nearby; for if he did, it is assumed he would have said so in his truly secret diaries which proudly list his other conquests. Any fantasies Byrd

---

[71] For example, Wright and Tinling, eds., *The Secret Diary, 1709–1712*, 15, 412, 419; and Tinling and Woodfin, eds., *Another Secret Diary, 1739–1741*, 1, 6, 7, 129, 171.
[72] *The Secret Diary, 1709–1712*, 205.
[73] *Ibid.*, 307.
[74] *Ibid.*, 22, 42, 79, 224.

may have had about his slave women were sublimated in the ritual games and whippings they used to establish physical contact, and in his keen observation of their marital and extra-marital sexual activities. Byrd, who had tumbled maids from London to Williamsburg, demanded fidelity among his servants. "In the afternoon I caused L-s-n to be whipped for beating his wife and Jenny was whipped for being his whore." . . .[75]

Byrd also liked to scrutinize Eugene, whose reactions indicated that household status for servants had more serious consequences than a few random beatings and scoldings. "Eugene was whipped again for his pissing in bed." Eighteen-year-old Eugene was a chronic bedwetter, in fact, and after Byrd had whipped him and used the branding iron, he wrote "I made Eugene drink a pint of piss." This type of "correction" obviously was not effective, but it does make an unforgettable comment upon the real nature of Byrd's view of Eugene. One June day in 1709, the young man ran away. Byrd's reaction was laconic, his explanation facile and insensitive: "my Eugene ran away this morning for no reason but because he had not done anything yesterday. I sent my people after him but in vain." [76]

Byrd's brutal humiliation of Eugene is partially understandable in the context of his society—one which legitimized such forms of violence as judicial torture. But these background factors do not illuminate the strain of perverse cruelty in Byrd's competitive reactions to the very few young black men in the Westover household; nor do they clarify such cloying, teasing games his servant women engaged him in, as watch-Jenny-throw-water-on-the-couch. Perhaps Byrd imagined that he and Eugene were engaged in a contest for control of the household women. If so this competitiveness would make more intelligible the relationships in Byrd's turbulent first marriage: his enthusiastic involvement in scenes with his wife, Anaka, and the ubiquitous Jenny; that girl's ability to argue with her mistress; and the uncivilized, unpatriarchal nature of Byrd's cruelty toward Eugene. . . .

Landon Carter, who was not as talented, cosmopolitan, or ambitious as Byrd, was obsessively preoccupied with the workings of his home plantation and the activities of all of its slaves. His direct supervision and surveys were in fact so extensive and exhaustive that virtually every slave at Sabine Hall was treated like a household servant. Consequently, his slaves—house, field, and artisans alike—knew his insecurities, and engaged in types of rebellious activities that gave the fullest expression to Carter's awkward execution of the patriarchal role, and the entire plantation family suffered.

[75] *Ibid.,* 192.
[76] *Ibid.,* 45, 46, 112, 113. The entry p. 46 reads "George B-th brought home my boy Eugene . . . [he] was whipped for running away and had the bit put on him." Byrd's style of paternalism was not simply restricted to his black "people." See, *ibid.,* 13, 75. "I proceeded to Falling Creek where I found Mr. Grills [an overseer] drunk. . . . I scolded at Mr. Grills till he cried and then was peevish." And "I denied my man Grills to go to a horse race because there was nothing but swearing and drinking there."

Landon Carter was a deeply embittered man. "For some reason," writes Professor [Jack P.] Greene, "he had failed—and he knew he had failed—to make any lasting impression upon his generation, to achieve that recognition among his contemporaries that would assure him a place in history." [77] Failure as a statesman underscored Carter's need to succeed as head of his large household.

Subordinates in this household were not playful as much as they were "impudent" and "unruly." When Carter's authority, self-respect, or dignity were compromised by their actions he quickly restored "order" by ritualized physical violence. But beating his servants did not lessen Carter's bitter disappointment in his son, Robert Wormeley. The planter spent his old age venting his anger and frustration in a running feud with his son. Painfully aware that Carter considered him a failure, Robert at one time sought his father's approval, which was not forthcoming because he lacked Landon's drive. Unfortunately for all, moreover, Robert and his family lived in the old man's household; consequently his behavior was often petty and self-defeating.[78]

The son's revenge was to waste himself by drinking, gambling, and squandering Landon's money—a type of negative rebelliousness that was especially effective because of Carter's drone-like preoccupation with plantation activities, and his sensitivity to insubordination. One "domestic gust," which Carter bitterly relived in his diary, began when his two granddaughters tattled on their brother. Robert's wife threatened to whip "young Landon." We can see the old man attempting to busy himself with his reading, yet incapable of remaining aloof since there was a lesson to be taught here. Landon sassed his mother, "telling her when she said she would whip him, that he did not care if she did." The boy's father, Carter's son, "heard this unmoved." So the patriarch assumed con-

---

[77] Jack P. Greene, Landon Carter: An Inquiry into the Personal Values and Social Imperatives of the Eighteenth-Century Virginia Gentry (Charlottesville, 1967), 10.

[78] Greene, Landon Carter, 76–83. For another side of Robert Wormeley—that is, more from the young man's point of view and less from his father's—see his daybooks and plantation records, which he kept for his father while acting in the capacity of a steward during the early 1770's. This material is in the Wellford Papers, UVA, and in the Carter Papers, William and Mary College Library. See also Louis Morton, ed., "The Daybook of Robert Wormeley Carter of Sabine Hall, 1766," VMHB, LXVIII (July 1960), 301–16. In Morton's article (313–14), Carter writes on Aug. 25, 1766: "Determined [to take up residence] at Hiccory Thicket [for] myself & Family, as the [only method] to avoid the frequent quarrels between Father & me; discoursing about the matter [with] Mr Parker I recd from him some hints, that Father looks upon it [gambling] in so heinous a light as to threaten to make an alteration in his will to the prejudice of me & my Children; upon this I discoursed with the old Gent on the affair; I understood from him that he would take away the maids that tended my Children, & that he would not aid me but distress me; this prevailing reason obliged me to lay aside my design & with it bid adieu to all Satisfaction, being compelled to live with him who told me I was his daily curse; and who [attributed] to me his Negroes running away, &c." Then after this intriguing observation, young Carter noted, "But he is still my Father & I must bear with every thing from him; in order [to lead a?] quiet life."

trol: "I bid him come and tell me what he did say for I could not bear a
child should be sawsy to his Mother." The boy ignored him; Carter
grabbed his arm and shook him. There were words between father and
son. The "gust" abated until breakfast, when the sulking youngster was
twice summoned to the table by his father, then by his grandfather. Again,
Carter, assuming command, was ignored. So he reached for his whip and
"gave" the child "one cut over the left arm," and "the other over the
banister by him." The outraged mother "then rose like a bedlamite," and
"up came her Knight Errant"; there were "some heavy God damnings,"
but the son, the old man took pains to note, "prudently did not touch
me. Otherwise my whip handle should have settled him if I could." [79]

Disappointment and frustration shadowed Carter even into his beloved kitchen garden. Here too he was clearly vulnerable because he had
to deal with another man, in this instance, his slave gardener Toney. One
morning after putting the slave to work fencing the plot, he rode out
and inspected the job. Concerned even with the width of the gate posts,
he dismounted:

> and showed [Toney] where the two concluding posts were to stand
> and the rest at 8 feet asunder from post to post . . . and I asked
> him if he understood me. He said he did and would do it so. I have
> been 2 hours out and when I came home nothing was done and he
> was gone about another jobb. I asked him why he served me so.
> He told me because it would not answer his design. The villain had
> so constantly interrupted my orders that I have given him about
> every jobb this year that I struck him about the shoulders with my
> stick.[80]

Predictably, Toney retaliated. The following morning he "laid himself
up and complained of a pain in his shoulder, which did not raise the least
swelling," Carter noted. "The idle dog," moreover, refused to come out
and take off a lock that he had previously returned from a locksmith, and
that only he could remove. "I might as well give up every Negroe if I
submit to this impudence," Carter concluded.[81]

In a fashion, masters such as Carter influenced the very nature of
their servants' rebelliousness, because they themselves provided "privileged" slaves with the means by which they could sabotage the plantation operation. Most larger planters maintained a revolving fund of odd
jobs, piecemeal work, outside the field. Although low in prestige and
virtually without any meaningful personal compensation for the slave,
these tasks were eagerly sought after nonetheless by those who wished
temporarily to escape the dulling monotony of field work. From the master's point of view, work in the garden, kitchen, or stable would hope-
fully serve as an incentive for good behavior. From the slave's point of
view, the new task was truly appreciated; but once obtained, the problem

[79] *Landon Carter's Diary*, I, 310.
[80] *Ibid.*, I, 369; see also, 378.
[81] *Ibid.*

was to keep it. The servant's feelings were highly ambivalent, because the assignment also presented itself as an opportunity for the slave to avenge himself. If the planter was present, so much the better. Although he was demoted to the field, Johnny, Landon Carter's herdsman, refused to be cowed. Carter was his audience.

> [He] was so pleased in being turned to the hoe that he came this morning at day break to tell me he was going and the rascal took his row next to hindmost man in my field. But to show him I did not intend the hoe to be his field of diversion I gave him the place of my fourth man and have ordered my overseers to keep him to that. I observed it made him quicken the motion of his arm which up here used to be one, two, in the time of a soldier's parade.[82]

Landon Carter was much too mistrustful, angry, and aggravated by the slightest threat to his person to perform well as a patriarch. This criticism of his son's handling of this role is informative, because it points to a major source of weakness in Carter's own performance:

> And for my Sons people I suppose the same [one cotton shift per slave] altho' perhaps he may have ordered two shirts and shifts apiece for his people for he differs from me he loves to encourage people for doing nothing when for my part I think they ought to be severely punished.[83]

Unhappy with himself and unable to maintain easily his position as head of the plantation family, Carter could not accept the fact that competent patriarchs tolerantly overlooked much of their servants' intransigent behavior. A patriarch had to be discreet and discriminating in his selection of the opportunities for "disciplining" slaves and instilling in them a sense of "duty." . . .

For many servants the problems encountered in adjusting to household status were especially critical because of an intimate relationship with their masters. Whatever the precise nature of this relationship, the slaves' emotional involvement was considerable. Close contact with the master, irrespective of what "good" treatment and "care" they received, was in many ways psychologically harmful. A study of the waitingman's problems of speech demonstrates that much of the servant's idiosyncratic behavior was symptomatic; that speech problems are another indication of the disturbed, neurotic nature of these fearful, hostile, and talented people; and that in the final analysis, a man-servant's speech impediments

[82] *Ibid.*, 397.
[83] [Landon Carter] to [John] Boughton, n.d. This document is labeled "Rough to Boughton," Wellford Papers, UVA.

or facial tics were manifestations of roles contrary to their true feelings and impulses. . . .

In the familial and domestic world of eighteenth-century plantation society, the location of a slave's job was an important part of his activities as a slave. "Outlandish" Africans often reacted to their new condition by attempting to escape, either to return to Africa or to form settlements of fugitives to re-create their old life in the new land. These activities were not predicated upon the Africans' experience of plantation life, but on a total rejection of their lot.

Most Africans who did not run off at this point were placed on the isolated, up-country quarters, where they remained for the rest of their lives, slowly learning the ways of their captors. This task assignment affected "new Negroes" in two ways. First, the quarter limited their contact with persons who spoke good English and possessed job skills, thus reducing the possibilities that they would readily acquire skills that would widen horizons and move them out of the plantation circuit. Second, since the quarter was isolated, it directed the slaves' rebelliousness toward the plantation itself, rather than toward the less accessible outer world. The field laborers' acts of defiance produced a satisfaction which, though often short-lived, was direct, and brought a quick and visible relief to immediate pressures.

This inward-directed rebelliousness included attacks on crops, stores, tools, and overseers, as well as deliberate laziness, feigned illness, and truancy. While this type of behavior on the part of one slave was ineffectual, slaves understood that if together they did a "little leaning," the overall effect on the plantation's efficiency could be considerable. Only rarely did the quarter slaves reject slavery completely by resisting it outwardly.

A few Africans and many of their children did gain the requisite linguistic and occupational skills to make the move from the quarter to the slightly larger world of the great planter's house, or, rarely, into an even larger arena by way of literate and technical skills. For the house servants, most rebelliousness was still manifested in inward-directed ways: in games with the master, drunkenness, and "laziness." Unlike the crop hands, house servants were also subjected to frequent and often frightening confrontations with the master himself; some of them exhibited neurotic symptoms during these encounters. For the artisans and waitingmen, who—because they traveled extensively—were more able to see their relatively "privileged" positions in relationship to the possibilities of life outside the plantation, rebelliousness became a matter of escaping from slavery itself, of turning their hostilities away from themselves and the plantation. Both their jobs and their facility in speaking English gave them an assurance that they did not need the paternalistic protection of their masters or the plantation environment to survive within the society. On reaching a high level of understanding of their masters' ways, artisans too desired an "independence on every one but Providence"; and although they also sometimes exhibited fear reactions when confronting their masters, they were resourceful runaways, and by the end of the century, had become insurrectionists.

Violence Over Stamps

HILLER B. ZOBEL

Although historians have lavished attention on political events in our history, they have seldom studied how politics affected the lives of common people, and, conversely, how common people affected politics. Yet political events were a part of the everyday lives of most colonists. This was especially true in New England, where the town meeting gave common folk an opportunity to make their opinions heard, and where most men in their lifetime were likely to occupy at least a minor office such as fence viewer or hogreeve.

At no time are common people more important in politics than when change occurs swiftly, for rapid political alterations are almost always associated with challenges to established authority. And these challenges are usually accompanied by violence. In most historical writing, however, only the leaders of political movements appear before our view. Behind the scenes operates the "mob"—a term which itself is loaded with emotional meaning. But who made up the mob, or "crowd," as we might better label a collection of individuals massed for political purposes? How did it come together? What did its members intend? How did they impose their collective will on those who held political power? Until questions of this kind are posed and answered, the political lives of ordinary people will be obscured, and those beneath the elite will remain historically voiceless.

Insofar as they have studied the political "crowd," American historians have employed several explanatory models. In the eighteenth century, upper-class targets of the crowd's wrath frequently described the mob as "frenzied," "mad," or "unthinking." This is the model of crowd behavior that historians have most often used, especially since the invention of the term "mass hysteria" by social psychologists. In this view the crowd is made up of lower-class individuals who act out of passion rather than reason. The "mob" surges through a town willy-nilly, feeding on its own passion, and striking out recklessly and wantonly at anything in its way. A second model of crowd behavior, equally condescending, presumes that most crowds are led and controlled by middle-class or upper-class individuals who manipulate the mob for their own purposes. Peter Oliver, one of the targets of the crowd's wrath in Boston in 1764, thus wrote: "As for the People in general, they were like the Mobility of all Countries, perfect Machines, wound up by any Hand who might first take the Winch."

The third model of crowd dynamics, formulated by historians only recently, sees most eighteenth-century mobs in a far different way. The urban mob is not mad with passion. It does not strike out indiscriminately. Instead it is highly rational in pursuing specific interests related to the lives of its members, who are often skilled artisans and small shopkeepers. Its targets are selected in advance and its goals are carefully calculated. No doubt this theory has only lately received attention from American historians partly because violent mass action has not been widely recognized in modern America as a legitimate form of protest.

But this was not the case in the eighteenth century. Popular expression of grievances, often accompanied by violence, was accepted as a proper antidote to unresponsive holders of political power. Moreover, mass disobedience often brought quick results, for in colonial America those in authority, as yet unshielded from the people by urban police forces, maintained only a frail grip on their offices. For example, mobs in Boston as early as 1709 used violence to prevent one of the town's richest merchants from shipping grain to the West Indies at a time when bread was in short supply among the lower class in the town. In the 1730s, crowds working by night destroyed the Boston public market, because it was regarded as a mechanism that enriched the affluent at the expense of the poor. In both cases the crowd acted out of calculated self-interest, and in both cases it successfully defied the authorities to take action against its members. Rather than being "irrational" or manipulated, these crowds were self-conscious and self-activating. Dozens of other examples of this phenomenon can be found.

Students will want to consider the words Hiller Zobel uses in the following selection to describe the motivation and activation of the Boston mob in August 1765. What does the author mean when he writes that the mob was "used" or "summoned" or "permitted to rear its way into the Stamp Act controversy"? If the mob could be "turned on or off to suit the policies of its directors," was this because the mob was easily gulled by those of higher social station with different interests to pursue, or because the interests of its members coincided with those of its leaders?

In considering the political role of the crowd and the political involvement of ordinary people in Boston in the 1760s, we do well to remember that every man and woman in the street on the night of August 26 was a member of a community that still only numbered about 16,000 and occupied less than a square mile of land. Boston, in other words, was not half as large in population or geographical area as many university campuses today. In such a setting most adults knew a large proportion of the townspeople and a good deal more about the activities of their neighbors than city dwellers do in today's mass society. In this sense political participation was highly public. Privacy, whether in personal or political affairs, was far more difficult to achieve.

The Sugar Act duties, onerous though they might be in the enforcement, were really only preludes to a more direct and insupportable
method of revenue raising. The possibility of Britain's imposing on America a scheme of "internal" taxation, divorced from the customs or the
regulation of trade, had existed even before the Sugar Act. In the Parliamentary discussions which preceded enactment of that measure, Grenville had clearly stated the possibility of "certain Stamp Duties" in America. The House, by resolution only, had approved the idea in principle;
but for about a year the proposal remained inert, while Grenville listened halfheartedly to assorted American suggestions for raising the
money which England needed. It is immaterial whether Grenville gave
sincere consideration to the possibility of the Americans' taxing themselves an equivalent of the expected revenue, or whether his offer to receive an alternate system to the stamp duties "had never been made in
•good faith." The fact is that Grenville did put a stamp bill to the House
of Commons in February [1764]. After a spirited debate, during which
Colonel Isaac Barre, veteran of the Canadian war and a friend of the
colonies, first introduced the phrase "Sons of Liberty," the bill passed the
Commons on February 27, the Lords on March 8, and received the sovereign's approval on March 22. But it was not the young king who signed
the bill into law. Illness or madness (neither doctors nor historians have
ever settled the question definitely) incapacitated him temporarily; a
specially appointed group of commissioners affixed the royal assent.[1]

News of the Parliamentary debates, and hence of the imminence of
the Stamp Act, reached Massachusetts in April. By May 27, the 117 sections of the statute itself had arrived. On and after November 1, taxes of
up to £10 would have to be paid for pre-stamped paper, the only sheets
on which the following documents could be printed, engrossed, or written: "fifteen classes of documents used in court proceedings (including
the licenses of attorneys), the papers used in clearing ships from harbors,
college diplomas, appointments to public office, bonds, grants and deeds
for land, mortgages, indentures, leases, contracts, bills of sale, articles of
apprenticeship, liquor licenses, . . . pamphlets, newspapers (and adver-

"Violence Over Stamps." From *The Boston Massacre* by Hiller B. Zobel, pp. 24–38.
Reprinted by permission of W. W. Norton & Company, Inc. Copyright © 1970 by
Hiller B. Zobel.

[1] Stamp Act generally: Edmund S. and Helen M. Morgan, *The Stamp Act Crisis*
(New York, 1963), 74–92; Lawrence Henry Gipson, *The British Empire Before
the American Revolution* (13 vols; Caldwell, Id., and New York, 1936–), 10:257–
271; Bernhard Knollenberg, *Origin of the American Revolution, 1759–1766* (New
York, 1965), 204–209; John C. Miller, *Origins of the American Revolution* (Boston, 1943), 110–112. No good faith: Morgan, *Stamp Act*, 91. "Sons of Liberty":
Knollenberg, *Origin*, 206. Passage and royal assent: *ibid.*, 207–209; Manfred S. Gutt-
macher, *America's Last King* (New York, 1941), 75–86.

tisements in them), and almanacs." Admissions to the Bar (£ 10), playing cards (one shilling per pack), and dice (ten shillings the pair) also came under the act; criminal matters did not.[2]

From this summary catalogue, it is obvious that the Grenville ministry was quite literally forcing its stamp on every aspect of American life. The individual taxes were not large, and the total sum to be taken out of America was not excessive, especially in comparison with the crushing taxation and serious economic unrest that were afflicting the mother country in 1764 and 1765. What seems to have caused the most grief in the colonies was the all-pervading nature of the duties, the requirement that the underlying blank paper be purchased ready-stamped (from ministerially selected "distributors" to whom the privilege would be worth at least £300 annually), and the enforcement provisions authorizing prosecutions before the juryless courts of vice-admiralty.[3]

The initial Massachusetts reaction was peaceable. At the first proposal of the stamp duties, in 1764, a rudimentary nonimportation association had been formed. This plan, forerunner of a special type of violent nonviolence which would not fully flower for another three years, bound its subscribers (who included some members of both legislative chambers) "to forbear the importation, or consumption, of English goods; and particularly to break off from the custom of wearing black clothes, or other mourning (it being generally of British manufacture) upon the death of relations." The first funeral "agreeable to the New Mode" took place September 17. The association assumed a gastronomic aspect in early 1765, when "a great proportion of the inhabitants of Boston" agreed to eat no lamb during the year, "in order to increase the growth, and, of course, the manufacture of wool in the province." [4]

Neither of these boycotts met particular success. Another Massachusetts suggestion found a readier reception. On June 8, only twelve days after official news of the act's passage reached Boston, the House resolved to write to every colonial assembly, urging that all "consult together on the present circumstances of the colonies, and the difficulties to which they are and must be reduced, by the operations of the acts of parliament for laying duties and taxes on the colonies." By October 7, eight colonies had accepted the invitation, and the Stamp Act Congress convened in New York City.[5]

Meanwhile, in Boston, the pressure rose with the New England summer temperature. On July 2, the radical Boston *Gazette* published the

---

[2] News of debates: Thomas Hutchinson, *The History of the Colony and Province of Massachusetts Bay*, ed. Lawrence Shaw Mayo (3 vols.; Cambridge, Mass., 1936), 3:84. Act: *ibid.*, 3:85; John Boyle, "Journal of Occurrences in Boston, 1759–1778," *New Eng. Historical and Genealogical Register*, 84 (1930), 118 (hereafter *NEGHR*). Catalogue: Morgan, *Stamp Act*, 96; see also the statute itself: 5 Geo. 3, c. 12 (1765).

[3] English taxation compared: Gipson, *Empire*, 10:279. Additional provisions: Miller, *Origins*, 114.

[4] Nonimportation and no lamb: Hutchinson, *History*, 3:84. Funeral: Boyle, "Journal," 166.

[5] News arrives: Boyle, "Journal," 168. Circular letter: Hutchinson, *History*, 3:85. Stamp Act Congress: Knollenberg, *Origin*, 210; Morgan, *Stamp Act*, 139–152.

resolves which the Virginia House of Burgesses had passed in late May. These had sprung from the heated brain of Patrick Henry, whose zeal in their support had driven him to rank his king with Caesar and Charles I. They flatly insisted that the Virginians (and by extension all Americans) "enjoyed the inestimable right of" internal self-government and self-taxation. Just as the Speaker of the Burgesses had admonished Henry for his words, so did the amazed Bostonians. James Otis even went so far as to say, before a group of interested listeners on King Street, that the resolves were downright treasonable. But whatever spirit of moderation greeted the Viriginia manifesto upon its first appearance soon vanished. At Harvard commencement on July 17, Elbridge Gerry, a young candidate for the master's degree, entertained his audience by arguing the affirmative of the *Quaestio*: "Can the new Prohibitary Duties, which make it useless for the People to engage in Commerce, be evaded by them as Faithful Subjects?" A week later, ironically, Gerry learned that H.M.S. *Niger* had taken one of his merchant father's "schooners out of the Harbour of St. Peters," Nova Scotia, presumably on suspicion of violating the customs laws.[6]

The time of purely verbal resistance had almost ended. In Boston, a secret group calling itself the Loyal Nine began meeting to plan active opposition to the Stamp Act and to the men who would effectuate it. From the start, the Loyal Nine seems to have decided on physical intimidation as the most effective means of resisting the Stamp Act. In this, they were only following Massachusetts tradition. No matter how peaceably and humbly the men of Massachusetts might phrase their petitions to the king and his government, when it came to dealing on this side of the water with their grievances, they had always resorted to the direct approach. In the 1740's, for instance, the Bostonians had staged three full-scale riots; the last, in 1747, arose out of objections to impressment of seamen by the Royal Navy, and lasted three days. Actually, rioting in Boston was almost a ritual. Every November 5 (or November 6 if November 5 fell on a Sunday), the town celebrated the anniversary of the infamous Gunpowder Plot, also known as Guy Fawkes Day, with a North End–South End battle royal. It is significant that the Bostonians called November 5 Pope's Day, and used the occasion to refuel their already warm anti-Catholic sentiments. This particular strain of bigotry, with its related anti-Irish and anti-Scottish biases, underlay much of the tension which later developed.[7]

[6] Patrick Henry: Morgan, *Stamp Act*, 122–123. Resolves: *Boston Gazette*, July 1, 1765. Otis on Resolves: Hutchinson, *History*, 3:86n. Commencement July 17: *Letters and Diary of John Rowe, Boston Merchant, 1759–1762, 1764–1779*, ed. Anne Rowe Cunningham (Boston, 1903), 86. Gerry: Samuel Eliot Morison, *Three Centuries of Harvard* (Cambridge, Mass., 1946), 91. Gerry Sr.'s ship: Rowe, *Diary*, 87.

[7] Loyal Nine: Morgan, *Stamp Act*, 160 and works there cited. Boston riots: Bernard Bailyn, *Pamphlets of the American Revolution, 1750–1776* (Cambridge, Mass., 1965), 582. Anti-Catholicism: Charles H. Metzger, *Catholics and the American Revolution* (Chicago, 1962), 7–24; see also John Adams, "A Dissertation on the Canon and Feudal Law," *The Works of John Adams*, ed. Charles Francis Adams (10 vols.; Boston, 1850–56), 3:449, 453, 456.

To the Loyal Nine and other opponents of English policy, the value of Boston's mobbish tradition lay in the immediate availability of a corps of husky, willing bully-boys and, more important, of a leadership cadre accustomed to the difficult job of directing and channeling the mob's energies. Chief of the South End mob, and by force of personality and arms head of the combined mob, was a twenty-eight-year-old shoemaker named Ebenezer Mackintosh. Born in Boston, Mackintosh lived in the South End's Ward Twelve (whose territory included the town gallows on Boston Neck). A volunteer in General James Abercromby's abortive Ticonderoga expedition of 1758, he had become a member of Engine Number Nine, one of the semiformal brigades which were Boston's only organized fire protection; oddly enough, the "master" of Number Nine, the man who had specially selected Mackintosh for inclusion in the Engine, was Stephen Greenleaf, the sheriff of Suffolk County.[8]

In the Pope's Day fracas of 1764, a boy was killed, "many were hurt & bruised on both sides," with "several thousand people following" the participants, "hallowing &c . . ." Mackintosh and others were arrested and charged; after a lengthy delay, they were on February 7, 1765, "tryed [i.e., made the subjects of a probable-cause hearing] before Mr Justice Dana & Justice Storey for the 5th of Nov. affair." Later, a superior court grand jury indicted them, although they were never tried. Mackintosh, already called "Captain," had established himself as a mob chieftain. This reputation did him no harm with the "Caucas Clubb," that informal political association which met in the garret of Thomas Dawes. There, Dawes, Samuel Adams, and an inchoate group of their friends "smoke tobacco till you cannot see from one End of the Garrett to the other. There they drink Phlip," John Adams supposed, "and there they choose a Moderator, who puts Questions to the Vote regularly, and select Men, Assessors, Collectors, Wardens, Fire Wards, and Representatives are Regularly chosen before they are chosen in the Town." At such a "Caucas," some time before the town meeting of March 12, 1765, Mackintosh was named "sealer of leather," a minor regulatory position. The meeting confirmed the Caucas choice, and did so again in 1766, 1767, and 1768. Patronage, artfully wielded, had bound Mackintosh's interest to that of the nascent Sons of Liberty.[9]

When the Loyal Nine allied itself with Boston's mob, opposition to the English colonial policy passed a watershed. Before, disagreement tended to be expressed abstractly, by petitions, newspaper screeds, private letters, even actions at law. In a very real sense, the issue of Britain's relationship with her colonies was being thrashed out, debated. The decision to use the mobs to achieve political ends represented a conscious conclusion that American words could not, alone or even combined with

[8] Mackintosh: George P. Anderson, "Ebenezer Mackintosh: Stamp Act Rioter and Patriot." *Colonial Society of Massachusetts Publications*, 26 (1924–26), *passim*.

[9] Pope's Day 1764: Rowe, *Diary*, 68. Mackintosh's hearing: *ibid.*, 76. Caucas Clubb: *Diary and Autobiography of John Adams*, ed. L. H. Butterfield, et al. (4 vols.; Cambridge, Mass., 1961), 1:238. Mackintosh's nomination: Anderson, "Mackintosh," 27.

the words of English friends, reach the ears of those who counted, those who could change the revenue policy. As Bernard Bailyn has written, "Force had been introduced into the Revolutionary movement in a form long familiar but now newly empowered by widely shared principles and beliefs. It would never threafter be absent." [10] The force which Samuel Adams and the Loyal Nine summoned into the argument destroyed the possibility of accommodation. When the Boston mob was permitted to roar its way into the Stamp Act controversy, the effect was frightening. Indeed, that was precisely what those who summoned the mob had in mind. Their object was simple: compel repeal of the Stamp Act by putting those who were to administer and enforce it in fear of their lives. The radicals sought a political goal by physical means, and they achieved it, as they were to achieve other such goals in the immediate and distant future. But in doing so at such an early stage in the dispute, they ensured that the future course of the disagreement could never be resolved without force.

It is not really an answer to argue, as some have done, that in fact the Boston mob did not cause wholesale or even retail slaughter, and that compared to the Paris rabble in 1789 the Bostonians acted decently and decorously. The essential characteristic of the mobs in pre-Revolutionary Boston, as of mobs anywhere at any time, was the impression they gave of unpredictability. He whom the mob threatened never knew just how far the crowd would go. He knew only that he faced a crew of bullies, rough, loud, frequently intoxicated. In some cases, the mob demanded of its victim that he do something—resign an office, swear not to import British goods. Here the mob's purpose, or rather the purpose of those who summoned up the mob, was to convey to the victim in the most explicit simple terms the frightening alternatives: Do what the mob asks, or the mob will destroy your property and perhaps destroy you. Sometimes, the mob's aim was entirely destructive. It did not seek to compel action by the victim; it reserved the action for itself, action like destruction of a house or tarring and feathering. To the victim, the purpose was really immaterial; the threat of physical harm, brutally and unreasoningly administered, lay behind the whistles and the shouts.

It is a paradox of the violence in Boston during the years from 1765 to 1770 that although the rioters seemed uncontrolled and uncontrollable, they were in fact under an almost military discipline. On one notable occasion, according to the Tory Peter Oliver, Mackintosh

> paraded the Town with a Mob of 2,000 Men in two Files, & passed by the Stadthouse, when the general Assembly were sitting, to display his Power: if a Whisper was heard among his Followers, the holding up of his Finger hushed it in a Moment: & when he had fully displayed his Authority, he marched his Men to the first Rendevouz, & Order'd them to retire peaceably to their several Homes; & was punctually obeyed.

[10] Bailyn, *Pamphlets*, 585.

The Boston mob's ardor, there is little doubt, could be turned on or off to suit the policies of its directors. It was a shaped political instrument, consciously used as such. The occasional excesses in which the mob indulged only emphasized its usual discipline; under stress of combat, even veteran troops sometimes temporarily get out of hand.

The Boston mob, as a political weapon, first came to life on the evening of August 14, 1765, "when the noble Ardour of Liberty" (or so the patriots were later to describe it) "burst thro' its long Concealment, o'erleap'd the Barriers of Oppression, and lifted its awful Crest amid the Group of lowering Dastards, haughty Tyrants, and merciless Paracides." The object of this o'erleaping ardour was Andrew Oliver, secretary of the province, brother to Judge Peter Oliver of the superior court, and stamp distributor-designate. A wealthy merchant and landowner, Oliver made no secret of his appointment; a little while earlier, when Jared Ingersoll landed at Boston from England, bearing his own commission as Connecticut's stamp master, Oliver had joined with other dignitaries in rendering him honors, and in escorting him on the first part of his journey south. The Boston *Gazette* flayed Oliver for his part in the ceremonies, and the night of August 13, the Loyal Nine prepared him a special treat. The next morning, "A Great Number of people assembled at Deacon Elliot's Corner" (at what is today the intersection of Essex and Washington Streets) "to see the Stamp Officer hung in Effigy with a Libel [i.e., label] on the Breast, on Deacon Elliot's tree." Oliver's figure remained all day high on the Liberty Tree—it was already called that—and within a month someone would nail a copper name-plate to its trunk: "The Tree of Liberty." Passers-by stopped to stare; word spread throughout Boston and even to some of the nearby towns; people came from all over. Samuel Adams was there; when someone asked him who and what the effigy was, Adams "said' he did not know, he could not tell. He wanted to enquire." Bernard convened the council while Sheriff Greenleaf reconnoitered and wisely or perhaps designedly "forebore any attempt to remove the image." The governor and the council debated throughout the day, with most of the councilors urging "that the people were orderly, and if left alone, would take down the image, and bury it without any disturbance; but an attempt to remove it would bring on a riot, the mischief designed to be prevented." [11] In fact, what choice did Bernard have? Boston possessed no police force, only a few Dogberry-Verges constables better equipped to serve court papers than to keep the peace. The nearest regular troops were in New York; neither the militia (if it could be assembled in time) nor the governor's cadets were reliable. And anyway, it was much simpler to believe that with darkness the fun would end, and the crowd would disperse.

[11] Parade: *Peter Oliver's Origin and Progress of the American Revolution*, ed. Douglass Adair and John A. Schutz (San Marino, Cal., 1961), 54. "Ardour of Liberty," etc.: *Boston Evening Post*, Aug. 18, 1765. Oliver and Ingersoll: Hutchinson, *History*, 3:85–86; *B. Gaz.*, Aug. 12, 1765. Effigy prepared by Loyal Nine: Anderson, "Mackintosh," 31. Crowd at Elliot's: Rowe, *Diary*, 88. "Tree of Liberty": *B. Gaz.*, Sept. 16, 1765. Sam Adams: Adams, *Diary and Autobiography*, 1:295. Council and sheriff: Hutchinson, *History*, 3:87.

But here as on other occasions, Bernard's hopes betrayed him. When night fell, the throng remained intact. The managers of the proceedings cut down the effigy "in Triumph amidst the acclamations of many thousands who were gathered together on that occasion." They proceeded in rowdy procession along what is now Washington Street toward the Town House (which we today call the Old State House) and poured into the building "in the chamber whereof the governor and council were sitting," still searching for a formula to meet the emergency. "Forty or fifty tradesmen, decently dressed," led the crowd, which now numbered "thousands," through the Town House and down along King Street (today's State Street) toward the waterfront. Oliver owned a dock near the foot of King Street where he had recently put up a small frame building. Assuming that this was to be stamp headquarters, the mob laid it "flat to the ground in a few minutes." A little to the southward, on a street which then as now was called Oliver, stood Oliver's opulent town house, furnished in the genteel, expensive style to which wealthy Bostonians were accustomed. The back gardens of the house ran to the slopes of a commanding eminence called Fort Hill (leveled in the nineteenth century). It was the mob's intention to burn Oliver's effigy atop the hill, and burned it was. But passing Oliver's house, some of them "endeavoured to force themselves into it, and being opposed, broke the windows, beat down the doors, entered, and destroyed part of his furniture." Hutchinson, who had been at the council meeting, had apparently raced the mob to Oliver's home, for he was there when it was assaulted. He tried to obtain help from the sheriff and the colonel of the militia, but neither the civil nor the military powers, nor Hutchinson himself, could stop the mob. By the time peace restored itself, "the blind, undistinguishing Rage of the Rabble," as John Adams called it the next day, had left Oliver's "Garden torn in Pieces, his House broken open, his furniture destroyed and his whole family thrown into Confusion and Terror." It was indeed "a very attrocious Violation of the Peace and of dangerous Tendency and Consequence." [12]

"Attrocious" though they may have been, the mob's actions bore immediate results. Oliver "came to a sudden resolution to resign his office before another night" and agreed in writing to submit his resignation to London forthwith. The news, which Oliver took pains to disseminate widely and promptly, occasioned great joy, another mob, and a second bonfire on Fort Hill, "not to insult the distributor, but to give him thanks." Few onlookers or participants were so shrewd as John Rowe, who noted that Oliver had only "resigned his Commission in Form." Generally, radicals and conservatives alike regarded the event as a "matter of triumph" for the Loyal Nine. Each year thereafter on the anniversary (or the following Monday if the anniversary fell on Sunday) the Sons of Liberty held a huge public celebration; this custom continued

---

[12] Crowd and cutting down image: Rowe, *Diary*, 89. Through Town House, assault on Oliver's house: Hutchinson, *History*, 3:87–88; for an excellent description of the outrage, see Morgan, *Stamp Act*, 161–165. Adams's report and reaction: Adams, *Diary and Autobiography*, 1:259–261.

even after the Declaration of Independence. Obviously, the patriots realized the significance of the mob's work; destruction of property and bodily harm, threatened and actual, in fact controlled but in appearance unchecked, had proven a successful revolutionary technique.[13]

The force which Mackintosh and the Loyal Nine led through the August night had crushed Oliver. But the real object was not he. In the very essay which deplored the "strange Conduct" toward Oliver, John Adams suggested the true target.

> Has not his Honour the Lieutenant Governor discovered [i.e., revealed] to the People in innumerable Instances, a very ambitious and avaricious Disposition? Has he not grasped four of the most important offices in the Province into his own Hands? . . . Is not this amazing ascendancy of one Family, Foundation sufficient on which to erect a Tyranny? Is it not enough to excite Jealousies among the People? . . . Would it not be Prudence then in those Gentlemen at this alarming Conjuncture, and a Condescention that is due to the present Fears and Distresses of the People, (in some manner consistent with the Dignity of their stations and Characters,) to remove these Jealousies [i.e., fears] from the Minds of the People by giving an easy solution of these Difficulties?

Irate though Adams was, he did not suggest that Hutchinson had supported the Stamp Act; apart from the charge of nepotism, the most damaging indictments he could bring against the lieutenant governor were his watering down of the remonstrance to Parliament in 1764 and his efforts to procure the appointment of Richard Jackson as the province's London agent. Not a word about the Stamp Act; not even a mention of Hutchinson's part in granting the writs of assistance. Nothing about Hutchinson's position against a gold standard in the currency dispute of 1762, which Hutchinson himself conceded had unaccountably raised resentments against him. Adams left all these out, and still considered Hutchinson's guilt large enough to justify the violence against Oliver. And even if he had mentioned them, could he seriously blame Hutchinson in the slightest for the mob's behavior? The answer seems obvious unless this is an example of the technique so well-practiced by the other Adams of putting one's enemy in the wrong and keeping him there.[14]

A more plausible, yet typically unjustified, source of the resentment which was building up and being built up against Hutchinson arose from a set of depositions or affidavits which Bernard had earlier collected and sent to England. Hutchinson was unconnected with any of these except for having sworn one of the deponents. Boston merchant Briggs Hallo-

---

[13] Resignation and reaction: Hutchinson, *History*, 3:88; Rowe, *Diary*, 89. Anniversary celebration: Rowe, *Diary*, 139, 172, 191, 205, 248, 316; Adams, *Diary and Autobiography*, 1:341–342.

[14] Adams, *Diary and Autobiography*, 1:260–261. Currency dispute: Hutchinson, *History*, 3:72. Sam Adams's technique: John C. Miller, *Sam Adams, Pioneer in Propaganda* (Boston, 1936), 24.

well, at the Plantation Office in London, saw the affidavits, noted their contents and attestations. When he returned to Boston in the summer of 1765, he "reported that complaint was made in them of John Rowe, Solomon Davy [Davis], and other merchants, as illicit traders, and that they were sworn to before" Hutchinson. The evening of August 15, a mob surrounded Hutchinson's North End house, inflamed by a further rumor that he "was a favourer of the stamp act, and had encouraged it by letters" to England. Through barred doors and windows, Hutchinson heard the shouts. "After attempting to enter, they called upon him to come into the balcony, and to declare that he had not written in favour of the act, and they would retire quite satisfied." Hutchinson stayed silent; the rabble debated. Finally a neighbor told them Hutchinson had left before dark for his country house in nearby Milton. "Upon this, they dispersed, with only breaking some of the glass" of the windows, each surmounted by the crown of Britain.[15]

It was plain that the mob, and whoever was directing it, controlled Boston. Bernard and the council had been unable to advance any sensible proposal for containing the violence other than to offer a £100 reward for the conviction of the Oliver mobbers. Ordinary people feared the dangers inherent in the mob's power, but, as Hutchinson observed, "would give no aid in discountenancing it, lest they should become obnoxious themselves." On Sunday, August 25, Jonathan Mayhew, cleric and radical pamphleteer, preached from his West Church pulpit a sermon on the text, "I would they were even cut off which trouble you. For, brethren, ye have been called unto liberty . . ." Unfortunately, Mayhew omitted the ensuing clause: "only *use* not liberty for an occasion to the flesh, but by love serve one another." The merchants, irked by the incident of the depositions, now made joint cause with the mob directors. John Rowe, according to Hutchinson, admitted that they proceeded to stir up the mob to attack "the houses of the Custom House officers, the Register of the Admiralty, and the Chief Justice, the last of whom was made the principal object." Rowe's diary for the essential dates is lost; the only documentary evidence so far unearthed to link him so directly with what followed Mayhew's sermon is Hutchinson's bald statement. Circumstantial evidence tying merchants and land speculators to the ensuing events will, however, shortly appear.[16]

There is some indication that Hutchinson's magnificent six-pilastered brick home had been marked for destruction even before Mayhew spoke. Hutchinson, who had arrived with his family from Milton the morning of August 26, heard "whispered" rumors in the late afternoon that "[Cus-

---

[15] Depositions and Hallowell's report: Hutchinson, *Diary*, 1:67. Events of Aug. 15: Hutchinson, *History*, 3:88–89. Hutchinson's windows: Samuel A. Drake, *Old Landmarks and Historic Personages of Boston* (Boston, 1873), 167.

[16] Reward: Hutchinson, *History*, 3:87; Boyle, "Journal," 169. Timidity: Hutchinson, *History*, 3:89. Mayhew's sermon (Galatians 5:12–13): Clifford K. Shipton and John L. Sibley, *Biographical Sketches of Graduates of Harvard University* (Cambridge, Mass., 1873–), 11:465 (hereafter *Sibley-Shipton*); Hutchinson, *History*, 3:89. Rowe's involvement: Hutchinson, *Diary*, 1:67; Rowe, *Diary*, 89.

toms Surveyor Charles] Paxton's, [Comptroller Benjamin] Hallowell's, &
the custom house & admiralty officers' houses would be attacked." But a
friend assured him that the window-breaking of August 15 had satisfied
the mob, and that he "was become rather popular." He changed his warm
suit coat for a thin dressing gown and, in the twilight heat, sat down
quietly to supper with his children. Outside, the rumors took violent
shape. A bonfire in King Street drew a large crowd which, "well-supplied
with strong drink," was easily led to the Hutchinson (now Pearl) Street
house (on ground now a part of the Federal Reserve Bank), where the
unpopular Paxton had rented lodgings. Paxton was fortunately away for
the evening, and his fast-thinking landlord saved the tenant from execution in absentia by standing treat for a barrel of punch. "Hurrah, hurrah," was the response. "He is a clever fellow and no Tory. So come along
and we'll drink his health and down with the Stamps." Thirst temporarily
slaked, the mob then apparently split up, some members heading for the
home and office of Register of the Admiralty William Story on King
Street, opposite what is today the Old State House, others for the Hanover Street house of Comptroller Hallowell. The mob at Story's "pulled
down the Windows of his Office and burnt all the [vice-admiralty] papers therein . . . broke all the rest of his Windows." This gang moved
on to Hallowell's, where another group had already "begun the Destruction. They broke all his Windows, took down some very curious carv'd
Work in one of his Rooms," and "plundered his cellars of the wine and
spirits in them." Now thoroughly warmed within and without, the mobs
converged and thundered into the North End, where Hutchinson, one of
the richest men in Boston, worth well over £15,000, still sat at his evening meal, his children around him.[17]

Suddenly, "somebody ran in and said the mob was coming." Hutchinson told his children "to fly to a secure place" and then he "shut up my
house as I had done before intending not to quit it." But daughter Sally,
having left once,

> repented her leaving me and hastened back and protested she
> would not quit the house unless I did. I could not stand against this
> and withdrew with her to a neighbouring house where I had been
> but a few minutes before the hellish crew fell upon my house with
> the rage of divels and in a moment with axes split down the door

[17] Hutchinson's home described in detail: Drake, *Boston Landmarks*, 167. Hutchinson's home as target: Diary of Ebenezer Parkman, cited in Morgan, *Stamp Act*,
166; *Sibley-Shipton*, 11:465. Hutchinson and the rumors: Hutchinson to Jackson,
Aug. 30, 1765, Mass. Arch., 26:146, printed with only minor errors in Anderson,
"Mackintosh," 32–34. The riot preliminaries: Hutchinson, *History*, 3:90. Locations:
of Paxton's house, Drake, *Boston Landmarks*, 273; Hallowell's house, *ibid.*, 148;
Story's house, Annie H. Thwing, *The Crooked and Narrow Streets of Boston, 1630–
1822* (Boston, 1920), 141. Activities: at Paxton's house, R. S. Longley, "Mob Activities in Revolutionary Massachusetts," *New England Quarterly* 6 (1933), 108–109;
at Story and Hallowell houses, Hutchinson, *History*, 3:90; Joshua Henshaw to ?,
NEHGR 32:268–269 (1878). Hutchinson's worth: AO 13/46.647, Public Record
Office, London. Hereafter PRO.

and entred. My son being in the great entry heard them cry damn him he is upstairs we'll have him. Some ran immediately as high as the top of the house, others filled the rooms below and cellars and others remained without the house to be employed there. Messages soon came one after another to the house where I was to inform me the mob were coming in Pursuit of me and I was obliged to retire thro yards and gardens to a house more remote where I remained until 4 o'clock by which time one of the best finished houses in the Province had nothing remaining but the bare walls and floors. Not contented with tearing off all the wainscot and hangings and splitting the doors to pieces they beat down the Partition walls and altho that alone cost them near two hours they cut down the cupola or lanthorn and they began to take the slate and boards from the roof and were prevented only by the approaching daylight from a total demolition of the building. The garden fence was laid flat and all my trees etc. broke down to the ground . . . Besides my plate and family pictures, household furniture of every kind my own my children and servants apparel they carried off about £900 sterling in money and emptied the house of every thing whatsoever except a part of the kitchen furniture not leaving a single book or paper in it and have scattered or destroyed all the manuscripts and other papers I had been collecting for 30 years together besides a great number of Publick papers in my custody.[18]

Hutchinson's description does not exaggerate. Joshua Henshaw, no Tory, wrote his cousin on August 28 "an Account of the base Proceedings of a Mob on Monday Evening, which in short overset all the approved of Measures the other [i.e., the Oliver mob] had taken."

With Respects to the Lieut. Governor's House, where they ended their vile Transactions [Henshaw continued], such as were never heard of here before, they had then rais'd a greater Number and were intoxicated with Liquor, broke his Windows, threw all his Furniture out of his House, stamp'd upon the Chairs, Mahogany Tables, very handsome large gilt-framed Pictures, the Peices of which lay in Piles in the Street, open'd his Beds and let all the Feathers out, took ten thousand Pounds in Cash, took all his Cloathes, Linnen, Plate and every Thing he had, cut the Balcony off of the Top of his House, pulled down all the Fruit-Trees in his Garden, and did him in all £25,000 Damage.

Henshaw's figure is quite exaggerated but there is no reason to doubt the accuracy of his description otherwise, especially as he "went over the ruins" the day after the riot. Josiah Quincy, a sadly cross-eyed young law

---

[18] Hutchinson to Richard Jackson, Aug. 30, 1765, Mass. Arch., 26:146; Sally's "Resolution fixed to stay and share his Fate" is confirmed in an apparently contemporaneous account by Josiah Quincy, Quincy, *Reports*, 169; see also Hutchinson, *History*, 3:90.

student only two years out of Harvard, wrote at the same time that the "Rage-intoxicated Rabble . . . beset the House on all Sides, and soon destroyed every Thing of Value. . . . The Destruction was really amazing, for it was equal to the Fury of the Onset." [19]

What reason lay behind this "unparalleled outrage," as Hutchinson called it? Who were the "demons" who perpetrated it? Hutchinson was admittedly not so "popular" as his friends had suggested, but he was certainly a public figure whose services to the province had been and would continue to be respected and sought after, a man, in John Adams's words, of "great Merit," whose "Countrymen loved, admired, revered, rewarded, nay almost adored him . . . 99 in an 100 of them really thought him, the greatest and best Man in America." Under those circumstances, Hutchinson's friends, although proved by the event to have been tragically misinformed, were not irrational in failing to attend him. Whether their presence would have averted the horrors, no one can say; it may be worth noting that at Philadelphia two months later, when reports formed of a planned assault on the home of Stamp Collector John Hughes, "several Hundreds" of his friends patrolled the streets, causing "the Collection of Rabble . . . to decrease visibly," and ultimately to disperse.[20]

Absent friends, but present enemies. Were their reasons for hating Hutchinson strong enough, valid enough to sanction the gutting of his home? We do not know, because we do not know the reasons themselves. Hutchinson thought the root lay in his unfortunate attestation of the depositions, and that "the merchants, as one of them, Mr. Rowe, acknowledged, stirred up the mob," making his house "the principal object." Samuel Adams offered a characteristic double set of what might properly be called non-explanations. On the one hand, he castigated the rioters as "a Lawless unknown Rabble," and the riot a "Transaction of a truly *mobbish* Nature," the cause of which was "not known publickly—some Persons have suggested their private thoughts of it." But he also cultivated the rumor that the rioters had discovered letters in the house establishing Hutchinson's authorship of the Stamp Act, Adams thus implying that the mob's subsequent destructiveness merely represented its just resentment at the lieutenant governor's perfidy. Since we know that the act was drafted by Thomas Whately of the Treasury Office in London, Adams's insinuations seem almost ridiculous. Far from fearing that his ransacked correspondence would link him to the act, Hutchinson knew that "he had, as far as with propriety he might, used his endeavours to prevent it; and he thought it probable some of his papers to evidence it, might fall into the hands of people who brought the charge against him." In other words, Hutchinson's real worry was that the mob (or whoever was be-

[19] Henshaw to ?, Aug. 28, 1765, *NEGHR* 32: 268–269 (1878); Josiah Quincy, Jr., *Reports of Cases Argued and Adjudged in the Superior Court of Judicature of the Province of Massachusetts Bay,* ed. Samuel M. Quincy (Boston, 1865), 169–170.
[20] Hutchinson to Richard Jackson, Aug. 30, 1765, Mass. Arch., 26:146. Adams, *Diary and Autobiography,* 1:306; on the Philadelphia incident, see Hughes' letters, extracted in Morgan, *Stamp Act,* 314–315.

hind it) would destroy the proof of Hutchinson's opposition to the act and would continue to charge him with having favored it.[21]

Hutchinson owned a large mercantile business, and it is possible that here as elsewhere in the colonies the mob's animus was commercial. The "Number of Persons in Disguise with axes Clubbs &c." which stormed the Scarborough, Maine home of Richard King a few months later (after having "talk'd about the Riots in the Prov[ince]"), likewise called themselves "Suns of liburty," but their real aim was the location and destruction of fifty-four notes of hand, three bonds, eight deeds, five executions, and one lease. The private Hutchinson papers which the mob destroyed may well have afforded a rough kind of debtor's relief. In Providence, they had a more facetious explanation. The members of a "Political Clubb" with whom John Adams's friend Daniel Leonard spent an evening, "Thought Hutchinson's History did not shine. Said his House was pulled down, to prevent his writing any more by destroying his Materials." [22]

This gallows humor may have come close to the truth. Among the documents Hutchinson had been collecting as the foundation of his *History* were various papers pertaining to land titles in Maine, at that time part of Massachusetts. This vast area provoked large-scale land and timber speculation, in which Hutchinson's family had participated, some of its claims conflicting with those of other Bostonians. Whether a desire to limit Hutchinson's title search was the ultimate motive behind the riot is still uncertain. Hutchinson's only known reference to the matter is too oblique to be helpful. It comes as a footnote to the posthumously published Volume III of the *History:*

> The lieutenant-colonel of the [Boston militia] regiment, observing two men disguised, with long staves in their hands, who seemed to be directors, expressed his concern at the damage other people, besides the lieutenant-governor, might sustain by the destruction of so many papers. Answer was made, that it had been resolved to destroy every thing in the house; and such resolve should be carried to effect.[23]

21 Merchants raising the mob: *The Diary and Letters of Thomas Hutchinson*, ed. Peter Orlando Hutchinson (2 vols.; Boston, 1884–86), 67. Adams on the mob: Adams to Dennys DeBerdt, Nov. 15, 1766; Adams, *Writings*, 1:100 and Adams to John Smith, [Dec.] 20, 1765, *ibid.*, 1:60. Adams on Hutchinson and the Stamp Act: *Sibley-Shipton*, 10:428. Whately drafter of Stamp Act: Morgan, *Stamp Act*, 78–80. Hutchinson's opposition: Hutchinson, *Diary*, 70; see also Morgan, *Stamp Act*, 269–274.

22 Richard King: *Legal Papers of John Adams*, ed. L. Kinvin Wroth and Hiller Zobel (3 vols.; Cambridge, Mass., 1965), 1:106–140. Providence: Adams, *Diary and Autobiography*, 1:300.

23 Maine land: Legal Papers, 2:255–258; (Miller, *Sam Adams*, 59, says without documentation that Samuel Adams took "a flyer in Maine lands."). Destruction to prevent title search: William Gordon, *The History of the Rise of the Independence of the United States of America* (4 vols.; London, 1788), 1:180. Hutchinson's allusion: Hutchinson, *History*, 3:90n.

Two men disguised. With blackened faces perhaps, and rough clothing? We do not know. We do not even know their names. Indeed few of the rioters escaped the anonymity that prudence, shame, and the nature of a mob imposed on the participants; Hutchinson has provided the only firm identification—Mackintosh. It is a characteristic of mobs that their whole is infinitely more notable than their parts. The crowd becomes an historical entity and later basks in the glare of its own notoriety; the individuals who comprise it remain through the centuries in the shadows which initially encouraged and protected them. Thus it has been with the "hellish crew" who trampled Hutchinson's opulence. In his *History* and his diary Hutchinson labeled Mackintosh as the principal participant; Bernard, some years later, called "one Moore a principal hand"; and Hutchinson's niece, writing more than a half-century afterwards, accused a North Square mason named Atkins of having helped. Other than these, and except for Hutchinson's comment about John Rowe, we have until now no positive identification of the men who stormed the lieutenant governor's house.[24]

The thick, unexplored files in the office of the Clerk of the Supreme Judicial Court for Suffolk County provide a little more evidence. A jail return, or list of prisoners, dated October 15, 1765, shows that Christopher Barrett, Samuel Taylor, and Stephen Grealy (Greeley) were charged "with being concerned in an Extraordinary Riot in the Evening the 26th day of August last and breaking open and entring the Dwelling house of the Honorable Thos. Hutchinson Esqr. and taking Stealing and Carrying away from thence great sums of his Money and quantitys of his Goods etc." None of these men ever stood trial for the alleged offense; so one cannot say for sure that they were part of the mob. Other evidence in the files, however, circumstantially suggests the makeup of at least a portion of the Boston mob. In early 1765, as a result of the Pope's Day rioting in November 1764, the Suffolk County Grand Jury returned indictments against members of the North End and South End gangs. From the mass of papers, it is possible to state with some certainty the sort of men who were concerned in the 1764 riots. Because we know that a year after the riots, the rival gangs merged under Mackintosh's leadership, it is reasonable to assume that some of the 1764 crowd participated in the 1765 outrages. Other evidence, shortly to be discussed, makes this assumption even more rational.[25]

Mackintosh (spelled McIntosh) was one of the accused, of course. So was another cordwainer, Benjamin Starr, and a leather dresser, Isaac Bowman Apthorp. The others came from various occupations, most in-

[24] Hutchinson on Mackintosh: Hutchinson, *History*, 3:91, 101; Hutchinson, *Diary*, 1:71. On Moore: Bernard to Hillsborough, Aug. 29, 1768, CO 5/767 PRO. On Atkins: recollection of Hannah Mather, quoted in Esther Forbes, *Paul Revere and the World He Lived In* (Boston, 1962), 172–173.

[25] Early Court Files and Papers, Office of the Supreme Judicial Court, Suffolk County Courthouse, Boston (hereafter SF), #100480, #100493, #100494; #100599 (jail return).

volving manual labor. There was a sizable contingent of maritime workers: shipwrights Henry Swift, John Blight, and William Blight, sailmaker
Zephaniah Bassett, ship joiner William Bovey, caulker William Larribee,
and ropemaker Thomas Rice. Samuel Richardson was a hatter, Ichabod
Simpson a housewright, George Hambleton a chaisemaker, John Corbit
a distiller, and Benjamin Wheeler a barber. Cornelius Abbot, Henry
Gardner, and Thomas Stimpson were bakers; Thomas Smith was simply
"laborer." These were apparently young apprentice types. The documents label as "infants," that is, minors, John Blight, Hambleton, Swift,
Richardson, Bassett, and Simpson.

Beyond telling us the names, occupations, and (in some cases) ages
of the putative mob members, the papers show clearly the people who
took an active interest in their fate. This evidence is the most useful of
all in connecting the Pope's Day brawlers of 1764 with the more serious
rioters of later years. The files contain a number of "recognizances," or
surety bonds binding the named individual (defendant or, possibly, witness) to appear at a designated future court session. Since each surety
made himself monetarily responsible for the "principal's" appearance, and
since provincial Massachusetts lacked anything like a compensated, pre-
mium-receiving bail bondsman, one can reasonably assume that a man who
stood surety on a recognizance was taking some kind of personal interest
in the principal. A surety for Simpson and for Smith was distiller William
Speakman, partner of Thomas Chase, one of the Loyal Nine; it was in a
"Compting Room" of the Chase & Speakman distillery that the Nine held
its meetings. And when the deputy sheriff sought to serve a warrant on
Corbit, John "Avarey" "gave his word" that Corbit would appear. John
Avery, Harvard 1759, also belonged to the Loyal Nine.[26]

The 1764 rioters, although arraigned, that is, required to plead to the
indictments—they all pleaded not guilty except John Blight, whose absence the file does not explain—were never tried. There is no formal indication that the charges were dropped; apparently the matter was permitted merely to die. It is possible that a dearth of evidence forced this
development; perhaps it would be fairer to say that the prosecution simply lacked witnesses, at least willing ones. Some time in March 1765, for
example, Richardson and Theodore Bliss (whom we shall meet again)
"were bro't into Court to give Evidence in behalf of the King." Upon
their refusal to be sworn, the court ordered them "committed to his
Majesty's gaol." The record is bare of any suggestion that Richardson's
recalcitrance stemmed from a reluctance to incriminate himself. Indeed,
he avoided punishment in an unusual way, one which reinforces the
proposition that a connection existed between Pope's Day 1764 and the
Hutchinson riot. He produced a kind of "excuse note," directed to the
judges:

26 Chase and Speakman firm: Adams, *Diary and Autobiography*, 1:294. Avery and
   the Loyal Nine: Morgan, *Stamp Act*, 160. Avery at Harvard: Harvard University,
   Quinquennial Catalogue of the Officers and Graduates, 1636–1922 (Cambridge,
   Mass., 1920), 158.

> This may certify that about six Weeks ago I was called to visit
> Samuel Richardson son of Capt. Nathl Richardson. I found his
> Nerves much disordered with frequent Twitchings and partial Con-
> vulsions attended with a Delirium. I bled him largely and gave him
> several Doses of Physick—upon which the Delirium ceased and his
> Nerves grew quiet. Upon Enquery I found that He had at Times
> been liable to Disorders of this Kind from his Childhood.

The note, dated March 21, 1765, bore the signature of Doctor Joseph
Warren, Avery's Harvard classmate, and already a rising figure in Samuel Adams's organization. A memorandum in Clerk Samuel Winthrop's
hand across the foot of the document records that "upon the above Certificate he was discharged." [27]

[27] Richardson and Bliss: Minute Books, Superior Court of Judicature, Office of the
Supreme Judicial Court, Suffolk County Courthouse, Boston, 81, March Term,
1765. Warren's note: SF #100482. Warren and Harvard: *Harvard Catalogue*, 158.
Warren and Samuel Adams: *Sibley-Shipton*, 10:425.

Suggestions for Further Reading

Religion has been a primary focus for colonial historians and yet most scholarship in this area deals with doctrinal and institutional aspects of Puritanism, Anglicanism, or other forms of Protestant commitment. For the personal experience of religion one must turn to a few scattered books. Among the best are Ola Winslow, *Meetinghouse Hill, 1630–1783** (New York, 1952); Norman Pettit, *The Heart Prepared: Grace and Conversion in Puritan Spiritual Life* (New Haven, Conn., 1966); and Perry Miller's essays in *Errand into the Wilderness** (Cambridge, Mass., 1956). The permeation of individual lives with religion is revealed in a number of biographies: among the best are Larzar Ziff, *The Career of John Cotton: Puritanism and the American Experience* (Princeton, N.J., 1962); Robert Middlekauff, *The Mathers: Three Generations of Puritan Intellectuals* (New York, 1971); Edmund S. Morgan, *The Gentle Puritan: A Life of Ezra Stiles, 1727–1795* (New Haven, Conn., 1962); and Perry Miller, *Jonathan Edwards** (New York, 1949).

Detailed information on the lives of indentured servants can be found in Abbot E. Smith, *Colonists in Bondage: White Servitude and Convict Labor in America, 1607–1776** (Chapel Hill, N.C., 1947). The student should turn next to Lawrence W. Towner, "A Fondness for Freedom: Servant Protest in Puritan Society," *William and Mary Quarterly* 19 (1962):201–19, and Russell R. Menard, "From Servant to Freeholder: Status Mobility and Property Accumulation in Seventeenth-Century Maryland," *William and Mary Quarterly* 30 (1973):37–64.

Studies of slavery are legion, but the inquiring student must be selective in order to find works about slaves themselves, rather than books on slaveowners. For the eighteenth century, Basil Davidson's *The African Slave Trade: Pre-Colonial History, 1450–1850** (Boston, 1961) is a good introduction to that subject. For slave life in the colonies consult Winthrop D. Jordan, *White Over Black: The Development of American Attitudes Toward the Negro, 1550–1812** (Chapel Hill, N.C., 1968), and Peter H. Wood, *Black Majority: Negroes in Colonial South Carolina from 1670 Through the Stono Rebellion* (New York, 1974). A comparative view, essential to understanding American slavery, can be developed by reading Carl N. Degler, *Neither Black Nor White: Slavery and Race Relations in Brazil and the United States** (New York, 1971); Richard S. Dunn, *Sugar and Slaves: The Rise of the Planter Class in the British West Indies, 1624–1713** (Chapel Hill, N.C., 1972); Marvin

* Available in paperback edition.

Harris, *Patterns of Race in the Americas* (New York, 1964); and Herbert S. Klein, *Slavery in the Americas: A Comparative Study of Virginia and Cuba* (Chicago, 1967).

For the role of politics in the lives of ordinary people, see Pauline Maier, "Popular Uprisings and Civil Authority in Eighteenth-Century America," *William and Mary Quarterly* 27 (1970): 3–35; Jesse Lemisch, "Jack Tar in the Streets: Merchant Seamen in the Politics of Revolutionary America," *William and Mary Quarterly* 25 (1968):371–407, and "Listening to the 'Inarticulate': William Widger's Dream and the Loyalties of American Revolutionary Seamen in British Prisons," *Journal of Social History* 3 (1969):1–29; Alan and Katherine Day, "Another Look at the Boston 'Caucus'," *Journal of American Studies* 3 (1971):19–42; G. B. Warden, "The Caucus and Democracy in Colonial Boston," *New England Quarterly* 43 (1970):19–45; and Gary B. Nash, "The Transformation of Urban Politics, 1700–1765," *Journal of American History* 60 (1973):605–32. Much is to be gained, in thinking about the role of the "mob" or the "crowd," by reading recent work on the eighteenth- and early nineteenth-century European crowd. See especially, E. J. Hobsbawm, *Primitive Rebels: Studies in Archaic Forms of Social Movement in the 19th and 20th Centuries** (New York, 1965); George Rudé, *The Crowd in History, 1730–1848** (New York, 1964); and E. P. Thompson, "The Moral Economy of the English Crowd in the Eighteenth Century," *Past and Present*, no. 50 (1971), pp. 76–136. On the American crowd of the Revolutionary period, see Gordon S. Wood, "A Note on Mobs in the American Revolution," *William and Mary Quarterly* 23 (1966):635–42, and John Shy, "The American Revolution: The Military Conflict Considered as a Revolutionary War," in Stephen G. Kurtz and James H. Hutson, *Essays on the American Revolution** (Chapel Hill, N.C., 1973).

1790–1830
The Early Republic

Mass Death in Philadelphia

J. H. POWELL

Not until recently has much importance been given to the history of diseases, or epidemiology, in the explanation of how societies evolve and why historical change occurs as it does. To overlook the history of disease in the first two centuries of American history, however, is a major error. Two disease phenomena make this clear. First, European conquest of North and South America could never have been carried out so rapidly had it not been for the epidemic diseases spread among Indian peoples by the colonizers. In Europe, bacteriological infections such as smallpox, diphtheria, scarlet fever, and yellow fever had wrought demographic disaster in the fifteenth and sixteenth centuries. But infected populations gradually built up immunities against these diseases. The Indians, however, had developed no such resistance when Europeans arrived in North America carrying deadly microorganisms. Whole tribes could be wiped out in a few years by smallpox or diphtheria. In fact, the latest research by anthropologists and demographers indicates that European viral infections may have wiped out 90–95 percent of the indigenous population of the New World within the first century of European colonization.

Bacteriological warfare, though unplanned, was thus the Europeans' most effective device in conquering the indigenous people of the Americas. To take but one specific example, Puritans arriving in southern New England in the 1630s found a region only sparsely populated by Indians. An epidemic virus, spread by visiting European fishermen in 1616–17, had claimed the lives of at least half of the native people. This process was repeated over and over again before the American Revolution. Tribe after tribe contracted the deadly smallpox or diphtheria from white traders or while serving as allies of the English on military expeditions against the French or Spanish. In Virginia, where there had been some 30,000 Indians before the arrival of Englishmen in 1607, only 130 remained in 1774. Many of these had been killed in intermittent warfare with colonists, but epidemic disease was by far the largest killer. In other colonies the story was much the same.

A second example of the crucial role of disease concerns the African people brought to the American colonies as slaves. It was their labor that built the plantation economies of Maryland, Virginia, the Carolinas, and Georgia in the eighteenth century. One of the reasons these economies prospered was that Africans thrived, demographically speaking, in the colonial South. This high rate of survival contrasts markedly with the decimation of slaves in the Caribbean and in some of the Spanish and Portuguese colonies of Latin America. In these regions tropical diseases swept slaves away like leaves in a windstorm. According to the demographic studies of Philip Curtin, only about 5 percent of all slaves brought to the New World were imported into the American mainland colonies. Yet 40 percent of the hemisphere's Afro-American peoples are now Americans—compelling evidence of the enormous effect tropical diseases had on enslaved Africans. A comparison of slave importations and slave populations in Virginia and Jamaica illustrates the point for the colonial period. The number of slaves in the two colonies was almost equal in 1775, with Virginians owning about 200,000 slaves and the Jamaicans about 193,000. But between 1700 and 1775, Virginia had imported about 100,000 slaves, while net imports in Jamaica exceeded 350,000. Greater numerical balance between male and female slaves in Virginia probably led to a higher birthrate among slaves there, but the disastrous mortality rate in the Caribbean, which affected blacks and whites alike, was the major force at work.

Diseases, of course, affected European-Americans as well as Afro-Americans and Native Americans. Virginians were plagued for almost a century by malaria and dysentery. For the first half-century of colonization not one of each five arrivals from England survived the first year, according to the testimony of Governor William Berkeley, who lived in the Chesapeake area for most of his life. More than 100,000 Englishmen immigrated to Virginia in the seventeenth century and yet at the end of that period the population of the colony stood at less than 75,000. The lowlands of South Carolina were equally destructive of human life for several generations. The smallpox epidemics in Philadelphia and New York in 1731–32 and the throat distemper epidemic of 1736–37 in Massachusetts carried off about 7 to 10 percent of the population in a single year. A comparable toll today in a major city such as Houston or Detroit would be 100,000 to 150,000 lives.

In spite of some advances in medical knowledge—inoculation against smallpox was probably the most important—American society was struck again and again by disease in the eighteenth century. The death of a relative or friend was thus a common occurrence in the lives of virtually everybody. Hardly a parent existed who had not watched disease carry off several children before they reached maturity. Similarly, large numbers of children were orphaned when their parents succumbed to epidemic disorder. Mortality rates were especially high in the cities, where population was most dense and where poverty consigned large numbers of people in the second half of the eighteenth century to crowded housing. During an epidemic in one of the eighteenth-century cities death was never far from anyone's door. Such was the case in Philadelphia in 1793. Yellow fever swept through the town, cutting across class, religious, and racial lines and devastating the lives of thousands. This was an unusually severe epidemic —the worst the city ever suffered. The following account by J. H. Powell therefore gives us the opportunity to see, in exaggerated form, how early Americans experienced the constant presence of sickness and death.

All the medicines in the pharmacopoeia—the doctors seemed determined to use them all—had not power enough to arrest disaster or erase the horrid scenes presented in these first two weeks of September [1793]. Terror and a numb dismay overwhelmed people. The poorest in spirit abandoned themselves to primitive efforts at self-preservation, sometimes forsaking the simplest decencies of human relationships. In the continual failure of the doctors even the bravest men lost hope. The city surrendered to a coarsening fear.

The very aspect of the disease was frightening to look upon. Patients had a brilliant, ferocious look, their faces dark with blood, their eyes sad, watery, and inflamed. They sighed constantly, their skin was dry and obscenely yellow. After September 10, Dr. [Benjamin] Rush noted, a new characteristic became universal: "the determination of blood to the brain." Laymen learned to recognize the disease on sight, and the sight was ghastly.

Horrors were common, but none the less horrid. They were consuming of the spirit, profane, atrocious, repulsive. The tales people told were of a fantastic spectre: a husband married twenty years deserted his wife in her last agonies. Wives fled from husbands, parents from children, children from parents. Masters hurried servants off to Bush Hill on the slightest suspicion of the disease, servants abandoned masters; "less concern was felt for the loss of a parent, a husband, a wife or an only child," Carey wrote, "than, on other occasions, would have been caused by the death of a servant, or even a favorite lap-dog."

Rich merchants who had given daily employment to dozens were abandoned by wives, children, friends, clerks, and servants, with only a Negro left in attendance, if that. The poor with no attendants and no money for medicines suffered dreadfully. Seven out of eight who died were of the poor, and of these a third at least died simply from want of proper treatment, Carey estimated. Many of them perished "without a human being to hand them a drink of water, to administer medicines, or to perform any charitable office for them." Bodies were found lying in the streets. A man and wife were discovered dead in bed, their little child between them still sucking at its mother's breasts. A woman, seized in labor just as her husband expired, crawled to a window and cried out for help. Two men went in from the street but arrived just in time to see her die. Midwives—those who remained in the city and escaped the plague— were unable to meet all their calls, and charged exorbitant rates.

"Panic" (Editor's title: "Mass Death in Philadelphia"). From J. H. Powell, *Bring Out Your Dead: The Great Plague of Yellow Fever in Philadelphia in 1793* (Philadelphia: University of Pennsylvania Press, 1949), pp. 90–113. Reprinted by permission of the publisher.

A servant girl started off to her home in the country but was taken sick on the road and returned to town, where no one would take her in. A Guardian [of the Poor] hauled her to the Almshouse in a cart, only to have her refused admission. The Guardian offered five dollars for a night's lodging for her, but no place was found; she died in the cart. Children were wandering in the streets, their parents dead at home. A laborer with the improbable name of Sebastian Ale hired out as a grave-digger. An old man, he had long since lost the sense of smell. He opened a grave to bury a wife with her husband who had died a few days before. His shovel struck and broke the husband's coffin, from which emitted such an "intolerable and deadly stench" that Sebastian Ale sickened imme-diately and in a day or two died.

A woman whose husband had died refused a coffin for him as too cheap. She bought instead an elaborate and expensive one, only to die herself the next week and be buried in the cheap box she had rejected. A Water Street man discovered his wife *in extremis*, and fled the house to avoid infection. Next morning he came back with a coffin he had pur-chased for her, only to find her recovered, while he himself died in a few days and his wife found a use for the coffin. One night a sailor lay drunk in a Northern Liberties street. Examining him from a discreet distance, some neighbors concluded he was dead, and called the carter. When he felt himself dragged by the heels toward a coffin the sailor awoke from his stupor and startled the carter by prodigious howls.

These were the stories people told. The sights they saw were pitiably worse. As mosquitoes buzzed in the damp heat, the citizens looked about them on a wretchedness they could not cure, the cause of which they did not know. The very air of the city was now infected, Rush wrote. Con-tagion would carry at least clear across the street.

Whole families were afflicted. Stevens the saddler was the sixth of his family to die; four persons in the household of George Hammond, the British Minister, were ill. William Young had ten in his house down at one time. The Reverend James Sproat, his wife, son, and daughter all died, as did Michael Hay, his wife, and three children, David Flickwir and five of his family, Samuel Weatherby, his wife, and four grown chil-dren. From one house more than twenty persons were carried away, some to Bush Hill, some to the grave. In other families five, six, eight, ten, and in Godfrey Gebler's family eleven, died.

All other diseases were forgotten. Indeed, Rush and some of his col-leagues assumed no others existed. The fever was "a monarchical disor-der," Rush told his wife on September 7. It had quite chased influenza from the city. He treated every illness as if it were the fever.

Yet in spite of the desperate panic some general observations were made. Oliver Wolcott noticed that every time the wind blew from the northern quarter patients improved and fewer new cases occurred. But whenever the wind shifted to the south, blowing across the rivers or up from the swamps and meadows below the city, the number of sick mul-tiplied, and the fever was more fatal. Therefore, he concluded, the malady increased with heat and diminished with cold.

Other thoughtful persons noticed that French exiles seemed to be immune. The doctors explained this to Mathew Carey in various ways. Some said it was because the French despised danger, others that the French made frequent use of *lavements* at all times, which purified the bowels, discharged foul matter, and removed costiveness, "one of the most certain supports of this and other disorders." The French themselves sometimes said it was because they did not, like Americans, eat unripe fruit. Neither Carey nor Rush counted the cases among the French and Santo Domingans treated by the foreign doctors.

To young people the fever seemed particularly fatal—everyone noted that—and to housemaids, to tipplers and drunkards and corpulent persons, to prostitutes, and to the poor who lived amid filth in airless tenements. Among the old and infirm, on the other hand, the disease claimed fewer victims and, on the whole, women were less susceptible than men. In wide, airy streets not many died, but in crowded, dark, and stagnant alleys no house remained uninfected. And frequently there were the "walking cases"—those who protested they were well, who would not lie abed, who went about their business as usual, grim spectres with yellow skin and bloodshot eyes, until suddenly they fell dead.

With the breakdown of civil government, distribution of food to the poor ceased almost entirely, so by the middle of September people were starving. Scenes so frightful, and the general despondency, caused all sorts of exaggerations. One Philadelphian wrote a friend in Norfolk that half the inhabitants had fled and the remaining were dying in such abundance "they drag them away, like dead beasts, and put ten, or fifteen, or more, in a hole together. All the stores are shut up."

Exaggeration at such a time was deplorable. For those who looked closely there were many comforting signs. The impetus of trading still carried people to business every day. Such stores as remained open did very well indeed, and those who had farms or country places to rent or carriages for hire, the two notaries who "protested for the banks," the makers of coffins, the apothecaries, bleeders, and doctors attained a sudden prosperity. Even ordinary business processes went on to some degree. A new countinghouse opened in Dock Street—almost unbelievably, the proprietor was named Blight. James Calbraith & Co. advertised for sale a shipment of elegant British goods just arrived. Samuel Benge, fresh from London, set up opposite the State House as an upholsterer and venetian-blind maker. M. Blanchard continued his amazing aerial experiments from the back yard of Governor Mifflin's closed house. And in the less infected residential district Folwell's Young Ladies' Drawing School commenced its fall term.

Ships continued to arrive—one day thirty came in, thirteen of them from the West Indies. The papers, doing what they could to calm the people, stopped publishing so many obituaries. "Amen" in Brown's *Federal Gazette* wrote praising the citizenry for their clean-up campaign, particularly the clerks of the markets who had removed "putrid sheep's heads and other noxious offals." He observed that areas formerly offensive were now "delightful to the olfactory nerves."

II

Yet such reassuring signs did not go very far, particularly as the number of deaths mounted higher and higher. Doctors turned away patients by the dozens. And no nurses were to be had. With the first recognition of the disease, it became impossible to hire anyone to attend the sick. Soon people noticed that Negroes seemed immune (a conclusion they would have to revise later) and this report gained such currency that a number of colored people, completely untrained, were persuaded to take service in infected houses. Rates offered for nurses and attendants, black or white, were exorbitant, and the Negroes were blamed for it. Nurses demanded three or four dollars a day. They exacted it "with the utmost rigor from starving families," Mathew Carey said, and then they failed to do their duties. The publisher charged further that Negroes even plundered houses. Ebenezer Hazard observed that since nurses received board and room in addition to their fees, their pay was as high as congressmen's. Vicious stories were circulated about the Negroes. Many blamed them for carrying contagion, or preying upon the diseased.

Later, when Negroes proved as susceptible to the fever as whites, some of their leaders intimated that the report of their immunity had been only a wily stratagem of white people to persuade them to serve. This was not true. Actually, Negroes were not infected (or at least, not seen to be) until the disease had raged a full month. The Negroes had no better friend in all America than Benjamin Rush, and Rush certainly thought them immune until after the middle of September. He wrote his "dear friends" Richard Allen and William Gray of the African Society, pleading that since God had granted them special exemption from the disease, they had a particular obligation to come forward and attend the sick of all ranks. The newspapers carried similar appeals, and in the first week of September the Negroes responded.

Now Philadelphia's Negro community, of over twenty-five hundred people, had never been dearly cherished by the city. There were great champions of the people of color, of course—the Reverend James Sproat, Dr. Rush, the leading Quakers; and the Abolition Society was the model for all such societies in America. But the Negroes, even the more than two thousand freedmen, had few economic opportunities, and no social equality. Graduation from the African School did not mean that a Negro could rise in business or the professions or in the world of affairs. It only meant he could bear his limited destiny more philosophically. Negroes were day laborers, domestic servants, or tradesmen in a small way. Women were cooks and laundresses. There were outstanding personalities among them, but the vast majority of the black people lived insecurely on the verge of starvation.

Yet from among these, the poorest, most despised of the city, came some of the most heroic figures of the plague year.

The elders of the African Society met on September 5 and decided they must see what the Negro inhabitants could do to help the stricken white citizens. Two by two, they set out on a tour of the city. Absalom Jones and Richard Allen went to a house on Emsley's Alley where they found a mother dead, a father dying, two small children hungry and frightened. They sent for the Guardians of the Poor, and moved on. That day they visited more than twenty families. Other Negroes did likewise, and afterwards all the elders came together again to tell what they had seen.

Next day Jones and Allen called on Mayor [Matthew] Clarkson to ask how the Negroes could be of most use. The Mayor received them gratefully. These two Negroes were the first volunteers that had come to him, the first Philadelphians prepared to accept the plague and over-come it. Most of Clarkson's Federalist friends had fled, and nearly his entire civil service, but the city was at last producing new and courageous leaders from its humblest people. The Mayor sent an announcement to the papers: anyone wishing help should apply to Jones and Allen of the African Society.

Absalom Jones and Richard Allen were men dismayed by neither the terrors of the pestilence nor the injustice of public slanders. Their lot as Negroes in white America had formed them to endure both. Born in slavery, they had earned their freedom—earned it by the long, hard way of purchase. Absalom Jones had learned to read in slavery. He bought a spelling book. He worked in his owner's store, packing and delivering goods. Somehow he learned to write. Somehow he attended night school. He borrowed money, bought his wife's freedom, saved a few more dol-lars, bought a home. Then, at the age of thirty-eight, he purchased his own freedom. He continued to work in the store, he prospered. He even built two houses and rented them. He was now a man of forty-five, large, rotund, impressive.

Richard Allen, thirty-three, had made his way in the world sheerly by the strength and appealing beauty of his spiritual force. Born a slave to Chief Justice Chew, sold as a child to the Stokeleys of lower Delaware, he experienced a conversion at seventeen, became a Methodist, began preaching. His mother, brother, and sister followed him to the new church. He learned to read and write. Finally for a great sum he pur-chased freedom. He drove a salt wagon, labored in the fields, preached Methodism to all who would listen—to white and black alike—in Dela-ware, Pennsylvania, Maryland, and Jersey, in cities, in towns, in forest glades of the frontier. At twenty-six he came to Philadelphia. He preached at St. George's Methodist Church, he worked as a cobbler.

The illiterate and poor among the Negroes needed help from their own. Absalom Jones and Richard Allen founded the Free African Society in 1787—first organization of Negroes, for Negroes, in all America. It was a social organization, a non-sectarian society designed to give mutual aid to members in sickness and to care for widows and fatherless children. Its leaders were Negroes of education and substance who worshiped with Jones and Allen at St. George's Church.

Then one day an appalling thing happened at St. George's. In the midst of prayer, white trustees of the church advanced on the kneeling Negroes and ordered them to go sit in the gallery. One tried to pull Ab

Jones to his feet, saying he could not kneel there. Jones said, "Wait until the prayer is over, and I will trouble you no more." But the trustee beckoned to another white to come and help him. The prayer ended, the Negroes talked together. They had helped build this church. Allen's preaching had been immensely popular, with the whites, too. This insult, this manhandling, they could not bear. They decided to leave. Led by Jones and Allen, the colored worshipers went out from St. George's, and, said Allen, white people "were no more plagued with us in the church."

Absalom Jones took one group with him, to establish St. Thomas', first Episcopal church for Negroes in America. Jones became deacon, then Bishop White ordained him priest, first Negro rector in the country. Richard Allen established a Methodist church, the mother church of all Negro Methodism. Eventually he rose to be first Bishop of the African Methodist Church of North America.

All Philadelphia knew Jones and Allen in 1793. All Philadelphia knew their piety, their honesty, their ability. Now all Philadelphia was to learn their courage. The African Society, intended for the relief of destitute Negroes, suddenly assumed the most onerous, the most disgusting burdens of demoralized whites.

The Society supplied nurses on demand, and when carriers of the dead were needed, Jones hired five Negroes to gather the bodies, put them in coffins, and haul them to the graveyards. Jones and Allen themselves shared this grim business, on regular schedules. They secured others to transport the sick to Bush Hill. There, they found things so deplorably inadequate and disorganized that they reported back to the elders of the Society. The elders asked the Mayor if he would not liberate certain Negro prisoners from the Walnut Street Jail on condition that they would serve as nurses at the lazaretto. The Mayor, confident of Jones and Allen, freed the prisoners, and those Negroes labored at Bush Hill with conspicuous devotion. Dr. Rush spoke with warm pride of his friends "Billy Grey and Ab Jones." He began a course of training for them. He directed them where to procure medicines, showed them how to bleed and when, asked them to send for him or his pupil Edward Fisher if they needed help. Jones, Gray, Allen and their helpers bled above eight hundred persons following Rush's prescriptions.

What time they could spare from carrying the dead, Jones and Allen devoted to visiting the sick, purging, and bleeding. For Dr. Rush they made careful notes on all their cases, and on the appearance of bodies immediately after death. The whole city watched them every day as they made their rounds, every night as they drove the dead carts. And, of course, the city shunned them as infected, vilified them as predatory. No conduct, however heroic, could expiate the original sin of a dark skin. Doctors who opposed Rush's great purge and copious bleedings attacked the Negroes for practicing his cure, and even citizens who bid highest for their services accused the Negroes of profiteering, plundering, extorting.

Actually the African Society was going in debt for its pains. Of course, there were some Negroes who plundered and extorted. Two thousand people of any color are not all saints. But the venal ones were not those supplied by the Society. The elders ultimately found the hire of carriers and purchase of coffins had been much more expensive than the small income received for interring the dead and burning the bedding of patients. The African Society ended the year with a deficit of £177/9/8. Jones and Allen rebelled at the aspersions of Mathew Carey. He, they observed, had first fled the city, then returned to profit from his tracts on the fever.

Mayor Clarkson was apprehensive, however, and called the two Negro leaders in to discuss the high prices. Jones and Allen told him they buried the poor with no charges at all; they never fixed rates, or asked for pay. They left this entirely to the stricken families. Yet sick people all over the city offered fantastic sums for their services. A few cases of payment were gaining public notice far beyond their importance. Clarkson realized that little could be done. He did, however, arrange that public authority should pay the charges of carrying the dead, and published notices in the papers asking people to add nothing to this in the way of remuneration. It had no effect, of course; but at least it offered official support to Jones and Allen in their attempt to keep prices down.

By mid-September, Negroes were beginning to take the disease. Overnight, it seemed, great numbers were seized. "If the disorder should continue to spread among them," Rush wrote, "then will the measure of our suffering be full." He cared for many, noting some curious differences between white and black patients—Negroes were more infected when it turned cool, no Negro ever hemorrhaged as whites did. Soon Richard Allen himself fell very ill, and called Dr. Rush. Jones for a while was left with the whole burden of the dead.

Absalom Jones and Richard Allen were not men to let insults and abuse go unnoticed. The accusations Carey and others had made were slurs on the colored race too base to stand unanswered. When they found time, Jones and Allen wrote a book about the plague and their experiences in it. They wrote with deep feeling and with honesty, these former slaves, founders of churches, social reformers. Their slender little volume was one of the most affecting records produced that whole tragic year. *A Narrative of the Proceedings of the Black People, during the Late Awful Calamity in Philadelphia, in the Year 1793: and a Refutation of Some Censures, Thrown upon Them in Some Late Publications* was printed by William Woodward at the sign of Franklin's Head. It reported in simple, unornamented prose the gruesome scenes the Negro carriers had witnessed.

They had seen many white people acting "in a manner that would make humanity shudder." They saw a white woman demand and get £6 for putting a corpse into a coffin. They saw four white men extort $40 for bringing it downstairs. They discovered a white nurse pilfering buckles and other valuables of Mr. and Mrs. Taylor, who died together in one night. They found the white nurse of an elderly lady who had died (a Mrs. Malony) lying drunk, with one of the patient's rings on her finger, another in her pocket. And they passed a white householder who threatened to shoot them if they carried a body by his house. Soon he himself was dead and in their coffin.

Sometimes Negro carriers were called to bury a patient whom they found still alive. Sometimes they found no one in the house of a dead person but helpless children. They picked up boys and girls wandering aimlessly on the streets and took them to the orphanage. Once a Negro saw a white man push a woman out of a house. She staggered to the gutter and fell there insensible. The black men found she was far gone in fever, and took her to Bush Hill.

Colored people exhibited, their leaders wrote, "more humanity, more sensibility" than the whites. A poor Negro named Sampson went from house to house caring for the sick and taking no reward. When he himself fell a victim of the fever, none of those he had helped would aid his family. Sarah Bass, a colored widow, went from one sickroom to another, taking only what was offered her. Mary Scott nursed for half a dollar a day, refusing more when she could have it—in gratitude, a white patient settled on her a pension of £6 a year. One elderly colored woman, when asked what her price was, answered "a dinner, master, on a cold winter's day." A young Negress refused to take money because God would see it and afflict her with the disorder, but if she nursed for nothing he would spare her. Caesar Cranchal, Negro, nursed without pay, declaring he would not sell his life for money, even though he should die —which he did.

Such examples of Negro heroism Jones and Allen proudly set down. They were "sensibly aggrieved" at the charges against them. Many of their people had given their time, their energies, their substance, their very lives in service. They did not deserve the calumny heaped upon them. And the two great leaders were manfully aware of the purity of their own conduct. Mayor Clarkson could bear witness to their labors, and Dr. Rush, and thousands whom they had aided, perhaps saved, and thousands whose dead they had buried.

And, indeed, many others. In Boston, a newspaper published a poetic "Eulogium" to Absalom Jones and Richard Allen:

> Brethren of Man, and friends of fairer clay!
> Your Godlike zeal in Death's triumphant day
> Benignant Angels saw—they lent a smile,
> 'Twas temper'd with the dew of sympathy divine. . . .

III

Not all white people were unmanned, of course. True, some men noted for their bravery behaved less than gallantly. Commodore Barry retired to the country and would permit no one from the city to come near his house. Captain Sharp, who had fought with distinction in the Revolution, one night heard his wife complain of feeling ill and, thinking she had the fever, jumped out of bed and shut himself in another room where he died in a day or two, though his wife recovered. It did not pass unnoticed that the intrepid Commodore Thomas Truxtun left the city. And Charles Biddle observed his clerk, a Hessian veteran of the war, weaken in his determination to stay at work when he saw twelve "corpuses" passing his house at one time on the way to Potter's Field.

Others, however, rose to nobility. "Amidst the general abandonment of the sick that prevailed," Carey wrote, "there were to be found many illustrious instances of men and women, some in the middle, others in the lower spheres of life, who, in the exercises of the duties of humanity, exposed themselves to dangers, which terrified men, who have hundreds of times faced death without fear, in the field of battle." When the disaster was over, many of these were dead. Ministers were as busy as the doctors, visiting the sick, comforting the bereaved, and feeding the hungry. The young Guardians Wilson, Sansom, and Tomkins labored endlessly day and night, and the stewards of the Almshouse attended to business without a break, doling out their supplies for the poor throughout the city.

Heroism of the few only pointed up the fearfulness of the many. Fear, said "A. B.," weakened the nerves, debilitated the constitution, depressed the mind. Fear could actually cause the fever. So could great exertion. Biddle believed that Captain Sharp had been "frightened into fever," and Rush found that the men who manned the fire engines, sprinkling the streets to lay the dust, were often overcome.

Fear could certainly cause disasters of more tangible kinds. A demoralized city is a city out of control, a city in which crime, decay, and fire are inevitable. On the night of September 7 fire broke out in Second Street below Market. It started in Kennedy's soap house, spread to Thomas Dobson's printing house and the stables and warehouses near-by. The engines came; some spirited citizens bathed their heads in vinegar, took tobacco in their mouths, and turned out to fight the blaze. It proved "one of the most obstinate fires to extinguish" that editor Andrew Brown could remember. One man in the bucket line looked at his companions on either side, reflecting that they might have come "from the gloomy chambers of debilitated friends or relatives."

Two persons were killed and several others badly hurt before the French frigate *La Precieuse* and the East Indiaman *La Ville de l'Orient* maneuvered their equipment into play and put out the fire. Republican seamen of France received for a day what praises the distrait city could spare from its preoccupation with a more general disaster, but Dr. Rush made the lugubrious note that strenuous exertions at the fire and the numerous colds taken caused many more persons to be seized with the fever. Dobson's stock of Currie's pamphlet, printed only the day before and but half sold, was burnt up; so was part of Hazard's *Historical Collections*. People thought of this as "the Great Fire in Second street." For weeks afterwards a long ladder belonging to one of the companies lay in Chestnut Street. No one was interested enough to remove it.

Panic was as contagious as sickness, as revolting as the black vomit, as formidable as death itself. There were those who remembered that a Methodist boy six months ago had predicted this fever, and years before Friend Jane Watson had told the Pine Street Meeting one First Day of the determination of the Most High against the inhabitants: He who sitteth upon the Pale Horse, He whose name is Death, would be sent through the streets of Philadelphia.

Now were visions made reality. A Marylander beheld two angels conversing with the watch at midnight, and heard the voice of Doom in Philadelphia's streets. Doom cried out in the words of Ezekiel against the modern Tyre that dwelt at the entry of the sea, perfected in its beauty by its builders. In the day of its ruin all its riches and its wares, its mariners, pilots and calkers, its dealers, and its men of war would fall into the waters. Its suburbs would shake. "The merchants among the people hiss at thee. Thou art become a terror, and thou shalt nevermore have any being."

IV

On that Saturday, September 7, members of Holy Congregation Mikveh Israel assembled in their little upper room on Cherry Street. It was Rosh Hashanah, the New Year 5554, a day of mighty holiness, of awe and terror. Outside, many Philadelphians were laid in hasty graves that day, while inside Parnas Benjamin Nones, Rabbi Jacob Cohen, and all the fifty families of Philadelphia's Jewry felt the imminence of death.

They had seen the fever in their own homes. They had nursed the sick, had endured the starvation, the lassitude, the obsceneness, and indignity of plague. Never in the fifty years of the synagogue's existence, not even that desperate time sixteen years before when Howe's army had come marching into the city during the month of Elul, had the Penitential Days brought such present griefs and fears. Sadness imbued the ancient pious words of old Amnon of Metz with a new and piteous understanding: *On the first day of the year it is written, and on the Day of Atonement the decree is sealed, how many shall pass away and how many shall be born, who shall live and who shall die, who at the measure of man's day and who before it, who shall perish by fire and who by water, who by sword and who by wild beasts, who by hunger and who by thirst, who by earthquake and who by plague . . .*

By fire, by earthquake, by plague . . . The great fire in Second Street on Rosh Hashanah tried the stricken city almost beyond endurance, and before the Day of Atonement came fantastic rumors of earthquakes: Reading, Lancaster, and Bethlehem felt severe shocks. Fugitives wrote back to the city describing them. The electric fluids of the earth, undispelled by lightnings, were restless. "Tremendous times!" Mrs. Henry Drinker wrote. "Wars, Pestilence, Earthquakes . . ."

Rabbi Cohen stayed in the city through Yom Kippur. Then he fled. It was his duty, he was told. Most of his congregation were sick or had left the city. He headed for the high and healthy country, taking lodging at Easton where he met Judge Bradford, there on judicial circuit. Bradford told him he was quite right to leave. The only protection was flight. This was an enemy to be conquered by distance, not by power. Bradford wished Rush had not started telling people to stay in the city. Of course, Dr. Kuhn's flight was a different matter, the Judge opined. It was desertion of duty, an act of cowardice.

Everyone felt the same about Kuhn's "craven flight," particularly as the need grew daily worse. Young Dr. Barton was down now, and Senator Anthony Morris was "on the verge of life." And John Barclay had to be carried home from the bank in a litter. Foreign ministers fled: George Hammond of Britain settled in Lansdowne, Don Joseph de Viar, Spanish Commissioner, took his family to Trenton, Citizen François Xavier Dupont, French Consul, fled to Bensalem in Bucks County, but not soon enough—he died there of the fever. Reports of hideous mismanagement of Bush Hill were whispered about the city. "Poor Philadelphia!" exclaimed Susan Dillwyn: "lately so full, so gay, and busy. Now a mournful solitude." Was there any prospect, she wondered, except the entire desolation of the town?

"'Tis really an alarming and serious time," Mrs. Henry Drinker confided to her diary. She was summering in Germantown, for the Drinker house on Front Street below Race was always unhealthy in the autumn. "Our House is left, filled with valuables, nobody to take care of it—ye Grapevines hanging in clusters, and some of ye fruit Trees loaded." Reports of the plague had come out to Germantown slowly at first, but soon the city road was crowded with fugitives. They applied at every house for lodging, everywhere they were turned down. They described the scenes in the city. Some citizens were dying of fear, Mrs. Drinker heard. Some died on the streets, or along the Germantown Pike. In the Drinker's neighborhood in the city lived a slatternly old hag named Clarey. She sold oysters in a cellar in Front Street below Elfreth's Alley. Clarey lost her senses and wandered out of town. Someone found her dead on the road. Hosts of rumors flew about—that five Negroes were arrested for poisoning pumps, that hundreds of French soldiers were marching on Philadelphia from New York, that all manner of disasters were impending.

Elizabeth Drinker went regularly to Meeting in Germantown, where every First Day she gathered more news, of a nursing mother refused admission to the hospital dying in a cart, of a fugitive from the city lying either drunk or feverish in a field near the eighth milestone (no one daring to go near him to find out which), of the deaths of dozens of friends and acquaintances, of a trench dug in Potter's Field for the pauper dead. Loaded wagons jamming the Germantown Pike in continuous line from the city made a melancholy sight. Dr. Lusby, who came out with his family from Second Street, told the Drinkers the frightful numbers of the dead.

By Tuesday, September 10, the deplorable state of the city was reflected in every line published on the fever. There seemed not space enough in the newspapers to relate all that was happening. Advertisements called for creditors of decedents' estates, and hawked the familiar nostrums. An appeal to bankers urged that all notes be renewed so the respectable inhabitants could leave the city—a live debtor was a better risk than a dead one, the writer seemed to think. Half a column was given to an earnest plea for removing the sick poor to Bush Hill as soon as they were infected; another urged masters to send servants to the country and urged that all infected people should be segregated and kept together. Since the city government had arrogated so much power to itself, it might do that, too. The emptiness of the streets, the furtive burials by night, the flight of thousands were all described.

But the worst news of the tenth was a tiny three-line item: "This morning, the PRESIDENT of the United States, set out from town, for Mount Vernon."

To his close associates, there was nothing particularly surprising about President Washington's departure. It was his custom every year to go off to Virginia in the early fall and stay until near the time for Congress to meet. Fifteen days during the latter half of August the newspapers had carried the familiar

NOTICE

All persons having accounts open with the household of the President of the United States, are requested to present them for settlement before the first day of September ensuing.

But this year the fever lent a disconsolate aspect to the President's move. Washington was officially the symbol of state, personally a figure to inspire confidence. His robust dignity, his commanding presence, gave the streets an air when he rode them, and made the city proud. His departure was noticed everywhere.

General Washington had had a miserable summer. His neutrality policy was difficult and unpopular, Jefferson was resigning; his personal secretary, Tobias Lear, had left. Alexander Hamilton was his principal support in public matters, but Hamilton came down with the fever. He was stricken on September 5, Mrs. Hamilton soon after. At once the Secretary of the Treasury called Dr. Stevens, whose method proved so successful that Hamilton sent a letter to the papers about it. He hoped, he said, to quiet "that undue panic which is fast depopulating the city, and suspending business both public and private." He wished to rouse the courage of the citizens to save lives, to prevent pain. He praised Stevens, whom he had known from their common boyhood in the West Indies, and announced that the Doctor would communicate his method either individually or in the papers before he left for New York on the next day. The Secretary told all who would listen how efficacious Stevens' cure was.

In Philadelphia Hamilton's illness became a controversial issue, because the Secretary so specifically opposed Dr. Rush and his method, so wholeheartedly endorsed Stevens' cure. In the rest of the nation his case had a different importance, for in the tense political situation Hamilton was the key figure. In every American city, anti-French partisans waited anxiously for word of "Col. Hamilton and his Lady." When his recovery was announced, letters of gratitude and relief from the most distant places appeared in Brown's *Federal Gazette*. For a while the Secretary's illness was the biggest news story of the capital city.

Public interest did not secure special privileges for the Hamiltons, however. When they left town they were shunned as infectious, refused admission to New York, had to go on up to "Green Bush" opposite Albany. There they were obliged to stay until all five physicians of Albany town trooped across the Hudson, examined them, pronounced them in good health and not likely to bring the Philadelphia pestilence to their fellow citizens.

Hamilton's support would have helped General Washington deal with neutrality matters, with Citizen Genêt, with other compelling problems. But even the presence of Hamilton that first fortnight in September could not have brought the federal government to life, for as a matter of obstinate fact public administration had come almost entirely to a standstill. Clerks in the departments could not be kept at their desks, and even heads of departments were (as Washington put it) finding "matters of private concernment which required them to be absent."

Six clerks of the Treasury Department had taken the fever, three of the Post Office, seven of the Customs Service. The Post Office Department simply shut up shop, moving the local mail service to the University building. Oliver Wolcott, Comptroller of the Treasury, tried in vain to preserve the routines of his department in spite of Hamilton's illness. He moved his family and office out to Falls of Schuylkill, to "Smith's Folly," a huge house Provost Smith of the University had built some years before. There he sought to assemble his staff. He wrote to five clerks who had fled to New York, demanding they return at once and get to work. But the clerks wrote back with wondrous excuses— the air was bad, they had no information of the fever, they had no friends in town to open their houses and send out beds and mattresses, they were not sure the government would pay their extra expenses. Wolcott was helpless. He could not in conscience demand that they endanger themselves by returning.

One Treasury clerk stayed at work, however. He was Joshua Dawson, of the Register's Office. His job was import tonnage and duties on spirits. Dawson continued at his Arch Street home, even though his little daughter died. Every day a courier came in from Wolcott, received a letter from the conscientious Dawson, and rode out again to the Falls. It was unsafe, Dawson thought, but necessary.

Public papers were locked up in closed houses when the clerks left. Postmaster-General Pickering and Attorney-General Randolph were off on an Indian treaty; their departments quickly fell apart, and they found nothing but confusion when they returned. President Washington had no one to inform him or bring him reports, none to advise or confer with him. The federal government had evaporated. No point could be gained by staying. He determined to speed his departure.

"It was my wish to have continued there longer," he wrote Lear; "but as Mrs. Washington was unwilling to leave me surrounded by the malignant fever wch. prevailed, I could not think of hazarding her and the Children any longer by *my* continuance in the City the house in which we lived being, in a manner, blockaded, by the disorder and was becoming every day more and more fatal. . . ."

He instructed Secretary of War Knox to send by every Monday's post concise information of the disease and its progress. He recommended removing the clerks and even the entire War Office out of town, and asked Knox to give advice to his housekeeper in case the presidential establishment "should be involved in any delicacy."

"I sincerely wish, and pray, that you and yours, may escape untouched and, when we meet again, that it may be under circumstances more pleasing than the present," he concluded to General Knox on the evening of the ninth.

Next morning, the tenth, the President and Lady Washington drove down to Gray's Ferry, where they visited with the Secretary of State. Jefferson was likewise preparing to leave, he told them. He handed Washington all the papers relating to the Spanish negotiation of Carmichael and Short. These Washington studied as his coach crossed the floating bridge and rumbled along down the Chester Pike. From Chester that evening he sent them back to Jefferson with his comments. From Elkton the next day (September 11) he posted another letter to Jefferson, on Saturday the fourteenth he passed through Alexandria in the afternoon, picking up a packet of Philadelphia mail that had preceded him, and reached Mount Vernon that night.

In the critical state of foreign affairs, he had planned to stay away only fifteen or eighteen days. He took no official papers with him. But as reports of the fever grew worse he postponed his return again and again. He rode about his farms, he sat endless hours at his desk writing letters, he received friends. Not for six weeks did he leave the fresh, healthy air of Mount Vernon.

V

About the time Washington left, Samuel Breck, merchant, found it necessary to return to Philadelphia. Late in August he had gone up the river to Bristol, where his family had fled. But he had a ship loading for Liverpool at the Walnut Street Wharf and wanted to see to its clearance. On September 9 he wandered clear up Front Street from Old Swedes Church to Walnut, observing the dismal scenes of the plague. As he started back to Bristol he passed the lodgings of Vicomte de Noailles. The Vicomte leaned out of his window and cried, "Fly as soon as you can, for pestilence is all around us!" Breck flew.

Charles Willson Peale, encumbered with his museum and a large family, could not leave. Peale's museum was famous over all America, an amazing collection of improving spectacles—paintings, stuffed animals and birds, fossils, botanic specimens, dioramas—displayed at the artist's residence at Third and Lombard. The engaging painter was, James Hardie wrote in his *Directory*, "remarkable for his ingenuity and perseverance rather than for pecuniary achievements." It was an observation all the artist's friends could agree with, for his twenty-five-cent show was far from profitable. It was absorbing to Peale, however, and to his children—those extraordinary children with their astonishing names— Raphael, Angelica Kaufmann, Rembrandt, Titian, Rubens, and baby Sophonisba Angusciola.

With his wife and some of the children, Peale had spent several weeks at Cape Henlopen collecting birds for the museum. They first learned of the city's disaster when the vessel bringing them up the river was warped into the dock in early September. The painter had trained one of the Santo Domingan refugees as a frame maker, so he had been directly in contact with the reputed carriers of the disease. He shut himself and his whole entourage in his house. The birds they had collected for specimens they cooked and ate—it saved going to the market—and the artist spent his time happily classifying his collection of American minerals. He sprinkled his family and all the furniture liberally with vinegar. Several times a day he marched somberly from room to room firing off a musket charge to fill the house with acrid smoke.

Little Rubens Peale, sickly all his nine years, had been supplied with a large amount of foul-tasting medicine by Dr. Hutchinson, the family physician. When that good man died, Rubens was delighted. He destroyed all his medicines, and from then on was his own doctor. To his father, Hutchinson's death was a cruel blow, however, for soon Mrs. Peale contracted the fever. She had experienced a disagreeable smell in the garden. Dr. Mease came twice, took a little blood the second time. But then he also fell ill, and Peale undertook to care for Betsy himself. For two weeks he did not remove his clothes. He administered barley water, laudanum, spread vinegar all around, purged and bled according to the prescription Dr. Rush published in the newspapers. Betsy recovered, and Peale himself survived a mild attack, but he dwelt in constant fear.

Fear, indeed, was in everyone's heart. "An universal trepidation benumbed people's faculties," Carey wrote, "and flight and trepidation seemed to engross the whole attention of a large proportion of the citizens."

Yet fear itself had to have an end. As the days wore slowly on, people became accustomed to the desperate scenes about them, accustomed even to the obscene and disgusting facts of disease. The heroism of a few induced an element of courage in many. The need for workmen brought out volunteers, first Jones and Allen, then others; and though there was no national, state, or city government left, the Mayor served as the symbol of calm, orderly procedures. Panic burned itself out. It was replaced in most hearts by a calloused, blunted acceptance of the horror, and by the determination to live with it.

A community cannot maintain panic long. Its people, in the ordinary course of surviving, develop such mechanisms of resistance as will first meet, then conquer, the operation of fear. In the first half of September, Philadelphians had been wasted by panic, but in the latter half of the month they were to pull themselves together. September 15 was the watershed of the plague. After that day, the pestilence would no longer be a terror without pity. It would be a fact to be confronted, and overcome. Even though the disease grew steadily worse, even though deaths mounted to ever higher numbers, the citizens were about to find resources within themselves to develop a program of control and achievement.

Panic had reduced the community to its basic components. Among these components was the quality of leadership. The fever was, as everyone knew, not yet half over. But from September 15 on, panic would meet its match in the leadership of three men—in Dr. Rush's serene confidence, in Stephen Girard's organizing genius, in Matthew Clarkson's cool and resolute determination.

These were the leaders who would refuse to fear fear. These were the men whose examples would bring the city out of its fantastic defeat.

Southern Folkways

FRANK LAWRENCE OWSLEY

The most persistent image of the South between the American Revolution and the Civil War is that of a society in which three kinds of people existed: wealthy planters, black slaves, and poor white farmers. Like most popular images, this one contains an element of truth. Each group was well represented in antebellum southern society. But the South also contained a sizeable number of free blacks; thousands of Creeks, Cherokees, Choctaws, and other Indian peoples; a large number of white agriculturalists who were neither rich nor poor; and many artisans and industrial workers living in growing urban centers.

All of these people were a part of the racially, ethnically, religiously, and economically diverse Southern society of the early nineteenth century. It was a society to which large numbers of people were migrating from the older seaboard states, in search of new land, greater opportunities, or perhaps simply an escape from problems accumulated over the years. The very magnitude of this migration indicates how much Anglo-Americans had chafed at being pinned to the coastal plain before the American Revolution by the power of the Cherokees, Creeks, and others, as well as by the presence of France and Spain in the trans-Allegheny region.

Most of the land sought by post-Revolutionary herdsmen and farmers moving into the South was in the possession of Indian peoples, and had been so for centuries. Thus it required a series of wars, reminiscent of the late seventeenth-century hostilities against the Indians of the Chesapeake and New England regions, to divest the Native Americans of their tribal homelands and forcibly remove them to remote trans-Mississippi regions. But the tide of frontiersmen was overwhelming. Nothing could hold them back, especially since the Revolution had militarized a large part of post-colonial society and thus prepared it for a task not contemplated by the idealistic Revolutionary leaders. These Southern frontiersmen appear in popular history as heroic figures such as Daniel Boone and Davy Crockett. But for the most part, as the following essay shows, they were common people, though people with a nearly insatiable hunger for land.

Frank Lawrence Owsley was one of a handful of historians of an earlier generation to interest himself in the daily lives of the people of the Southern frontier. From his work, one can gain a vivid sense of the pleasures and problems that filled their lives. While considering the everyday existence of these Southern folk, however, the student should remember that Owsley, like any historian, was selective in what he chose to describe. Thus the violence inherent in the process of occupying land belonging to another people, who would not willingly surrender their territory, is ignored. So are the brutalities and daily

anxieties associated with slaveholding, which, at one point or another in life, became the experience of about one of every two white
Southerners. But in spite of these omissions, one can gain access
through Owsley's work to some of the least examined parts of the
"Southern experience."

The term "folk" has for its primary meaning a group of kindred people, forming a tribe or nation; a people bound together by ties of race,
language, religion, custom, tradition, and history. Such a common tie we
call folkways. A folk thus possesses a sense of solidarity and is quite different from a conglomerate mass of people. It has most if not all of the
characteristics of nationalism. Indeed, it may be contended with much
force that there can be no true nationalism where the population does
not constitute a folk. The Southern people, according to these several
characteristics, were a genuine folk long before the Civil War. Even the
Southern aristocracy, who were generally of plebeian origin, were folk-
ish in their manners and customs, and shared to a marked degree in this
sense of solidarity. This was especially true after the War of 1812, when
the Great Migration to the West dispersed and diluted the remnants of
the old colonial aristocracy, itself descended largely from the yeomanry
and middle class of England.

The greatest single factor, perhaps, in developing the Southern population into a genuine American folk was the common national origin of
the bulk of the people. With the exception of the large French element
in Louisiana the Southern people prior to 1860 were predominantly
British, being a mixture of English and Scotch, with here and there a
dash of German, French, or Irish. As a rule they were more English
than Scotch in blood, but in physical appearance they probably resembled the Scotch more than they did the English or even the other Americans except in the lower part of the Midwest where so many Southern
folk had settled. The English and Scotch temperaments were blended in
the Southerners. They usually had the steady, easygoing nature of the
English combined with an underlying Gaelic temper and humor. Fat or
lean, blond or brunet, the Southern type could be discerned by travelers
from abroad and from other parts of America. Appearance, the inde-
finable qualities of personality, and their manners and customs, particularly their distinctive speech, set them apart from the inhabitants of the
other sections of the United States, and in this way strengthened their
sense of kinship.

Southern folkways were in part the folkways of rural England,
Scotland, and North Ireland of the sixteenth and seventeenth centuries,

"Southern Folkways." From Frank Lawrence Owsley, *Plain Folk of the Old South*
(Baton Rouge, La.: Louisiana State University Press, 1949), pp. 90–105, 108–15. Reprinted by permission of the publisher.

modified by the impact of the New World environment; and in part
they were an indigenous growth of the South.

The spoken English of the South was as distinctive a characteristic
of the Southern folk as corn bread, turnip greens, and sweet potatoes
and, romance to the contrary, was considered outlandish by the Northerners and the English. True, it was soft and pleasant in tone and inflection; but it had characteristics that were considered as serious defects by
outsiders. Such, for example, were the drawl, the guttural "r" pronounced "ah"—and the omission of the "r" in such words as court so as
to pronounce it "cote." The drawl positively irritated the English,
though it usually—but not always—amused the Northerners; and the
Southern use or lack of use of the "r" made the speech of the Southerners sound effeminate except to the English who treated their "r's" in
a similar fashion. The employment of archaic word forms was a characteristic of the speech of the plain folk, such, for example as "yaller" for
"yellow," "holped" for "helped," "fotched" for "fetched"—itself archaic
in America—"ile" for "oil" and "bile" for "boil."

Though it usually has been assumed that the Southern drawl is of
Negro origin, it is in reality impossible to ascertain by historical investigation the truth or falsity of this assumption. Considerable doubt, however, may be raised concerning this theory by asking the following questions. First, where did the Negro acquire his drawl, since he learned his
speech from the whites? Second, from whence came the drawl of the
people of the upper Great Plains and of the Blue Ridge, Smoky, and
Cumberland Mountains, who have had little or no contact with the
Negro? I am of the opinion that the drawl, wherever found, was originally developed by the whites in response to psychological factors, and
that the Negro slave, who acquired his speech from the whites, further
decreased its tempo in response to similar though not identical psychological causes. The prolongation of a word by the whites was, according
to this theory, a form of politeness, and by the slave, one of deference.
Here one probably finds the combination of frontier or rural influence
and race temperament. To the white man on the frontier and in rural
isolation, contacts with those outside the family were usually infrequent
and were either highly prized or greatly dreaded—where potential enemies were involved. Under such conditions men would, so it appears,
have a tendency to speak both slowly and softly to one another; for to
speak quickly and in a gruff tone would sound unneighborly or unfriendly. To be unneighborly was not the desire of people of a frontier
or of a rural community. To be unfriendly was dangerous, for it was
regarded as a challenge to a personal encounter by people whose fighting
spirit and mores did not permit the refusal of such a challenge.

The natural impulse of the Negro to be friendly and sociable and
his desire to ingratiate himself with his master in order to fend off punishment or finagle the latter's best suit of broadcloth caused him to reduce the tempo of his words more than simple politeness required. Once
this excessive drawl was acquired, it would be transmitted to white children who were in frequent and often constant association with Negroes.

The complex inflection, rising or falling at the sensitive points, was a characteristic of Southern speech. When combined with a soft drawl and the slight "r," it made a command sound like a request, and a request like a casual inquiry. It was, indeed, a cushion, a shock absorber for unpleasant but necessary communications; it was a balm to wounded pride and sorrow; it was also a honeyed persuader that would cause any but a Southern girl to sue a young man for breach of promise, usually—but not always—with no tangible evidence to present to court.

The speech of the plain folk and that of the more cultivated Southern people was basically the same, except, of course, the well educated would not customarily use archaic word forms. It was a speech that could not be successfully imitated. It was and is, indeed, as difficult to master as a foreign language. Few persons outside the South have ever mastered it so as to carry on a conversation without introducing false elements. For example, "you all" will be used in speaking to and of one person, whereas in true Southern English, though "you all" may be addressed to one person, its reference is always plural; it means you and your family, you and your friends, or you and your group—never just *you*. Then the drawl will be prolonged where it is not needed, and the inflection will rise or fall at the wrong spot.

The closely knit family with its ramified and widespreading kinship ties was a folk characteristic which the Southerners possessed to a degree second only to the Highland Scots of an earlier time. Though families were frequently scattered by the westward migration, they more often than not migrated and settled together. The father or the elder brother of a large family, though comfortably situated, frequently moved to the public domain or where land was cheap and plentiful to be near his sons and daughters with their husbands, or brothers and brothers-in-law with their families. Senator Charles Tait of Georgia gave expression to this pattern of behavior in a letter to his son, James, when they were preparing to migrate to Alabama: "I wish you to go where you think it will be best for you to go—where you can be more prosperous and happy. I will go where you go and stay where you stay." [1] An examination of county records, older county histories with the genealogical sketches, and, of course, the numerous genealogical works will reveal ample evidence of the cohesive quality of the family group even under the dispersive impact of the public domain.

The family was not patriarchal in the European or Oriental sense, where parental authority could usually be enforced by the ability of the father to cut the son or daughter off from an inheritance. In a country where a son and even a daughter could leave the parental roof and make his or her way in the new country to the West, discipline by such economic coercion was not feasible. We cannot, however, apply the escape-valve theory to the situation and thus come out with the conclusion that the presence of the frontier destroyed family discipline; for, as a rule, parents and grandparents exercised great influence and authority over their sons and daughters and grandsons and granddaughters, even after

[1] February 26, 1819, Tait Papers, Family Letters I (A), Alabama Department of Archives and History, Montgomery, Ala.

they were grown and married. Apparently, among the Southern folk, as among rural folk generally, age was supposed to bring wisdom rather than senility. The idea of Junior and "Honey Child" that the "old man" and the "old lady" are out of date and senile at the age of forty is decidedly an urban development.

The rural environment of the Old South where the whole family worked together, hunted together, went to church and parties together, and expected to be buried together and to come to judgment together on the Last Day, helps explain the closely knit family group. Certainly it helps explain the deference of younger persons to their parents and elders, for daily association demonstrated that "pa" knew the seasons, the habits and peculiarities of the crops; that he was a master of woodcraft, and he knew the stratagems of the chase and many other fascinating matters that only long experience and reflection could teach. "Pa" could also cut a smarter step in the reel and square dance and play the fiddle better than the boys could, and they knew it. As for "ma," it would take a lot of hard apprenticeship for the daughters to learn to cook, quilt, knit, garden, and "manage" like she could. As likely as not, too, she could dance forty different square-dance figures—and call them. In other words pa's and ma's opinions were respected because they demonstrated in their day-long work with their sons and daughters in field and house and in their play that skill and wisdom come from experience.

Religion was also a vital part of Southern folkways. Indeed, it is difficult to conceive of a genuine folk without religion. The same or similar religious beliefs and practices are an important factor in the creation of a folk, for they help bind together both the family group and the community. The Southern people, inland from the coast where the Episcopal and Catholic Churches were strong, adhered generally to the Methodist, Baptist, Presbyterian, and Church of Christ denominations with their evangelical characteristics.

The rural church, whether a small log house or a pretentious structure, was the center of a community. Here gathered rich and poor, slave and master, to hear the uncompromising champion of righteousness proclaim a gospel of eternal reward for the faithful, and for the wicked, one of eternal punishment varying from Milton's outer darkness to lakes of molten lead. To those believing but sinful souls who still had a large acreage to be sown to wild oats, such sermons were too horrible to contemplate; and they did not contemplate them. Such sinners usually stopped short of the church door and spent their time outside. They were the young bucks whom the county grand jury sometimes indicted for disturbing public worship by discharging firearms, profane swearing, and fighting near the church ground. To the saints and to those who had placed their feet upon the path of righteousness—though they might occasionally take a little detour—it was a joyous religion proclaiming a loving and forgiving God, a God who watched over the lives of his poor, earthly creatures with such care that He marked the sparrow's fall. Their happiness not infrequently moved them to loud amens and occasional loud exclamations of joy.

The church house, though reverently called the "House of God," was also a social center, where friends and neighbors met. Many would gather on the church grounds long before services began and many would linger after the preacher had finished. The older men, singly or in small groups, would visit the graveyard. After that they discussed politics, the crops, the prospects for rain if the weather was dry, and their hopes for dry weather if it was rainy; and they laid plans for corn shuckings, logrollings, house-raisings, and other co-operative enterprises that usually combined business and pleasure. Nor was any occasion permitted to come to an end without tall tales and spicy anecdotes going their rounds. The older women, breaking quietly into little groups, would visit the churchyard, where each, perhaps, had laid away one or more children and other close relatives; and where inevitably other children and other members of the family would be buried. The churchyard was a sacred place. But these women were not overwhelmed by death. They were borne up by their religion, which promised the resurrection of the body and which taught that to give way to unrestrained grief over the death of a loved one was to question God's wisdom and His love. This sorrowful duty being performed, they chatted about their family, their gardens, flowers, chickens, clothes, and the forthcoming wedding; and planned the dinners and quiltings that accompanied the logrolling, corn shucking, or other co-operative work their menfolk had arranged.

The young men and young ladies were, of course, more preoccupied with jollification and lovemaking. They usually paired off and strolled to the spring or well. Here they conspired to gather at some neighbor's house in the afternoon to sing, and to meet again at Wednesday-night prayer services. But while plans were made for further pleasure, the pilgrimage to the well or spring was not wasted. Perhaps some couple would become engaged; and certainly each young beau would return triumphantly bearing the spoils of conquest—a rose or a cape jessamine or a bouquet as large as his mother's feather duster pinned on his lapel.

The younger children played games, hunted snakes and lizards in the woods, boasted of the prowess of their dogs or their father's mules and horses, all of which not infrequently and most naturally ended in a fight.

When at last the crowd broke up, it was not unusual for over half the congregation to go home with the others to eat late Sunday dinner. The cakes, pies, and meats—baked ham, turkey, roast pork—were already cooked and waiting in anticipation of this, for word that they were "expected" next Sunday would already have reached the ones to be invited. Only the chicken had to be fried, the biscuits cooked, and the huge pot of coffee boiled. It was not at all against the principles of the most devout for the menfolk to go to the smokehouse and uncork the wine barrel or the brown jug, to put a razor edge on the already sharp appetite in preparation for the meal that was being laid on the table in such quantities that the legs were almost buckling under the load.

The greatest social and religious events of the year were the revivals, called "protracted meetings" when held in churches, and "camp meetings" when conducted out-of-doors at regular camp grounds. They were held in the late summer after the crops were laid by and before gathering season. The best known of the camp meetings, and one that prejudiced many good people against such, was the Kentucky Cane Ridge Revival of 1800, where 20,000 or 30,000 attended, and the mighty congregation, saints and sinners, were affected by strange religious exercises, including the holy dance, the jerks, the weird holy laugh, and mass swooning. Such a camp meeting was, however, unusual both in size and in behavior. The normal camp meeting was attended by a few hundred families at most, and was usually a very orderly and, to the participants, a very enjoyable social and religious occasion.

In Georgia, the New England schoolteacher, Emily Burke, attended such a camp meeting, of which she has left an excellent account. Though she was probably a member of the Congregational Church, which generally disapproved of revivals and especially camp meetings as encouraging indecorous emotional outbursts, she was deeply impressed by the beauty and serenity of the meeting place and by the religious services. She described the camp ground as "a beautiful square lot of forest land about one acre and a half in extent, laid out amid a native and gigantic growth of oaks." On one corner of the lot was the old church which accommodated "the usual Sabbath day congregation," and on another stood a large building called "the Tabernacle" erected for the purpose of sheltering the large assemblies of the annual camp meeting. "On every side of the square, all fronting the center," says Miss Burke, "the fathers of the principal families constituting these assemblies, have each their own family residence. These little habitations are built of logs, having a piazza in front, and their number is sufficient to enclose the entire square." For the purpose of illuminating the camp grounds each householder had "erected in front of his own house a platform about six feet from the ground and four feet square, upon which . . . [was] laid earth to the depth of about one foot for the purpose of making a foundation for a fire." At twilight, fires were lighted, which "at this elevation sent forth such a broad and brilliant sheet of light in all directions, that those who seated themselves in front of their dwellings could read with perfect ease without the aid of another light."

This camp meeting was the great social event of the year, comments Miss Burke. Everyone who could possibly do so attended—rich and poor, old and young, black and white. Everything was dated with reference to whether it happened before or after the camp meeting. Young ladies planned their clothes for months in advance, and young gentlemen certainly did not neglect this matter. When all had gathered at the camp grounds, this finery was unpacked and tidied up, and in the evenings and during the intervals between services, writes Miss Burke, these "young and joyous people, richly and gaily dressed, could be seen moving in all directions, or standing in small groups beneath the shade of some widespreading tree, in this little city of oaks." [2]

Miss Burke speaks with admiration of the "commanding eloquence"

[2] Emily Burke, *Reminiscences of Georgia* (Oberlin, Ohio, 1850), 238, 242.

of the ministers who preached at this camp meeting; and she felt that "on such occasion, one would not fail of having at least, an intellectual feast if not a spiritual one." But she was most deeply stirred by the simple, informal early-morning prayer services.

"The first thing in the morning [she writes], just as the sun is rising, this sleeping congregation is aroused from its slumbers by several loud and long blasts from a hunting trumpet [horn], to attend early prayers. Consequently with a slight attention to the toilet, the members of each family are soon collected together for worship. The master of the family in which I was most hospitably entertained for several days was a young man of about the age of twenty six or eight, yet he presided over one of these extensive household establishments with all that ease and dignity becoming a patriarch of three score and ten. . . . As soon as we were assembled he arose and in a sweet, clear and strong voice, sung [the song] 'A Charge to keep I have, A God to glorify. . . .' We were assembled in that part of the house called the 'dining hall,' the front of which was all open to the public view, and as all the other families were similarly situated, the songs of praise which went up from each could be distinctly heard by all the rest, as they resounded that morning through every part of the camp ground." It was an experience Miss Burke would not forget. "I never expect to enjoy another scene like this beneath the skies," she later wrote.[3]

Timothy Flint, another New Englander and a missionary to the West, like Miss Burke came to regard the revival and camp meeting as a useful and beneficial institution. He describes one of the large meetings held in Tennessee in the early part of the nineteenth century.

"The notice has been [sent out] two or three months. On the appointed day, coaches, chaises, wagons, carts, people on horseback, and multitudes travelling from a distance on foot, wagons with provisions, mattresses, tents, and arrangements for the stay of a week, are seen hurrying from every point toward the central spot. It is in the midst of a grove of those beautiful and lofty trees, natural to the valleys of Tennessee, in its deepest verdue and beside a spring branch, for the requisite supply of water." [4]

All classes are there: the ambitious and the wealthy, aspirants for office, curiosity seekers, the young and the beautiful, children, the middle aged, and the old.[5]

"The line of tents is pitched; and the religious city grows up in a few hours under the trees beside the stream. Lamps are hung in lines among the branches; and the effect of their glare upon the surrounding forest is, as magic. The scenery of the most brilliant theatre in the world is a painting only for children, compared with it. . . . By this time the moon . . . begins to show its disk above the dark summits of the mountains; and a few stars are seen glimmering through the intervals of

3 Ibid., 244–45.
4 Timothy Flint, The History and Geography of the Mississippi Valley (Cincinnati, 1832), 144.
5 Ibid., 145.

branches. The whole constitutes a temple worthy of the grandeur of God." [6]

Such a setting stimulates the imagination and arouses the emotions. As the time for the opening of the services approaches and the vast audience settles into its place, it is in a receptive, even an exalted mood. Suddenly the murmuring of the excited multitude ceases, and there is a strange, momentary silence of anticipation. Then "an old man, in a dress of quaintest simplicity, ascends a platform, wipes the dust from his spectacles, and in a voice of suppressed emotion, gives out the hymn, of which the whole assembled multitude can recite the words. . . . We should deem poorly of the heart, that would not thrill, as the song is heard, like the 'sound of many waters' echoing among the hills and mountains." [7]

The song being finished, silence again settles upon the multitude, as the old man pauses for a moment before beginning his sermon. Then, continues Flint, "the hoary orator talks of God, of eternity, a judgment to come, and all that is impressive beyond. He speaks of his [religious] 'experiences,' his toil and travels, his persecutions and welcomes, and how many he has seen in hope, in peace and triumph, gathered to their fathers; and when he speaks of the short space that remains to him, his only regret is, that he can no more proclaim, in the silence of death the mercies of his crucified savior.

"There is no need of the studied trick of oratory, to produce in such a place the deepest movements of the heart. No wonder, as the speaker pauses to dash the gathering moisture from his eye, that his audience are dissolved in tears, or uttering the exclamation of penitence." [8]

But there was always, according to the view, ofttimes exaggerated of course, of the less worldly, another camp meeting only a few hundred yards away being conducted by Satan himself, where, according to Miss Burke, the schoolma'am, the "rowdy element" congregated in another tabernacle "to drink whiskey, smoke cigars, play cards, and steal horses." Miss Burke was convinced that " 'when the sons of God assembled together, Satan came also.' . . . for while the fervent and incessant prayers of the righteous ascended on high like holy incense from within, . . . the curses and blasphemies that were poured forth from the throats of those who had encamped round about this place of prayer and praise, were sufficient to induce one to conclude he must have fallen somewhere near the precincts of the infernal regions." [9]

But Satan's hosts were not invincible; for vigorous preachers like Peter Cartwright frequently invaded the precincts of the devil and, with a good hefty stick to whack young sinners over the back, put the armies of darkness to flight. Simon Peter Richardson, the Methodist presiding elder, scattered such an unholy band at St. Mary's, Georgia, by sheer lung power. Satan's followers were having a ball in the customhouse

[6] *Ibid.*
[7] *Ibid.*
[8] *Ibid.*, 145–46.
[9] Burke, *Reminiscences of Georgia*, 240–41.

only sixty yards from the church and had assured the preacher that they would dance him down. The dance and music had scarcely got under way, however, when Richardson sent one of the assistant preachers to the gallery to stir up the Negroes. As Richardson puts it, they "turned them loose" and their shouting drowned the music of the dance, and the "dancers left in every direction" as if pursued. "When the meeting was over," says Richardson, "we passed the custom house, and all was dark and still." [10]

In turning now to the more earthly folkways, it should be remarked that rural Southerners did not divide their lives into well-separated compartments as do their urban and even rural descendants. They often made little distinction between work and play, for all co-operative work was accompanied by play and was almost invariably followed by a party. A few examples of this co-operative work will be described, such as house-raisings, logrollings, the burning of the woods, and corn shuckings.

When a new family moved into a community and purchased land on which there was no house, or when a home burned or a couple married, it was the custom for the neighbors to gather and build a house for the homeless family or the newly wed couple. This was not just a frontier custom, though it doubtless originated on the frontier, but a rural folkway practiced in many parts of the South as late as World War I. Nor were the houses thus co-operatively raised necessarily of logs as they had been in the frontier days. On the contrary, in a country where the vast pine forests were considered encumbrances and there were numerous small sawmills, plank houses were as often put up as log. If the houses were to be built of planks, the cooperative task would consist chiefly of constructing what was called "the shell"—the framework, the flooring, roof, and weatherboarding. The shell could usually be built in one or two days; and then the family could move in. After that, individual neighbors might contribute two or three days each as the time could be spared, for putting in ceiling, windows, doors, and for the general finishing. More often than not, perhaps, the finishing process was done by the owner of the house, and might extend over a number of years. One room would be ceiled one year and another later. Frequently in the warmer parts of the South nothing but doors, window shutters, a chimney, and stove flue were added after the shell was built. . . .

Perhaps the next co-operative jobs would be a series of logrollings. These affairs usually took place in the late winter and early spring just before spring plowing was begun. In the South, the farmers never cleared their lands by cutting the trees down and removing them, but girdled them with an ax, which would cause them to die very quickly. A crop would then be grown in this "deadening" or "new ground" with no further clearing, for there was seldom any underbrush, because of the habit, first of the Indians and then of the farmers, of burning the woods annually. During the fall and winter the deadened trees would be set

[10] Simon P. Richardson, *Lights and Shadows of Itinerant Life; An Autobiography* (Nashville, 1901), 97, 98.

on fire and many would burn in two, where they had been girdled, and would fall; others would be weakened at this point by fire and would be blown down during the year. In the spring the farmer and his boys and two or three slaves, if he owned any, would cut the branches from the fallen trees and pile them in what was nearly always called a "bresh heap." The logs were then cut into ten- or twelve-foot lengths and the neighbors were invited to a logrolling which would usually be a few days after the invitation was sent out.

On the appointed day the neighbors would gather and proceed to the field. Here they paired off, each pair having a hand stick or hand spike between them. This hand stick, made of a hickory sapling, was about five feet long and three inches in diameter and was tapered at the ends to make it easy to grasp. It was flattened on top to prevent it from turning. From two to four pairs of men with hand sticks were assigned to each piece of log or "cut." The hand sticks were then thrust under the log so that it would rest on the center of the sticks, and at a signal the men stooped down and grasped the ends firmly. Then, at the signal "ready," the men in a squatting position braced themselves, keeping their bodies erect and alert; and at the next signal, such as "heave," "up," or "go," they all lifted in unison, planted their feet firmly, and then walked slowly and often in step, as if marching, to the place designated for the log heap. Here they lowered the log to the ground by squatting, but taking care to keep their backs as erect as possible. The log was then rolled from the hand sticks and the men returned for another log. These men were skilled weight lifters, for it will be observed that the log was actually raised and lowered primarily by leg power. Among these people size and heft and symmetry of muscle made no impression. A man's strength was judged by his lifting power; and ofttimes a man of 140 pounds with no bulging muscles, but with sinews like steel cables, would bring up his end of the hand stick under the "butt cut" of a huge pine, while his 200-pound partner, unable to rise, would have his knuckles buried in the ground under his end of the hand stick. Such feats were called "pulling down," and no logrolling was a success in which some champion did not thus go down.

When the log pile was waist high another would be started, and in this way hundreds of such heaps would be made in a day.

While the men were thus "toting" the logs—not rolling them except to get them off the hand sticks onto the log heap—the mothers and their daughters were cooking dinner and quilting. Ward in his *History of Coffee County, Georgia*, gives some of the chief items of one of these dinners: A sixty-gallon sugar boiler filled with rice, chicken, and fresh pork backbone—a sort of camp stew; a large pot of turnip greens and corn-meal dumplings, served with a boiled ham sliced and laid on top; crackling or shortening bread; Irish potatoes; sweet potatoes; a variety of cakes; two-story biscuits; and, of course, the huge pot of coffee, so strong that it could walk, or float an iron wedge, as these folk would have expressed it. When dinnertime came, a loud and long blast or two on a hunting horn would make the announcement; whereupon all hands would lay aside their hand sticks, dispose of their tobacco cuds, take a few gulps from the jug, and lose no time in getting to the dinner table. The logrolling was usually followed by a square dance, the music for which would be furnished by a fiddler and banjo picker who played such tunes as "One Eyed Gopher" and "Squirrel Gravey" until bribed to play some other dance tune such as the "Arkansas Traveller" and "Turkey in the Straw." [11]

After the logrollings usually came the woods burning. The woods were fired each spring when the leaves and grass had dried sufficiently to burn thoroughly. This was no cabalistic ritual, as a psychologist, employed by the Bureau of Forestry during the leaf-raking era of CWA, suggested to a faculty group at Vanderbilt. It was for the practical purposes of removing dead grass and young underbrush from the cattle range and protecting the rail fences from wildfires set in the forests by careless or mischievous persons. Burning off the woods was always an exciting affair because of the inherently dramatic and fascinating power of fire and because of the actual hazards involved.

Neighbors agreed to fire the woods on a certain date. The first step was to clear a wide strip of leaves and brush near the rail fences, either by raking or burning with a well-controlled fire. In thus creating a firebreak by the use of fire, the men and boys (this was an occasion the boys liked almost as well as Christmas) would arm themselves with long-leaf pine brushes, with which they constantly beat down any unruly flames getting too near the fence or threatening to break loose in the woods. Sometimes, of course, a gust of wind would scatter burning leaves, and like magic a great fire would spring up and go galloping and roaring through the woods. Strategy usually rendered such wild charges harmless. A portion of the men, and probably all the boys, like a good army would rush to the flanks and rear of the forest fire and set backfires which soon met and stemmed the onslaught of the conflagration. When the firebreaks were finished the forest would then be set ablaze. After that men and boys patrolled the fences to extinguish fires set by burning leaves and sparks. Occasionally, however, fire would cunningly and quietly sneak up from an unexpected direction, on the side where there were no firebreaks, and then suddenly charge the lightwood fence, pounce upon it, and devour a hundred panels and, occasionally, a mile before it could be stopped. Sometimes houses, especially barns, were burned in this way, in which case both a house-raising and a rail splitting would be necessary.

Another interesting and exciting custom was the corn shucking. On an appointed night the neighbors gathered in the barn lot and shucked a quantity of corn, sometimes as much as one hundred bushels in an evening. There were evidently several ways of conducting a corn shucking, most of which contained some element of rivalry. Often two captains would be appointed by the host, and each would choose a team.

[11] *Ibid.*, 192–96; Warren P. Ward, *Ward's History of Coffee County, Georgia* (Atlanta, 1930), 159–61; and Timothy H. Ball, *A Glance into the Great South-East; or Clarke County, Alabama and Its Surroundings from 1540 to 1877* (Grove Hill, Ala., 1882), 187; Luke E. Tate, *History of Pickens County, Georgia* (Atlanta, 1935), 63. The older county histories usually contain descriptions of logrollings.

The corn would then be divided into two piles of equal size. Then came the race, the shouting and the singing of corn songs, long ago forgotten. Soon the bottle of brandy or whiskey would be put into circulation, and the tempo of the corn shucking and of the corn songs would be increased. During the evening a few would show their liquor to some extent, though it was considered disgraceful to become intoxicated. The winning team would march around their pile of corn, carrying their captain on their shoulders, singing a corn song of triumph. Sometimes but not often, some disgruntled member of the losing team, who had had too much to drink, would send a well-aimed ear of corn at the exposed head of a member of the rival team, and a fight would promptly follow, in which most would enthusiastically participate. After the corn was shucked came the shucking supper. The following is a partial list of the dishes served at a corn shucking in Rowen County, North Carolina: loaf bread, biscuits, ham, fresh pork, chicken pie, pumpkin custard or pie, apple pie, grape pie, cakes, coffee, sweet milk, buttermilk, and preserves. One type of corn shucking was that in which the young men and girls were the chief participants. The prize went to the boy or girl who found the largest number of red or multicolored ears of corn. The lucky boy could kiss any girl he chose—which would, for policy's sake and other reasons, be the girl he brought to the party. The girl who won the prize could kiss any boy she chose or make any other demand, which had to be fulfilled, even to having some silly oaf jump into a cattle pool. This kind of corn shucking was usually a very hilarious occasion. A great deal of hard work was performed with little feeling of weariness. After the corn was shucked, the supper and dance would inevitably follow, and the party would hardly break up before dawn.

Another type of corn shucking apparently had no element of rivalry in it, but was a co-operative task lightened by corn songs and rhythmic potations of corn liquor. The Reverend George Brewer, who participated in these affairs, has left a description of such a corn shucking. The portion dealing with the corn songs is worth quoting: "There were usually two or more recognized leaders in singing the corn songs, and as they would chant or shout their couplet, all the rest would join in the chorus. There was no poetry or metre, to these songs, but there was a thrill from the melody welling up with such earnestness from the singers that it was so inspiring that the hands would fly with rapidity in tearing off the shucks, and the feet [would] kick back the shucks with equal vigor. The leader would shout:

'Pull off the shucks boys, pull off the shucks,' the crowd [would] shout out in a singing chorus:

'Round up the corn boys, round up the corn'

The leader would then chant:

'The night's getting off boys, the night's getting off'

The crowd would again sing the chorus:

'Round up the corn boys, Round up the corn.'

The leader would chant:

'Give me a dram, sir, Give me a dram.'

The chorus:

'Round up the corn boys, Round up the corn' "

"This singing," says Brewer, "could be heard on a still night 2 miles."

The Reverend further recalled that when the corn was shucked, "The leaders would pick up the owner on their shoulders and carry him several times around the house, followed closely by all the others singing some of their most stirring corn songs, and praising him in their songs. After thus carrying him around in triumph, they would enter the hall-way with him on their shoulders, and seat him in a chair, and with a shuffling dance, go out into the yard. A hearty dram was then given them and they were seated to a rich supper around an improvised table. Negroes and whites enjoyed these shuckings very much . . . [and] there was the best of feeling mutually among them." [12]

The most noteworthy of all co-operative undertakings was the folk custom of taking over and working or gathering the crops of a neighbor who was handicapped by his own illness or that of a member of his family. The fields would be plowed and hoed, and, in the fall, fodder would be pulled and cotton picked or tobacco cut and stripped. The women and girls ofttimes shared equally with the men in such work. Indeed, in stripping tobacco and picking cotton, the girls often excelled the men. This relief work would be done usually by the neighbors con-tributing hoe hands, teams, and plow hands for a certain number of days each. Another method of extending this kind of relief was what was called "swapping work," a custom that still lingers in some communi-ties. The number of days work contributed by each neighbor would be paid back hand for hand, team for team, and day for day at a suitable time. It is probable that most farmers preferred to repay in this fashion rather than accept as a gift the aid which they had received during their illness. It should be observed, however, that "swapping work" was also a community custom practiced as a matter of economy and sociability and in no way connected with illness or hardship cases. For example when a farmer had fully hoed and plowed all his fields, and had several days of idleness in prospect, he and his sons—and his slaves if he had a few—would ofttimes go into a neighbor's fields and "catch him up with his work" as the phrase went. Later, when needed, this work would be repaid. This was putting not money, but work in the bank to be drawn on when it was required.[13]

[12] Jethro Rumple, *A History of Rowan County, North Carolina* (Salisbury, 1881), 172; George E. Brewer, "History of Coosa County, Alabama" (ms. in Alabama Department of Archives and History), 197–200; Nettie Powell, *History of Marion County, Georgia* (Columbus, Ga., 1931), 33; Tate, *History of Pickens County, Georgia*, 63–64, have accounts of corn shuckings.

[13] The writer was well acquainted with this custom and shared in its practice when a boy. According to the old people of the community it was an old, neighborly custom.

Beauty, the Beast and the Militant Woman: A Case Study in Sex Roles and Social Stress in Jacksonian America

CARROLL SMITH-ROSENBERG

By the 1830s, women's roles in America had changed considerably since the days of William Bradford's Plymouth Plantation or John Winthrop's Massachusetts Bay Colony. In the colonial era a woman such as Anne Hutchinson was scourged as a "leper" by the Boston magistrates, not only because she preached a variant form of Puritan theology, but because she dared to preach at all. Women were regarded as intellectually inferior, incapable of instructing others in doctrinal matters. Anne Hutchinson challenged not only the religious teachings of the Massachusetts clergy but also the exclusion of women from traditionally male activities. She was punished for her autonomous behavior by banishment from the colony.

As American society developed in the eighteenth and early nineteenth centuries, women's place in society was enlarged in one way. The function of nurturing and educating children, defined as women's primary role, became invested with new importance by the arbiters of cultural norms. Moreover, the work of child-rearing was left primarily to women. In the nineteenth century, the locus of men's work began to change from the farm, where they had always been in close contact with their wives and children throughout the day, to the factory or the office, where they saw nothing of their families from early morning to evening, six days a week. Domestic authority and responsibility fell more heavily upon women as a consequence of this alteration in the nature of men's work.

But at the same time, women were forced into a narrower sphere of activity, especially if they rose into the middle class. Where once the family had worked together as an economic unit, now the husband was the "breadwinner" and the woman was guardian of the home. As the "cult of domesticity" grew in nineteenth-century America, middle-class women found themselves objects of admiration and praise; but at the same time they were excluded from activities where they had once been important. In a society that heralded individualism, personal autonomy, and an experimental approach to life, the young married woman found herself chained to the hearth. Alexis de Tocqueville, whose observations exposed America to the Americans, put it this way in the 1830s in his extraordinary work **Democracy in America:**

In America the independence of woman is irrecoverably lost in the bonds of matrimony: if an unmarried woman is less constrained there than elsewhere, a wife is subjected to stricter obligations. The former makes her father's house an abode of freedom and of pleasure; the latter lives in the home of her husband as if it were a cloister.

Escaping "the quiet circle of domestic employments," as de Tocqueville put it, became increasingly difficult in the era of "Jacksonian democracy."

It was against this trend that some middle-class women began to revolt in the 1830s. Offended by the prevailing sexual double standard, restricted and alienated in their domestic roles, unwilling to accept the passive existence to which they had been assigned, they began reform movements that were intended to change their own lives as well as society at large. Only a small number of women became actively involved, but what they did and said and wrote touched the lives of many more.

Carroll Smith-Rosenberg's essay takes us into the experiences of a few of these women—those who began the New York Female Reform Society, an organization that hoped to change the attitudes and behavior of both women and men. Through the work of such groups, which proliferated in the antebellum period, the lives of middle-class and lower-class women intersected. The double standard required that middle-class women remain chaste before marriage and virtuous afterward, while allowing men sexual license at all times. But this social arrangement required the availability of lower-class prostitute women, whose sexual service to men permitted upper-class women to remain pure. The Female Reform Society brought the two kinds of women together. Nevertheless, this crossing of paths did not create a sisterhood between middle- and lower-class women, because the reformers offered prostitutes no viable economic alternative to plying their trade.

The antebellum women's movements provide a clear example of conjunction between the private and public sides of life. Many middle-class women, restricted and frustrated in their private domains, sought expanded lives and self-activation in the public sphere. Although operating in the name of religious reform, usually of the evangelical type, they were finding ways, as Smith-Rosenberg writes, "to manifest a discontent with their comparatively passive and constricted social role."

On a spring evening in May 1834, a small group of women met at the revivalist Third Presbyterian Church in New York City to found the New York Female Moral Reform Society. The Society's goals were ambitious indeed; it hoped to convert New York's prostitutes to evangeli-

"Beauty, the Beast and the Militant Woman: A Case Study in Sex Roles and Social Stress in Jacksonian America," by Carroll Smith-Rosenberg. From *American Quarterly* 23 (1971):562–84. Published by the University of Pennsylvania. Copyright, 1971, Trustees of the University of Pennsylvania. Reprinted by permission of the author and the publisher.

cal Protestantism and close forever the city's numerous brothels. This bold attack on prostitution was only one part of the Society's program. These self-assertive women hoped as well to confront that larger and more fundamental abuse, the double standard, and the male sexual license it condoned. Too many men, the Society defiantly asserted in its statement of goals, were aggressive destroyers of female innocence and happiness. No man was above suspicion. Women's only safety lay in a militant effort to reform American sexual mores—and, as we shall see, to reform sexual mores meant in practice to control man's sexual values and autonomy. The rhetoric of the Society's spokesmen consistently betrayed an unmistakable and deeply felt resentment toward a male-dominated society.[1]

Few if any members of the Society were reformed prostitutes or the victims of rape or seduction. Most came from middle-class native American backgrounds and lived quietly respectable lives as pious wives and mothers. What needs explaining is the emotional logic which underlay the Society's militant and controversial program of sexual reform. I would like to suggest that both its reform program and the anti-male sentiments it served to express reflect a neglected area of stress in mid-19th century America—that is, the nature of the role to be assumed by the middle-class American woman.

American society from the 1830s to the 1860s was marked by advances in political democracy, by a rapid increase in economic, social and geographic mobility, and by uncompromising and morally relentless reform movements. Though many aspects of Jacksonianism have been subjected to historical investigation, the possibly stressful effects of such structural change upon family and sex roles have not. The following pages constitute an attempt to glean some understanding of women and women's role in antebellum America through an analysis of a self-consciously female voluntary association dedicated to the eradication of sexual immorality.

Women in Jacksonian America had few rights and little power. Their role in society was passive and sharply limited. Women were, in general, denied formal education above the minimum required by a literate early industrial society. The female brain and nervous system, male physicians and educators agreed, were inadequate to sustained intellectual

---

[1] "Minutes of the Meeting of the Ladies' Society for the Observance of the Seventh Commandment held in Chatham Street Chapel, May 12, 1834," and "Constitution of the New York Female Moral Reform Society," both in ledger book entitled "Constitution and Minutes of the New York Female Moral Reform Society, May, 1834 to July 1839," deposited in the archives of the American Female Guardian Society (hereinafter referred to as A.F.G.S.), Woodycrest Avenue, Bronx, New York. (The Society possesses the executive committee minutes from May 1835–June 1847, and from Jan. 7, 1852–Feb. 18, 1852.) For a more detailed institutional history of the Society see Carroll Smith Rosenberg, *Religion and the Rise of the American City* (Ithaca, N.Y.: Cornell Univ. Press, 1971), chaps. 4 and 7. The New York Female Moral Reform Society changed its name to American Female Guardian Society in 1849. The Society continues today, helping children from broken homes. Its present name is Woodycrest Youth Service.

effort. They were denied the vote in a society which placed a high value upon political participation; political activity might corrupt their pure feminine nature. All professional roles (with the exception of primary school education) were closed to women. Even so traditional a female role as midwife was undermined as male physicians began to establish professional control over obstetrics. Most economic alternatives to marriage (except such burdensome and menial tasks as those of seamstress or domestic) were closed to women. Their property rights were still restricted and females were generally considered to be the legal wards either of the state or of their nearest male relative. In the event of divorce, the mother lost custody of her children—even when the husband was conceded to be the erring party.[2] Women's universe was bounded by their homes and the career of father or husband; within the home it was woman's duty to be submissive and patient.

Yet this was a period when change was considered a self-evident good, and when nothing was believed impossible to a determined free will, be it the conquest of a continent, the reform of society or the eternal salvation of all mankind. The contrast between these generally accepted ideals and expectations and the real possibilities available to American women could not have been more sharply drawn. It is not implausible to assume that at least a minority of American women would find ways to manifest a discontent with their comparatively passive and constricted social role.

Only a few women in antebellum America were able, however, to openly criticize their socially defined sexual identity. A handful, like Fanny Wright, devoted themselves to overtly subversive criticism of the social order.[3] A scarcely more numerous group became pioneers in women's education. Others such as Elizabeth Cady Stanton, Lucretia Mott and Susan B. Anthony founded the women's rights movement. But most respectable women—even those with a sense of ill-defined grievance—were unable to explicitly defy traditional sex-role prescriptions.

I would like to suggest that many such women channeled frustration, anger and a compensatory sense of superior righteousness into the reform movements of the first half of the 19th century; and in the controversial moral reform crusade such motivations seem particularly apparent. While unassailable within the absolute categories of a pervasive evangelical world-view, the Female Moral Reform Society's crusade against illicit sexuality permitted an expression of anti-male sentiments.

---

[2] For a well-balanced though brief discussion of American women's role in antebellum America see Eleanor Flexner, *A Century of Struggle* (Cambridge: Harvard Univ. Press, 1959), chaps. 1–4.

[3] There are two modern biographies of Fanny Wright, both rather thin: W. R. Waterman, *Frances Wright* (New York: Columbia Univ. Press, 1924); Alice J. Perkins, *Frances Wright, Free Enquirer* (New York: Harper & Bros., 1939). Fanny Wright was one of the first women in America to speak about women's rights before large audiences of both men and women. Yet she attracted very few women into the women's rights movement, probably because her economic and political views and her emphatic rejection of Christianity seemed too radical to most American women.

And the Society's "final solution"—the right to control the mores of men—provided a logical emotional redress for those feelings of passivity which we have suggested. It should not be surprising that between 1830 and 1860 a significant number of militant women joined a crusade to establish their right to define—and limit—man's sexual behavior.

Yet adultery and prostitution were unaccustomed objects of reform even in the enthusiastic and millennial America of the 1830s. The mere discussion of these taboo subjects shocked most Americans; to undertake such a crusade implied no ordinary degree of commitment. The founders of the Female Moral Reform Society, however, were able to find both legitimization for the expression of grievance normally unspoken and an impulse to activism in the moral categories of evangelical piety. Both pious activism and sex-role anxieties shaped the early years of the Female Moral Reform Society. This conjunction of motives was hardly accidental.

The lady founders of the Moral Reform Society and their new organization represented an extreme wing of that movement within American Protestantism known as the Second Great Awakening. These women were intensely pious Christians, convinced that an era of millennial perfection awaited human effort. In this fervent generation, such deeply felt millennial possibilities made social action a moral imperative. Like many of the abolitionists, Jacksonian crusaders against sexual transgression were dedicated activists, compelled to attack sin wherever it existed and in whatever form it assumed—even the unmentionable sin of illicit sexuality.

New Yorkers' first awareness of the moral reform crusade came in the spring of 1832 when the New York Magdalen Society (an organization which sought to reform prostitutes) issued its first annual report. Written by John McDowall, their missionary and agent, the report stated unhesitatingly that 10,000 prostitutes lived and worked in New York City. Not only sailors and other transients, but men from the city's most respected families, were regular brothel patrons. Lewdness and impurity tainted all sectors of New York society. True Christians, the report concluded, must wage a thoroughgoing crusade against violators of the Seventh Commandment.[4]

The report shocked and irritated respectable New Yorkers—not only by its tone of righteous indignation and implied criticism of the city's old and established families. The report, it seemed clear to many New Yorkers, was obscene, its author a mere seeker after notoriety.[5]

[4] John R. McDowall, *Magdalen Report*, rpr. *McDowall's Journal*, 2 (May 1834), 33–38. For the history of the New York Magdalen Society see *First Annual Report of the Executive Committee of the New York Magdalen Society, Instituted January 1, 1830*. See as well, Rosenberg, *Religion*, chap. 4.

[5] Flora L. Northrup, *The Record of a Century* (New York: American Female Guardian Soc., 1934), pp. 13–14; cf. *McDowall's Defence*, 1, No. 1 (July 1836), 3; *The Trial of the Reverend John Robert McDowall by the Third Presbytery of New York in February, March, and April, 1836* (New York, 1836). [Thomas Hastings Sr.], *Missionary Labors through a Series of Years among Fallen Women by the New-York Magdalen Society* (New York: N.Y. Magdalen Soc., 1870), p. 15.

Hostility quickly spread from McDowall to the Society itself; its members were verbally abused and threatened with ostracism. The Society disbanded.

A few of the women, however, would not retreat. Working quietly, they began to found church-affiliated female moral reform societies. Within a year, they had created a number of such groups, connected for the most part with the city's more evangelical congregations. These pious women hoped to reform prostitutes, but more immediately to warn other God-fearing Christians of the pervasiveness of sexual sin and the need to oppose it. Prostitution was after all only one of many offenses against the Seventh Commandment; adultery, lewd thoughts and language, and bawdy literature were equally sinful in the eyes of God. These women at the same time continued unofficially to support their former missionary, John McDowall, using his newly established moral reform newspaper to advance their cause not only in the city, but throughout New York State.[6]

After more than a year of such discreet crusading, the women active in the moral reform cause felt sufficiently numerous and confident to organize a second city-wide moral reform society, and renew their efforts to reform the city's prostitutes. On the evening of May 12, 1834, they met at the Third Presbyterian Church to found the New York Female Moral Reform Society.[7]

Nearly four years of opposition and controversy had hardened the women's ardor into a militant determination. They proposed through their organization to extirpate sexual license and the double standard from American society. A forthright list of resolves announced their organization:

> Resolved, That immediate and vigorous efforts should be made to create a public sentiment in respect to this sin; and also in respect to the duty of parents, church members and ministers on the subject, which shall be in stricter accordance with . . . the word of God.
>
> . . . .
>
> Resolved, That the licentious man is no less guilty than his victim, and ought, therefore, to be excluded from all virtuous female society.
>
> Resolved, That it is the imperious duty of ladies everywhere, and of every religious denomination, to co-operate in the great work of moral reform.

[6] Northrup, *Record of a Century*, pp. 14–15; only two volumes of *McDowall's Journal* were published, covering the period Jan. 1833 to Dec. 1834. Between the demise of the New York Magdalen Society and the organization of the New York Female Moral Reform Society (hereinafter, N.Y.F.M.R.S.), McDowall was connected, as agent, with a third society, the New York Female Benevolent Society, which he had helped found in February of 1833. For a more detailed account see Carroll S. Rosenberg, "Evangelicalism and the New City," Ph.D. Diss. Columbia University, 1968, chap. 5.

[7] *McDowall's Journal*, 2 (Jan. 1834), 6–7.

A sense of urgency and spiritual absolutism marked this organizational meeting, and indeed all of the Society's official statements for years to come. "It is the duty of the virtuous to use every consistent moral means to save our country from utter destruction," the women warned. "The sin of licentiousness has made fearful havoc . . . drowning souls in perdition and exposing us to the vengeance of a holy God." Americans hopeful of witnessing the promised millennium could delay no longer.[8]

The motivating zeal which allowed the rejection of age-old proprieties and defied the criticism of pulpit and press was no casual and fashionable enthusiasm. Only an extraordinary set of legitimating values could have justified such commitment. And this was indeed the case. The women moral reformers acted in the conscious conviction that God imperiously commanded their work. As they explained soon after organizing their society: "As Christians we must view it in the light of God's word—we must enter into His feelings on the subject—engage in its overthrow just in the manner he would have us. . . . We must look away from all worldly opinions or influences, for they are perverted and wrong; and individually act only as in the presence of God." [9] Though the Society's pious activism had deep roots in the evangelicalism of the Second Great Awakening, the immediate impetus for the founding of the Moral Reform Society came from the revivals Charles G. Finney conducted in New York City between the summer of 1829 and the spring of 1834.[10]

Charles Finney, reformer, revivalist and perfectionist theologian from western New York State, remains a pivotal figure in the history of American Protestantism. The four years Finney spent in New York had a profound influence on the city's churches and reform movements, and upon the consciences generally of the thousands of New Yorkers who crowded his revival meetings and flocked to his churches. Finney insisted that his disciples end any compromise with sin or human injustice. Souls were lost and sin prevailed, Finney urged, because men chose to sin—

[8] "Minutes of the Meeting of the Ladies' Society for the Observance of the Seventh Commandment . . . May 12, 1834," and "Preamble," "Constitution of the New York Female Moral Reform Society."

[9] *Advocate of Moral Reform* (hereinafter, *Advocate*) 1 (Jan.–Feb. 1835), 6. The *Advocate* was the Society's official journal.

[10] Close ties connected the N.Y.F.M.R.S. with the Finney wing of American Protestantism. Finney's wife was the Society's first president. The Society's second president, Mrs. William Green, was the wife of one of Finney's closest supporters. The Society's clerical support in New York City came from Finney's disciples. Their chief financial advisers and initial sponsors were Arthur and Lewis Tappan, New York merchants who were also Charles Finney's chief financial supporters. For a list of early "male advisers" to the N.Y.F.M.R.S. see Joshua Leavitt, *Memoir and Select Remains of the Late Reverend John R. McDowall* (New York: Joshua Leavitt, Lord, 1838), p. 248, also pp. 99, 151, 192. See as well L. Nelson Nichols and Allen Knight Chalmers, *History of the Broadway Tabernacle of New York City* (New Haven: Tuttle, Morehouse & Taylor, 1940), pp. 49–67, and William G. McLoughlin Jr., *Modern Revivalism* (New York: Ronald Press, 1959), pp. 50–53.

because they chose not to work in God's vineyard converting souls and reforming sinners.[11] Inspired by Finney's sermons, thousands of New Yorkers turned to missionary work; they distributed Bibles and tracts to the irreligious, established Sunday schools and sent ministers to the frontier.[12] A smaller, more zealous number espoused abolition as well, determined, like Garrison, never to be silent and to be heard. An even smaller number of the most zealous and determined turned—as we have seen— to moral reform.[13]

The program adopted by the Female Moral Reform Society in the spring of 1834 embraced two quite different, though to the Society's founders quite consistent, modes of attack. One was absolutist and millennial, an attempt to convert all of America to perfect moral purity. Concretely the New York women hoped to create a militant nationwide women's organization to fight the double standard and indeed any form of licentiousness—beginning of course in their own homes and neighborhoods. Only an organization of women, they contended, could be trusted with so sensitive and yet monumental a task. At the same time, the Society sponsored a parallel and somewhat more pragmatic attempt to convert and reform New York City's prostitutes. Though strikingly dissimilar in method and geographic scope, both efforts were unified by an uncompromising millennial zeal and by a strident hostility to the licentious and predatory male.

The Society began its renewed drive against prostitution in the fall of 1834 when the executive committee appointed John McDowall their missionary to New York's prostitutes and hired two young men to assist him.[14] The Society's three missionaries visited the female wards of the almshouse, the city hospital and jails, leading prayer meetings, distributing Bibles and tracts. A greater proportion of their time, however, was spent in a more controversial manner, systematically visiting—or, to be more accurate, descending upon—brothels, praying with and exhorting both the inmates and their patrons. The missionaries were specially fond of arriving early Sunday morning—catching women and customers as they awoke on the traditionally sacred day. The missionaries would

---

11 For an excellent modern analysis of Finney's theology and his place in American Protestantism see McLoughlin, *Modern Revivalism*. McLoughlin has as well edited Finney's series of New York Revivals which were first published in 1835. Charles Grandison Finney, *Lectures on Revivals of Religion*, ed. William G. McLoughlin (Cambridge: Harvard Univ. Press, 1960). McLoughlin's introduction is excellent.

12 Rosenberg, *Religion*, chaps. 2 and 3.

13 These reforms were by no means mutually exclusive. Indeed there was a logical and emotional interrelation between evangelical Protestantism and its missionary aspects and such formally secular reforms as peace, abolition and temperance. The interrelation is demonstrated in the lives of such reformers as the Tappan brothers, the Grimké sisters, Theodore Dwight Weld, Charles Finney and in the overlapping membership of the many religious and "secular" reform societies of the Jacksonian period. On the other hand, the overlap was not absolute, some reformers rejecting evangelical Protestantism, others pietism, or another of the period's reforms.

14 *Advocate*, 1 (Jan.–Feb. 1835), 4; Northrup, *Record*, p. 19.

announce their arrival by a vigorous reading of Bible passages, followed
by prayer and hymns. At other times they would station themselves
across the street from known brothels to observe and note the identity
of customers. They soon found their simple presence had an important
deterring effect, many men, with doggedly innocent expressions, pausing momentarily and then hastily walking past. Closed coaches, they also
reported, were observed to circle suspiciously for upwards of an hour
until, the missionary remaining, they drove away.[15]

The Female Moral Reform Society did not depend completely on
paid missionaries for the success of such pious harassment. The Society's
executive committee, accompanied by like-thinking male volunteers,
regularly visisted the city's hapless brothels. (The executive committee
minutes for January 1835, for example, contain a lengthy discussion of
the properly discreet makeup of groups for such "active visiting.")[16]
The members went primarily to pray and to exert moral influence. They
were not unaware, however, of the financially disruptive effect that frequent visits of large groups of praying Christians would have.[17] The
executive committee also aided the concerned parents (usually rural) of
runaway daughters who, they feared, might have drifted to the city and
been forced into prostitution. Members visited brothels asking for information about such girls; one pious volunteer even pretended to be
delivering laundry in order to gain admittance to a brothel suspected of
hiding such a runaway.[18]

In conjunction with their visiting, the Moral Reform Society opened
a House of Reception, a would-be refuge for prostitutes seeking to reform. The Society's managers and missionaries felt that if the prostitute
could be convinced of her sin, and then offered both a place of retreat
and an economic alternative to prostitution, reform would surely follow.
Thus they envisioned their home as a "house of industry" where the
errant ones would be taught new trades and prepared for useful jobs—
while being instructed in morality and religion. When the managers felt
their repentant charges prepared to return to society, they attempted to
find them jobs with Christian families—and, so far as possible, away
from the city's temptations.[19]

Despite their efforts, however, few prostitutes reformed; fewer still
appeared, to their benefactresses, to have experienced the saving grace of
conversion. Indeed, the number of inmates at the Society's House of
Reception was always small. In March 1835, for instance, the executive
committee reported only fourteen women at the House. A year later,

---

[15] *Advocate*, 1 (Mar. 1835), 11–12; 1 (Nov. 1835), 86; N.Y.F.M.R.S., "Executive
Committee Minutes, June 6, 1835 and April 30, 1836." These pious visitors received
their most polite receptions at the more expensive houses, while the girls and customers of lower-class, slum brothels met them almost uniformly with curses and
threats.

[16] N.Y.F.M.R.S., "Executive Committee Minutes, Jan. 24, 1835."

[17] *Advocate*, 1 (Jan.–Feb. 1835), 7.

[18] For a description of one such incident see *Advocate*, 4 (Jan. 15, 1838), 15.

[19] *Advocate*, 1 (Sept. 1, 1835), 72; Northrup, *Record*, p. 19.

total admissions had reached but thirty—only four of whom were considered saved.[20] The final debacle came that summer when the regular manager of the House left the city because of poor health. In his absence, the executive committee reported unhappily, the inmates seized control, and discipline and morality deteriorated precipitously. The managers reassembled in the fall to find their home in chaos. Bitterly discouraged, they dismissed the few remaining unruly inmates and closed the building.[21]

The moral rehabilitation of New York's streetwalkers was but one aspect of the Society's attack upon immorality. The founders of the Female Moral Reform Society saw as their principal objective the creation of a woman's crusade to combat sexual license generally and the double standard particularly. American women would no longer willingly tolerate that traditional—and role-defining—masculine ethos which allotted respect to the hearty drinker and the sexual athlete. This age-old code of masculinity was as obviously related to man's social preeminence as it was contrary to society's explicitly avowed norms of purity and domesticity. The subterranean mores of the American male must be confronted, exposed and rooted out.

The principal weapon of the Society in this crusade was its weekly, *The Advocate of Moral Reform*. In the fall of 1834, when the Society hired John McDowall as its agent, it voted as well to purchase his journal and transform it into a national women's paper with an exclusively female staff. Within three years, the *Advocate* grew into one of the nation's most widely read evangelical papers, boasting 16,500 subscribers. By the late 1830s the Society's managers pointed to this publication as their most important activity.[22]

Two themes dominated virtually every issue of the *Advocate* from its founding in January 1835, until the early 1850s. The first was an angry and emphatic insistence upon the lascivious and predatory nature of the American male. Men were the initiators in virtually every case of adultery or fornication—and the source, therefore, of that widespread immorality which endangered America's spiritual life and delayed the promised millennium. A second major theme in the *Advocate's* editorials and letters was a call for the creation of a national union of women. Through their collective action such a united group of women might ultimately control the behavior of adult males and of the members' own children, particularly their sons.

The founders and supporters of the Female Moral Reform Society entertained several primary assumptions concerning the nature of human sexuality. Perhaps most central was the conviction that women felt little

[20] *Advocate*, 1 (Mar. 1835), 11; N.Y.F.M.R.S., "Executive Committee Minutes, Apr. 5, 1836, May 30, 1835."

[21] N.Y.F.M.R.S., "Executive Committee Minutes, Oct. 4, 1836."

[22] N.Y.F.M.R.S., "Executive Committee Minutes, June 6 and June 25, 1835, June (n.d.), 1836"; N.Y.F.M.R.S., *The Guardian or Fourth Annual Report of the New York Female Moral Reform Society presented May 9, 1838*, pp. 4–6.

sexual desire; they were in almost every instance induced to violate the Seventh Commandment by lascivious men who craftily manipulated not their sensuality, but rather the female's trusting and affectionate nature. A woman acted out of romantic love, not carnal desire; she was innocent and defenseless, gentle and passive.[23] "The worst crime alleged against [the fallen woman] in the outset," the *Advocate's* editors explained, "is . . . 'She is without discretion.' She is open-hearted, sincere, and affectionate. . . . She trusts the vows of the faithless. She commits her all into the hands of the deceiver." [24]

The male lecher, on the other hand, was a creature controlled by base sexual drives which he neither could nor would control. He was, the *Advocate's* editors bitterly complained, powerful and decisive; unwilling (possibly unable) to curb his own willfulness, he callously used it to coerce the more passive and submissive female. This was an age of rhetorical expansiveness, and the *Advocate's* editors and correspondents felt little constraint in their delineation of the dominant and aggressive male. "Reckless," "bold," "mad," "drenched in sin" were terms used commonly to describe erring males; they "robbed," "ruined" and "rioted." But one term above all others seemed most fit to describe the lecher—"The Destroyer." [25]

A deep sense of anger and frustration characterized the *Advocate's* discussion of such all-conquering males, a theme reiterated again and again in the letters sent to the paper by rural sympathizers. Women saw themselves with few defenses against the determined male; his will was far stronger than that of woman.[26] Such letters often expressed a bitterness which seems directed not only against the specific seducer, but toward all American men. One representative rural subscriber complained, for example: "Honorable men; they would not plunder; . . . an imputation on their honour might cost a man his life's blood. And yet they are so passingly mean, so utterly contemptible, as basely and treacherously to contrive . . . the destruction of happiness, peace, morality, and all that is endearing in social life; they plunge into degradation, misery, and ruin, those whom they profess to love. O let them not be trusted. Their 'tender mercies are cruel.' " [27]

The double standard seemed thus particularly unjust; it came to symbolize and embody for the Society and its rural sympathizers the callous indifference—indeed at times almost sadistic pleasure—a male-

---

23 "Budding," "lovely," "fresh," "joyous," "unsuspecting lamb," were frequent terms used to describe innocent women before their seduction. The *Advocate* contained innumerable letters and editorials on this theme. See, for example, *Advocate,* 4 (Jan. 1, 1838), 1; *Advocate,* 10 (Mar. 1, 1844), 34; *Advocate and Guardian* (the Society changed the name of its journal in 1847), 16 (Jan. 1, 1850), 3.

24 Letter in *Advocate,* 1 (Apr. 1835), 19.

25 "Murderer of Virtue" was another favorite and pithy phrase. For a sample of such references see: *Advocate,* 4 (Feb. 1, 1838), 17; *Advocate,* 10 (Jan. 1, 1844), 19–20; *Advocate,* 10 (Jan. 15, 1844), 29; *Advocate,* 10 (Mar. 1, 1844), 33.

26 *Advocate,* 1 (Jan.–Feb. 1835), 3; *Advocate,* 1 (Apr. 1835), 19; *Advocate. and Guardian,* 16 (Jan. 1, 1850), 3.

27 Letter in *McDowall's Journal,* 2 (Apr. 1834), 26–27.

dominated society took in the misfortune of a passive and defenseless woman. The respectable harshly denied her their friendship; even parents might reject her. Often only the brothel offered food and shelter. But what of her seducer? Conventional wisdom found it easy to condone his greater sin: men will be men and right-thinking women must not inquire into such questionable matters.[28]

But it was just such matters, the Society contended, to which women must address themselves. They must enforce God's commandments despite hostility and censure. "Public opinion must be operated upon," the executive committee decided in the winter of 1835, "by endeavoring to bring the virtuous to treat the guilty of both sexes alike, and exercise toward them the same feeling." "Why should a female be trodden under foot," the executive committee's minutes questioned plaintively, "and spurned from society and driven from a parent's roof, if she but fall into sin—while common consent allows the male to habituate himself to this vice, and treats him as not guilty. Has God made a distinction in regard to the two sexes in this respect?" [29] The guilty woman too should be condemned, the Moral Reform Society's quarterly meeting resolved in 1838: "But let not the most guilty of the two—the deliberate destroyer of innocence—be afforded even an 'apron of fig leaves' to conceal the blackness of his crimes." [30]

Women must unite in a holy crusade against such sinners. The Society called upon pious women throughout the country to shun all social contact with men suspected of improper behavior—even if that behavior consisted only of reading improper books or singing indelicate songs. Churchgoing women of every village and town must organize local campaigns to outlaw such men from society and hold them up to public judgment.[31] "Admit him not to your house," the executive committee urged, "hold no converse with him, warn others of him, permit not your friends to have fellowship with him, mark as an evildoer, stamp him as a villain and exclaim, 'Behold the Seducer.' " The power of ostracism could become an effective weapon in the defense of morality.[32]

A key tactic in this campaign of public exposure was the Society's willingness to publish the names of men suspected of sexual immorality. The *Advocate's* editors announced in their first issue that they intended to pursue this policy, first begun by John McDowall in his *Journal.*[33]

---

[28] Many subscribers wrote to the *Advocate* complaining of the injustice of the double standard. See, for example: *Advocate*, 1 (Apr. 1835), 22; *Advocate*, 1 (Dec. 1835), 91; *Advocate and Guardian*, 16 (Jan. 1, 1850), 5.

[29] *Advocate*, 1 (Jan.–Feb. 1835), 6–7.

[30] Resolution passed at the Quarterly Meeting of the N.Y.F.M.R.S., Jan. 1838, printed in *Advocate*, 4 (Jan. 15, 1838), 14.

[31] This was one of the more important functions of the auxiliaries, and their members uniformly pledged themselves to ostracize all offending males. For an example of such pledges see *Advocate*, 4 (Jan. 15, 1838), 16.

[32] *Advocate and Guardian*, 16 (Jan. 1, 1850), 3.

[33] McDowall urged his rural subscribers to report any instances of seduction. He dutifully printed all the details, referring to the accused man by initials, but otherwise giving the names of towns, counties and dates. Male response was on occasion bitter.

"We think it proper," they stated defiantly, "even to expose names, for the same reason that the names of thieves and robbers are published, that the public may know them and govern themselves accordingly. We mean to let the licentious know, that if they are not ashamed of their debasing vice, we will not be ashamed to expose them. . . . It is a justice which we owe each other." [34] Their readers responded enthusiastically to this invitation. Letters from rural subscribers poured into the *Advocate*, recounting specific instances of seduction in their towns and warning readers to avoid the men described. The editors dutifully set them in type and printed them. [35]

Within New York City itself the executive committee of the Society actively investigated charges of seduction and immorality. A particular target of their watchfulness was the city's employment agencies —or information offices as they were then called; these were frequently fronts for the white-slave trade. The *Advocate* printed the names and addresses of suspicious agencies, warning women seeking employment to avoid them at all costs. [36] Prostitutes whom the Society's missionaries visited in brothels, in prison or in the city hospital were urged to report the names of men who had first seduced them and also of their later customers; they could then be published in the *Advocate*. [37] The executive committee undertook as well a lobbying campaign in Albany to secure the passage of a statute making seduction a crime for the male participant. [38] While awaiting the passage of this measure, the executive committee encouraged and aided victims of seduction (or where appropriate their parents or employers) to sue their seducers on the grounds of loss of services. [39]

Ostracism, exposure and statutory enactment offered immediate, if unfortunately partial, solutions to the problem of male licentiousness. But for the seduced and ruined victim such vengeance came too late. The tactic of preference, women moral reformers agreed, was to educate children, especially young male children, to a literal adherence to the Seventh Commandment. This was a mother's task. American mothers, the *Advocate's* editors repeated endlessly, must educate their sons to re-

[34] *Advocate*, 1 (Jan.–Feb. 1835), 2.

[35] Throughout the 1830s virtually every issue of the *Advocate* contained such letters. The *Advocate* continued to publish them throughout the 1840s.

[36] For detailed discussions of particular employment agencies and the decision to print their names see: N.Y.F.M.R.S., "Executive Committee Minutes, Feb. 12, 1845, July 8, 1846."

[37] N.Y.F.M.R.S., "Executive Committee Minutes, Mar. 1, 1838, Mar. 15, 1838"; *Advocate*, 4 (Jan. 15, 1838), 15.

[38] The Society appears to have begun its lobbying crusade in 1838. N.Y.F.M.R.S., "Executive Committee Minutes, Oct. 24, 1838, Jan. 4, 1842, Feb. 18, 1842, Apr. 25, 1844, Jan. 8, 1845"; American Female Moral Reform Society (the Society adopted this name in 1839), *Tenth Annual Report for . . . 1844*, pp. 9–11; American Female Moral Reform Soc., *Fourteenth Annual Report for . . . 1848*.

[39] The N.Y.F.M.R.S.'s Executive Committee Minutes for the years 1837, 1838, 1843 and 1844 especially are filled with instances of the committee instituting suits against seducers for damages in the case of loss of services.

ject the double standard. No child was too young, no efforts too diligent in this crucial aspect of socialization.[40] The true foundations of such a successful effort lay in an early and highly pietistic religious education and in the inculcation of a related imperative—the son's absolute and unquestioned obedience to his mother's will. "Obedience, entire and un-questioned, must be secured, or all is lost." The mother must devote herself whole-heartedly to this task for self-will in a child was an ever-recurring evil.[41] "Let us watch over them continually. . . . Let us . . . teach them when they go out and when they come in—when they lie down, and when they rise up. . . ."[42] A son must learn to confide in his mother instinctively; no thought should be hidden from her.

Explicit education in the Seventh Commandment itself should begin quite early for bitter experience had shown that no child was too young for such sensual temptation.[43] As her son grew older, his mother was urged to instill in him a love for the quiet of domesticity, a repugnance for the unnatural excitements of the theater and tavern. He should be taught to prefer home and the companionship of pious women to the temptations of bachelor life.[44] The final step in a young man's moral edu-cation would come one evening shortly before he was to leave home for the first time. That night, the *Advocate* advised its readers, the mother must spend a long earnest time at his bedside (ordinarily in the dark to hide her natural blushes) discussing the importance of maintaining his sexual purity and the temptations he would inevitably face in attempting to remain true to his mother's religious principles.[45]

Mothers, not fathers, were urged to supervise the sexual education of sons. Mothers, the Society argued, spent most time with their chil-dren; fathers were usually occupied with business concerns and found little time for their children. Sons were naturally close to their mothers and devoted maternal supervision would cement these natural ties. A mother devoted to the moral reform cause could be trusted to teach her son to reject the traditional ethos of masculinity and accept the higher —more feminine—code of Christianity. A son thus educated would be inevitably a recruit in the women's crusade against sexual license.[46]

The Society's general program of exposure and ostracism, lobbying and education depended for effectiveness upon the creation of a national association of militant and pious women. In the fall of 1834, but a few

[40] *Advocate,* 1 (Jan.–Feb. 1835), 6–7; 4 (Jan. 1, 1838), 1.

[41] *Advocate,* 10 (Feb. 1, 1844), 17–18; *Advocate and Guardian,* 16 (Jan. 1, 1850), 3–4.

[42] *Advocate,* 10 (Jan. 1, 1844), 7–8.

[43] *Advocate,* 2 (Jan. 1836), 3; *Advocate,* 4 (Jan. 15, 1838), 13.

[44] *Advocate,* 4 (Jan. 1, 1838), 1–2; *Advocate,* 10 (Feb. 15, 1844), 26; *Advocate and Guardian,* 16 (Jan. 15, 1850), 15.

[45] *Advocate,* 1 (Jan.–Feb. 1835), 5–6.

[46] An editorial in the *Advocate* typified the Society's emphasis on the importance of child rearing and religious education as an exclusively maternal role. "To a mother.—You have a child on your knee. . . . It is an immortal being; destined to live forever! . . . And who is to make it happy or miserable? You—the mother! You who gave it birth, the mother of its body, . . . its destiny is placed in your hands" (*Advocate,* 10 [Jan. 1, 1844], 8).

months after they had organized their Society, its New York officers
began to create such a woman's organization. At first they worked
through the *Advocate* and the small network of sympathizers John Mc-
Dowall's efforts had created. By the spring of 1835, however, they were
able to hire a minister to travel through western New York State "in
behalf of Moral Reform causes." [47] The following year the committee
sent two female missionaries, the editor of the Society's newspaper and
a paid female agent, on a thousand-mile tour of the New England states.
Visiting women's groups and churches in Brattleboro, Deerfield,
Northampton, Pittsfield, the Stockbridges and many other towns, the
ladies rallied their sisters to the moral reform cause and helped organize
some forty-one new auxiliaries. Each succeeding summer saw similar
trips by paid agents and managers of the Society throughout New York
State and New England.[48] By 1839, the New York Female Moral Reform Society boasted some 445 female auxiliaries, principally in greater
New England.[49] So successful were these efforts that within a few years
the bulk of the Society's membership and financial support came from
its auxiliaries. In February 1838, the executive committee voted to invite
representatives of these auxiliaries to attend the Society's annual meeting.
The following year the New York Society voted at its annual convention to reorganize as a national society—the American Female Moral
Reform Society; the New York group would be simply one of its many
constituent societies.[50]

This rural support was an indispensable part of the moral reform
movement. The local auxiliaries held regular meetings in churches, persuaded hesitant ministers to preach on the Seventh Commandment, urged
Sunday school teachers to confront this embarrassing but vital question.
They raised money for the executive committee's ambitious projects,
convinced at least some men to form male moral reform societies, and
did their utmost to ostracize suspected lechers. When the American Female Moral Reform Society decided to mount a campaign to induce the
New York State legislature to pass a law making seduction a criminal offense, the Society's hundreds of rural auxiliaries wrote regularly to their
legislators, circulated petitions and joined their New York City sisters in
Albany to lobby for the bill (which was finally passed in 1848).[51]

[47] N.Y.F.M.R.S., "Executive Committee Minutes, June 25, 1835."
[48] N.Y.F.M.R.S., "Executive Committee Minutes, Oct. 4, 1836, and May 22, 1837, and
Sept. 11, 1839." Indeed, as early as 1833 a substantial portion of John McDowall's
support seemed to come from rural areas. See, for example, *McDowall's Journal*, 1
(Aug. 1833), 59–62.
[49] N.Y.F.M.R.S., "Executive Committee Minutes, Oct. 4, 1838"; Northrup, *Record*,
p. 22.
[50] N.Y.F.M.R.S., "Executive Committee Minutes, May 10, 1839"; N.Y.F.M.R.S.,
"Quarterly Meeting, July, 1839." Power within the new national organization was
divided so that the president and the board of managers were members of the
N.Y.F.M.R.S. while the vice-presidents were chosen from the rural auxiliaries. The
annual meeting was held in New York City, the quarterly meetings in one of the
towns of Greater New England.
[51] Virtually every issue of the *Advocate* is filled with letters and reports from the
auxiliaries discussing their many activities.

In addition to such financial and practical aid, members of the moral reform society's rural branches contributed another crucial, if less tangible, element to the reform movement. This was their commitment to the creation of a feeling of sisterhood among all morally dedicated women. Letters from individuals to the *Advocate* and reports from auxiliaries make clear, sometimes even in the most explicit terms, that many American women experienced a depressing sense of isolation. In part, this feeling merely reflected a physical reality for women living in rural communities. But since city- and town-dwelling women voiced similar complaints, I would like to suggest that this consciousness of isolation also reflected a sense of status inferiority. Confined by their non-maleness, antebellum American women lived within the concentric structure of a family organized around the needs and status of husbands or fathers. And such social isolation within the family—or perhaps more accurately a lack of autonomy both embodied in and symbolized by such isolation—not only dramatized, but partially constituted, a differentiation in status.[52] The fact that social values and attitudes were established by men and oriented to male experiences only exacerbated women's feelings of inferiority and irrelevance. Again and again the Society's members were to express their desire for a feminine-sororial community which might help break down this isolation, lighten the monotony and harshness of life, and establish a countersystem of female values and priorities.

The New York Female Moral Reform Society quite consciously sought to inspire in its members a sense of solidarity in a cause peculiar to their sex, and demanding total commitment, to give them a sense of worthiness and autonomy outside woman's traditionally confining role. Its members, their officers forcefully declared, formed a united phalanx twenty thousand strong, "A UNION OF SENTIMENT AND EFFORT AMONG . . . VIRTUOUS FEMALES FROM MAINE TO ALABAMA." [53] The officers of the New York Society were particularly conscious of the emotional importance of female solidarity within their movement—and the significant role that they as leaders played in the lives of their rural supporters. "Thousands are looking to us," the executive committee recorded in their minutes with mingled pride and responsibility, "with the expectation that the

---

[52] The view that many women held of their role is perhaps captured in the remarks of an editorialist in the *Advocate* in 1850. Motherhood was unquestionably the most correct and important role for women. But it was a very hard role. "In their [mothers'] daily rounds of duty they may move in a retired sphere—secluded from public observation, oppressed with many cares and toils, and sometimes tempted to view their position as being adverse to the highest usefulness. The youthful group around them tax their energies to the utmost limit—the wants of each and all . . . must be watched with sleepless vigilance; improvement is perhaps less marked and rapid than is ardently desired. . . . Patience is tried, faith called into exercise; and all the graces of the Spirit demanded, to maintain equanimity and exhibit a right example. And *such* with all its weight of care and responsibility is the post at which God in his providence has placed the mothers of our land." The ultimate reward of motherhood which the writer held out to her readers, significantly, was that they would be the ones to shape the character of their children. *Advocate and Guardian*, 16 (Jan. 15, 1850), 13.

[53] N.Y.F.M.R.S., *Guardian*, p. 8.

principles we have adopted, and the example we have set before the world will continue to be held up & they reasonably expect to witness our *united onward* movements till the conflict shall end in Victory." [54]

For many of the Society's scattered members, the moral reform cause was their only contact with the world outside farm or village— the *Advocate* perhaps the only newspaper received by the family.[55] A sense of solidarity and of emotional affiliation permeated the correspondence between rural members and the executive committee. Letters and even official reports inevitably began with the salutation, "Sisters," "Dear Sisters" or "Beloved Sisters." Almost every letter and report expressed the deep affection Society members felt for their like-thinking sisters in the cause of moral reform—even if their contact came only through letters and the *Advocate.* "I now pray and will not cease to pray," a woman in Syracuse, New York, wrote, "that your hearts may be encouraged and your hands strengthened." [56] Letters to the Society's executive committee often promised unfailing loyalty and friendship; members and leaders pledged themselves ever ready to aid either local societies or an individual sister in need.[57] Many letters from geographically isolated women reported that the Society made it possible for them for the first time to communicate with like-minded women. A few, in agitated terms, wrote about painful experiences with the double standard which only their correspondence with the *Advocate* allowed them to express and share.[58]

Most significantly, the letters expressed a new consciousness of power. The moral reform society was based on the assertion of female moral superiority and the right and ability of women to reshape male behavior.[59] No longer did women have to remain passive and isolated

---

[54] N.Y.F.M.R.S., "Executive Committee Minutes, Oct. 24, 1836."

[55] See two letters, for example, to the *Advocate* from rural subscribers. Although written fifteen years apart and from quite different geographic areas (the first from Hartford, Conn., the second from Jefferson, Ill.), the sentiments expressed are remarkably similar. Letter in *Advocate*, 1 (Apr. 1835), 19; *Advocate and Guardian*, 16 (Jan. 15, 1850), 14.

[56] Letter in *Advocate*, 4 (Jan. 1, 1838), 6.

[57] Letters and reports from rural supporters expressing such sentiments dotted every issue of the *Advocate* from its founding until the mid-1850s.

[58] The editors of the *Advocate* not infrequently received (and printed) letters from rural subscribers reporting painfully how some young woman in their family had suffered social censure and ostracism because of the machinations of some lecher— who emerged from the affair with his respectability unblemished. This letter to the *Advocate* was the first time they could express the anguish and anger they felt. For one particularly pertinent example see an anonymous letter to the *Advocate*, 1 (Mar. 1835), 15–16.

[59] N.Y.F.M.R.S., "Executive Committee Minutes, Oct. 4, 1836"; *Advocate*, 1 (Apr. 1835), 19–20; *Advocate*, 3 (Jan. 15, 1837), 194; *Advocate*, 4 (Jan. 1, 1838), 5, 7–8; *Advocate*, 4 (Apr. 1838), 6–7. An integral part of this expression of power was the women's insistence that they had the right to investigate male sexual practices and norms. No longer would they permit men to tell them that particular questions were improper for women's consideration. See for example, N.Y.F.M.R.S.,

within the structuring presence of husband or father. The moral reform movement was, perhaps for the first time, a movement within which women could forge a sense of their own identity.

And its founders had no intention of relinquishing their new-found feeling of solidarity and autonomy. A few years after the Society was founded, for example, a group of male evangelicals established a Seventh Commandment Society. They promptly wrote to the Female Moral Reform Society suggesting helpfully that since men had organized, the ladies could now disband; moral reform was clearly an area of questionable propriety. The New York executive committee responded quickly, firmly—and negatively. Women throughout America, they wrote, had placed their trust in a female moral reform society and in female officers. Women, they informed the men, believed in both their own right and ability to combat the problem; it was decidedly a woman's, not a man's issue.[60] "The paper is now in the right hands," one rural subscriber wrote: "This is the appropriate work for *women.* . . . Go on Ladies, go on, in the strength of the Lord." [61]

In some ways, indeed, the New York Female Moral Reform Society could be considered a militant woman's organization. Although it was not overtly part of the woman's rights movement, it did concern itself with a number of feminist issues, especially those relating to woman's economic role. Society, the *Advocate's* editors argued, had unjustly confined women to domestic tasks. There were many jobs in society that women could and should be trained to fill. They could perform any light indoor work as well as men. In such positions—as clerks and artisans—they would receive decent wages and consequent self-respect.[62] And this economic emphasis was no arbitrary or inappropriate one, the Society contended. Thousands of women simply had to work; widows, orphaned young women, wives and mothers whose husbands could not work because of illness or intemperance had to support themselves and their children. Unfortunately, they had now to exercise these responsibilities on the pathetically inadequate salaries they received as domestics, washerwomen or seamstresses—crowded, underpaid and physically unpleasant occupations.[63] By the end of the 1840s, the Society had adopted the cause of the working woman and made it one of their principal concerns—in the 1850s even urging women to join unions and, when

---

"Circular to the Women of the United States," rpr. in *Advocate,* 1 (Jan.–Feb. 1835), 6–7, 4.

[60] N.Y.F.M.R.S., "Executive Committee Minutes, June 28, 1837."

[61] Letter in *Advocate,* 1 (Apr. 1835), 19.

[62] *Advocate and Guardian,* 16 (Jan. 15, 1850), 9.

[63] *Advocate,* 1 (May 1835), 38; N.Y.F.M.R.S., *Guardian,* pp. 5–6. The Society initially became concerned with the problems of the city's poor and working women as a result of efforts to attack some of the economic causes of prostitution. The Society feared that the low wages paid seamstresses, domestics or washerwomen (New York's three traditional female occupations) might force otherwise moral women to turn to prostitution. The Society was, for example, among the earliest critics of the low wages and bad working conditions of New York's garment industry.

mechanization came to the garment industry, helping underpaid seamstresses rent sewing machines at low rates.[64]

The Society sought consciously, moreover, to demonstrate woman's ability to perform successfully in fields traditionally reserved for men. Quite early in their history they adopted the policy of hiring only women employees. From the first, of course, only women had been officers and managers of the Society. And after a few years, these officers began to hire women in preference to men as agents and to urge other charitable societies and government agencies to do likewise. (They did this although the only salaried charitable positions held by women in this period tended to be those of teachers in girls' schools or supervisors of women's wings in hospitals and homes for juvenile delinquents.) In February 1835, for instance, the executive committee hired a woman agent to solicit subscriptions to the *Advocate*. That summer they hired another woman to travel through New England and New York State organizing auxiliaries and giving speeches to women on moral reform. In October of 1836, the executive officers appointed two women as editors of their journal—undoubtedly among the first of their sex in this country to hold such positions.[65] In 1841, the executive committee decided to replace their male financial agent with a woman bookkeeper. By 1843 women even set type and did the folding for the Society's journal. All these jobs, the ladies proudly, indeed aggressively stressed, were appropriate tasks for women.[66]

The broad feminist implications of such statements and actions must have been apparent to the officers of the New York Society. And indeed the Society's executive committee maintained discreet but active ties with the broader woman's rights movement of the 1830s, 40s and 50s; at one point at least, they flirted with official endorsement of a bold woman's rights position. Evidence of this flirtation can be seen in the minutes of the executive committee and occasionally came to light in articles and editorials appearing in the *Advocate*. As early as the mid-

---

[64] Significantly, the Society's editors and officers placed the responsibility for the low wages paid seamstresses and other female workers on ruthless and exploitative men. Much the same tone of anti-male hostility is evident in their economic exposés as in their sexual exposés.

[65] N.Y.F.M.R.S., "Executive Committee Minutes, Feb. 20, 1835, Oct. 4 and Oct. 5, 1836"; N.Y.F.M.R.S., *Fifth Annual Report*, p. 5.

[66] A.F.G.S., *Eleventh Annual Report*, pp. 5-6. For details of replacing male employees with women and the bitterness of the male reactions, see N.Y.F.M.R.S., "Executive Committee Minutes," *passim*, for early 1843. Nevertheless, even these aggressively feminist women did not feel that women could with propriety chair public meetings, even those of their own Society. In 1838, for instance, when the ladies discovered that men expected to attend their annual meeting, they felt that they had to ask men to chair the meeting and read the women's reports. Their decision was made just after the Grimké sisters had created a storm of controversy by speaking at large mixed gatherings of men and women. Northrup, *Record*, pp. 21-25. For the experiences of the Grimké sisters with this same problem, see Gerda Lerner's excellent biography, *The Grimké Sisters from South Carolina* (Boston: Houghton Mifflin, 1967), chaps. 11-14.

1830s, for instance, the executive committee began to correspond with a number of women who were then or were later to become active in the woman's rights movement. Lucretia Mott, abolitionist and pioneer feminist, was a founder and secretary of the Philadelphia Female Moral Reform Society; as such she was in frequent communication with the New York executive committee.[67] Emma Willard, a militant advocate of women's education and founder of the Troy Female Seminary, was another of the executive committee's regular correspondents. Significantly, when Elizabeth Blackwell, the first woman doctor in either the United States or Great Britain, received her medical degree, Emma Willard wrote to the New York executive committee asking its members to use their influence to find her a job.[68] The Society did more than that. The *Advocate* featured a story dramatizing Dr. Blackwell's struggles. The door was now open for other women, the editors urged; medicine was a peculiarly appropriate profession for sensitive and sympathetic womankind. The Society offered to help interested women in securing admission to medical school.[69]

One of the most controversial aspects of the early woman's rights movement was its criticism of the subservient role of women within the American family, and of the American man's imperious and domineering behavior toward women. Much of the Society's rhetorical onslaught upon the male's lack of sexual accountability served as a screen for a more general—and less socially acceptable—resentment of masculine social preeminence. Occasionally, however, the *Advocate* expressed such resentment overtly. An editorial in 1838, for example, revealed a deeply felt antagonism toward the power asserted by husbands over their wives and children. "A portion of the inhabitants of this favored land," the Society admonished, "are groaning under a despotism, which seems to be modeled precisely after that of the Autocrat of Russia. . . . We allude to the tyranny exercised in the HOME department, where lordly man, 'clothed with a little brief authority,' rules his trembling subjects with a rod of iron, conscious of entire impunity, and exalting in his fancied superiority." The Society's editorialist continued, perhaps even more bitterly: "Instead of regarding his wife as a help-mate for him, an equal sharer in his joys and sorrows, he looks upon her as a useful article of furniture, which is valuable only for the benefit derived from it, but which may be thrown aside at pleasure." [70] Such behavior, the editorial carefully emphasized, was not only commonplace, experienced by many of the Society's own members—even the wives of "Christians" and of ministers—but was accepted and even justified by society; was it not sanctioned by the Bible?

At about the same time, indeed, the editors of the *Advocate* went

[67] N.Y.F.M.R.S., "Executive Committee Minutes, Aug. 3, 1837."

[68] N.Y.F.M.R.S., "Executive Committee Minutes, June 2, 1847, Mar. 28, 1849." The *Advocate* regularly reviewed her books, and indeed made a point of reviewing books by women authors.

[69] *Advocate and Guardian*, 16 (Jan. 15, 1850), 10.

[70] *Advocate*, 4 (Feb. 15, 1838), 28.

so far as to print an attack upon "masculine" translations and interpretations of the Bible, and especially of Paul's epistles. This appeared in a
lengthy article written by Sarah Grimké, a "notorious" feminist and abolitionist.[71] The executive committee clearly sought to associate their organization more closely with the nascent woman's rights movement.
Calling upon American women to read and interpret the Bible for themselves, Sarah Grimké asserted that God had created woman the absolute
equal of man. But throughout history, man, being stronger, had usurped
woman's natural rights. He had subjected wives and daughters to his
physical control and had evolved religious and scientific rationalizations
to justify this domination. "Men have endeavored to entice, or to drive
women from almost every sphere of moral action." Miss Grimké
charged: "'Go home and spin' is the . . . advice of the domestic ty-
rant. . . . The first duty, I believe, which devolves on our sex now is
to think for themselves. . . . Until we take our stand side by side with
our brother; until we read all the precepts of the Bible as addressed to
woman as well as to man, and lose . . . the consciousness of sex, we
shall never fulfil the end of our existence." "Those who do undertake to
labor," Miss Grimké wrote from her own and her sister's bitter experiences, "are the scorn and ridicule of their own and the other sex." "We
are so little accustomed *to think for ourselves*," she continued,

> that we submit to the dictum of prejudice, and of usurped author-
> ity, almost without an effort to redeem ourselves from the unhal-
> lowed shackles which have so long bound us; almost without a de-
> sire to rise from that degradation and bondage to which we have
> been consigned by man, and by which the faculties of our minds,
> and the powers of our spiritual nature, have been prevented from
> expanding to their full growth, and are sometimes wholly crushed.

Each woman must re-evaluate her role in society; no longer could she
depend on husband or father to assume her responsibilities as a free individual. No longer, Sarah Grimké argued, could she be satisfied with
simply caring for her family or setting a handsome table.[72] The officers
of the Society, in an editorial comment following this article, admitted
that she had written a radical critique of woman's traditional role. But
they urged their members, "It is of immense importance to our sex to
possess clear and *correct* ideas of our rights and duties." [73]
    Sarah Grimké's overt criticism of woman's traditional role, contain-
ing as it did an attack upon the Protestant ministry and orthodox interpretations of the Bible, went far far beyond the consensus of the *Advocate's* rural subscribers. The following issue contained several letters
sharply critical of her and of the managers, for printing her editorial.[74]
And indeed the *Advocate* never again published the work of an overt

[71] See Lerner, *The Grimké Sisters*.
[72] *Advocate*, 4 (Jan. 1, 1838), 3–5.
[73] *Ibid.*, p. 5.
[74] See, for example, *Advocate*, 4 (Apr. 1, 1838), 55; 4 (July 16, 1838), 108.

feminist. Their membership, the officers concluded, would not tolerate explicit attacks upon traditional family structure and orthodox Christianity. Anti-male resentment and anger had to be expressed covertly. It was perhaps too threatening or—realistically—too dangerous for respectable matrons in relatively close-knit semi-rural communities in New York, New England, Ohio or Wisconsin so openly to question the traditional relations of the sexes and demand a new and ominously forceful role for women.

The compromise the membership and the officers of the Society seemed to find most comfortable was one that kept the American woman within the home—but which greatly expanded her powers as pious wife and mother. In rejecting Sarah Grimké's feminist manifesto, the Society's members implicitly agreed to accept the role traditionally assigned woman: the self-sacrificing, supportive, determinedly chaste wife and mother who limited her "sphere" to domesticity and religion. But in these areas her power should be paramount. The mother, not the father, should have final control of the home and family—especially of the religious and moral education of her children. If the world of economics and public affairs was his, the home must be hers.[75]

And even outside the home, woman's peculiar moral endowment and responsibilities justified her in playing an increasingly expansive role, one which might well ultimately impair aspects of man's traditional autonomy. When man transgressed God's commandments, through licentiousness, religious apathy, the defense of slavery, or the sin of intemperance—woman had both the right and duty of leaving the confines of the home and working to purify the male world.

The membership of the New York Female Moral Reform Society chose not to openly espouse the woman's rights movement. Yet many interesting emotional parallels remain to link the moral reform crusade and the suffrage movement of Elizabeth Cady Stanton, the Grimké sisters and Susan B. Anthony. In its own way, indeed, the war for purification of sexual mores was far more fundamental in its implications for woman's traditional role than the demand for woman's education—or even the vote.

Many of the needs and attitudes, moreover, expressed by suffragette leaders at the Seneca Falls Convention and in their efforts in the generation following are found decades earlier in the letters of rural women in the *Advocate of Moral Reform*. Both groups found woman's traditionally passive role intolerable. Both wished to assert female worth and values in a heretofore entirely male world. Both welcomed the creation of a sense of feminine loyalty and sisterhood that could give emotional strength and comfort to women isolated within their homes—whether in a remote farmstead or a Gramercy Park mansion. And it can hardly be assumed that the demand for votes for women was appreciably more radical than a moral absolutism which encouraged women to invade

---

[75] For examples of the glorification of the maternal role see *Advocate*, 10 (Mar. 15, 1844), 47, and *Advocate and Guardian*, 16 (Jan. 15, 1850), 13–14.

bordellos, befriend harlots and publicly discuss rape, seduction and prostitution.

It is important as well to re-emphasize a more general historical perspective. When the pious women founders of the Moral Reform Society
gathered at the Third Free Presbyterian Church, it was fourteen years
before the Seneca Falls Convention—which has traditionally been accepted as the beginning of the woman's rights movement in the United
States. There simply was no woman's movement in the 1830s. The future
leaders were either still adolescents or just becoming dissatisfied with
aspects of their role. Women advocates of moral reform were among
the very first American women to challenge their completely passive,
home-oriented image. They were among the first to travel throughout
the country without male chaperones. They published, financed, even set
type for their own paper and defied a bitter and long-standing male opposition to their cause. They began, in short, to create a broader, less
constricted sense of female identity. Naturally enough, they were dependent upon the activist impulse and legitimating imperatives of evangelical religion. This was indeed a complex symbiosis, the energies of
pietism and the grievances of role discontent creating the new and activist female consciousness which characterized the history of the American Female Moral Reform Society in antebellum America. Their experience, moreover, was probably shared, though less overtly, by the thousands of women who devoted time and money to the great number of
reform causes which multiplied in Jacksonian America. Women in the
abolition and the temperance movements (and to a less extent in more
narrowly evangelical and religious causes) also developed a sense of their
ability to judge for themselves and of their right to publicly criticize
the values of the larger society. The lives and self-image of all these
women had changed—if only so little—because of their new reforming
interests.

Slave Songs and Slave Consciousness: An Exploration in Neglected Sources

LAWRENCE W. LEVINE

Explorations of the ordinary aspects of American life often require the traveling of roads unfamiliar to traditional historians. This is especially true of attempts to discover what life was like for the "historically inarticulate"—those Americans, usually at the bottom of the social scale, who left behind few diaries, autobiographies, or letters. As Lawrence W. Levine points out, such people were not, however, inarticulate. But we must go to unaccustomed sources in order to reconstruct their daily experiences, their values, their anxieties and aspirations, and, ultimately, the role they played in history.

Music has always reflected the ethos of plain people. Through music the most vibrant human emotions are often expressed—and with instruments that poor people have hand-fashioned for centuries, as well as with the voice. By employing slave music as a historical source, Levine has been able to delve into Afro-American life in the nineteenth-century South with unusual success. He shows us how slaves kept alive elements of African culture; they did so, he argues, for the good reason that African oral traditions, music, and religious outlooks provided a way of "protecting their personalities from some of the worst ravages of the slave system." Preserving cultural traits, in other words, was vitally important to the daily life of Afro-Americans. It kept them from becoming the "samboes" white slavemasters liked to see, and often imagined they saw, when they looked at their bondsmen and bondswomen.

In slave spirituals, Levine believes, we are admitted to many daily occurrences in the life of American slaves. Through slave songs we can glean an understanding of Southern slaves' attitudes toward work; of their feelings about resistance and accommodation to the slave system; of their innermost emotions of hope and despair; and of a religious belief in which they attempted to join the past, the present, and the future in a way that made life under slavery bearable.

Almost all of the songs on which Levine bases his analysis date from the period after the slave trade was closed. The end of the trade may have made an important difference in slaves' cultural patterns and modes of resistance, for after 1807 Afro-Americans were cut off from Africa. "Salt water slaves," as newly imported Africans were called, no longer arrived on Southern plantations, and Afro-Americans experienced no fresh infusions of language, music, folk art, dance, and so forth from their homelands. Africans born in America quickly dominated the black population numerically in the nineteenth century, and African cultural traditions were perpetuated with greater and greater difficulty. With Gerald Mullin's study of African acculturation in the American South (p. 123), based on eighteenth-century sources,

and Levine's study, founded on nineteenth-century sources, both
ready to hand, the student can compare the daily lives of Afro-Americans in two distinctly different eras.

N̲egroes in the United States, both during and after slavery, were
anything but inarticulate. They sang songs, told stories, played verbal
games, listened and responded to sermons, and expressed their aspirations,
fears, and values through the medium of an oral tradition that had characterized the West African cultures from which their ancestors had
come. By largely ignoring this tradition, much of which has been preserved, historians have rendered an articulate people historically inarticulate, and have allowed the record of their consciousness to go unexplored.

Having worked my way carefully through thousands of Negro
songs, folktales, jokes, and games, I am painfully aware of the problems
inherent in the use of such materials. They are difficult, often impossible, to date with any precision. Their geographical distribution is usually unclear. They were collected belatedly, most frequently by men
and women who had little understanding of the culture from which they
sprang, and little scruple about altering or suppressing them. Such major
collectors as John Lomax, Howard Odum, and Newman White all admitted openly that many of the songs they collected were "unprintable"
by the moral standards which guided them and presumably their readers. But historians have overcome imperfect records before. They have
learned how to deal with altered documents, with consciously or unconsciously biased firsthand accounts, with manuscript collections that were
deposited in archives only after being filtered through the overprotective
hands of fearful relatives, and with the comparative lack of contemporary sources and the need to use their materials retrospectively. The
challenge presented by the materials of folk and popular culture is
neither totally unique nor insurmountable.

In this essay I want to illustrate the possible use of materials of this
kind of discussing the contribution that an understanding of Negro songs
can make to the recent debate over slave personality. In the process I
will discuss several aspects of the literature and problems related to the
use of slave songs.

The subject of Negro music in slavery has produced a large and
varied literature, little of which has been devoted to questions of meaning and function. The one major exception is Miles Mark Fisher's 1953

"Slave Songs and Slave Consciousness: An Exploration in Neglected Sources" by
Lawrence W. Levine. From *Anonymous Americans: Explorations in Nineteenth-
Century Social History*, Tamara K. Hareven, ed., © 1971, pp. 99–126. Reprinted by
permission of Prentice-Hall, Inc., Englewood Cliffs, N.J.

study, *Negro Slave Songs in the United States,* which attempts to get at the essence of slave life through an analysis of slave songs. Unfortunately, Fisher's rich insights are too often marred by his rather loose scholarly standards, and despite its continuing value his study is in many respects an example of how *not* to use Negro songs. Asserting, correctly, that the words of slave songs "show both accidental and intentional errors of transmission," Fisher changes the words almost at will to fit his own image of their pristine form. Arguing persuasively that "transplanted Negroes continued to promote their own culture by music," Fisher makes their songs part of an "African cult" which he simply wills into existence. Maintaining (again, I think, correctly), that "slave songs preserved in joyful strains the adjustment which Negroes made to their living conditions within the United States," Fisher traces the major patterns of that adjustment by arbitrarily dating these songs, apparently unperturbed by the almost total lack of evidence pertaining to the origin and introduction of individual slave songs.[1]

Fisher aside, most other major studies of slave music have focused almost entirely upon musical structure and origin. This latter question especially has given rise to a long and heated debate.[2] The earliest collectors and students of slave music were impressed by how different that music was from anything familiar to them. Following a visit to the Sea Islands in 1862, Lucy McKim despaired of being able "to express the entire character of these negro ballads by mere musical notes and signs. The odd turns made in the throat; and that curious rhythmic effect produced by single voices chiming in at different irregular intervals, seem almost as impossible to place on score, as the singing of birds, or the tones of an Aeolian Harp."[3] Although some of these early collectors maintained, as did W. F. Allen in 1865, that much of the slave's music "might no doubt be traced to tunes which they have heard from the whites, and transformed to their own use, . . . their music . . . is rather European than African in its character,"[4] they more often stressed the distinctiveness of the Negro's music and attributed it to racial characteristics, African origins, and indigenous developments resulting from the slave's unique experience in the New World.

This tradition, which has had many influential twentieth-century adherents,[5] was increasingly challenged in the early decades of this cen-

[1] Miles Mark Fisher, *Negro Slave Songs in the United States* (New York, 1963, orig. pub. 1953), 14, 39, 132, and *passim.*

[2] The contours of this debate are judiciously outlined in D. K. Wilgus, *Anglo-American Folksong Scholarship Since 1898* (New Brunswick, 1959), App. One, "The Negro-White Spirituals."

[3] Lucy McKim, "Songs of the Port Royal Contrabands," *Dwight's Journal of Music,* XXII (November 8, 1862), 255.

[4] W. F. Allen, "The Negro Dialect," *The Nation,* I (December 14, 1865), 744–745.

[5] See, for instance, Henry Edward Krehbiel, *Afro-American Folksongs* (New York. 1963, orig. pub. 1914); James Wesley Work, *Folk Song of the American Negro* (Nashville, 1915); James Weldon Johnson, *The Book of American Negro Spirituals* (New York, 1925), and *The Second Book of Negro Spirituals* (New York, 1926); Lydia Parrish, *Slave Songs of the Georgia Sea Islands* (Hatboro, Penna., 1965, orig. pub. 1942); LeRoi Jones, *Blues People* (New York, 1963).

tury. Such scholars as Newman White, Guy Johnson, and George Pullen Jackson argued that the earlier school lacked a comparative grounding in Anglo-American folk song. Comparing Negro spirituals with Methodist and Baptist evangelical religious music of the late eighteenth and early nineteenth centuries, White, Johnson, and Jackson found similarities in words, subject matter, tunes, and musical structure.[6] Although they tended to exaggerate both qualitatively and quantitatively the degrees of similarity, their comparisons were often a persuasive and important corrective to the work of their predecessors. But their studies were inevitably weakened by their ethnocentric assumption that similarities alone settled the argument over origins. Never could they contemplate the possibility that the direction of cultural diffusion might have been from black to white as well as the other way. In fact, insofar as white evangelical music departed from traditional Protestant hymnology and embodied or approached the complex rhythmic structure, the percussive qualities, the polymeter, the syncopation, the emphasis on overlapping call and response patterns that characterized Negro music both in West Africa and the New World, the possibility that it was influenced by slaves who attended and joined in the singing at religious meetings is quite high.

These scholars tended to use the similarities between black and white religious music to deny the significance of slave songs in still another way. Newman White, for example, argued that since white evangelical hymns also used such expressions as "freedom," the "Promised Land," and the "Egyptian Bondage," "without thought of other than spiritual meaning," these images when they occurred in Negro spirituals could not have been symbolic "of the Negro's longing for physical freedom."[7] The familiar process by which different cultural groups can derive varied meanings from identical images is enough to cast doubt on the logic of White's argument.[8] In the case of white and black religious music, however, the problem may be much less complex, since it is quite possible that the similar images in the songs of both groups in fact served similar purposes. Many of those whites who flocked to the camp meetings of the Methodists and Baptists were themselves on the social and economic margins of their society, and had psychic and emotional needs which, qualitatively, may not have been vastly different from those of black slaves. Interestingly, George Pullen Jackson, in his attempt to prove the white origin of Negro spirituals, makes exactly this point: "I may mention in closing the chief remaining argument of the die-hards for the Negro source of the Negro spirituals. . . . How could any, the argument runs, but a natively musical

[6] Newman I. White, *American Negro Folk-Songs* (Hatboro, Penna., 1965, orig. pub. 1928); Guy B. Johnson, *Folk Culture on St. Helena Island, South Carolina* (Chapel Hill, 1930); George Pullen Jackson, *White and Negro Spirituals* (New York, 1943).
[7] White, *American Negro Folk-Songs*, 11–13.
[8] Professor John William Ward gives an excellent example of this process in his discussion of the different meanings which the newspapers of the United States, France, and India attributed to Charles Lindbergh's flight across the Atlantic in 1927. See "Lindbergh, Dos Passos, and History," in Ward, *Red, White, and Blue* (New York, 1969), 55.

and sorely oppressed race create such beautiful things as 'Swing Low,' 'Steal Away,' and 'Deep River'? . . . But were not the whites of the mountains and the hard-scrabble hill country also 'musical and oppressed'? . . . Yes, these whites were musical, and oppressed too. If their condition was any more tolerable than that of the Negroes, one certainly does not get that impression from any of their songs of release and escape." [9] If this is true, the presence of similar images in white music would merely heighten rather than detract from the significance of these images in Negro songs. Clearly, the function and meaning of white religious music during the late eighteenth and early nineteenth centuries demands far more attention than it has received. In the interim, we must be wary of allowing the mere fact of similarities to deter us from attempting to comprehend the cultural dynamics of slave music.

Contemporary scholars, tending to transcend the more simplistic lines of the old debate, have focused upon the process of syncretism to explain the development of Negro music in the United States. The rich West African musical tradition common to almost all of the specific cultures from which Negro slaves came, the comparative cultural isolation in which large numbers of slaves lived, the tolerance and even encouragement which their white masters accorded to their musical activities, and the fact that, for all its differences, nothing in the European musical tradition with which they came into contact in America was totally alien to their own traditions—all these were conducive to a situation which allowed the slaves to retain a good deal of the integrity of their own musical heritage while fusing to it compatible elements of Anglo-American music. Slaves often took over entire white hymns and folk songs, as White and Jackson maintained, but altered them significantly in terms of words, musical structure, and especially performance before making them their own. The result was a hybrid with a strong African base.[10]

One of the more interesting aspects of this debate over origins is that no one engaged in it, not even advocates of the white derivation theory, denied that the slaves possessed their own distinctive music. Newman White took particular pains to point out again and again that the notion that Negro song is purely an imitation of the white man's music "is fully as unjust and inaccurate, in the final analysis, as the Negro's assumption that his folk-song is entirely original." He observed that in the slaves' separate religious meetings they were free to do as they would with the music they first learned from the whites, with the result that their spirituals became "the greatest single outlet for the expression of the

[9] George Pullen Jackson, "The Genesis of the Negro Spiritual," *The American Mercury*, XXVI (June 1932), 248.

[10] Richard Alan Waterman, "African Influence on the Music of the Americas," in Sol Tax (ed.), *Acculturation in the Americas: Proceedings and Selected Papers of the XXIXth International Congress of Americanists* (Chicago, 1952), 207–218; Wilgus, *Anglo-American Folksong Scholarship Since 1898*, 363–364; Melville H. Herskovits, "Patterns of Negro Music" (pamphlet, no publisher, no date); Gilbert Chase, *America's Music* (New York, 1966), Chap. 12; Alan P. Merriam, "African Music," in William R. Bascom and Melville J. Herskovits (eds.), *Continuity and Change in African Cultures* (Chicago, 1959), 76–80.

Negro folk-mind." [11] Similarly, George Pullen Jackson, after admitting that he could find no white parallels for over two-thirds of the existing Negro spirituals, reasoned that these were produced by Negro singers in true folk fashion "by endless singing of heard tunes and by endless, inevitable and concomitant singing differentiation." Going even further, Jackson asserted that the lack of deep roots in Anglo-American culture left the black man "even freer than the white man to make songs over unconsciously as he sang . . . the free play has resulted in the very large number of songs which, though formed primarily in the white man's moulds, have lost all recognizable relationship to known individual white-sung melodic entities." [12] This debate over origins indicates clearly that a belief in the direct continuity of African musical traditions or in the process of syncretism is not a necessary prerequisite to the conclusion that the Negro slaves' music was their own, regardless of where they received the components out of which it was fashioned; a conclusion which is crucial to any attempt to utilize these songs as an aid in reconstructing the slaves' consciousness.

Equally important is the process by which slave songs were created and transmitted. When James McKim asked a freedman on the Sea Islands during the Civil War where the slaves got their songs, the answer was eloquently simple: "Dey make em, sah." [13] Precisely *how* they made them worried and fascinated Thomas Wentworth Higginson, who became familiar with slave music through the singing of the black Union soldiers in his Civil War regiment. Were their songs, he wondered, a "conscious and definite" product of "some leading mind," or did they grow "by gradual accretion, in an almost unconscious way"? A freedman rowing Higginson and some of his troops between the Sea Islands helped to resolve the problem when he described a spiritual which he had a hand in creating:

Once we boys went for some rice and de nigger-driver he keep a-callin' on us; and I say, "O de ole nigger-driver!" Den anudder said, "Fust ting my mammy tole me was, notin' so bad as nigger-driver." Den I made a sing, just puttin' a word, and den anudder word.

He then began to sing his song:

O, de ole nigger-driver!
O, gwine away!
Fust ting my mammy tell me,
O, gwine away!

11 White, *American Negro Folk-Songs*, 29, 55.
12 Jackson, *White and Negro Spirituals*, 266–267.
13 James Miller McKim, "Negro Songs," *Dwight's Journal of Music*, XXI (August 9, 1862), 149.

> Tell me 'bout de nigger-driver,
>   O, gwine away!
> Nigger-driver second devil,
>   O, gwine away!

Higginson's black soldiers, after a moment's hesitation, joined in the singing of a song they had never heard before as if they had long been
familiar with it. "I saw," Higginson concluded, "how easily a new 'sing'
took root among them." [14]

   This spontaneity, this sense of almost instantaneous community which
so impressed Higginson, constitutes a central element in every account
of slave singing. The English musician Henry Russell, who lived in the
United States in the 1830's, was forcibly struck by the ease with which
a slave congregation in Vicksburg, Mississippi, took a "fine old psalm
tune" and, by suddenly and spontaneously accelerating the tempo, transformed it "into a kind of negro melody." [15] "Us old heads," an ex-slave
told Jeanette Robinson Murphy, "use ter make 'em up on de spurn of de
moment. Notes is good enough for you people, but us likes a mixtery."
Her account of the creation of a spiritual is typical and important:

> We'd all be at the "prayer house" de Lord's day, and de white
> preacher he'd splain de word and read whar Esekial done say—
>
> *Dry bones gwine ter lib ergin.*
>
> And, honey, de Lord would come a-shinin' thoo dem pages and re-
> vive dis ole nigger's heart, and I'd jump up dar and den and holler
> and shout and sing and pat, and dey would all cotch de words and
> I'd sing it to some ole shout song I'd heard 'em sing from Africa,
> and dey'd all take it up and keep at it, and keep a-addin' to it, and
> den it would be a spiritual.[16]

   This "internal" account has been verified again and again by the
descriptions of observers, many of whom were witnessing not slave services but religious meetings of rural southern Negroes long after emancipation. The essential continuity of the Negro folk process in the more
isolated sections of the rural South through the early decades of the twentieth century makes these accounts relevant for the slave period as well.
Natalie Curtis Burlin, whose collection of spirituals is musically the most
accurate one we have, and who had a long and close acquaintance with

---

[14] Thomas Wentworth Higginson, *Army Life in a Black Regiment* (Beacon Press
   edition, Boston, 1962, orig. pub. 1869), 218–219.

[15] Henry Russell, *Cheer! Boys, Cheer!*, 84–85, quoted in Chase, *America's Music*,
   235–236.

[16] Jeanette Robinson Murphy, "The Survival of African Music in America," *Popular
   Science Monthly*, 55 (1899), 660–672, reprinted in Bruce Jackson (ed.), *The
   Negro and His Folklore in Nineteenth-Century Periodicals* (Austin, 1967), 328.

Negro music, never lost her sense of awe at the process by which these songs were molded. On a hot July Sunday in rural Virginia, she sat in a Negro meeting house listening to the preacher deliver his prayer, interrupted now and then by an "O Lord!" or "Amen, Amen" from the congregation.

> Minutes passed, long minutes of strange intensity. The mutterings, the ejaculations, grew louder, more dramatic, till suddenly I felt the creative thrill dart through the people like an electric vibration, that same half-audible hum arose,—emotion was gathering atmospherically as clouds gather—and then, up from the depths of some "sinner's" remorse and imploring came a pitiful little plea, a real "moan," sobbed in musical cadence. From somewhere in that bowed gathering another voice improvised a response: the plea sounded again, louder this time and more impassioned; then other voices joined in the answer, shaping it into a musical phrase; and so, before our ears, as one might say, from this molten metal of music a new song was smithied out, composed then and there by no one in particular and by everyone in general.[17]

Clifton Furness has given us an even more graphic description. During a visit to an isolated South Carolina plantation in 1926, he attended a prayer meeting held in the old slave cabins. The preacher began his reading of the Scriptures slowly, then increased his tempo and emotional fervor, assuring his flock that "Gawd's lightnin' gwine strike! Gawd's thunder swaller de ert!"

> Gradually moaning became audible in the shadowy corners where the women sat. Some patted their bundled babies in time to the flow of the words, and began swaying backward and forward. Several men moved their feet alternately, in strange syncopation. A rhythm was born, almost without reference to the words that were being spoken by the preacher. It seemed to take shape almost visibly, and grow. I was gripped with the feeling of a mass-intelligence, a self-conscious entity, gradually informing the crowd and taking possession of every mind there, including my own.

In the midst of this increasing intensity, a black man sitting directly in front of Furness, his head bowed, his body swaying, his feet patting up and down, suddenly cried out: "Git right—sodger! Git right—sodger! Git right—wit Gawd!"

> Instantly the crowd took it up, moulding a melody out of half-formed familiar phrases based upon a spiritual tune, hummed here and there among the crowd. A distinct melodic outline became

[17] Natalie Curtis Burlin, "Negro Music at Birth," *Musical Quarterly*, V (January 1919), 88. For Mrs. Burlin's excellent reproductions of Negro folk songs and spirituals, see her *Negro Folk-Songs* (New York, 1918–1919), Vol. I–IV.

more and more prominent, shaping itself around the central theme of the words, "Git right, sodger!"

Scraps of other words and tunes were flung into the medley of sound by individual singers from time to time, but the general trend was carried on by a deep undercurrent, which appeared to be stronger than the mind of any individual present, for it bore the mass of improvised harmony and rhythms into the most effective climax of incremental repetition that I have ever heard. I felt as if some conscious plan or purpose were carrying us along, call it mob-mind, communal composition, or what you will.[18]

. . . These accounts and others like them make it clear that spirituals both during and after slavery were the product of an improvisational communal consciousness. They were not, as some observers thought, totally new creations, but were forged out of many preexisting bits of old songs mixed together with snatches of new tunes and lyrics and fit into a fairly traditional but never wholly static metrical pattern. They were, to answer Higginson's question, *simultaneously* the result of in-dividual and mass creativity. They were products of that folk process which has been called "communal re-creation," through which older songs are constantly recreated into essentially new entities.[19] Anyone who has read through large numbers of Negro songs is familiar with this process. Identical or slightly varied stanzas appear in song after song; identical tunes are made to accommodate completely different sets of lyrics; the same song appears in different collections in widely varied forms. In 1845 a traveler observed that the only permanent elements in Negro song were the music and the chorus. "The blacks themselves leave out old stanzas, and introduce new ones at pleasure. Travelling through the South, you may, in passing from Virginia to Louisiana, hear the same tune a hundred times, but seldom the same words accompanying it." [20] Another observer noted in 1870 that during a single religious meeting the freedmen would often sing the words of one spiritual to several different tunes, and then take a tune that particularly pleased them and fit the words of several different songs to it.[21] Slave songs, then, were never static; at no time did Negroes create a "final" version of any spiritual. Always the community felt free to alter and recreate them.

The two facts that I have attempted to establish thus far—that slave music, regardless of its origins, was a distinctive cultural form, and that

[18] Clifton Joseph Furness, "Communal Music Among Arabians and Negroes," *Musical Quarterly*, XVI (January 1930), 49–51.

[19] Bruno Nettl, *Folk and Traditional Music of the Western Continents* (Englewood Cliffs, 1965), 4–5; Chase, *America's Music*, 241–243.

[20] J. K., Jr., "Who Are Our National Poets?," *Knickerbocker Magazine*, 26 (October 1845), 336, quoted in Dena J. Epstein, "Slave Music in the United States Before 1860: A Survey of Sources (Part I)," *Music Library Association Notes*, XX (Spring 1963), 208.

[21] Elizabeth Kilham, "Sketches in Color: IV," *Putnam's Monthly*, XV (March 1870), 304–311, reprinted in Jackson, *The Negro and His Folklore in Nineteenth-Century Periodicals*, 129.

it was created or constantly recreated through a communal process—are essential if one is to justify the use of these songs as keys to slave consciousness. But these facts in themselves say a good deal about the nature and quality of slave life and personality. That black slaves could create and continually recreate songs marked by the poetic beauty, the emotional intensity, the rich imagery which characterized the spirituals—songs which even one of the most devout proponents of the white man's origins school admits are "the most impressive religious folk songs in our language" [22]—should be enough to make us seriously question recent theories which conceive of slavery as a closed system which destroyed the vitality of the Negro and left him a dependent child. For all of its horrors, slavery was never so complete a system of psychic assault that it prevented the slaves from carving out independent cultural forms. It never pervaded all of the interstices of their minds and their culture, and in those gaps they were able to create an independent art form and a distinctive voice. If North American slavery eroded the African's linguistic and institutional life, if it prevented him from preserving and developing his rich heritage of graphic and plastic art, it nevertheless allowed him to continue and to develop the patterns of verbal art which were so central to his past culture. Historians have not yet come to terms with what the continuance of the oral tradition meant to blacks in slavery.

In Africa, songs, tales, proverbs, and verbal games served the dual function of not only preserving communal values and solidarity, but also of providing occasions for the individual to transcend, at least symbolically, the inevitable restrictions of his environment and his society by permitting him to express deeply held feelings which he ordinarily was not allowed to verbalize. Among the Ashanti and the Dahomeans, for example, periods were set aside when the inhabitants were encouraged to gather together and, through the medium of song, dance, and tales, to openly express their feelings about each other. The psychological release this afforded seems to have been well understood. "You know that everyone has a *sunsum* (soul) that may get hurt or knocked about or become sick, and so make the body ill," an Ashanti high priest explained to the English anthropologist R. S. Rattray:

> Very often . . . ill health is caused by the evil and the hate that another has in his head against you. Again, you too may have hatred in your head against another, because of something that person has done to you, and that, too, causes your *sunsum* to fret and become sick. Our forbears knew this to be the case, and so they ordained a time, once every year, when every man and woman, free man and slave, should have freedom to speak out just what was in their head, to tell their neighbours just what they thought of them, and of their actions, and not only their neighbours, but also the king or chief. When a man has spoken freely thus, he will feel his *sunsum* cool and quieted, and the *sunsum* of the other person against whom he has now openly spoken will be quieted also.

[22] White, *American Negro Folk-Songs*, 57.

Utilization of verbal art for this purpose was widespread throughout
Africa, and was not confined to those ceremonial occasions when one
could directly state one's feelings. Through innuendo, metaphor, and
circumlocution, Africans could utilize their songs as outlets for individual
release without disturbing communal solidarity.[23]

There is abundant internal evidence that the verbal art of the slaves
in the United States served many of these traditional functions. Just as
the process by which the spirituals were created allowed for simultaneous
individual and communal creativity, so their very structure provided
simultaneous outlets for individual and communal expression. The over-
riding antiphonal structure of the spirituals—the call and response pattern which Negroes brought with them from Africa and which was
reinforced by the relatively similar white practice of "lining out" hymns
—placed the individual in continual dialogue with his community, allowing him at one and the same time to preserve his voice as a distinct entity
and to blend it with those of his fellows. Here again slave music con-
fronts us with evidence which indicates that however seriously the slave
system may have diminished the strong sense of community that had
bound Africans together, it never totally destroyed it or left the individual atomized and emotionally and psychically defenseless before his
white masters. In fact, the form and structure of slave music presented the
slave with a potential outlet for his individual feelings even while it continually drew him back into the communal presence and permitted him
the comfort of basking in the warmth of the shared assumptions of those
around him.

Those "shared assumptions" can be further examined by an analysis
of the content of slave songs. Our preoccupation in recent years with
the degree to which the slaves actually resembled the "Sambo" image
held by their white masters has obscured the fact that the slaves developed images of their own which must be consulted and studied before
any discussion of slave personality can be meaningful. The image of
the trickster, who through cunning and unscrupulousness prevails over
his more powerful antagonists, pervades slave tales. The trickster figure
is rarely encountered in the slave's religious songs, though its presence
is sometimes felt in the slave's many allusions to his narrow escapes from
the devil.

> The Devil's mad and I'm glad,
> He lost the soul he thought he had.[24]

[23] Alan P. Merriam, "Music and the Dance," in Robert Lystad (ed.), *The African
World: A Survey of Social Research* (New York, 1965), 452–468; William Bascom,
"Folklore and Literature," in *Ibid.*, 469–488; R. S. Rattray, *Ashanti* (Oxford, 1923),
Chap. XV; Melville Herskovits, "Freudian Mechanisms in Primitive Negro Psy-
chology," in E. E. Evans-Pritchard *et al.* (eds.), *Essays Presented to C. G. Seligman*
(London, 1934), 75–84; Alan P. Merriam, "African Music," in Bascom and Hersko-
vits, *Continuity and Change in African Cultures*, 49–86.

[24] William Francis Allen, Charles Pickard Ware, and Lucy McKim Garrison, com-
pilers, *Slave Songs of the United States* (New York, 1867, Oak Publications ed.,
1965), 164–165.

> Ole Satan toss a ball at me.
> O me no weary yet . . .
>
> Him tink de ball would hit my soul.
> O me no weary yet . . .
>
> De ball for hell and I for heaven.
> O me no weary yet . . .[25]
>
> Ole Satan thought he had a mighty aim;
> He missed my soul and caught my sins.
> Cry Amen, cry Amen, cry Amen to God!
>
> He took my sins upon his back;
> Went muttering and grumbling down to hell.
> Cry Amen, cry Amen, cry Amen to God! [26]

The single most persistent image the slave songs contain, however, is that of the chosen people. The vast majority of the spirituals identify the singers as "de people dat is born of God," "We are the people of God," "we are de people of de Lord," "I really do believe I'm a child of God," "I'm a child ob God, wid my soul sot free," "I'm born of God, I know I am." Nor is there ever any doubt that "To the promised land I'm bound to go," "I walk de heavenly road," "Heav'n shall-a be my home," "I gwine to meet my Saviour," "I seek my Lord and I find Him," "I'll hear the trumpet sound/In that morning." [27] The force of this image cannot be diminished by the observation that similar images were present in the religious singing of white evangelical churches during the first half of the nineteenth century. White Americans could be expected to sing of triumph and salvation, given their long-standing heritage of the idea of a chosen people which was reinforced in this era by the belief in inevitable progress and manifest destiny, the spread-eagle oratory, the bombastic folklore, and, paradoxically, the deep insecurities concomitant with the tasks of taming a continent and developing an identity. But for this same message to be expressed by Negro slaves who were told endlessly that they were members of the lowliest of races *is* significant. It offers an insight into the kinds of barriers the slaves had available to them against the internalization of the

---

[25] *Ibid.,* 43.

[26] Harriet Jacobs, *Incidents in the Life of a Slave Girl* (Boston, 1861), 109.

[27] Lines like these could be quoted endlessly. For the specific ones cited, see the songs in the following collections: Higginson, *Army Life in a Black Regiment,* 206, 216–217; Allen *et al., Slave Songs of the United States,* 33–34, 44, 106–108, 131, 160–161; Thomas P. Fenner, compiler, *Religious Folk Songs of the Negro as Sung on the Plantations* (Hampton, Virginia, 1909, orig. pub. 1874), 10–11, 48; J. B. T. Marsh, *The Story of the Jubilee Singers; With Their Songs* (Boston, 1880), 136, 167, 178.

stereotyped images their masters held and attempted consciously and unconsciously to foist upon them.

The question of the chosen people image leads directly into the
larger problem of what role religion played in the songs of the slave.
Writing in 1862, James McKim noted that the songs of the Sea Island
freedmen "are all religious, barcaroles and all. I speak without exception.
So far as I heard or was told of their singing, it was all religious." Others
who worked with recently emancipated slaves recorded the same experience, and Colonel Higginson reported that he rarely heard his troops
sing a profane or vulgar song. With a few exceptions, "all had a religious
motive." [28] In spite of this testimony, there can be little doubt that the
slaves sang nonreligious songs. In 1774, an English visitor to the United
States, after his first encounter with slave music, wrote in his journal:
"In their songs they generally relate the usage they have received from
their Masters or Mistresses in a very satirical stile and manner." [29] Songs
fitting this description can be found in the nineteenth-century narratives
of fugitive slaves. Harriet Jacobs recorded that during the Christmas
season the slaves would ridicule stingy whites by singing:

> Poor Massa, so dey say;
> Down in de heel, so dey say;
> Got no money, so dey say;
> God A'mighty bress you, so dey say.[30]

"Once in a while among a mass of nonsense and wild frolic," Frederick
Douglass noted, "a sharp hit was given to the meanness of slaveholders."

> We raise de wheat,
> Dey gib us de corn;
> We bake de bread,
> Dey gib us de crust;
> We sif de meal,
> Dey gib us de huss;
> We peal de meat,
> Dey gib us de skin;
> And dat's de way
> Dey take us in;
> We skim de pot,

[28] McKim, "Negro Songs," 148; H. G. Spaulding, "Under the Palmetto," *Continental
Monthly*, IV (1863), 188–203, reprinted in Jackson, *The Negro and His Folklore in
Nineteenth-Century Periodicals*, 72; Allen, "The Negro Dialect," 744–745; Higgin-
son, *Army Life in a Black Regiment*, 220–221.

[29] *Journal of Nicholas Cresswell, 1774–1777* (New York, 1934), 17–19, quoted in
Epstein, *Music Library Association Notes*, XX (Spring 1963), 201.

[30] Jacobs, *Incidents in the Life of a Slave Girl*, 180.

> Dey gib us de liquor,
> And say dat's good enough for nigger.[31]

Both of these songs are in the African tradition of utilizing song to by-pass both internal and external censors and give vent to feelings which could be expressed in no other form. Nonreligious songs were not limited to the slave's relations with his masters, however, as these rowing songs, collected by contemporary white observers, indicate:

> We are going down to Georgia, boys,
>   Aye, aye.
> To see the pretty girls, boys,
>   Yoe, yoe.
> We'll give 'em a pint of brandy, boys,
>   Aye, aye.
> And a hearty kiss, besides, boys,
>   Yoe, yoe.[32]

> Jenny shake her toe at me,
>   Jenny gone away;
> Jenny shake her toe at me,
>   Jenny gone away.
> Hurrah! Miss Susy, oh!
>   Jenny gone away;
> Hurrah! Miss Susy, oh!
>   Jenny gone away.[33]

The variety of nonreligious songs in the slave's repertory was wide. There were songs of in-group and out-group satire, songs of nostalgia, nonsense songs, songs of play and work and love. Nevertheless, our total stock of these songs is very small. It is possible to add to these by incorporating such post-bellum secular songs which have an authentic slavery ring to them as "De Blue-Tail Fly," with its ill-concealed satisfaction at the death of a master, or the ubiquitous

> My ole Mistiss promise me,
> W'en she died, she'd set me free,

---

[31] *Life and Times of Frederick Douglass* (rev. ed., 1892, Collier Books Edition, 1962), 146–147.

[32] John Lambert, *Travels Through Canada and the United States of North America in the Years, 1806–1807 and 1808* (London, 1814), II, 253–254, quoted in Dena J. Epstein, "Slave Music in the United States Before 1860: A Survey of Sources (Part 2)," *Music Library Association Notes*, XX (Summer 1963), 377.

[33] Frances Anne Kemble, *Journal of a Residence on a Georgian Plantation in 1838–1839* (New York, 1863), 128.

>She lived so long dat 'er head got bal',
>An' she give out'n de notion a dyin' at all.[34]

The number can be further expanded by following Constance Rourke's suggestion that we attempt to disentangle elements of Negro origin from those of white creation in the "Ethiopian melodies" of the white minstrel shows, many of which were similar to the songs I have just quoted.[35] Either of these possibilities, however, forces the historian to work with sources far more potentially spurious than those with which he normally is comfortable.

Spirituals, on the other hand, for all the problems associated with their being filtered through white hands before they were published, and despite the many errors in transcription that inevitably occurred, constitute a much more satisfactory source. They were collected by the hundreds directly from slaves and freedmen during the Civil War and the decades immediately following, and although they came from widely different geographical areas they share a common structure and content, which seems to have been characteristic of Negro music wherever slavery existed in the United States. It is possible that we have a greater number of religious than nonreligious songs because slaves were more willing to sing these ostensibly innocent songs to white collectors who in turn were more anxious to record them, since they fit easily with their positive and negative images of the Negro. But I would argue that the vast preponderance of spirituals over any other sort of slave music, rather than being merely the result of accident or error, is instead an accurate reflection of slave culture during the ante-bellum period. Whatever songs the slaves may have sung before their wholesale conversion to Christianity in the late eighteenth and early nineteenth centuries, by the latter century spirituals were quantitatively and qualitatively their most significant musical creation. In this form of expression slaves found a medium which

---

[34] For versions of these songs, see Dorothy Scarborough, *On the Trail of Negro Folk-Songs* (Cambridge, 1925), 194, 201–203, 223–225, and Thomas W. Talley, *Negro Folk Rhymes* (New York, 1922), 25–26. Talley claims that the majority of the songs in his large and valuable collection "were sung by Negro fathers and mothers in the dark days of American slavery to their children who listened with eyes as large as saucers and drank them down with mouths wide open," but offers no clue as to why he feels that songs collected for the most part in the twentieth century were slave songs.

[35] Constance Rourke, *The Roots of American Culture and Other Essays* (New York, 1942), 262–274. Newman White, on the contrary, has argued that although the earliest minstrel songs were Negro derived, they soon went their own way and that less than ten per cent of them were genuinely Negro. Nevertheless, these white songs "got back to the plantation, largely spurious as they were and were undoubtedly among those which the plantation-owners encouraged the Negroes to sing. They persist to-day in isolated stanzas and lines, among the songs handed down by plantation Negroes . . ." White, *American Negro Folk-Songs*, 7–10 and Appendix IV. There are probably valid elements in both theses. A similarly complex relationship between genuine Negro folk creations and their more commercialized partly white influenced imitations was to take place in the blues of the twentieth century.

resembled in many important ways the world view they had brought with them from Africa, and afforded them the possibility of both adapting to and transcending their situation.

It is significant that the most common form of slave music we know of is sacred song. I use the term "sacred" not in its present usage as something antithetical to the secular world; neither the slaves nor their African forebears ever drew modernity's clear line between the sacred and the secular. The uses to which spirituals were put are an unmistakable indication of this. They were not sung solely or even primarily in churches or praise houses, but were used as rowing songs, field songs, work songs, and social songs. On the Sea Islands during the Civil War, Lucy McKim heard the spiritual "Poor Rosy" sung in a wide variety of contexts and tempos.

> On the water, the oars dip "Poor Rosy" to an even andante; a stout boy and girl at the hominy-mill will make the same "Poor Rosy" fly, to keep up with the whirling stone; and in the evening, after the day's work is done, "Heab'n shall-a be my home" [the final line of each stanza] peals up slowly and mournfully from the distant quarters.[36]

For the slaves, then, songs of God and the mythic heroes of their religion were not confined to any specific time or place, but were appropriate to almost every situation. It is in this sense that I use the concept sacred—not to signify a rejection of the present world but to describe the process of incorporating within this world all the elements of the divine. The religious historian Mircea Eliade, whose definition of sacred has shaped my own, has maintained that for men in traditional societies religion is a means of extending the world spatially upward so that communication with the other world becomes ritually possible, and extending it temporally backward so that the paradigmatic acts of the gods and mythical ancestors can be continually reenacted and indefinitely recoverable. By creating sacred time and space, man can perpetually live in the presence of his gods, can hold on to the certainty that within one's own lifetime "rebirth" is continually possible, and can impose order on the chaos of the universe. "Life," as Eliade puts it, "is lived on a twofold plane; it takes its course as human existence and, at the same time, shares in a transhuman life, that of the cosmos or the gods." [37]

This notion of sacredness gets at the essence of the spirituals, and through them at the essence of the slave's world view. Denied the possibility of achieving an adjustment to the external world of the ante-bellum South which involved meaningful forms of personal integration, attainment of status, and feelings of individual worth that all human beings

---

[36] McKim, "Songs of the Port Royal Contrabands," 255.

[37] Mircea Eliade, *The Sacred and the Profane* (New York, 1961), Chaps. 2, 4, and *passim*. For the similarity of Eliade's concept to the world view of West Africa, see W. E. Abraham, *The Mind of Africa* (London, 1962), Chap. 2, and R. S. Rattray, *Religion and Art in Ashanti* (Oxford, 1927).

crave and need, the slaves created a new world by transcending the narrow confines of the one in which they were forced to live. They extended
the boundaries of their restrictive universe backward until it fused with
the world of the Old Testament, and upward until it became one with
the world beyond. The spirituals are the record of a people who found
the status, the harmony, the values, the order they needed to survive by
internally creating an expanded universe, by literally willing themselves
reborn. In this respect I agree with the anthropologist Paul Radin that

> The ante-bellum Negro was not converted to God. He converted
> God to himself. In the Christian God he found a fixed point and
> he needed a fixed point, for both within and outside of himself, he
> could see only vacillation and endless shifting. . . . There was no
> other safety for people faced on all sides by doubt and the threat
> of personal disintegration, by the thwarting of instincts and the an-
> nihilation of values.[38]

The confinement of much of the slave's new world to dreams and fantasies
does not free us from the historical obligation of examining its contours,
weighing its implications for the development of the slave's psychic and
emotional structure, and eschewing the kind of facile reasoning that leads
Professor Elkins to imply that, since the slaves had no alternatives open
to them, their fantasy life was "limited to catfish and watermelons." [39]
Their spirituals indicate clearly that there *were* alternatives open to them
—alternatives which they themselves fashioned out of the fusion of their
African heritage and their new religion—and that their fantasy life was
so rich and so important to them that it demands understanding if we
are even to begin to comprehend their inner world.

The God the slaves sang of was neither remote nor abstract, but as
intimate, personal, and immediate as the gods of Africa had been. "O
when I talk I talk wid God," "Mass Jesus is my bosom friend," "I'm
goin' to walk with [talk with, live with, see] King Jesus by myself, by
myself," were refrains that echoed through the spirituals.[40]

> In de mornin' when I rise,
>   Tell my Jesus huddy [howdy] oh,
> I wash my hands in de mornin' glory,
>   Tell my Jesus huddy oh.[41]

[38] Paul Radin, "Status, Phantasy, and the Christian Dogma," in Social Science Institute, Fisk University, *God Struck Me Dead: Religious Conversion Experiences and
Autobiographies of Negro Ex-Slaves* (Nashville, 1945, unpublished typescript).
[39] Stanley Elkins, *Slavery* (Chicago, 1959), 136.
[40] Allen *et al.*, *Slave Songs of the United States*, 33–34, 105; William E. Barton, *Old
Plantation Hymns: A Collection of Hitherto Unpublished Melodies of the Slave
and the Freedmen* (Boston, 1899), 30.
[41] Allen *et al.*, *Slave Songs of the United States*, 47.

> Gwine to argue wid de Father and chatter wid de son,
> The last trumpet shall sound, I'll be there.
> Gwine talk 'bout de bright world dey des' come from.
> The last trumpet shall sound, I'll be there.[42]

> Gwine to write to Massa Jesus,
> To send some Valiant soldier
> To turn back Pharaoh's army, Hallelu![43]

The heroes of the Scriptures—"Sister Mary," "Brudder Jonah," "Brudder Moses," "Brudder Daniel"—were greeted with similar intimacy and immediacy. In the world of the spirituals, it was not the masters and mistresses but God and Jesus and the entire pantheon of Old Testament figures who set the standards, established the precedents, and defined the values; who, in short, constituted the "significant others." The world described by the slave songs was a black world in which no reference was ever made to any white contemporaries. The slave's positive reference group was composed entirely of his own peers: his mother, father, sister, brother, uncles, aunts, preacher, fellow "sinners" and "mourners" of whom he sang endlessly, to whom he sent messages via the dying, and with whom he was reunited joyfully in the next world.

The same sense of sacred time and space which shaped the slave's portraits of his gods and heroes also made his visions of the past and future immediate and compelling. Descriptions of the Crucifixion communicate a sense of the actual presence of the singers: "Dey pierced Him in the side . . . Dey nail Him to de cross . . . Dey rivet His feet . . . Dey hanged Him high . . . Dey stretch Him wide. . . ."

> Oh sometimes it causes me to tremble,—tremble,—tremble,
> Were you there when they crucified my Lord? [44]

The Slave's "shout"—that counterclockwise, shuffling dance which frequently occurred after the religious service and lasted long into the night —often became a medium through which the ecstatic dancers were transformed into actual participants in historic actions: Joshua's army marching around the walls of Jericho, the children of Israel following Moses out of Egypt.[45]

The thin line between time dimensions is nowhere better illustrated than in the slave's visions of the future, which were, of course, a direct

---

[42] Barton, *Old Plantation Hymns*, 19.

[43] Marsh, *The Story of the Jubilee Singers*, 132.

[44] Fenner, *Religious Folk Songs of the Negro*, 162; E. A. McIlhenny, *Befo' De War Spirituals: Words and Melodies* (Boston, 1933), 39.

[45] Barton, *Old Plantation Hymns*, 15; Howard W. Odum and Guy B. Johnson, *The Negro And His Songs* (Hatboro, Penn., 1964, orig. pub. 1925), 33–34; for a vivid description of the "shout" see *The Nation*, May 30, 1867, 432–433; see also Parrish, *Slave Songs of the Georgia Sea Islands*, Chap. III.

negation of his present. Among the most striking spirituals are those
which pile detail upon detail in describing the Day of Judgment: "You'll
see de world on fire . . . see de element a meltin', . . . see the stars a
fallin' . . . see the moon a bleedin' . . . see the forked lightning, . . .
Hear the rumblin' thunder . . . see the righteous marching, . . . see my
Jesus coming . . . ," and the world to come where "Dere's no sun to
burn you . . . no hard trials . . . no whips a crackin' . . . no stormy
weather . . . no tribulation . . . no evil-doers . . . All is gladness in de
Kingdom." [46] This vividness was matched by the slave's certainty that
he would partake of the triumph of judgment and the joys of the new
world:

> Dere's room enough, room enough, room enough in de heaven, my Lord
> Room enough, room enough, I can't stay behind.[47]

Continually, the slaves sang of reaching out beyond the world that confined them, of seeing Jesus "in de wilderness," of praying "in de lonesome
valley," of breathing in the freedom of the mountain peaks:

> Did yo' ever
> Stan' on mountun,
> Wash yo' han's
> In a cloud? [48]

Continually, they held out the possibility of imminent rebirth; "I look
at de worl' an' de worl' look new, . . . I look at my hands an' they look
so too . . . I looked at my feet, my feet was too." [49]

These possibilities, these certainties were not surprising. The religious revivals which swept large numbers of slaves into the Christian
fold in the late eighteenth and early nineteenth centuries were based upon
a *practical* (not necessarily theological) Arminianism: God would save all
who believed in Him; Salvation was there for all to take hold of if they
would. The effects of this message upon the slaves who were exposed
to and converted by it have been passed over too easily by historians.
Those effects are illustrated graphically in the spirituals which were the
products of these revivals and which continued to spread the evangelical
word long after the revivals had passed into history.

The religious music of the slaves is almost devoid of feelings of de-
pravity or unworthiness, but is rather, as I have tried to show, pervaded

---

[46] For examples of songs of this nature, see Fenner, *Religious Folk Songs of the Negro*, 8, 63–65; Marsh, *The Story of the Jubilee Singers*, 240–241; Higginson, *Army Life in a Black Regiment*, 205; Allen *et al.*, *Slave Songs of the United States*, 91, 100; Burlin, *Negro Folk-Songs*, I, 37–42.

[47] Allen *et al.*, *Slave Songs of the United States*, 32–33.

[48] *Ibid.*, 30–31; Burlin, *Negro Folk-Songs*, II, 8–9; Fenner, *Religious Folk Songs of the Negro*, 12.

[49] Allen *et al.*, *Slave Songs of the United States*, 128–129; Fenner, *Religious Folk Songs of the Negro*, 127; Barton, *Old Plantation Hymns*, 26.

by a sense of change, transcendence, ultimate justice, and personal worth. The spirituals have been referred to as "sorrow songs," and in some respects they were. The slaves sang of "rollin' thro' an unfriendly world," of being "a-trouble in de mind," of living in a world which was a "howling wilderness," "a hell to me," of feeling like a "motherless child," "a po' little orphan chile in de worl'," a "home-e-less child," of fearing that "Trouble will bury me down.' " [50]

But these feelings were rarely pervasive or permanent; almost always they were overshadowed by a triumphant note of affirmation. Even so despairing a wail as "Nobody Knows the Trouble I've Had" could suddenly have its mood transformed by lines like: "One morning I was a-walking down, . . . Saw some berries a-hanging down, . . . I pick de berry and I suck de juice, . . . Just as sweet as de honey in de comb." [51] Similarly, amid the deep sorrow of "Sometimes I feel like a Motherless chile," sudden release could come with the lines: "Sometimes I feel like/A eagle in de air. . . . Spread my wings an'/Fly, fly, fly." [52] Slaves spent little time singing of the horrors of hell or damnation. Their songs of the Devil, quoted earlier, pictured a harsh but almost semicomic figure (often, one suspects, a surrogate for the white man), over whom they triumphed with reassuring regularity. For all their inevitable sadness, slave songs were characterized more by a feeling of confidence than of despair. There was confidence that contemporary power relationships were not immutable: "Did not old Pharaoh get lost, get lost, get lost, . . . get lost in the Red Sea?"; confidence in the possibilities of instantaneous change: "Jesus make de dumb to speak. . . . Jesus make de cripple walk. . . . Jesus give de blind his sight. . . . Jesus do most anything"; confidence in the rewards of persistence: "Keep a' inching along like a poor inch-worm,/ Jesus will come by'nd bye"; confidence that nothing could stand in the way of the justice they would receive: "You kin hender me here, but you can't do it dah," "O no man, no man, no man can hinder me"; confidence in the prospects of the future: "We'll walk de golden streets/Of de New Jerusalem." Religion, the slaves sang, "is good for anything, . . . Religion make you happy, . . . Religion gib me patience . . . O member, get Religion . . . Religion is so sweet." [53]

The slaves often pursued the "sweetness" of their religion in the face of many obstacles. Becky Ilsey, who was 16 when she was emancipated, recalled many years later:

> 'Fo' de war when we'd have a meetin' at night, wuz mos' always
> 'way in de woods or de bushes some whar so de white folks

[50] Allen et al., Slave Songs of the United States, 70, 102–103, 147; Barton, Old Plantation Hymns, 9, 17–18, 24; Marsh, The Story of the Jubilee Singers, 133, 167; Odum and Johnson, The Negro And His Songs, 35.

[51] Allen et al., Slave Songs of the United States, 102–103.

[52] Mary Allen Grissom, compiler, The Negro Sings A New Heaven (Chapel Hill, 1930), 73.

[53] Marsh, The Story of the Jubilee Singers, 179, 186; Allen et al., Slave Songs of the United States, 40–41, 44, 146; Barton, Old Plantation Hymns, 30.

couldn't hear, an' when dey'd sing a spiritual an' de spirit 'gin to
shout some de elders would go 'mongst de folks an' put dey han'
over dey mouf an' some times put a clof in dey mouf an' say:
"Spirit don talk so loud or de patterol break us up." You know dey
had white patterols what went 'roun' at night to see de niggers
didn't cut up no devilment, an' den de meetin' would break up an'
some would go to one house an' some to er nudder an' dey would
groan er w'ile, den go home.[54]

Elizabeth Ross Hite testified that although she and her fellow slaves on
a Louisiana plantation were Catholics, "lots didn't like that 'ligion."

We used to hide behind some bricks and hold church ourselves.
You see, the Catholic preachers from France wouldn't let us shout,
and the Lawd done said you gotta shout if you want to be saved.
That's in the Bible.

Sometimes we held church all night long, 'til way in the
mornin'. We burned some grease in a can for the preacher to see
the Bible by. . . .

See, our master didn't like us to have much 'ligion, said it made
us lag in our work. He jest wanted us to be Catholicses on Sundays
and go to mass and not study 'bout nothin' like that on week days.
He didn't want us shoutin' and moanin' all day long, but you gotta
shout and you gotta moan if you wants to be saved.[55]

The slaves clearly craved the affirmation and promise of their religion. It would be a mistake, however, to see this urge as exclusively other-
worldly. When Thomas Wentworth Higginson observed that the spirituals exhibited "nothing but patience for this life,—nothing but triumph in
the next," he, and later observers who elaborated upon this judgment,
were indulging in hyperbole. Although Jesus was ubiquitous in the spirituals, it was not invariably the Jesus of the New Testament of whom the
slaves sang, but frequently a Jesus transformed into an Old Testament
warrior: "Mass' Jesus" who engaged in personal combat with the Devil;
"King Jesus" seated on a milk-white horse with sword and shield in
hand. "Ride on, King Jesus," "Ride on, conquering King," "The God I
serve is a man of war," the slaves sang.[56] This transformation of Jesus is
symptomatic of the slaves' selectivity in choosing those parts of the Bible
which were to serve as the basis of their religious consciousness. Howard
Thurman, a Negro minister who as a boy had the duty of reading the
Bible to his grandmother, was perplexed by her refusal to allow him to
read from the Epistles of Paul.

[54] McIlhenny, *Befo' De War Spirituals*, 31.

[55] *Gumbo Ya-Ya: A Collection of Louisiana Folk Tales*, compiled by Lyle Saxon,
Edward Dreyer, and Robert Tallant from materials gathered by workers of the
WPA, Louisiana Writer's Project (Boston, 1945), 242.

[56] For examples, see Allen *et al.*, *Slave Songs of the United States*, 40–41, 82, 97, 106–
108; Marsh, *The Story of the Jubilee Singers*, 168, 203; Burlin, *Negro Folk-Songs*,
II, 8–9; Howard Thurman, *Deep River* (New York, 1945), 19–21.

When at length I asked the reason, she told me that during the days of slavery, the minister (white) on the plantation was always preaching from the Pauline letters—"Slaves, be obedient to your masters," etc. "I vowed to myself," she said, "that if freedom ever came and I learned to read, I would never read that part of the Bible!" [57]

Nor, apparently, did this part of the Scriptures ever constitute a vital element in slave songs or sermons. The emphasis of the spirituals, as Higginson himself noted, was upon the Old Testament and the exploits of the Hebrew children.[58] It is important that Daniel and David and Joshua and Jonah and Moses and Noah, all of whom fill the lines of the spirituals, were delivered in *this* world and delivered in ways which struck the imagination of the slaves. Over and over their songs dwelt upon the spectacle of the Red Sea opening to allow the Hebrew slaves past before inundating the mighty armies of the Pharaoh. They lingered delightedly upon the image of little David humbling the great Goliath with a stone—a pretechnological victory which post-bellum Negroes were to expand upon in their songs of John Henry. They retold in endless variation the stories of the blind and humbled Samson bringing down the mansions of his conquerors; of the ridiculed Noah patiently building the ark which would deliver him from the doom of a mocking world; of the timid Jonah attaining freedom from his confinement through faith. The similarity of these tales to the situation of the slave was too clear for him not to see it; too clear for us to believe that the songs had no worldly content for the black man in bondage. "O my Lord delivered Daniel," the slaves observed, and responded logically: "O why not deliver me, too?"

> He delivered Daniel from de lion's den,
>   Jonah from de belly ob de whale,
>   And de Hebrew children from de fiery furnace,
>   And why not every man? [59]

These lines state as clearly as anything can the manner in which the sacred world of the slaves was able to fuse the precedents of the

---

[57] Thurman, *Deep River*, 16–17.

[58] Higginson, *Army Life in a Black Regiment*, 202–205. Many of those northerners who came to the South to "uplift" the freedmen were deeply disturbed at the Old Testament emphasis of their religion. H. G. Spaulding complained that the ex-slaves needed to be introduced to "the light and warmth of the Gospel," and reported that a Union army officer told him: "Those people had enough of the Old Testament thrown at their heads under slavery. Now give them the glorious utterances and practical teachings of the Great Master." Spaulding, "Under the Palmetto," reprinted in Jackson, *The Negro and His Folklore in Nineteenth-Century Periodicals*, 66.

[59] Allen *et al.*, *Slave Songs of the United States*, 148; Fenner, *Religious Folk Songs of the Negro*, 21; Marsh, *The Story of the Jubilee Singers*, 134–135; McIlhenny, *Befo' De War Spirituals*, 248–249.

past, the conditions of the present, and the promise of the future into one connected reality. In this respect there was always a latent and symbolic element of protest in the slave's religious songs which frequently became overt and explicit. Frederick Douglass asserted that for him and many of his fellow slaves the song, "O Canaan, sweet Canaan,/I am bound for the land of Canaan," symbolized "something more than a hope of reaching heaven. We meant to reach the *North*, and the North was our Canaan," and he wrote that the lines of another spiritual, "Run to Jesus, shun the danger,/I don't expect to stay much longer here," had a double meaning which first suggested to him the thought of escaping from slavery.[60] Similarly, when the black troops in Higginson's regiment sang:

> We'll soon be free, [three times]
> When de Lord will call us home.

a young drummer boy explained to him, "Dey think *de Lord* mean for say *de Yankees*." [61] Nor is there any reason to doubt that slaves could have used their songs as a means of secret communication. An ex-slave told Lydia Parrish that when he and his fellow slaves "suspicioned" that one of their number was telling tales to the driver, they would sing lines like the following while working in the field:

> O Judyas he wuz a 'ceitful man
> He went an' betray a mos' innocen' man.
> Fo' thirty pieces a silver dat it wuz done
> He went in de woods an' e' self he hung.[62]

And it is possible, as many writers have argued, that such spirituals as the commonly heard "Steal away, steal away, steal away to Jesus!" were used as explicit calls to secret meetings.

But it is not necessary to invest the spirituals with a secular function only at the price of divesting them of their religious content, as Miles Mark Fisher has done.[63] While we may make such clear-cut distinctions, I have tried to show that the slaves did not. For them religion never constituted a simple escape from this world, because their conception of the world was more expansive than modern man's. Nowhere is this better illustrated than during the Civil War itself. While the war gave rise to such new spirituals as "Before I'd be a slave/I'd be buried in my grave,/ And go home to my Lord and be saved!" or the popular "Many thousand Go," with its jubilant rejection of all the facets of slave life—"No more peck o' corn for me, . . . No more driver's lash for me, . . . No more pint o' salt for me, . . . No more hundred lash for me, . . . No more

---

[60] *Life and Times of Frederick Douglass*, 159–160; Marsh, *The Story of the Jubilee Singers*, 188.

[61] Higginson, *Army Life in a Black Regiment*, 217.

[62] Parrish, *Slave Songs of the Georgia Sea Islands*, 247.

[63] "Actually, not one spiritual in its primary form reflected interest in anything other than a full life here and now." Fisher, *Negro Slave Songs in the United States*, 137.

mistress' call for me" [64]—the important thing was not that large numbers of slaves now could create new songs which openly expressed their views of slavery; that was to be expected. More significant was the ease with which their old songs fit their new situation. With so much of their inspiration drawn from the events of the Old Testament and the Book of Revelation, the slaves had long sung of wars, of battles, of the Army of the Lord, of Soldiers of the Cross, of trumpets summoning the faithful, of vanquishing the hosts of evil. These songs especially were, as Higginson put it, "available for camp purposes with very little strain upon their symbolism." "We'll cross de mighty river," his troops sang while marching or rowing,

> We'll cross de danger water, . . .
> O Pharaoh's army drownded!
> My army cross over.

"O blow your trumpet, Gabriel," they sang,

> Blow your trumpet louder;
> And I want dat trumpet to blow me home
> To my new Jerusalem.

But they also found their less overtly militant songs quite as appropriate to warfare. Their most popular and effective marching song was:

> Jesus call you, Go in de wilderness,
>   Go in de wilderness, go in de wilderness,
> Jesus call you. Go in de wilderness
> To wait upon de Lord.[65]

Black Union soldiers found it no more incongruous to accompany their fight for freedom with the sacred songs of their bondage than they had found it inappropriate as slaves to sing their spirituals while picking cotton or shucking corn. Their religious songs, like their religion itself, was of this world as well as the next.

Slave songs by themselves, of course, do not present us with a definitive key to the life and mind of the slave. They have to be seen within the context of the slave's situation and examined alongside such other cultural materials as folk tales. But slave songs do indicate the need to rethink a number of assumptions that have shaped recent interpretations of slavery, such as the assumption that because slavery eroded the linguistic and institutional side of African life it wiped out almost all the more fundamental aspects of African culture. Culture, certainly, is more than merely the sum total of institutions and language. It is also expressed by something less tangible, which the anthropologist Robert Redfield has

[64] Barton, *Old Plantation Hymns,* 25; Allen *et al., Slave Songs of the United States,* 94; McKim, "Negro Songs," 149.
[65] Higginson, *Army Life in a Black Regiment,* 201–202, 211–212.

called "style of life." Peoples as different as the Lapp and the Bedouin, Redfield has argued, with diverse languages, religions, customs, and institutions, may still share an emphasis on certain virtues and ideals, certain manners of independence and hospitality, general ways of looking upon the world, which give them a similar life style.[66] This argument applies to the West African cultures from which the slaves came. Though they varied widely in language, institutions, gods, and familial patterns, they shared a fundamental outlook toward the past, present, and future and common means of cultural expression which could well have constituted the basis of a sense of community and identity capable of surviving the impact of slavery.

Slave songs present us with abundant evidence that in the structure of their music and dance, in the uses to which music was put, in the survival of the oral tradition, in the retention of such practices as spirit possession which often accompanied the creation of spirituals, and in the ways in which the slaves expressed their new religion, important elements of their shared African heritage remained alive not just as quaint cultural vestiges but as vitally creative elements of slave culture. This could never have happened if slavery was, as Professor Elkins maintains, a system which so completely closed in around the slave, so totally penetrated his personality structure as to infantalize him and reduce him to a kind of *tabula rasa* upon which the white man could write what he chose.[67]

Slave songs provide us with the beginnings of a very different kind of hypothesis: that the preliterate, premodern Africans, with their sacred world view, were so imperfectly acculturated into the secular American society into which they were thrust, were so completely denied access to the ideology and dreams which formed the core of the consciousness of other Americans, that they were forced to fall back upon the only cultural frames of reference that made any sense to them and gave them any feeling of security. I use the word "forced" advisedly. Even if the slaves had had the opportunity to enter fully into the life of the larger society, they might still have chosen to retain and perpetuate certain elements of their African heritage. But the point is that they really had no choice. True acculturation was denied to most slaves. The alternatives were either to remain in a state of cultural limbo, divested of the old cultural patterns but not allowed to adopt those of their new homeland—which in the long run is no alternative at all—or to cling to as many as possible of the old ways of thinking and acting. The slaves' oral tradition, their music, and their religious outlook served this latter function and constituted a cultural refuge at least potentially capable of protecting their personalities from some of the worst ravages of the slave system.

The argument of Professors Tannenbaum and Elkins that the Protestant churches in the United States did not act as a buffer between the slave and his master is persuasive enough, but it betrays a modern pre-

---

[66] Robert Redfield, *The Primitive World and Its Transformations* (Ithaca, 1953), 51–53.
[67] Elkins, *Slavery*, Chap. III.

occupation with purely institutional arrangements.[68] Religion is more than an institution, and because Protestant churches failed to protect the slave's inner being from the incursions of the slave system, it does not follow that the spiritual message of Protestantism failed as well. Slave songs are a testament to the ways in which Christianity provided slaves with the precedents, heroes, and future promise that allowed them to transcend the purely temporal bonds of the Peculiar Institution.

Historians have frequently failed to perceive the full importance of this because they have not taken the slave's religiosity seriously enough. A people cannot create a music as forceful and striking as slave music out of a mere uninternalized anodyne. Those who have argued that Negroes did not oppose slavery in any meaningful way are writing from a modern, political context. What they really mean is that the slaves found no *political* means to oppose slavery. But slaves, to borrow Professor Hobsbawm's term, were prepolitical beings in a prepolitical situation.[69] Within their frame of reference there were other—and from the point of view of personality development, not necessarily less effective—means of escape and opposition. If mid-twentieth-century historians have difficulty perceiving the sacred universe created by slaves as a serious alternative to the societal system created by southern slaveholders, the problem may be the historians' and not the slaves'.

Above all, the study of slave songs forces the historian to move out of his own culture, in which music plays a peripheral role, and offers him the opportunity to understand the ways in which black slaves were able to perpetuate much of the centrality and functional importance that music had for their African ancestors. In the concluding lines of his perceptive study of primitive song, C. M. Bowra has written:

> Primitive song is indispensable to those who practice it. . . . they cannot do without song, which both formulates and answers their nagging questions, enables them to pursue action with zest and confidence, brings them into touch with gods and spirits, and makes them feel less strange in the natural world. . . . it gives to them a solid centre in what otherwise would be almost chaos, and a continuity in their being, which would too easily dissolve before the calls of the implacable present . . . through its words men, who might otherwise give in to the malice of circumstances, find their old powers revived or new powers stirring in them, and through these life itself is sustained and renewed and fulfilled.[70]

This, I think, sums up concisely the function of song for the slave. Without a general understanding of that function, without a specific understanding of the content and meaning of slave song, there can be no full comprehension of the effects of slavery upon the slave or the meaning of the society from which slaves emerged at emancipation.

68 *Ibid.*, Chap. II; Frank Tannenbaum, *Slave and Citizen* (New York, 1946).
69 E. J. Hobsbawm, *Primitive Rebels* (New York, 1959), Chap. I.
70 C. M. Bowra, *Primitive Song* (London, 1962), 285–286.

Suggestions for Further Reading

On disease and death, an ever present part of daily life, the inquiring student can learn much from Alfred W. Crosby, Jr., *The Columbian Exchange: Biological and Cultural Consequences of 1492* (Westport, Conn., 1972); Allen E. Stearn, *The Effect of Smallpox on the Destiny of the Amerindian* (Boston, 1945); John Duffy, *Epidemics in Colonial America** (Baton Rouge, La., 1953); and Charles E. Rosenberg, *The Cholera Years: The United States in 1832, 1849, and 1866* (Chicago, 1962). Also of importance is David E. Stannard, "Death and Dying in Puritan New England," *American Historical Review* 78 (1973):1305–30.

Public responsibility for the care of both the diseased and the insane can be traced in Dora Mae Blackmon, *The Care of the Mentally Ill in America, 1604–1812* (Washington, D.C., 1964); John B. Blake, *Public Health in the Town of Boston, 1630–1822* (Cambridge, Mass., 1959); John Duffy, *A History of Public Health in New York City, 1625–1866* (New York, 1968); Norman Dain, *Disordered Minds: The First Century of Eastern State Hospital in Williamsburg, Virginia, 1766–1866* (Charlottesville, Va., 1971); David J. Rothman, *The Discovery of the Asylum: Social Order and Disorder in the New Republic* (Boston, 1971); and Gerald N. Grob, "Mental Illness, Indigency, and Welfare: The Mental Hospital in Nineteenth-Century America," in Tamara K. Hareven, ed., *Anonymous Americans: Explorations in Nineteenth-Century Social History** (Englewood Cliffs, N.J., 1971).

Women's roles, as they changed from the colonial period to the nineteenth century, are the subject of much new historical inquiry. For the eighteenth century, see Mary S. Benson, *Women in Eighteenth-Century America: A Study of Opinion and Social Usage* (New York, 1935), and Julia C. Spruill, *Women's Life and Work in the Southern Colonies** (Chapel Hill, N.C., 1938). Patterns of early education in the nineteenth century are traced in Bernard Wishy, *The Child and the Republic: The Dawn of Modern American Child Culture* (Philadelphia, 1967). But more important was the changing role of women in the work force, which can be studied in Edith Abbott, *Women in Industry* (New York, 1915); Hannah Josephson, *The Golden Thread: New England Mill Girls and Magnates* (New York, 1949); Caroline Ware, *Early New England Cotton Manufacturing* (Cambridge, Mass., 1931); and Gerda Lerner, "The Lady and the Mill Girl: Changes in the Status of Women in the Age of Jackson," *Midcontinent American Studies Journal* 10 (1969):5–15. Other aspects of women's life in the ante-

* Available in paperback edition.

bellum period can be studied in William R. Taylor and Christopher Lasch, "Two Kindred Spirits: Sorority and Family in New England, 1839–1846," *New England Quarterly* 36 (1963):23–41; Barbara Welter, "The Cult of True Womanhood, 1820–1860," *American Quarterly* 18 (1966):151–74; and David M. Kennedy, *Birth Control in America* (New Haven, Conn., 1970).

Antebellum slave life is a subject surrounded with controversy. For three contrasting views the student can read John Blassingame, *The Slave Community: Plantation Life in the Ante-Bellum South** (New York, 1972); Robert W. Fogel and Stanley L. Engerman, *Time on the Cross: The Economics of American Negro Slavery** (Boston, 1974); and Eugene D. Genovese, *Roll, Jordan, Roll: The World the Slaves Made* (New York, 1974). Also valuable are Kenneth Stampp, *The Peculiar Institution: Slavery in the Ante-Bellum South** (New York, 1956); Vincent Harding, "Religion and Resistance Among Antebellum Negroes," in August Meier and Elliott Rudwick, *The Making of Black America** (New York, 1969):179–97; George P. Rawick, *From Sundown to Sunup: The Making of the Black Community* (Westport, Conn., 1972); Raymond A. Bauer and Alice H. Bauer, "Day-to-Day Resistance to Slavery," *Journal of Negro History* 27 (1942):388–419; and John Lovell, Jr., *Black Song: The Forge and the Flame* (New York, 1972).

The lives of agricultural people of the South in the era from the American Revolution to the Civil War is largely still to be written. But for the earlier period, a good start can be made in Carl Bridenbaugh, *Myths and Realities: Societies of the Colonial South** (Baton Rouge, La., 1952). Useful for the nineteenth century are Everett Dick, *The Dixie Frontier: A Social History of the Southern Frontier from the First Transmontane Beginnings to the Civil War* (New York, 1948); Avery Craven, "Poor Whites and Negroes in the Antebellum South," *Journal of Negro History* 15 (1930):14–25; Roger Shugg, *Origins of the Class Struggle in Louisiana: A Social History of White Farmers and Laborers During Slavery and After, 1840–1875* (Baton Rouge, La., 1939); and Dickson D. Bruce, Jr., *And They All Sang Hallelujah: Plain-Folk Camp-Meeting Religion, 1800–1845* (Knoxville, Tenn., 1974).

1830–1877
The Expanding Nation

Schoolhouses and Scholars

STANLEY K. SCHULTZ

In modern America we think of education as the concern of schools and universities. But for the first two centuries of our history secondary schools existed for only a small minority of Americans, and universities served only a tiny fraction of that minority. This lack of schools did not mean that only the advantaged "received an education." Rather, it signified that the family and the church, rather than formal institutions of instruction, were the primary means by which skills, knowledge, moral precepts, and attitudes were transmitted from one generation to another.

In nineteenth-century America public education was extended to a far broader segment of society. At the same time, schools began to perform many of the functions previously performed by parents and religious leaders. Accordingly, not only the three R's but religious and moral instruction fell within the schoolteacher's responsibilities. The public school movement became an important part of the process of democratization that reformers of the antebellum period sought to extend to every aspect of society. And the public school became an important part of the life of nearly every child growing up in America. Before the century was over a great majority of young Americans, for most of their formative years, would spend a significant part of their waking day within the walls of the public school classroom. Public education, partially eclipsing the role of family and church, became a profoundly important part of everyday life.

The educational reform movement of the first half of the nineteenth century proclaimed the right of every child to free public education. Universal free public education soon became an irreducible article of faith among virtually all reformers, for it was argued that a democracy could not stand without an educated citizenry, and that an egalitarian society could not survive unless, through universal education, all persons were equally equipped to compete in an open marketplace of talent. Thus, it has been argued, an enlightened and insistent lower class, led by humanitarian reformers, fought an entrenched upper class in antebellum America for the right to public education. And won.

It is only recently that historians have challenged this view. But from recent scholarship we are learning that one of the primary aims, if not the central goal, of the public school movement was to impose social control on an increasingly multi-ethnic, urban, and impoverished lower class. Close examination of the curriculum, pedagogical techniques, and leadership of the school reform movement has led some historians to the conclusion that schools were designed to inculcate values and patterns of behavior that served those whose place in society was already secure. In this sense, the main legacy of the public school movement, as social historian Michael Katz has written in **The Irony of School Reform,** was the principle that "education was something the better part of the community did to the others to make them orderly, moral, and tractable." The research of Katz and others suggests that the public schools were widely supported by the upper classes, often against lower-class opposition, because the elite saw the public school as an instrument for arresting the social chaos and disintegration of family life that they identified as the most fearful side-effects of immigration, urbanization, and industrialization, and that together were transforming the social contours of the nation before the Civil War.

Nowhere was the educational reform movement more vibrant than in nineteenth-century Boston. In Stanley Schultz's analysis of the controversy over public education that preoccupied that city in the Jacksonian era, we can see how education touched the lives of most of the city's inhabitants. The confusion surrounding the school reform movement, which was partly a product of the conflict between the mythical image of the ideal rural schoolhouse and the realities of an urban setting, also tells us much about how Bostonians' lives were being affected by the advent of industrialization, immigration, and urban growth in this period. Many of the reformers hoped that somehow the schools could deal with these problems. Because the schoolteacher had been charged with many of the tasks performed in earlier eras by the parent and clergyman, it now seemed especially important that the schools rise to the challenge.

B etween 1820 and 1860 Boston and New England educators increasingly came to view the common school as a "community in miniature." There, the child could mature in an environment created especially for him, in surroundings tailored to fit his needs as separate from those of the adult community. There, the teacher could stand in place of the parent, examining the character, morals, and habits of each child, and exercising the moral authority that had once belonged exclusively to the family. There, also, the schoolmaster could impart the moral instruction that had once come from the pulpit, an agency whose orthodoxy and social prestige appeared ever more questionable.[1] The public school was to be a classroom, a family room, a church house—all things to all children. The school was to nurture the child to adulthood, equip him with necessary

"Schoolhouses and Scholars." From *The Culture Factory: Boston Public Schools, 1789–1860* by Stanley K. Schultz, pp. 69–92. Copyright © 1973 by Oxford University Press, Inc. Reprinted by permission.

[1] George B. Emerson and Alonzo Potter, *The School and the Schoolmaster* (New York, 1842), pp. 79–90, 128–40, 350–51.

skills of a livelihood, and familiarize him with the rigors and dangers of life in the city. In short, the school was to be the social incubator of responsible citizens.

While the goal was ambitious, the optimism of Bostonians appeared equal to the task. By the mid-1820's enthusiastic citizens had erected a year-round system of primary schools, and had done so in spite of determined opposition from conservatives. Boston leaders had expanded grammar school instruction throughout the city. They had also provided a Latin High School for boys, an English High School for boys and a similar experimental school for girls (schools with less emphasis on the classics than in Latin schools), two classrooms in the House of Industry (the city poorhouse), and two separate schools for Negro children. Although total private contributions for private education still surpassed city taxes for public schools, expenditures for public education averaged nearly $60,000 over the decade, or more than 16 per cent of total public expenditures.[2]

Boston seemed to deserve the praises bestowed by visitor and native alike. "The means of education are the same to all," marveled Mrs. Anne Royall, a usually cantankerous and cynical widow who supported herself by writing travelogues of American towns and cities. "There are not less than an hundred schools in Boston and vicinity, free to all, many of them without money and without price. . . . Never were the means so ample as in Boston; the whole state is one seminary of education; no excuse for ignorance; the poor are taught gratis." Educational critic James G. Carter testified that Boston alone had spent nearly as much for schooling as had the rest of the state combined. And referring to Carter's evaluation of Massachusetts' public schools, Harvard scholar George Ticknor, then a member of the Primary School Board, commented that the best proof of Boston's educational excellence was that wealthy citizens could find no better schools anywhere for their children. Indeed, by 1826, members of the City Council were suggesting that the city had built too well. Other New Englanders, they warned, heard of the superior public schools and moved to Boston to reap the advantages of free education. Yet even this criticism was a backhanded compliment, an indication of the pride that Bostonians had in their schools.[3]

Beneath the pride and optimism, however, lurked doubt. If the schools

[2] *Report of the School Committee of the City of Boston on the State of the Schools. May, 1826* (Boston, 1826), pp. 8–9. Excluding expenditures for primary schools, the city spent $45,193.56 on all schools during 1826. See Charles Phillips Huse, *The Financial History of Boston: From May 1, 1822, to January 31, 1909* (vol. XV, *Harvard Economic Studies*, Cambridge, Mass., 1916), Appendix I, "Schools, 1818–1859," p. 364.

[3] Anne Royall, *Sketches of History, Life, and Manners in the United States* (New Haven, 1826), p. 324; James G. Carter, *Letters to the Hon. William Prescott, LL.D., on the Free Schools of New England, with Remarks upon the Principles of Instruction* (Boston, 1824), p. 34; George S. Hillard, Mrs. Anna E. Ticknor, and Miss Anna E. Ticknor, eds., *Life, Letters and Journals of George Ticknor* (2 vols., Boston, 1877), II, 188; George Ticknor, "Free Schools of New England," *North American Review*, XIX (1824), 448–57; *Bowen's Boston News-Letter*, I (1825), 224.

were as good as everyone said, why weren't they even better? If Boston was so dedicated to the principle of free public education, why weren't all of the children attending the public schools? During the late 1820's approximately 45 per cent of the city's school-age population attended the primary and grammar schools, a commendable number but not enough, according to the critics. Clearly, remarked some citizens, educational problems were far from solution. The City Council, wary of large expenditures in the face of a mounting public debt, refused to allocate funds for new schools. The Council was willing to build onto existing schools to provide rooms for ward political meetings, thereby satisfying two city needs with one sum. But it balked at other additions or repairs. In 1826, for example, expenditures for all public obligations exceeded income. Councilmen pointed to generous allotments to schools as partially responsible for the fiscal crisis. It was to be nearly a decade before the Council would grant funds for construction of the city's first primary school building.[4]

Although the Primary School Board and the School Committee often trumpeted their successes, they also bemoaned the failure of the general public and the city to give more support to schools. As early as 1820 the School Committee had observed that "though the present system of public education, and the munificence with which it is supported, are highly beneficial and honorable to the town," yet it could be perfected. The ominous facts, charged the Primary School Board in 1824, "that in this city a considerable number of youth should be suffered to grow up destitute of the advantages secured to the children generally, and be abandoned to idleness, vagrancy, ignorance, and crime, reflects no honor on the citizens or on our institutions, and demands prompt attention."[5]

Such comments characterized the curious mixture of praise and condemnation that filled the rhetoric of the common school movement in Boston and elsewhere. The very educators and reformers who advertised the need for common schools were the first to decry current school conditions. To be sure, their carpings were partly promotional devices. The public hardly would have voted higher taxes for new schools, equipment, and more highly paid teachers if it believed all was well. To shatter public complacency about school conditions was an educator's self-imposed duty. The criticisms of educators and reformers also were signs of healthful self-criticism. James G. Carter illustrated this tendency in noting that "the success of the free school system is just cause of congratulation; but

---

[4] Enrollment figure an educated guess, derived from 1826 *Boston School Reports* (hereafter *BSR*) attendance of 7,044 and school-age population figures for 1830—see Table 3, Chapter 5, p. 110, *infra*. See also *Bowen's Boston News-Letter*, I (1825), 168, 270, and II (1826), 211; Joseph M. Wightman, comp., *Annals of the Boston Primary School Committee, From Its First Establishment in 1818, to Its Dissolution in 1855* (Boston, 1860), p. 153; James G. Carter, *Essays upon Popular Education, Containing a Particular Examination of the Schools of Massachusetts, and an Outline of an Institution for the Education of Teachers* (Boston, 1826), p. 41.

[5] "Actions of Boston School Committee of 1820–1821," in *BSR, 1864* (Boston, 1864), pp. 153–55; 1824 quotation in Wightman, *Annals*, p. 91.

. . . their influence has not been the greatest and best which the *same means,* under better management, might produce." [6]

Neither promotionalism nor self-criticism, however, explained the exuberance for public education on the one hand, and, on the other, the ever-present sense of dismay and defeat. However attractive a picture they painted, school authorities and educational reformers rarely failed to edge it with darker hues. "The public schools, in this city of Boston, are, we believe now, and have long been, comparatively in a prosperous state," commented Stephen Farley, a speaker before the 1834 meeting of the American Institute of Instruction. "We believe" and "comparatively"— these were words tinged with doubt. Boston schools, Farley concluded, tended toward *"what they ought to be;* and what all schools should be throughout the country." In 1845 the Boston School Committee reversed Farley's judgment. The annual report, written by Horace Mann's close friend and follower Samuel Gridley Howe, reluctantly charged that "the Grammar Schools of Boston have not the excellence and usefulness they should possess. We cannot but believe, for we see, that the other Schools [of the state] are better than most of ours." The report for the following year, prepared by Committee members less interested in reform, refuted Howe's declaration. In a metaphor that was to be oft-repeated the report asserted that "the common-school system of New England is its pride and strength; and the public schools of Boston are the richest jewel in its crown." Yet even this report dimmed its own lustrous praise of schools by exhorting citizens to "let us make them what they should be." [7]

Arguments for improving the schools invariably were accompanied by complaints about their present state. A comparison of the "is" and the "ought-to-be" was the reformers' stock-in-trade. As school systems expanded and as larger public funds for schools became available, the criticisms became more strident. Rising expectations of what an adequate system of public education could accomplish made present realities appear shoddy by comparison.

By 1855, for example, statesman Edward Everett could maintain that Boston schools had improved over the past fifty years "beyond what any one will readily conceive" who had not witnessed the changes for himself. But less than two years later, the celebrated Harvard philosopher Francis Bowen, whose chief experience had been with Boston schools, could observe of the entire New England school system: "any hovel would answer for a school-house, any primer would do for a textbook, any farmer's apprentice was competent to 'teach school.' " Boston schoolmen had been hurling the same invectives against their own schools for many years. A gulf existed between what educators and reformers believed the schools could become, and what they observed the schools to

---

[6] Carter quoted in Henry Barnard, ed., "James G. Carter," *Educational Biography: Teachers and Educators* (2nd ed., New York, 1859), pp. 185–86.

[7] Stephen Farley, "On the Improvement Which May Be Made in the Condition of the Common Schools," *Introductory Discourse and Lectures . . . American Institute of Instruction . . . Boston, August, 1834* (Boston, 1835), p. 70; *BSR, 1845* (Boston, 1845), p. 30; *BSR, 1846* (Boston, 1846), p. 160.

be. This disparity between expectations and realities gave rise to the educational jeremiad, that peculiar blend of praise and vilification that permeated school board reports and the pronouncements of reformers throughout the antebellum years.[8]

Educators and reformers had to adjust their conceptions of the ideal public school to fit the physical realities of an urban environment. Many persisted in measuring the city schools by a rural standard, as, indeed, they often measured the quality of urban life itself by a pastoral ideal. Since the public school was to be a model miniature community, educators stressed that the physical settings of classroom and school buildings inevitably would influence the quality of education. The school, they argued, could not be parent and clergyman unless it provided for the complete needs of the child—and these were physical as well as intellectual and moral. Much of the idealistic debate, therefore, about the social role of common schools centered around mundane matters such as the best location for the schoolhouse, the proper size of classrooms, and the need for playgrounds. In discussing the daily functioning of the public schools, educators and reformers revealed their idealistic conceptions of the perfect school for perfecting the child.

EXPECTATIONS AND REALITIES

Educators and school reformers—as college graduates, lawyers, physicians, and men in various other professions—could not help but breathe the intellectual atmosphere of their times. Whatever else was true, during the years of the common school movement a pastoral imagery suffused the intellectual horizons of America. Though the forty-year period from 1820 to 1860 saw proportionately the largest increase in urban population in the nation's history (with the peak urbanization of New England occurring in the 1840's),[9] many American intellectuals rejected that present in favor of the idyllic past. Novelists and essayists like Nathaniel Hawthorne, Herman Melville, James Fenimore Cooper, Henry David Thoreau, and Ralph Waldo Emerson perceived the nation in transition from an agrarian to an industrial society. Reacting against a prophesied age of the machine (most often symbolized by the railroad engine) these and other writers looked romantically over their shoulders to the alleged simplicity of by-gone days. In Nature—an abstract metaphor for simplicity and order—they found virtue and innocence; in the City or the Machine—

---

[8] Edward Everett, "The Boston Schools," *Barnard's American Journal of Education* (hereafter *BAJE*), I (May 1856), 643; Bowen, quoted *ibid.*, IV (September 1857), 14; I am indebted to Richard Hofstadter for pointing out that "the educational jeremiad is as much a feature of our literature as the jeremiad in the Puritan sermons," *Anti-Intellectualism in American Life* (New York, 1963), p. 301.

[9] *The Statistical History of the United States from Colonial Times to the Present* (Stamford, Conn., 1965), Chapter A, Series A 181–94 and 195–209, p. 14; Jeffrey G. Williamson, "Antebellum Urbanization in the American Northeast," *Journal of Economic History*, XXV (December 1965), 597–98 and *passim.*

verbal shorthand for complexity and disorder—they beheld decadence and artificiality.

Thus the political symbols of the period became Andrew Jackson—historian George Bancroft's "unlettered man of the West," the "nursling of the wilds"—and the log cabin. Thus the humor was wrapped in homespun and personified by riverboatman Mike Fink, backwoodsman Davy Crockett, and Yankee Colonel Jack Downing. Thus the Christian church became the Church Evangelical, crusading with its rural revivalism into the heart of even the great cities. Thus the characteristic philosophy of the period was Transcendentalism—a blend of two parts Nature and one part Mysticism—served up at the side of a pond by a man who had failed as a teacher in urban schools.[10]

Even city-born and bred Bostonians expressed this vague longing for a simplified, rural, or village past. In his *The Companion to Spelling Books*, a widely used textbook in Boston grammar schools, William Bentley Fowle wrote of innocence versus artificiality, "the town for manners, the country for morals." Ralph Waldo Emerson, who wished to demonstrate that one man could be a counterpoise to the city, still had to admit: "I wish to have rural strength and religion for my children, and I wish city facility and polish. I find with chagrin that I cannot have both." And, by the mid-1840's, the Brahmin educator and author George Ticknor could sadly recount that the Boston of his youth at the turn of the century was gone forever. Then "we . . . felt involved in each other's welfare and fate as it is impossible we should now, when our numbers are trebled, and our affairs complicated and extended till their circumference is too wide to be embraced by any one mind, and till the interests of each individual are grown too separate and intense to be bound in by any general sympathy with the whole." Ticknor could only grieve for the days when "we were then a more compact, united, and kindly community than we have ever been since, or ever can be again." [11]

Undoubtedly these pastoral longings, so pervasive in the intellectual climate of the period, influenced the attitudes of educators about the

---

10 For interpreting the intellectual currents of the period I have relied upon the perceptive discussions in Leo Marx, *The Machine in the Garden: Technology and the Pastoral Ideal in America* (New York, 1964); R. W. B. Lewis, *The American Adam: Innocence, Tragedy, and Tradition in the Nineteenth Century* (Chicago, 1955); Marvin Meyers, *The Jacksonian Persuasion: Politics and Belief* (Vintage ed., New York, 1960); John William Ward, *Andrew Jackson: Symbol for an Age* (New York, 1955); Constance Rourke, *American Humor: A Study of the National Character* (New York, 1931); Timothy L. Smith, *Revivalism and Social Reform: American Protestantism on the Eve of the Civil War* (1957; reprinted, New York, 1965); Louis B. Salomon, "The Straight-Cut Ditch: Thoreau on Education," *American Quarterly*, XIV (Spring 1962), 19–36; Octavius Brooks Frothingham, *Transcendentalism in New England: A History* (1876; reprinted, New York, 1959).

11 William B. Fowle, *The Companion to Spelling Books* (Boston, 1843), p. 17; Bliss Perry, ed., *The Heart of Emerson's Journals* (New York, 1958), entries for October 17, 1840, and March 1844, pp. 157, 208; George Ticknor, "Memoirs of the Buckminsters," *Christian Examiner*, XLVII (1849), 171–73.

conditions of Boston schools. Who could admire the congested urban classroom when comparing it to the literary commonplace of the day, Ichabod Crane's schoolhouse in Sleepy Hollow? There "the schoolhouse stood just at the foot of a woody hill, with a brook running close by. From hence the low murmur of his pupils' voices conning their lessons might be heard in a drowsy summer's day, like the hum of a bee-hive." Indeed, who could admire the city itself when even the textbooks used by children in rural and urban schools alike painted it as artificial and corrupt when compared with the virtuous, idyllic life of the countryside? Certainly the most familiar building in all of American folklore was the "Little Red Schoolhouse," the traditional symbol of American education. Educational reformers found it far more pleasant to imagine a little red schoolhouse in the country, bordered by vines and flowers, standing sentinel near a wooded hill, than to conjure up a rather dirty, wooden or stone, one or two story building on a crowded street, surrounded by tailors' shops, wagon depots, saloons, and other sights and sounds of the city. That many Boston and New England educators fancied the image of the rural school and rejected the urban school as educationally unworthy was not surprising.[12]

Occasionally someone might rise to the defense of the urban classroom. Stephen Farley, calling for improvement, nonetheless praised the schools of Boston, New Haven, and other New England cities, regretting only that their examples did not reach and reform the country schools. In 1848, commenting on the recent annual report of the Boston schools, a writer in the *North American Review* observed that "in some respects, the city schools have advantages over those of the country. The city is the centre of intelligence, as well as of wealth. Ideas, no less than money, circulate with greater rapidity there. Books are more abundant and accessible, and the national powers are more speedily brought into activity. Talent of all kinds naturally concentrates in the city." Yet even this admirer felt compelled to warn that the activity of the city intellect might be superficial or showy.[13]

But for every admirer, there were many more detractors. Leading the chorus of jeremiads were such men as Warren Colburn, James G.

---

[12] Washington Irving, "The Legend of Sleepy Hollow," *Sketch-Book* (New York, 1820), p. 253. On schoolbooks, see the brilliant discussion by Ruth Miller Elson, *Guardians of Tradition: American Schoolbooks of the Nineteenth Century* (Lincoln, Neb., 1964), pp. 25–35. A starting point for comparison of the portrayal of schoolhouse and teacher in nineteenth-century fiction and poetry with actual physical and social conditions includes Arthur Foff, "Teacher Stereotypes in the American Novel" (unpublished Ph.D. dissertation, School of Education, Stanford University, 1953); Richard Allan Foster, *The School in American Literature* (Baltimore, 1930); and Maxine Greene, *The Public School & the Private Vision: A Search for America in Education and Literature* (New York, 1965). For a typical idealization of American education employing the rural symbol, see A. H. Nelson, "The Little Red Schoolhouse," *Educational Review*, XXIII (March 1901), 304–15.

[13] Farley, "On the Improvement of Schools," p. 70; "Boston Public Schools," *North American Review*, LXVI (April 1848), 447–48.

Carter, William A. Alcott, George B. Emerson, Samuel G. Goodrich, and Horace Mann—each a major figure of the day. Colburn was a founder of the American Institute of Instruction, a Boston schoolteacher, for a brief period a member of the Boston School Committee, and the author of *Colburn's First Lessons, Intellectual Arithmetic upon the Inductive Method of Instruction* (1826), the standard mathematics textbook in Boston, and throughout much of the nation as well. Carter, through his *Essays upon Popular Education* (1826), and his activities as chairman of the state House Committee on Education that created the Board of Education in 1837, fostered much of the debate on the common school movement in New England. Alcott was a tireless writer in educational campaigns, a former teacher in district schools, editor of the *Annals of Education* in Boston during the 1830's, and one of the most influential propagandists in the discovery of the childhood movement. Emerson, second only to Mann in public esteem as an educational missionary, served on both the Primary School Board and the School Committee in Boston. In addition, he was a co-author of *The School and the Schoolmaster* (1842), the leading manual for schoolteachers and administrators during the period. Goodrich was the author and publisher of the famous "Peter Parley" series—collections of didactic stories and moral aphorisms—as well as the compiler of numerous school textbooks.[14]

Each of these men had been born, raised, and educated in small town, rural surroundings. Each had attended a New England district school. Their childhood experiences led them to be sharply critical of urban schools. A realization that education in the city posed more difficult problems than existed in the countryside kindled their enthusiasm for reform. Although in numerous ways they measured the physical realities of urban schools by pastoral expectations, paradoxically these reformers did not urge a return to the rural, district school. They knew it too well.

The early training of Horace Mann was typical. Born in the small town of Franklin, Massachusetts, in 1796, he was one of five children whose father meagerly supported the family by cultivating a small farm. Mann's early education was limited to a district school that belonged to the smallest district, had the poorest schoolhouse, and employed the cheapest teachers in a town that itself was small and poor. Among his first teachers was an itinerant master named Samuel Barrett, a gentleman learned in languages who would teach for six months, then lose his post

---

[14] Theodore Edson, *Memoir of Warren Colburn, Written for the American Journal of Education* (Boston, 1856); Walter Scott Monroe, "Development of Arithmetic As a School Subject," U.S. Bureau of Education *Bulletin, 1917*, No. 10 (Washington, D.C., 1917); "James G. Carter," in Barnard, ed., *Educational Biography*, pp. 182–94; "William A. Alcott," *ibid.*, pp. 249–67; "George B. Emerson," *ibid.*, pp. 333–43; Robert C. Waterson, *Memoir of Geo. Barrell Emerson* (Boston, 1884), reprinted from the *Proceedings* of the Massachusetts Historical Society, XX (Boston, 1882–83); "Boston Public Schools," *North American Review*, p. 453; Samuel G. Goodrich, *Recollections of a Lifetime* (2 vols., New York, 1856); William B. Cairns, "Samuel Griswold Goodrich," Allen Johnson and Dumas Malone, eds., *Dictionary of American Biography* (11 vols., Subscription ed., New York, 1959), IV, Part I, 402–3.

because of a prolonged drunken binge. In later life Mann regretted his unhappy childhood, the "continual privations," the few and miserable books for children, the very poor teachers, and the fact that "until the age of fifteen I had never been to school more than eight or ten weeks in a year." [15]

To outsiders the district schools appeared praiseworthy. The usually critical Harriet Martineau, for example, on her visit through rural New England in the mid-1830's, marveled that "the provision of schools is so adequate, that any citizen who sees a child at play during school-hours may ask 'Why are you not at school?' and, unless a good reason be given, may take him to the schoolhouse of the district." [16] But those who had been trained in such schools could only criticize.

"Two principal causes have operated from the first establishment of the free schools," explained James G. Carter of the district schools, "to impair and pervert their influence. 1st, Incompetent instructors; 2d, Bad school books." Carter could not overemphasize the shabby quality of teaching in the district schools. Teachers were usually very young; they were constantly changing their employment in search of higher wages or more interesting work; worst of all, they rarely had undergone any direct training for their work. Other reformers joined in raising a familiar lament: "shall those who despair of success in any employment, be allowed to take up school-keeping as an ultimate resource?" It was not uncommon for school boards throughout New England to complain of applicants, as did one board in 1847, that "he thinks of turning peddler, or of working at shoemaking. But the one will expose him to storms, the other he fears will injure his chest. . . . He will nevertheless teach school for a meagre compensation." As was often the case, Horace Mann came closest to explaining the reasons for inadequate teaching. He noted: "we pay best,—1st, those who destroy us,—generals; 2nd, those who cheat us,—politicians and quacks; 3rd, those who amuse us,—singers and dancers; and last of all those who instruct us,—teachers." [17]

While rural teachers were incompetent, smalltown and district school-

---

[15] This account of Mann, including excerpts from a letter describing his early experiences, appeared in Barnard, ed., *Educational Biography*, pp. 365–68. Cf. Jonathan C. Messerli, "Horace Mann: The Early Years, 1796–1837" (unpublished Ph.D. dissertation, Department of Education, Harvard University, 1963).

[16] *Society in America* (2 vols., London, 1837), II, 163.

[17] Carter, *Letters . . . on the Free Schools*, p. 55; "The Common School System of Massachusetts," *New Englander*, XIII (February 1855), 55; *Reports of the Connecticut Board of Education, 1847* (New Haven, 1847), p. 48; Mann, *Common School Journal*, IX (1847), p. 48. There was a plethora of literature on the inadequacies of teachers and teacher-training during the period. For examples, see William A. Alcott, *Confessions of a Schoolmaster* (Boston, 1839), pp. 13, 17, 136–38; Rev. Samuel Read Hall, "On the Necessity of Educating Teachers," *Lectures before the American Institute of Instruction* (hereafter *LAII*) . . . *1834* (Boston, 1835), pp. 257ff.; David Mack, "The Claims of Our Age and Country Upon Teachers," *LAII* . . . *1839* (Boston, 1840), pp. 137–54; and, "P," "Definition of a Good School," *Common School Journal* (hereafter *CSJ*), VIII (January 15, February 2, March 2, November 2, 16, December 1, 1846), 17–20, 42–47, 71–76, 329–31, 344–49, 353–58.

houses were even more inadequate. "The site for a schoolhouse," wrote Samuel G. Goodrich in 1838, "is generally in the most neglected, because the cheapest, spot in town. . . . For the sheepfold and the cow-house, sheltered situations are carefully selected; but a bleak hill-top, swept by the winter blast, or a sandy plain, scorched by the dog-day sun, will do for a schoolhouse, especially if it is so useless for everything else as to be given gratis to the district." [18] Goodrich did not exaggerate. Down through the 1840's small, wood-frame, one-room schoolhouses were common in most districts. Built usually at the juncture of several roads the schools rarely had any enclosures or trees nearby. They were centers of noise and potential danger from passing vehicles when located in populous areas; or simply dirty, sun-baked and snow-swept, ramshackle huts when built in more isolated surroundings. If the structure was fortunate enough to have windows, the glass usually was broken, giving the building the appearance from the outside of an eyeless derelict. Inside, the one room was generally no larger than thirty feet square. Next to the entrance was a fireplace and the master's desk. Against the three remaining walls, in tiers from the oldest children next to the walls to younger children nearer the center of the room, were narrow, backless benches on which the youth sat for six or more hours a day.

Such schools often accommodated over one hundred children, crammed together on benches. Neither inside nor outside were there any sanitation facilities. Ventilation was so inadequate that during the twenty-week summer term, beginning about the first of May, students broiled, while during the twelve-to-sixteen-week winter term, starting about the first of December, they chilled. Discipline was harsh, with instructors brandishing and using rattan ferules (rulers). In one Massachusetts school there was even a five-foot whipping post in the center of the room. The level of education was no better than the physical surroundings, and the physical surroundings were such that an 1838 Massachusetts report on district schoolhouses accused that "there is no other class of buildings within our limits, erected for the permanent or temporary residence of our native population, so inconvenient, so uncomfortable, so dangerous to health by their construction within, or without, abandoned to cheerlessness and dilapidation." Horace Mann exaggerated only slightly when he wrote a friend that "I have no hesitation in repeating what I have so often publicly declared, that, from the bad construction of our schoolhouses, there is more physical suffering endured by our children in them, than by prisoners in our jails and prisons." [19]

[18] *Fireside Education* (New York, 1838), pp. 338–39.

[19] This characterization derived from a number of sources. The best starting point is Warren Burton, *The District School as It Was* (1833; reprinted, New York, 1928). Cf. Orville J. Taylor, *The District School; Or, National Education* (Philadelphia, 1835); *American Annals of Education*, II (August, October 1831), 380–83, 468–72; Thomas H. Palmer, "The Teacher's Manual," prize essay in an 1838 contest sponsored by the American Institute of Instruction, printed in Boston, 1840, and reprinted in *CSJ*, II (September 1, 15; October 1, 15; November 2, 16, 1840), 265–72, 281–87, 297–302, 303–18, 329–32; and Clifton Johnston, *Old-Time Schools and*

If the rural schoolhouse was a symbol of pastoral virtue to some, to others it was at best a tarnished symbol. It gleamed, in unsullied splendor, only to those who never had been confined within its walls. For those who had, perhaps a popular poem by John Greenleaf Whittier best recalled "In School-Days":

> Still sits the school-house by the road,
>   A ragged beggar sleeping;
> Around it still the sumachs grow,
>   And blackberry-vines are creeping.[20]

FROM COUNTRY TO CITY

While rural district schools were inadequate, educators and reformers had greater expectations for urban classrooms. Country schools usually suffered from lack of funds and public apathy, but urban schools generally enjoyed more tax support and public enthusiasm. Boston especially commanded the financial resources necessary to build a first-rate system of schools. And, over the years, city fathers proved reasonably generous in allocating funds for public education.

By the mid-nineteenth century, Bostonians could boast of a longer tradition of tax support for public education than any other community in America. Within a decade after settlement public expenditures for schooling had become one of the young community's major expenses. Although the amounts spent fluctuated widely during succeeding years, as did the general state of the city's economy, the principle of taxation for education remained firm. Individuals might occasionally question the need for dramatically increasing the allotted funds, but few, if any, attacked the principle.

Throughout the years of educational reform efforts within the city, the Commonwealth, and in New England, Boston citizens showed an uncommon willingness to see their tax monies spent on education. Over the period between 1820 and 1865 the city's tax expenditures on public education (including teachers' salaries, new construction, and maintenance) averaged slightly more than 18 per cent, or nearly one-fifth of public expenditures in an arena of competing municipal interests. Even the drop after 1845 in education's share of the total city budget did not reflect a declining enthusiasm for public schools. Rather, a reallocation of resources signalled recognition by city officials that other municipal needs —including professional police and fire departments, acceptance of responsibility for a public water works, expansion of sewers, more paved

---

School-books (New York, 1904), pp. 100–34. The 1838 Massachusetts Report quotation came from Johnson, pp. 130–31; Horace Mann quoted by Palmer (September 15, 1840), p. 282.

[20] Whittier, *The Complete and Poetical Works* (Cambridge, Mass., 1848), reprinted in Carl H. Gross and Charles C. Chandler, eds., *The History of American Education Through Readings* (Boston, 1964), pp. 127–28.

streets, and a burst of expenditures on welfare institutions—required public support at least equal to that given education. Between 1845 and 1865 education's share of the total budget averaged 16.5 per cent while per-pupil expenditures gradually rose over the period. In September 1846 Horace Mann compared Boston's per-pupil expenditure with those of Providence, Rhode Island, and Philadelphia, both communities known for their support of public schools. Providence averaged $5.57 per pupil, Philadelphia $5.67, and Boston about $13.00. By 1860 Boston was spending $20.50 per pupil.

Boston maintained its generally high level of public support for schools without significant state aid. Despite the prophecy of reformer James G. Carter in 1826 that public schools would become extinct in the city and throughout the commonwealth if the legislature failed to shoulder some of the fiscal burdens of education, Boston's school system grew in size. Even when the state did establish a common School Fund in 1834, Boston's annual share was a pittance, averaging between 1836 and 1865 only some 2 per cent of the city's total receipts. The state law required each town or city to raise by taxation a certain amount for the education of each child (no less than $1.50 for each person between the ages of five and fifteen), and Boston always exceeded that minimum by a wide margin. The city's mayors repeatedly praised their constituents for generous support of public schools and the School Committee echoed that praise.[21] "In no city in the world," asserted committeemen in 1845 in typical booster fashion, "has there been one-half so much pecuniary liberality for the maintenance of Common Schools, as in the city of Boston." The Committee bolstered its claim with figures "proving" the "extraordinary fact" that appropriations for popular education in Boston alone were far larger than those for all of England, ignoring the fact that in early Victorian England public educational facilities largely received support from voluntary philanthropic agencies.[22] Regardless of booster exaggerations, one claim was certain: Boston did commit a substantial amount of public tax monies to the support of schools. If the quality of public schools could be measured solely or even principally by monetary standards, Boston citizens evidently were willing to pay handsomely for public education.

But the educational critics who held high expectations for the superiority of urban classrooms over rural district schools did not judge by such standards. Educational reformers and school authorities leveled more damning charges against the Boston schools than even against the poor district schools of their youth. Because the city was rich, because it could provide generously for education, Boston schools should have surpassed the rural schools in every respect. Yet, according to the critics, they had not. Nor would more money alone solve the problems of the schools,

[21] Carter, *Letters . . . on the Free Schools*, pp. 34–35: *Laws and Acts of Massachusetts, 1834* (March 31, 1834), Chapter 169; *ibid., 1841*, Chapter 17; *ibid., 1854*, Chapter 300; Josiah Quincy, "Taking Leave of Office, January 3, 1829," in *The Inaugural Addresses of the Mayors of Boston* (2 vols., Boston, 1894), I, 103–4; Theodore Lyman, "Inaugural Address," in *ibid.*, I, 183.

[22] "Boston Grammar and Writing Schools," *CSJ*, VII (November 15, 1845), 344–45; *CSJ*, VIII (September 1, 1846), 270. Cf. *BSR, 1856* (Boston, 1856), Table I.

although the reformers and schoolmen usually requested more funds with each passing year. As the critics saw them, the problems were not primarily monetary, but moral; not fiscal but locational; the worst one could say about city schools was that they were located in the city.

Most of the critics doubted whether schools in the city could ever provide a proper climate for the nurture of moral virtues and citizen responsibility in a republican government. They "knew" that Boston schools did not offer that climate. They based their "knowledge" on certain environmental assumptions about the ideal physical setting for a school and the distance between that ideal and the reality of city schools.

Evaluating the physical facilities of common schools in the city proved a difficult task for the critics. While the district schools of their experience tended to be much alike, schoolrooms and schoolhouses in the city varied greatly. Periodic bursts of population growth necessitated make-shift provisions. Rising land costs often brought the destruction and relocation of schoolhouses to make way for new commercial activities. The annexations of South and East Boston, of portions of Chelsea, Cambridge, and Roxbury, and landfill operations to form the West End demanded new school construction to keep up with residential shifts in neighborhoods. Not until 1845 were residential areas at all well fixed, nor would they long remain so with the rush of immigration during the late 1840's and early 1850's and a beginning suburban trend by middle-class citizens.[23] Schoolhouses and schoolrooms therefore rarely were uniform in size or style. The critics, nonetheless, were able to make several telling generalizations about school locations, the uses of school buildings for other than educational purposes, and the quality of school construction.

Schools often were located in undesirable areas. Compared with relatively isolated rural schoolhouses, urban schools usually were squeezed onto narrow lots on busy streets, surrounded by buildings that served numerous and varied functions. Throughout most of the antebellum years, except for the suburban areas, undifferentiated land usage was as common in Boston as in other cities. Places of residence, business, and entertainment on the same block often sided with one another. Churches and schools stood hard fast warehouses, business offices, and private dwellings.[24]

A typical example of undifferentiated land usage was School Street,

23 Oscar Handlin, *Boston's Immigrants: A Study in Acculturation* (rev. ed., Cambridge, Mass., 1959), pp. 14–15.
24 Edward Stanwood, "Topography and Landmarks of the Last Hundred Years," in Justin Winsor, ed., *The Memorial History of Boston* (4 vols., Boston, 1881), IV, 25–65; Alex C. Porter, "Changes in the Value of Real Estate in Boston: The Past One Hundred Years," Bostonian Society *Collections*, I (1880), 57–74; Walter Muir Whitehill, *Boston: A Topographical History* (Cambridge, Mass., 1959), pp. 73–140; David Ward, "The Industrial Revolution and the Emergence of Boston's Central Business District," *Economic Geography* (1966), pp. 152–71; Sam Bass Warner, Jr., *Streetcar Suburbs: The Process of Growth in Boston, 1870–1900* (Cambridge, Mass., 1962), pp. 1–34; Walter Firey, *Land Use in Central Boston* (Cambridge, Mass., 1947), pp. 44–55.

a short street that cornered with the major thoroughfare of Tremont
Street, just off The Common, in the heart of the city. In 1830, at the
corner of Tremont and School stood the mansion of a famous Boston
physician. Next door, down School Street, was a stable belonging to a
three-story brick public house, the Boylston Hotel. Next to the hotel
was the most celebrated of all the city's schools, the Boston Latin School.
Between the stable and the hotel ran a passageway to the rear of the
Tremont Theater, a walkway in which the Latin School boys often
lingered "at the risk of being late at morning prayers" to see famous ac-
tors on their way to rehearsals. Adjoining the schoolhouse was Cook
Court, an area about twenty feet wide, which contained private residences. Beyond Cook Court was the home of another physician who
maintained a pasture with sheep who were the constant targets of coal
and wood chips thrown by the boys from the windows of the school.
Continuing down the street a visitor would find small shops, the Second
Universalist Church—pastorate of the abolitionist and communitarian reformer Hosea Bellow—a Five Cents Savings Bank, grocery stores, a well-
known saddle and harness store, a book bindery, a boarding house, artists'
studios, lawyers' offices, and a volunteer firemen's engine house.[25] These
various businesses and residences occupied an area of less than two city
blocks.

The Latin School was small but impressive. Originally it had only
one room, but boasted an imposing granite façade, and a bell-towered
cupola. By the 1830's, when the later popular writer Edward Everett
Hale began attending at the age of nine, the school contained a number
of small rooms on three stories. This most exclusive of Boston's schools
had only one playground—a yard some thirty feet square—behind the
school. Recesses during the day were short since only the children in the
ground-floor rooms could conveniently use the playground. And, as Hale
recalled, the masters did not want the rest of the children out in the street.
On the whole, Hale testified, "school life of itself had little to relieve it
of its awful monotony." [26]

The Latin School catered to a small number of children, and, despite its surroundings, was in a more favorable location than many of the
grammar schools and most of the primary schools of the city. The lower
schools especially did not fare well. Established to train those children
whose "mass of mind," according to educators, was to exert the strongest
influence on the commonwealth in coming years, these schools demonstrated the triumph of necessity over desirability.[27]

From their founding in 1818, primary schools had occupied whatever

[25] Rev. Edward Everett Hale, D.D., "School Street in 1830," *Proceedings* of the Bostonian Society, VIII (1923), 35–37.

[26] Hale, *A New England Boyhood* (1893; new ed., Boston, 1964), p. 38. Cf. "Edward
Everett Among the School Children of Boston," *BAJE,* I (May 1856), 642–43.

[27] *Report of the Committee of Conference with the Committee of Primary Schools,*
City of Boston, City Doc. No. 13 (1843), bound in *School Reports* (1842–43), III,
Suffolk, Essex, Middlesex Counties, Massachusetts State Archives, Boston (here-
after MSA).

quarters could be found in the city, desirable or not. The Primary School Board had attempted initially to open classrooms in every area of the city's twelve wards so that young pupils would not have to travel far from home. But the city made no provisions for schoolrooms or schoolhouses, and the Board had insufficient funds to build needed structures. The early method, therefore, of establishing schools was to require the women teachers to find suitable locations. After obtaining a classroom, the teacher herself had to pay the annual rent from a salary which, during the 1820's, averaged $250 a year. Annual rents in different parts of the city varied from $40 to $80 for a single, small room. Teachers who had to support themselves on such meager salaries naturally tried to find the cheapest locations for schoolrooms. In some cases women who owned their own homes used one room for school. More often, they located class-rooms in buildings that had available space and disregarded the building's function.[28]

Primary schools met in unlikely locations. Stores and the basements of public buildings often housed schoolrooms. Teachers held classes in church vestries, on the upper floors of warehouses with noisy mechanics' shops above and below, and in rooms adjoining the shops of blacksmiths. Two critics—physicians John D. Fisher, a member of the Primary School Board, and William C. Woodbridge, editor of the *Annals of Education*—investigated the schools during the early 1830's and reported that "we often found the entrance to the room through the filthy back-yard of a house, or in the neighborhood of a stable, or a blacksmith's shop, or a carriage manufactory house, where the children could scarcely pass in safety. . . . Several rooms are in the second or third stories, with steep and narrow stair cases, entirely unsafe for children." Referring to those upper-story rooms, another critic observed that "the school-room is in an old shell of a house, and is small, badly ventilated, and unpleasant. The floor seems ready to fall through into the room below, and the windows rattle in their casements, most ominously." Fisher and Woodbridge were shocked to discover that "in one case . . . we were assured the houses in the narrow passage to the school, were the resorts of licentiousness!" Because of the physical locations of many schools, parents were reluctant to send their children. At one school, for instance, located on the busy thoroughfare of Washington Street, attendance dropped by almost one-half during the winter because parents and teachers were afraid to let young children cross the streets owing to sleigh racing by "youngbloods" of the area. Other parents understandably refused to send their youngsters to backroom and basement schools located in some of the city's worst areas.[29]

---

[28] "First Report of Primary School Board, May 31, 1819," in Wightman, *Annals*, p. 42; "Report of the Primary School Board to the Sub-Committee of the Boston School Committee, March 11, 1828," *ibid.*, p. 109; Nathan Bishop, *Third Annual Report of the Superintendent of Public Schools of the City of Boston* (Boston, 1853), pp. 35–36.

[29] *Report of the Primary School Committee on Improvements* (Boston, 1833), quoted extensively in "Primary Schools of Boston," *American Annals of Education and*

The Primary School Board worked long and hard throughout the antebellum years to improve school facilities. But a growing urban population and intransigent City Fathers, preoccupied with a host of problems concerning the welfare of citizens, often defeated their best efforts.

In 1828 a Primary School Board committee composed of merchant Moses Grant, lawyer Thomas Wells, and the Reverend Joseph Tuckerman, the official "minister to the poor" of the Unitarian Church, presented a memorial to the City Council describing the "serious evils and bad consequences" of the lack of suitable rooms for schools. The Council agreed that changes were called for, and suggested a way to improve the situation while saving the city money at the same time. The School Committee, after consulting with the Primary Board, was to rent a suitable number of rooms for a period not longer than ten years, drawing the money from the city appropriation for primary schools. The total, however, was not to exceed $2,700. This limited sum meant an average of only $48 for each room. Considering the disparity of rents in the city, many rooms which could be obtained for that annual sum necessarily would not be much better than those currently occupied. But the City Council was interested in money. The Council argued that since it was providing funds for rent, teachers' salaries no longer had to provide for classrooms, and therefore could be reduced by $50 a year. The Primary Board had little choice but to accept the action of the Council. The city was willing to spend comparatively large amounts on the grammar schools, but relatively nothing on primary schools. All the talk about the necessity of primary schools for the lower classes was silenced by economics. The new provisions lessened the responsibilities and incomes of the teachers, while they also failed to ensure better schoolrooms for the students.[30]

Again in 1829 the Primary Board petitioned the city to purchase or build decent schools; again it failed. Over the ensuing five years the Board sought better rooms from the city, eventually obtaining space in grammar schoolhouses, gun-houses, engine-rooms, ward rooms, and church vestries. Finally in 1834 the City Council appropriated sufficient funds to erect Boston's first publicly owned primary school house. The building was of wood and brick, two stories high, and contained two separate schools. In the following two years the city built four more schools. The Board members felt proud of their achievements, limited though they were. To numerous critics the Board responded "that the rooms occupied by *our* Primary Schools have at all times been equal to, and will now compare advantageously, with those used by any city in the United States." The Board may have been engaging in hyperbole, or it may have been correct. Either way there was little cause for complacency. Throughout the 1830's most children who attended the pri-

---

Instruction (December 1833), pp. 584–87; John Odin, Jr., *Report of the Committee of Conference, Thirty-Fifth Annual Report of the Executive Committee of the Primary Schools, City of Boston, 1853* (Boston, 1853), pp. 37–38.

[30] "Resolution of a Committee of the City Council, July 14, 1828," reprinted in Wightman, *Annals*, pp. 110–11.

mary schools spent their days in classrooms like those of the previous decade.

The building program of the city did not keep pace with the need for classrooms. By 1842 there were 7,403 pupils attending 104 primary schools scattered throughout Boston. The city still rented 42 schoolhouses, of which 41 were primary schools. Since most schoolhouses contained at least two separate schools under different masters, possibly more than 80 of the 104 schools still rented were in undesirable locations. Nor did matters measurably change during the remaining years before the Civil War.[31]

Throughout the antebellum years grammar schools generally fared better in location than did the more numerous primary schools. The city had founded them long before it had created the lower schools and even after introducing primary education in 1818, the city fathers continued the practices of the past in lavishing more attention and funds on the grammar schools. Despite the better physical surroundings, however, the grammar schools faced many of the same problems as the primary schools. Despite the rhetoric about the value of public education and the need for more satisfactory physical plants, school buildings and locations usually remained secondary to the city's requirements for other public facilities such as water reservoirs and transportation lines.[32] And, when the city did authorize new school construction, the Council often designated the buildings to serve the public in several capacities at once.

Schools often served more than one purpose. While educational reformers condemned the undesirable locations of many city schools, they likewise denounced the practice of using school buildings for other than educational purposes. School buildings serving more than one public function were common. The Johnson School, located on bustling Tremont Street near The Common, for example, served as a public meeting house, a watch house for police, and as a fire station—as well as providing classrooms. In 1837 a group of parents complained to the City Council about the presence of the fire engine, claiming that it disrupted the process of education. The Council agreed, and moved the engine to a small station house—one built on the same lot, in back of the Johnson School. Other school buildings were also used for more than schooling. The basement of the Hancock School, on Hanover Street in the northeast section of the city, housed a Sunday school class, while a sub-cellar served a local merchant as a warehouse for his casks of molasses. Throughout the

---

31 *Ibid.*, p. 153; "Report of a Special Committee . . . 1838," reprinted in *ibid.*, pp. 181–83; Ms. School Census Schedule, bound in *School Reports* (1842–43), III, Suffolk, Essex, Middlesex Counties, MSA. Each group of children under one teacher was called a "school" by the Primary Board. It was not uncommon by the 1850's for six or more independent "schools" to be located in the same building; see Bishop, *Third Annual Report*, p. 36.

32 For example, Theodore Lyman, Jr., *Communication to the City Council on the Subject of Introducing Water into the City* (Boston, 1834); "Annual Appropriations, 1846–47," *Boston City Documents, 1846*, Doc. No. 15.

city, schoolhouses provided the wardrooms for neighborhood political meetings.[33]

The history of one school was typical of the multiple uses to which school buildings were put. In 1790 the town fathers provided for the construction of the Franklin School on Common Street, in the south-central area of Boston. For convenient access, the school was located just off the major artery of Washington Street. Unlike its namesake, Benjamin Franklin, the school did not serve community needs long. In 1819, due to population pressures in the area, the School Committee established a second school on the top floor of the two-story wooden building. The basement housed an old hand-engine which students often helped pull to the scene of a fire. By 1826 increased enrollment required larger quarters, and the classes moved to another location. The city made certain that the old building was well occupied, using it for primary schools, ward meetings, police and fire stations, religious services, and as a distribution center for medical supplies during a cholera epidemic in 1832. The new Franklin School was located further south on Washington Street, near Dover Street, then the extreme limits of the city. The city experienced difficulty in obtaining the land for the school, due to the demands for space by local businessmen. Once acquired, the land was hardly ideal for school purposes. It fronted the mud-flats and open marshes of the Back Bay, a swampland that many citizens considered an unsightly, stinking nuisance. The mud-flats offered an exciting, but dangerous, playground for adventuresome youth.

Like the old building and like many other schools throughout Boston, the new schoolhouse was constructed of wood. In a city plagued by fires, this type of construction threatened the existence of the building. In 1833 the threat became reality. The school had just been remodeled inside and was back in session during the fall when a fire destroyed most of the building. While repairs were being made, children shuffled back and forth to attend school in the old building on Common Street and in the vestry of the Pine Street Church. The City rebuilt Franklin School on the site of the fire only to see it again consumed in 1844. Once again rebuilding took place. But by then Franklin School was too small to accommodate the neighborhood population. The city therefore erected another new schoolhouse, back on Common Street, adjacent to the original location of the first Franklin School.

The School Committee considered this new Brimmer School building a model school. Constructed of brick, the building was safer than its predecessors, and roomier as well. On the first story was a ward room, and two primary and intermediate schools. On the two floors above were two large halls, with smaller adjacent recitation rooms. But neither this, nor the new Otis School—another model school built at the same time— served solely educational purposes. Nor were the model schools built in the most desirable locations as the School Committee attested in 1848 of

[33] Arthur Wellington Brayley, *Schools and Schoolboys of Old Boston* (Boston, 1894), esp. pp. 101, 104–5.

the Otis School: "during the late examination, the noise and smoke from the neighboring work shops were excessively annoying." [34]

The story of the Franklin School—and its adjuncts, the Brimmer and Otis schools—illustrated the larger problems faced by all grammar schools in the city. School buildings could not be used for educational purposes alone. The needs for space to carry on the daily activities of the city were too pressing.

Schools suffered from inadequate construction. The third generalization that educational reformers offered about Boston schools was that most were unsafe and unhealthy. The charge was true that most schools built before 1840 were firetraps. Modeled after the district schools of the countryside, many primary and grammar school buildings were constructed of wood and contained only one large room. By 1829 the Primary School Board had to report that of the fifty-seven schools in the city, twenty-eight met in "rather commodious rooms" (though only one-third of these could be called "large"), while the remaining twenty-nine rooms were inadequate for classes of forty and fifty pupils. The Board considered such schoolrooms "too small, badly ventilated, crowded and, in consequence, unhealthy and unpropitious for discipline." [35]

If the Board itself was dissatisfied, critics were even more disdainful. The extensive investigation of the primary schools by Dr. John Fisher and William C. Woodbridge in 1833 reflected the disparagement of educational reformers. Fisher and Woodbridge reported their findings to the Primary School Board, and, in the hope of arousing public opinion, published them in the *American Annals of Education.* The two rejoiced that the Board itself found the schools inadequately constructed, and deplored the fact that such a statement had to be presented to the world about Boston schools. They declared their concern for the schools had been piqued by the remark of a gentleman "familiar with our prisons, that *the children of the city of Boston were,* in many cases, confined for the day, in rooms so unsuitable and unhealthy, that they would not be assigned *to the convicts of our penitentiaries.*" [36] That statement strikingly presaged Horace Mann's depiction of the rural district schools.

---

[34] For the history of the Franklin-Brimmer Schools, see Brayley, *Schools and School-boys,* pp. 87–89, 91; and Charles J. Prescott, "The Brimmer School, 1844–1911," *Proceedings* of the Bostonian Society, VII (1919), 31–46. For similar developments in other schools, see Thomas C. Simonds, *History of South Boston* (Boston, 1857), pp. 111–53; Leah L. Wellington, *History of the Bowdoin School, 1821–1907* (Boston, 1912); Amos M. Leonard, "History of the Lawrence and Mather Schools, South Boston," *Proceedings* of the Bostonian Society, VIII (1922), 24–45. An excellent brief description of the physical facilities of the schools may be found in *Report of the Committee on Public Instruction Respecting the Consolidation of Grammar Schools, Boston City Documents, 1852,* Doc. No. 27. On the Back Bay during the period, see Whitehill, *Boston,* pp. 120–29. The quotation comes from the *Minutes* of the School Committee of Boston, ms. bound in separate volumes in Rare-Book Room, Boston Public Library, IV, August 2, 1848, 215; hereafter cited as *SCM.*

[35] "Semi-Annual Report of the Standing Committee, April 21, 1829," Wightman, *Annals,* p. 116; "Report . . . March 11, 1828," *ibid.,* p. 109.

[36] *Report of the Primary School Committee on Improvements,* p. 583.

The report of Fisher and Woodbridge clearly demonstrated the problems of founding and maintaining decently constructed schools in a city growing in population and hard-pressed for usable space. The authors discovered that the average schoolroom measured nineteen feet in width, twenty-six feet in length, and eight to nine feet in height. The average number of students occupying those cramped quarters was sixty-two. Judged against even the minimum standards for adequate classrooms established by a widely accepted *Essay on the Construction of School-Houses* in 1832 by William A. Alcott, the construction of Boston schools was shoddy. Fisher and Woodbridge charged that the schools having the most influence on the health and morals of the city's children failed, in most instances, to allow even one-half the smallest amount of space considered safe.[37]

Their report, and others similar in tone, prompted the Primary School Board to deny the "gross and false attack upon the character" of the schools. The Board pointed out that it had done all it could to build better schools. Still, the schools remained poorly constructed. In 1837 a respected Boston physician, one Dr. Perry, visited a primary school of sixty children and voiced the opinion that no child could remain in the school six hours a day for two years without risking consumption. Heating in the winter was either non-existent or dangerously hot. Ventilation was equally inadequate. In 1838 William A. Alcott visited the primary schools and found that the good doctor had not exaggerated. "There was hardly a healthy face to be seen," Alcott reported. Whether health could be judged by appearance alone was debatable. But Alcott's statistics for one school, in which over a third of the students were absent for 136 days during the year, due to ill health, suggested the dimensions of the problem.[38]

Even when the city built new and presumably better schools during the late 1830's and early 1840's, construction was often less than desirable. The greatest fault, declared the Primary School Board, lay in not providing adequate ventilation. For without a proper flow of fresh air, "the foetid air, produced by the respiration and the exhalation from the persons and clothing of fifty or sixty children, whose poverty may prevent the necessary change for cleanliness, will, in a short time, render the odor and atmosphere of the room intolerable." Despite repeated discussion about the best means of ventilating the schools, the Primary Board members and other concerned individuals found it difficult to convince the City Council to make changes. Council members, jealous of their prerogatives, often reacted hostilely to the suggestions of the educators. In 1846, for example, the Council's chairman of the Committee of Public Buildings reportedly asked what schoolmen could possibly know about construction. They may know how to care for children, he said, but not

---

37 *Essay on the Construction of School-Houses, to Which Was Awarded the Prize Offered by the American Institute of Instruction, August, 1831* (Boston, 1832); *Report of the Primary School Committee on Improvements*, p. 586.

38 "Report of a Special Committee . . . 1838," Wightman, *Annals*, p. 181; "Health in Common Schools," *CSJ*, II (November 2, 1840), 343, and 337–43, *passim*.

how to build, "while the Committee . . . is composed of *practical* men, who know all about the matter." There was no record of the chairman's probable chagrin when, in one new schoolhouse under his direction, the schoolmen discovered that the ventilating flues extending to the rooftop had been covered by stone coping, while in several others the flues terminated in attics which had no outlet to fresh air.[39]

By the 1840's the educational reformers had established a solid case against the adequacy of urban schools. The schools were badly located, served other than educational purposes, and were poorly constructed. For all three reasons the schools were unhealthy for their youthful occupants. And, schoolmen reasoned, if schools were unhealthy, they were also immoral. Seeing an intimate connection between the physical nature of the schools and the moral and social goals they were to serve, educators believed that urban schools were no more adequate than their rural counterparts.

[39] See reports in Wightman, *Annals*, pp. 224, 225, 241.

The Shuttle and the Cross:
Weavers and Artisans
in Kensington, 1844

DAVID MONTGOMERY

Daily life for the lower-class American worker changed radically in the nineteenth century. In an earlier epoch most men had worked at agricultural labor. The rising and setting of the sun, the weather, the seasons, and the cycle of crops calibrated their lives. When the ground lay fallow in winter, the pace of work slowed, just as it quickened at seed time and harvest time. But in the nineteenth century, with the advent of industrial capitalism, more and more people worked at machines. The clock measured out the pace of toil, and their tasks were repeated again and again. They had entered a world where the rationalized, mechanized division of labor was the key to profit. The profits, however, went most often to a small number of investors and entrepreneurs at the top.

The swiftness of the growth of industrialism is well illustrated by the case of Philadelphia. Less than three-quarters of a century before the Kensington and Southwark riots of the 1840s, this had been the city of Benjamin Franklin, an urban center containing only about 25,000 people. Most of them had labored independently and most had enjoyed at least a modest success. Growth and commercialization had brought change, of course, even in Franklin's lifetime. Already the entrepreneur who could organize and capitalize the production and distribution of goods had begun to replace the independent artisan. But the full development of the factory system would take another half-century. Similarly, poverty had blighted the lives of many Philadelphians in Franklin's day. But it was not until steam-driven machines replaced the old handicrafts that one could speak of mass poverty.

In three generations after the American Revolution, the population of Philadelphia grew from 25,000 to 230,000. This growth brought a yawning gap between rich and poor and a redistribution of the community's resources that left almost nothing in the hands of the bottom half. The Jacksonian era is often called the "Age of the Common Man." Insofar as the phrase refers to broadened political participation, it has historical meaning; but in economic terms the common man was as often the victim as the beneficiary of the new order. There lay the central paradox of the age of industrialization: the cultural myth proclaimed that every hardworking person could rise from the bottom; but the social reality was that most of the new wage-earning laboring class was permanently relegated to lower-class status.

The background David Montgomery provides for the Philadelphia labor riots of the 1840s takes us into all of the vital aspects of everyday life for the urban worker of the antebellum period. The nature of work, chances for upward mobility, religion, ethnic affiliation, and political participation are all included in his analysis. In fact they are closely linked. Focusing on the Philadelphia weavers, Montgomery demonstrates that the adjustment to industrial capitalism in nineteenth-century America was a long, bloody, and unrewarding process for many workers.

Much of the Philadelphia workers' antagonism toward their employers was displaced upon fellow workers of a different ethnic or religious group. This displacement, Montgomery writes, has given "the illusion of a society lacking in class conflict." But the lack of political unity among Protestant and Catholic workers or Irish and native American workers should not be confused with a passive acceptance of the new industrial order. Because religion and ethnic identity were parts of their daily existence—a way of giving sense and order to the precarious economic environment—the protest of urban workers was often fragmented. This pattern of "cultural politics" as opposed to class politics is of exceptional importance in understanding American labor history and the lives of urban workers. It must be considered in relation to the confusion that antebellum working people, many of them recent immigrants, experienced concerning the American class structure. All around them rang the Jacksonian rhetoric, which denied the permanence of social classes and perpetuated the idea that only the lazy or shiftless could fail to improve their class standing. Only generations of daily experience to the contrary could abolish the myth and thus restructure labor protest.

American workers in the nineteenth century engaged in economic conflicts with their employers as fierce as any known to the industrial world, yet in their political behavior they consistently failed to exhibit a class-consciousness. This paradox was evident as early as 1844, when nativist parties triumphed at the polls in Philadelphia, Boston and New York. At the close of a decade and a half of hotly-contested strikes and severe economic hardship, climaxed by the bitter depression of 1837–43, workingmen had divided their votes along ethnic lines. The greater part of them were swept up into an enthusiastic political movement whose negative reference group was not the capitalists, but Roman Catholics. Other workers found their enemy in evangelical Protestantism.

Analysis of the nativist movement and of the bloody riots it spawned in the Philadelphia area suggests that the political behavior of American workingmen in the 1840s was fashioned not so much by the economic

From "The Shuttle and the Cross: Weavers and Artisans in the Kensington Riots of 1844" by David Montgomery. *Journal of Social History* 5 (1972):411–31, 439. Copyright © by Peter N. Stearns. Reprinted by permission.

impact of industrialization as by the workers' reactions to the political demands made by evangelical Protestantism: the moral content of education, liquor licensing and prohibition, Sabbath closing and the suppression of popular "lewd and tumultous" conduct. Such moral policing as evangelists demanded was in turn urgently needed by the new industrialists, to be sure, for it promised them a disciplined labor force, pacing its toil and its very life cycle to the requirements of the machine and the clock, respectful of property and orderly in its demeanor.[1] Because the responses of various groups of workers to these evangelical issues were determined by their religious outlooks, rather than their economic conditions, however, the working classes were fragmented on election day. Class interests were most clearly evident in trade union activity and in tensions *within* the political parties over questions like the legal ten hour day. Such issues, rising directly from the economic impact of industrialization, set working class against middle class. The pattern of cultural politics generated by the religious impact of industrialization, on the other hand, attached workers to the political leadership of the middle classes of their particular ethnic groups.

The counterpoint of class and ethnic conflict in working-class life was clearly visible in Kensington, a manufacturing suburb of Philadelphia, where crowds of Irishmen and native Americans battled each other for four days in May 1844. While the city proper contained some of the most advanced iron rolling mills, machine shops and locomotive works in the country, only 54 percent of its 16,600 working adults were listed in manufacturing and trades by the census of 1840. Commerce, navigation and the learned professions absorbed the rest. By way of contrast, in Kensington 89 percent of the labor force of slightly under 3,000 people was classified in manufacturing and trades.[2] Few really wealthy men lived there. The richest residents were master weavers, shoemakers, victuallers, gunsmiths and ship builders, whose holdings census takers in 1850 assessed mostly between $2,000 and $10,000. By the Delaware River waterfront one could find the old Pennsylvania Wainwright family, lumber dealers and co-owners of two large piers. Jonathan Wainwright's real estate holdings valued at $20,000 in 1850 were remarkably large for Kensington, yet his wealth was surpassed by that of the acknowledged leader of the Catholic community, boss weaver Hugh Clark. Michael Keenan, another Catholic master weaver, whose houses were burned by rioters in 1844, estimated his real estate at $18,000 in 1850. Only the most prosperous of the Vandusens, a large clan of lumber merchants, ship builders and ship

[1] See Liston Pope, *Millhands and Preachers, A Study of Gastonia* (New Haven, 1965) and E. P. Thompson, "Time, Work-Discipline, and Industrial Capitalism," *Past and Present*, No. 38 (Dec., 1967), 56–97. Lee Benson, *The Concept of Jacksonian Democracy* (Princeton, 1961) is the classic work on "ethnocultural" determinants of American political behavior, but the book shows no awareness of the interaction between those determinants and class relations in the setting of industrialization.

[2] U.S. Census Office, *Sixth Census or Enumeration of the Inhabitants of the United States . . . in 1840* (Washington, 1841), 151.

carpenters who helped lead the Protestant cause, approached this level of wealth.[3]

This was a community of working men and women, and among them that division of labor which Adam Smith termed the mainspring of economic growth was evident in profusion.[4] Interspersed with the larger occupational categories were solitary cloth measurers, artificial limb makers, tooth manufacturers, bird stuffers, lime burners and saw handle makers, not to mention two perfumers, a drum maker and a "comedean." More important, the major occupations encompassed superior craftsmen whose style of work had changed little since the eighteenth century (butchers, cabinet makers, ship carpenters), some factory operatives (in metals and glass works), swarms of outworkers (weaving, tailoring and shoemaking) and the inevitable impoverished laborers, carters, draymen and boatmen.

With the notable exception of the weavers, most of the workmen had been born in the United States. In fact, the manuscript census returns of 1850, the first to record age, occupation and birthplace for each individual, indicate that most were native Pennsylvanians. In contrast to the heavily immigrant weaving areas, concentrated in the second and fifth wards of 1844, the waterfront first, third and fourth wards with their vast tracts of lumberyards, furniture shops, shipbuilding facilities and fishermen's wharves were the special domain of the natives. Alongside only five Englishmen and four Irishmen who worked in shipyard trades could be found 433 Americans. Many of their neighbors on the Delaware's shore worked at one of the two paternalistically managed glass works, where more than 70 percent of the employees were native born.[5] Not only were 92 of the 103 fishermen Pennsylvanian by birth, but they shared among themselves only a handful of family names.

Shoemaking, one of Kensington's largest occupations in 1850, involved 343 natives, 128 Germans, 70 Irishmen, 19 Englishmen, 3 Frenchmen, 2 Scots and a Dutchman. In the newer metal trades of the same area—machinists, boiler makers, molders and rolling mill hands—more than half were Pennsylvanians, and 63 percent were Americans, though numerous Englishmen were to be found in their ranks. Among tailors, on the other hand, German immigrants were preponderant; and in the ranks of cabinet makers Germans almost equalled the natives in number. At the bottom of the occupational ladder, the laborers included 405 Irishmen, 99 Germans and 205 natives.[6]

---

[3] U.S. National Archives, 1850 Census Population Schedules. Pennsylvania (microfilm rolls 806–07), 4th ward, dwellings 72, 74, 78 (p. 245); 3d ward, dwellings 621–22 (p. 170) 1071 (p. 205); 5th ward, p. 324. Hereafter these schedules will be cited as 7th Census MSS.

[4] Adam Smith, *An Inquiry into the Nature and Causes of the Wealth of Nations* (London, 1822), Book I, chap. 1.

[5] See T. W. Dyott, *An Exposition of the System of Moral and Mental Labor Established at the Glass Factory of Dyottville* (Philadelphia, 1833) for a description of this works when it employed about 400 people. The calculation of nativity of glass workers is mine, from 7th Census MSS.

[6] All figures are calculated from 7th Census MSS.

Among the wage earners were many young recent arrivals in Kensington. The town's population almost doubled between 1840 and 1850, on top of an increase of 88 percent during the twenties and 66 percent in the thirties.[7] Many of the residents lived in boardinghouses, kept mostly by widows or by workingmen's wives. In the home of a New York-born bootmaker dwelt three young families (his own and those of two youthful locally born machinists) and no fewer than four other machinists, one pattern maker, two blacksmiths, two iron molders and a stray cigar maker. All the boarders were Americans in their twenties, except for a molder and a machinist from England.[8] An inn, not far from this menagerie of metallurgists, bore a more cosmopolitan aspect. In addition to the owner's family, it housed an Irish hostler and his 18-year-old wife, an English bartender and his blacksmith compatriot, a painter, a ship carpenter, an accountant, a house carpenter and a cordwainer—all from Pennsylvania —a ship carpenter and a ship joiner from New York state, another ship carpenter from Vermont, and a house carpenter who had come up from Maryland.[9]

Kensington's main industry was weaving, both cotton cloth and, to a lesser extent, woolen. Its output, combined with that of other suburbs like Manayunk and Moyamensing, helped keep Philadelphia County the leading textile producing region of the country down to the Civil War. After the city of Philadelphia had absorbed these suburbs by the consolidation act of 1854, it boasted 260 separate cotton and woolen factories which was more, its champions claimed, than any other city in the world.[10] But most of its weaving was not carried on in these factories. Weaving was basically a cottage industry, based on the putting-out system and the use of handlooms. As early as 1827 the local Society of Weavers boasted, probably with some exaggeration, that 104 warping mills in the region supplied about 4,500 weavers. On the eve of the Civil War Edwin Freedley estimated that 6,000 handloom frames were in use in the county.[11]

Kensington alone had 2,238 weavers when the 1850 census was taken.[12] During the preceding decade some rooms used for cloth weaving and more of those used for carpet weaving had "assumed more of a 'factory' air, and a few really important establishments [had begun] their career." [13] Some large manufacturers put out yarn to as many as 100 weavers each, while many more supplied but half a dozen cottages. Spools of yarn for the journeymen's shuttles were wound either by their own

---

[7] Sixth Census, 151; Sam Bass Warner, Jr., The Private City: Philadelphia in Three Periods of Its Growth (Philadelphia, 1968), 51.

[8] 7th Census MSS, 2d ward, dwelling 757, p. 106.

[9] Ibid., 1st ward, dwelling 682, p. 41.

[10] Edwin T. Freedley, Philadelphia and Its Manufactures (Philadelphia, 1858), 234, 250–51.

[11] Samuel Hazard, ed., The Register of Pennsylvania, I (Jan., 1828), 28 (hereinafter cited as HR); Freedley, 250–54.

[12] My count from 7th Census MSS.

[13] Pennsylvania Bureau of Industrial Statistics, Report, XVII (1889), 4D (hereinafter cited as Pa. Bis).

families or by women and children employed by the master. In that case the master passed on the cost of winding to the journeyman at a rate of 75 cents a week, a rate which remained quite constant from the 1820s through the 1840s.[14] For the most part as Edwin T. Freedley observed, "the persons engaged in the production have no practical concern with the ten-hour system, or the factory system, or even with the solar system. They work at such hours as they choose in their own homes, and their industry is mainly regulated by the state of the larder." [15] A starker description by the contemporary novelist, George Lippard, suggested perhaps luridly, but nonetheless accurately, that the "state of the larder" was usually far from good: "Here we behold a house of time-worn brick, there a toppling frame; on every side the crash of looms, urged by weary hands even at this hour, disturbs the silence of the night." [16]

The neighborhood Lippard described surrounded the Nanny Goat Market, storm center of the great riots of 1844. In that neighborhood the census takers of 1850 confirmed the literary images of Lippard and Freedley. They found, for example, an Irish-born master weaver, Alexander Myers, living with his American wife and three small children, as well as a laborer and his wife who performed domestic service. Six Irish weavers with their families tenanted the surrounding buildings. The whole complex was valued at some $3,000.[17] Not far off lived Jacob Hopes, who similarly had come from Ireland early in the 1830s, married an American woman and now boarded seven single men, all weavers and presumably his journeymen.[18] John Lavery, another boss weaver, had lost in the 1844 riots a $2,000 establishment described by a metropolitan newspaper as "a large and handsome brick house with brick back buildings." The journeyman weaver, whose $150 two-story frame house next door was also wrecked, was a tenant as were the weaver residents of the next eight houses burned down the street.[19]

As these few examples suggest, both masters and workmen in the weaving business were predominantly Irish. In fact, 78 percent of the weavers were of Irish birth. In wards three and six (of 1850), where 70 percent of the town's weavers dwelt, 85 percent of them were Irish. The 5 percent who were born in America and the 9 percent born in England seem to have been largely children of Irish immigrants.[20] The ages of the weavers' oldest children born in the United States indicate that the parents

[14] HR, I (Jan., 1828), 28; letter of "One Who Knows, and a Weaver" to Spirit of the Times, Sept. 13, 1848; "Meeting of the Weavers," Philadelphia Public Ledger, March 2, 1845 (hereinafter cited as PPL).

[15] Freedley, 241–42.

[16] George Lippard, The Nazarene; or, The Last of the Washingtonians, A Revelation of Philadelphia, New York, and Washington, in the Year 1844 (Philadelphia, 1846), 161.

[17] 7th Census MSS, 2d ward, dwellings 98–102, pp. 63–64.

[18] Ibid., 3d ward, dwelling 1329, p. 231. The date of emigration in this and later cases is guessed from the age of the oldest child born in America.

[19] PPL, May 11, 1844.

[20] My count from 7th Census MSS. Of 2,238 weavers, 1,758 were born in Ireland. Of the weavers not born in Ireland 204 were English, 114 American, and 105 German by birth. The rest were from Scotland (55), France (2), and Switzerland (1). Of

came to Kensington in two great waves, one about 1828–33 and the second in the latter half of the forties, after the riot of 1844.[21]

Although the immigrant weavers seem to have been predominantly Roman Catholic, there was a significant Protestant minority among them. The precise division cannot be known because the census takers specified the religion of no one but clergymen. Just to the east of Second Street, the north-south axis of the weaving district, lived many Irish weavers with such names as Montgomery, Campbell, McTaige and Stewart. Though it is always dubious to guess an Irishman's faith by his family name, firmer evidence of Protestantism lies in the presence among these weavers of a Presbyterian minister, a Methodist minister and an Irish-born agent of the American Tract Society. One Presbyterian preacher shared the home of an Irish boss weaver, William Wallace. Two Catholic priests, presumably serving the large St. Michael's Church, were their close neighbors.[22] In a word, Catholics and Protestants were found in almost random dispersal among both boss and journeyman weavers, but almost all were Irish. Their ethnic cohesiveness was epitomized by the case of Bernard Sherry, a master weaver who lost one frame and three brick houses inhabited by his journeymen during the riot. After his buildings had been burned, Sherry was arrested on charges of having armed his workmen to defend them against the nativists.[23]

The ethnic cohesiveness of the weaving community did not preclude sharp economic conflict within it. From the end of the 1820s through the 1840s, the weavers fought a running battle against the constantly re-curring efforts of their countrymen-masters to reduce piece rates. When times were hard, as they were in 1833–34 or in 1837, or desperate as they were from 1839 to 1843, the masters claimed the fierce competition of the market compelled them to lower prices for weaving. When times were good, as in the flourishing years of 1835–36, the same masters argued that the high price of cotton threatened to wipe out profits if produc-tion costs did not fall. The dilemma of American hand weavers was pre-cisely what Frederick Engels described in England at the same time: "One class of woven goods after another is annexed by the power-loom, and hand-weaving is the last refuge of workers thrown out of employ-ment in other branches, so that the trade is always overcrowded." [24] Well might the Royal Commission on Handloom Weavers of 1838 warn British workers "to flee from the trade, and to beware of leading their children into it, as they would beware of the commission of the most atrocious of crimes." [25] But the supply of weavers stubbornly refused

the 114 born in the U.S., 33 were clearly sons of Irish immigrants, as were many of those born in England. The 3rd and 6th wards of 1850 were made from the 5th ward of 1844, focal point of the riots, as was the rural 7th ward.

21 A significant but smaller peak of immigration was reached between 1836 and 1838.
22 7th Census MSS, 6th ward, dwellings 70 (p. 406), 103 (p. 408), 96 (p. 408), 528 (p. 440).
23 *PPL*, May 11, 1844.
24 Frederick Engels, *The Condition of the Working-Class in England in 1844* (translated by Florence Kelley Wischnewetzky, London, 1892), 140.
25 Quoted in Asa Briggs, ed., *Chartist Studies* (London, 1962), 8–9.

to fall. From the manufacturing towns of Yorkshire to the banks of the Delaware River, the rural poverty of Ireland kept the weaving cottages full from the late 1820s onward.[26]

In 1827 an English emigrant warned weavers of Yorkshire not to expect to improve their lot by coming to America. In Philadelphia, he wrote, a "smart weaver . . . by a fair week's work of 12 hours per day" would do well to acquire gross earnings of $4.50 a week. Some did no better than $4.00.[27] A press statement of master weavers the same year claimed $5.00 as a weekly average for journeymen.[28] There seemed general agreement throughout this period that 100 yards of three shuttle gingham was something of a standard week's work, 120 yards the fruit of an extremely intensive week's application. From the late twenties through the mid-thirties, prices paid to journeymen hovered around 4 cents a yard for this rather common style of cloth. If a weaver had a family, their work at spooling could save the journeyman a charge of 75 cents weekly and possibly, with enough children, earn a pittance more for the household by winding spools for the use of other journeymen who had no children. Customarily part of the worker's pay was given in store goods rather than cash.

Wages were fixed by agreements negotiated each spring and fall between the manufacturers and committee representing the weavers. Kensington and Moyamensing rates were governed by separate but usually similar scales at least from the mid-1830s on.[29] Often the agreements were reached only after severe strikes, and during the 1830s these conflicts brought the weavers into affiliation with the General Trades' Union of the City and County of Philadelphia, an assembly of delegates from all the organized trades of the area. During the weavers' strike in the fall of 1836 their societies received $1,500 in aid from the Trades' Union.[30] In turn the weavers contributed one of the most prominent leaders of the local workers' movement, John Ferral. To accommodate both immigrants and the native American craftsmen the Trades' Union banned from its midst all "party, political, or religious sectarian" questions. "The followers of Christ acknowledge a time for all things," explained the American-born saddler John Crossin on behalf of the Trades' Union, and "we do the same." [31]

As the depression of 1839–43 deepened, weavers' strikes became in-

26 Engels, 93, 138–40, 183–84; E. P. Thompson, *The Making of the English Working Class* (London, 1963), 296, 431; A. Redford, *Labor Migration in England, 1800–1850* (Manchester, 1964), 144–64. See also K. H. Connell, *The Population of Ireland, 1750–1845* (Oxford, 1950).

27 An Intelligent Emigrant at Philadelphia, *A Letter on the Present State of the Laboring Classes in America* (Bury, 1827), 5–6.

28 *HR*, I (Jan., 1828), 28.

29 Carpet weavers' assemblies of the Knights of Labor continued this practice in Kensington into the 1870s. See *Pa. Bis*, XVII (1889), 18D–19D; Terence V. Powderly, *Thirty Years of Labor, 1859–1889* (Columbus, 1889), 183.

30 John R. Commons, et al., *A Documentary History of American Industrial Society* (Cleveland, 1910), V, 351, 377, 384.

31 *Ibid.*, V, 391.

creasingly violent. The basic gingham scale (which was used as the yard-stick throughout this discussion) was cut to 3 cents a yard in 1841, yet scabs were available in abundance especially from the most recent immigrants. From August of 1842 until January of the next year Kensington weavers refused to work at the fall scale offered by their employers. When some workers broke ranks, stalwarts staged parades of 150 to 500 participants through the streets, entered the houses of non-strikers and hurled their unfinished chains into bonfires in the streets. Early in November they dispersed a meeting of their masters by threatening to tear down the house where it was taking place, and two months later a sheriff's posse attempting to arrest some strikers was routed by a charge of over 400 weavers armed with muskets and brickbats. Three military companies arrived during the night, and in their presence the workers and masters reached agreement on a scale which left hundreds of families living on less than three dollars a week.[32]

A strike in the spring of 1843 won a small raise, which was celebrated by a massive unity parade of Kensington and Moyamensing weavers.[33] That August improving market conditions, optimism over the new tariff and a very effective one-month strike allowed the Kensington weavers to negotiate an enormous raise—to 5¼ cents a yard for the standard gingham. When three of the largest employers refused to accede to the new scale and demanded that other masters support them in continuing to resist, the employers' conference broke up in a brawl.[34] As the early glimmerings of returning prosperity shone over the land, the weavers' incomes actually moved upwards.

The trend did not last long. The following May saw the Kensington weaving district gutted by nativist rioters. Ten days after the disturbance, the handloom weavers' committee announced that a number of manufacturers, "willing to take advantage of the then existing circumstances to enrich themselves," had reduced "our wages at a time when it is uncalled for by the markets" and when journeymen could not respond because the authorities had banned all meetings. The committee spoke the truth. The basic gingham price had been slashed from 5¼ cents a yard back to 3¼ cents.[35]

The key to the weavers' downfall lay in the fact that no longer did they enjoy the support of the other workmen of Philadelphia. Quite the contrary; the final defeat had come in the wake of actual physical assault by other workers, for the most part native-born Protestant artisans. The

[32] *Pa. Bis*, VIII (1880–81), 266–68.

[33] *PPL*, June 6, 1843.

[34] Letter of "One Who Knows, and a Weaver" to *Spirit of the Times*, Sept. 13, 1848; *Pa. Bis*, VIII (1880–81), 269; *PPL*, Aug. 11, 16, 1843. This rate may have been as much as one cent per yard higher than the season's scale in Moyamensing, but a march of weavers from that town to Kensington failed to inspire a sympathy strike there. See *PPL*, Aug. 12, 15, 16, 1843; "Meeting of the Weavers," *ibid.*, March 2, 1845.

[35] *PPL*, May 24, 1844; "One Who Knows, and a Weaver" to *Spirit of the Times*, Sept. 13, 1848. In 1848 Freedley was to find the going rate no higher than three cents. Freedley, 254.

central problem for this study, therefore, is to explain the rift between the weavers and their fellow workmen of Philadelphia County.

During the 1830s all groups of Philadelphia workmen—Protestant and Catholic, native and immigrant, superior craftsmen, outworkers, factory operatives and laborers—had been caught up in an awakening of class solidarity as significant as any in American history. The formation of the General Trades' Union, which included delegates from some 50 organized trade societies by 1836, and the successful general strike for the ten-hour day in 1835 epitomized this movement.[36] With revenues of $400 to $500 a month from its constituent unions, the Trades' Union could boast early in 1836: "Within the last six months more than one half of the Societies in the Union have struck, and no instance is known where a Society has struck, under the sanction of the Union, and failed in that strike." [37] Most significant of all, these successful strikes were conducted by workers who ranged in status from laborers and factory operatives at one end of the scale to bookbinders and jewelers at the other. Even journeymen cabinet makers (whose primary concerns were to collect debts due them from merchants and to halt competition from auction sales) and butchers and victuallers (struggling to hold down stall rent charged by the city and impede the "shaving" practices of cattle dealers) participated in the Trades' Union.[38]

From the ranks of these diverse groups, the Trades' Union could summon up what a local paper called "one of the largest meetings ever held in this city," conducted "with strict order and propriety" to protest the conviction of striking coal heavers, who were among the poorest but also the most militant of the city's working people. The rally demanded the defeat of Mayor John Swift for "the false imprisonment and un-constitutional bail [he] demanded of the Schuylkill laborers . . . whose only crime consisted in asking 25 cents per day addition to former wages." [39]

Many prominent workingmen plunged into the county's political struggles, for the most part supporting the anti-bank wing of the Democratic Party. Ferral of the weavers, Benjamin Sewell the tanner, William Thompson the carpenter, William English, William Gilmore and Samuel Thompson, all shoemakers, and Edward A. Penniman and Joshua Fletcher of the coachmakers were but some of the Trades' Union leaders who promoted Henry A. Muhlenberg's gubernatorial campaign as an anti-monopoly Democrat, sent their champion Lemuel Paynter to Congress from the Southwark area (the manufacturing suburb to the south of

[36] See Commons, *Documentary History*, V, 325–92; William A. Sullivan, *The Industrial Worker in Pennsylvania, 1800–1840* (Harrisburg, 1955), 133–36; Leonard Bernstein, "The Working People of Philadelphia from Colonial Times to the General Strike of 1835," *Pennsylvania Magazine of History and Biography*, LXXIV (July, 1950), 322–39.

[37] Commons, *Documentary History*, V, 390.

[38] On the special demands of cabinet makers, see *PPL*, Oct. 15, 1841; Sept. 4, 1843. On those of butchers, see *PPL*, May 9, 1839.

[39] *PPL*, Aug. 25, 1836.

Philadelphia which was the birthplace of the artisans' movement), and
helped maintain a consistent Democratic majority of almost two to one
in Kensington elections.[40] After the depression struck, they organized mass
rallies to support President Van Buren's Independent Treasury scheme,
demand resumption of specie payments and suppression of "shin plaster"
small notes by banks and dispatched committees to visit each of the city's
banks with these demands.[41] Ferral proudly boasted to Senator James
Buchanan that "the working classes" had frustrated the efforts of pro-
bank "shin plaster democrats" to dominate the local party. He concluded
that "all is well with the bone and sinew" who had rededicated the Democratic organization to the "emancipation of our Country from the bondage in which it is at present held by chartered Monopolists." [42]

At the very time Ferral wrote, however, the impact of the depression
was relentlessly undermining the working-class cohesiveness which the
Trades' Union had built up on both the economic and political fronts.
As a prominent Philadelphian confided to his diary in the summer of
1842: "The streets seem deserted, the largest houses are shut up and to
rent, there is no business, there is no money, no confidence & little hope,
property is sold every day by the sheriff at a 4th of the estimated value
of a few years ago, nobody can pay debts, the miseries of poverty are
felt by both rich & poor. . . ." [43] In this setting most trade societies
collapsed, and the General Trades' Union disintegrated with the evapo-
ration of its once munificent treasury.

With the demise of the Trades' Union, Philadelphia lacked any institution uniting the Catholic weaver, the Methodist shoemaker and the Presbyterian ship carpenter as members of a common working class. Strikes
became as uncommon as they were hopeless, except among the handloom
weavers. Artisan struggles of other types excited the county. In the spring
of 1839, for example, the butchers waged a brilliantly executed campaign
against "shaver" cattle dealers. Through great public fanfare they enlisted the support of their impoverished customers behind the butchers'
concerted refusal to pay more than 10 cents a hundredweight for live
cattle.[44] The next year shoemakers set up a committee to aid their Boston
counterparts then being prosecuted in the famous case of *Commonwealth
v. Hunt*.[45]

From August to October 1842, a Workingmen's Convention met
weekly, organized ward clubs and staged street meetings throughout the

---

40 Bruce G. Laurie, "The Working People of Philadelphia, 1827–1853," unpublished
   doctoral dissertation (University of Pittsburg, 1971), 79–90, 253–65; Sullivan, 196–
   207; Warner, 90–91. On Kensington votes see *PPL*, Oct. 14, 1837; Oct. 12, 1839.
41 *PPL*, April 28, Sept. 8, 1838.
42 John Ferral to James Buchanan, Feb. 19, 1838 (Buchanan Papers, Box 92, Historical
   Society of Pennsylvania).
43 Sidney G. Fisher, *A Philadelphia Perspective, The Diary of Sidney George Fisher
   Covering the Years 1834–1871*, edited by Nicholas B. Wainwright (Philadelphia,
   1967), 134–35.
44 *PPL*, May 9, 1839.
45 *PPL*, Nov. 21, 1840.

county to protest unemployment and "to guard their more indigent brethren against the inclemencies of the coming winter." An Equal Rights Party which was launched by the movement, however, failed abysmally at the polls.[46]

When prominent mechanics convened a series of meetings during January and February of 1839 in an effort to revive their trades movement, laborers, factory operatives and even the struggling weavers were conspicuously absent. An address signed by well known spokesmen of the coach makers, shoemakers, painters, bricklayers, tailors, cabinet makers and others blamed the economic crisis on "corrupt legislation," stressed the theme of self-help and made its chief demand "a system of education which shall teach every child in the Commonwealth his duty and interests as a citizen and freeman." It argued that "the old system of pecuniary benefits through the assistance of Trades' Unions seems to have fallen into disrepute" and criticized the "old Union" for "indiscriminate association of all the Trades without any regard to their assimilation or affinity." [47]

It was precisely by making strikes futile, destroying the Trades' Union beyond even hope of resurrection and stimulating this new emphasis on self-improvement that the depression opened the way for the rise of nativism among the artisans. By magnifying the importance to artisans of the temperance and public education movements, these developments set their aspirations on a collision course with those of Catholic immigrants.

The temperance movement paved the way. Like the stress on education, it involved nothing new to artisan culture. In his eloquent pleas for working-class unity at the founding of the Mechanics Union of Trade Associations in 1827, William Heighton had implored his fellow craftsmen to put aside their "drinking, gaming, and frolicking," and devote themselves to self-education.[48] Almost 40 years before that a commentator describing the gathering of 17,000 Philadelphians, proudly arrayed by trades to celebrate the newly-adopted federal constitution, had attributed their orderliness to their drinking nothing but "Americn Beer and Cyder," and admonished his readers to "despise SPIRITOUS LIQUORS, as *Anti-Federal*, and to consider them as companions to all those vices, that are calculated to dishonor and enslave our country." [49]

The depression cast this traditional artisan virtue in a new light. The hard times made temperance societies with middle-class evangelical leadership ubiquitous in the manufacturing districts, infused a new sense of crusading militancy into their ranks and made them an integral part of

[46] *PPL*, Aug. 1, 8, 13, Sept. 16, Oct. 19, 24, 1842.

[47] E. A. Penniman, etc., *An Address to the Workingmen of the City and County of Philadelphia* (Philadelphia, 1839), 2, 3. On the mechanics' meetings see John R. Commons, et al., *History of Labour in the United States* (4 vols., New York, 1918–35), I, 469–71.

[48] William Heighton, *An Address Delivered Before the Mechanics and Working Classes, Generally of the City and County of Philadelphia* (Philadelphia, 1827), 13. See also Heighton, *An Address to the Members of Trade Societies and to the Working Classes Generally* (Philadelphia, 1827).

[49] *American Museum*, IV (July, 1788), 78.

artisan life. When the Journeymen House Carpenters prepared their futile strike for a wage increase in March 1839, they appealed publicly for help from the "friends of temperance," arguing that under current wages carpenters "are frequently driven by poverty and care to intemperance, to dispel for a season, the horrid gloom which envelopes their homes," thereby "encompassing their families with misery." [50] The Temperance Society responded with a public letter endorsing the carpenters' demands and calling upon them to make total abstinence a condition of membership in their society.[51] By 1842–43 the temperance societies in almost every ward were supplemented by others organized on trade lines, like the Cordwainers' Beneficial Temperance Association. A new labor-for-labor exchange, The First Co-operative Labor Association of Philadelphia, met in a city temperance house.[52]

In 1838 the movement acquired a new leader of increasing prominence named Lewis C. Levin. This Charleston-born lawyer, described by Alexander McClure as "one of the most brilliant and unscrupulous orators I have ever heard," both lectured for the cause and edited the *Temperance Advocate*.[53] In January 1842, he attracted attention to a new temperance society in the waterfront woodworking district of Kensington, which then had only 15 members, by staging a spectacular bonfire of booze obtained from a converted saloon keeper before the eyes of thousands of spectators. Gathering as much of his audience as would fit into a nearby church, he blamed drunkenness on "the prodigality of the mushroom aristocracy of the country," appealed to the "steady habits of old times" and demanded that the public be allowed to vote on whether taverns should be tolerated in neighborhoods.[54]

It was this demand for popular control of liquor licensing which brought the temperance movement with its new evangelical leadership and artisan base into the political arena.[55] There its impact blended with that of an even more emotionally-charged controversy over reading the Bible in the common schools.

There is no end of irony in the Bible-reading issue, and most of it stems from the fact that two very divergent groups had been involved in the struggle for free public education in Philadelphia in the 1820s and 1830s. One group was the artisans, starting with those involved in the Mechanics' Union of Trade Associations, founded in 1827 with the quest for "equal education" one of its foremost goals. "The original element

[50] *PPL*, March 22, 1839.

[51] *PPL*, March 29, 1839.

[52] *PPL*, Feb. 21, 1842; Dec. 13, 1843. Artisans supporting Whig candidates had organized their efforts in temperance halls as early as 1838. See the account of the Naylor meeting, *PPL*, Sept. 24, 1838.

[53] A. K. McClure, *Old Time Notes of Pennsylvania* (2 vols., Philadelphia, 1905), I, 89. On Levin see *Dictionary of American Biography* (New York, 1937), VI, 200–01 (hereinafter cited as *D.A.B.*).

[54] *PPL*, Jan. 24, 1842.

[55] For a good discussion of the transition from temperance to prohibition see Joseph Gusfield, *Symbolic Crusade. Status Politics and the American Temperance Movement* (Urbana, Ill., 1963).

of *despotism*," argued one of its reports, "is a MONOPOLY OF TAL-
ENT." The republican alternative, it contended, was the extension of
the same education to all citizens "as a matter of right." [56] This theme
was repeated at the 1836 Trades' Union mass meeting in defense of the
coal heavers. Resolutions adopted there denounced government grants
"to colleges, academies and seminaries, where the children of the wealthy
alone are taught, that they may move in the same sphere of life as their
parents," while "our children are destined to hereditary bondage, in consequence of the prevailing ignorance of the poorer classes." [57] Similarly
the artisans' convention of 1839 demanded a "levelling system . . . of
education," in the belief that "intelligence is a passport everywhere." [58]
That artisan devotion to education was not simply rhetorical is suggested
by a list of the students admitted from the city's common schools to its
select Central High School in 1844. Of the 90 students admitted that year,
37 were sons of artisans and four were sons of laborers. Together they
almost equalled in number the children of merchants, manufacturers and
professional men admitted. Not one weaver's child was on the list.[59]

The other, and ultimately more effective promoter of free public
education, was a band of paternalistic merchants and professional men,
largely old Federalists, led by Roberts Vaux and Samuel Breck. These
men spoke not of "levelling education" to emancipate the working man,
but of "universal education" as "a powerful check on vice," to use the
words of Governor Wolf's message in support of the Public School Bill
which became law in 1834.[60]

Prominent evangelists endorsed this effort. Albert Barnes, the "New
School" leader of Philadelphia's First Presbyterian Church, took a com-
prehensive view of the problem when he warned that "the lower stratum
of society . . . that dense and dark mass, the population of alleys and
cellars, and garrets—the ignorant, the degraded, the grossly sensual, the
idle, the worthless—the refuse of society . . . are not in a condition
where revivals of religion can be expected such as I am advocating." The
remedy, he suggested, was to elevate "that dark mass" by closing the
city's "fountains of poison," placing the Bible in the homes of the poor,
providing them "self-denying instruction," and ensuring that "these
hordes of wandering and wretched children [are] to be gathered into
schools and taught." [61]

[56] Report of the Joint Committe on the Common Schools, New York *Daily Sentinel*,
Feb. 20, 22, 1830.
[57] *PPL*, Aug. 25, 1836.
[58] Penniman, 2.
[59] *PPL*, July 10, 1844.
[60] Warren F. Hewitt, "Samuel Breck and the Pennsylvania School Law of 1834,"
Pennsylvania History, I (April, 1934), 63–75; Joseph J. McCadden, "Roberts Vaux
and His Associates in the Pennsylvania Society for the Promotion of Public
Schools," *ibid.*, III (Jan., 1936), 1–8; Warner, 111–23. The quotation from Wolf is
in Hewitt, 68.
[61] Albert Barnes, *Sermons on Revivals* (New York, 1841), 155–57. See also Timothy
L. Smith, "Protestant Schooling and American Nationality, 1800–1850," *Journal of
American History*, LIII (March, 1967), 679–95.

More secular objectives for the same crusade were expressed by the
Reverend Orville Dewey of Massachusetts in a review of two new ele-
mentary school textbooks. Dewey saw "combinations of the employed
to procure higher wages" and "political workingmen's parties" as threats
to "tear up every social institution by the roots, and leave nothing behind
but disorder, waste, and ruin." The remedy for such evils lay in looking
"to the very power which has given the impulse to control it. That power,
undoubtedly, is education" of the common people. To fulfill its function
of preserving social order, education must above all be moral, Dewey concluded. "Conscience," and he repeated, "conscience is our safeguard!" [62]

It was fine to have available such spelling lessons as "Obedience to
superiors is requisite in all society; it is consistent with propriety and adds
to general convenience," [63] but what better text for the safeguarding conscience was available than the Bible? The study of the scriptures was seen
by these reformers not as peripheral to the purposes of the common
schools, but central.

Now every good American Protestant knew that the volume God
had written personally was that authorized by King James. To the Roman
Catholic clergy, however, that translation was anathema. Its use in classrooms endangered the very souls of Catholic pupils. The dramatic expansion of the common school system in Philadelphia County in the
decade following the 1834 act added urgency to the issue. All the while
Protestants simply found Catholic objections incomprehensible. "We have
never discovered anything in that book, the reading of which we could
suppose would injure the morals of either Catholic children or their
parents!" wrote one indignant Protestant.[64]

Bishop Francis Patrick Kenrick of Philadelphia fought relentlessly and
skillfully to protect his Catholic flock from the Protestant Bible. He
realized that the Protestant clergy were adamant and very vocal in their
insistance that the Bible remain in the schools. He also realized that news
of the burning of King James Bibles by a Catholic missionary priest in a
small town in upstate New York and of Bishop John Hughes' call to
New York City's Catholics to form a separate political party around the
Bible issue had inflamed Philadelphia's Protestant establishment. Consequently Bishop Kenrick issued a discreet but firm public appeal to the
Board of Controllers of the Pennsylvania common schools to allow Catholic children to use their own version of the Bible in class and to be excused from other religious instruction. He was partially successful. The
Board of Controllers ruled in January 1843, that children whose "parents

---

[62] [Orville Dewey], "Popular Education. 1. The Political Class Book . . . by WIL-
LIAM SULLIVAN . . . 2. The Moral Class Book . . . by the SAME . . ." *North
American Review*, XXXVI (Jan., 1833), 73–99. The quotations are on pp. 81 and 96.

[63] B. Brandneth, *A New System for the Instruction of Youth* (New York, 1836),
quoted in Ruth Elson, *Guardians of Tradition* (Lincoln, Nebraska, 1964), 102.

[64] J. H. Lee, *History of the American Party in Politics: Embracing a Complete His-
tory of the Philadelphia Riots in May and July, 1844* (Philadelphia, 1855), 29–30.
On the expansion of the schools during 1834–44, see Warner, 117–18. On anti-
Catholic bias in school textbooks, see Elson, 47–55, 123–28.

were conscientiously opposed" might be excused from class during Bible readings.[65]

Agitation over the Bible in schools, like the excitement over liquor licensing, aroused both Catholic and Protestant workingmen with several important consequences. The first was the rise of Democratic politicians in Kensington and similar towns who were closely tied to the Irish weavers, but who defended them on cultural, rather than economic grounds. Leaders of the stripe of John Ferral, who had fought manufacturers and bankers in the political arena, were shunted aside by men like Hugh Clark, a boss weaver who fought "Puritan fanaticism." Born in Ireland in 1796, Clark came to the United States around 1813 and by 1827 was a member of the masters' Society of Weavers. His brother Patrick was a tavern keeper, and Hugh himself was a police magistrate of such prominence in the Catholic community that Protestant rioters made a point of sacking both of their homes and Patrick's tavern in 1844. When listed by the census-takers six years later, Hugh was an alderman and manufacturer, the owner of $30,000 of real estate, more than was reported by any other individual in the town. With him lived his 70-year-old mother and his two younger brothers, both weavers. Next door dwelt Patrick, who had replaced his lost tavern with a dyeing establishment valued at $6,700.[66] Here was the political leader of Kensington's Irish weavers, a man who opposed them in a succession of bitter strikes, then mounted the hustings to champion their right to a drink and the consciences of their children.

Second, Democratic artisans, among them some of the party's most consistent anti-monopolists, reacted angrily to the new prominence of Irish ethnic politics in their party. A revolt of the self-styled "Incorruptibles" against Clark's nomination for County Treasurer in 1841 split the Democratic Party and helped defeat Clark in his own home town.[67] Two years later an insurrection was mounted by Thomas Grover, Lemuel Paynter and William D. Kelley, the leaders of the artisan wing of the Democratic Party in Southwark, against the party's nomination of an Irishman for that district's Congressional seat. The result again was victory for the Whigs.[68] The whole Incorruptible movement was remarkably similar to the struggle in Williamsburg (Brooklyn) which the emigre Irish Chartist and land reformer Thomas A. Devyr described in his mem-

[65] Hugh J. Nolan, *The Most Reverend Francis Patrick Kenrick, Third Bishop of Philadelphia, 1830–1851* (Washington, D.C., 1948), 289–96; Ray A. Billington, *The Protestant Crusade, 1800–1860* (New York, 1938), 142–66; Lee, 17–21. On Bishop Hughes in New York see Charles H. Haswell, *Reminiscences of an Octogenarian of the City of New York* (New York, 1897), 372–75; Thomas A. Devyr, *The Odd Book of the Nineteenth Century* (Greenpoint, N.Y., 1882), American Section, 33–38; Anna E. Carroll, *The Great American Battle; Or, The Contest between Christianity and Political Romanism* (New York and Auburn, 1856), *passim*.

[66] 7th Census MSS, 3d ward, dwellings 621–22, p. 170; *PPL*, May 11, 1844; *HR*, I (Jan., 1928), 28; letter of "A NATURALIZED CITIZEN: A DEMOCRAT AND AN IRISHMAN FOREVER" to *PPL*, Oct. 7, 1843.

[67] *PPL*, Oct. 14, 1841. Plankenton, the Whig candidate, carried Kensington with 852 votes. Clark came second with 821. Faunce, the Incorruptible, got 679 votes.

[68] *PPL*, Oct. 12, 1843.

oirs. Furiously opposing Catholic sectarian politics in the name of the
local Democratic Party's Jacksonian economic program, Devyr found
himself denounced by his fellow Irishmen and hailed by the nativists.[69]

Third, the cleavages opened in Democratic ranks by the issues of
liquor and schools tempted prominent Whigs to try to strike bargains
with Democrats like Clark in order to capture county offices. In fact,
nativist publicists charged that Whig lust for such votes lay behind the
decision of the Whig-dominated Board of Controllers of the common
schools to accede to Bishop Kenrick's demand on the Bible reading question. Whether or not there was any truth in that charge, it is certain
that when Morton McMichael ran for sheriff on the Whig ticket in 1843
he received considerable support from Irish Catholics out to avenge their
recent defeats at the hands of native Democrats. An open letter in the
press from "A NATURALIZED CITIZEN; A DEMOCRAT AND AN
IRISHMAN FOREVER" accused the Democratic party of proscribing
Irish candidates both in 1841 and in the current Congressional elections in
Southwark. The remedy it proposed was for Irishmen to vote Whig so
that they could later return to the chastised Democratic fold. "The Whig
County Ticket," it claimed, "is made up of known and ardent friends
of Ireland, and is headed with the name of Morton McMichael, who, like
General Jackson, is the son of Irish parents, and, like him, every inch
an Irishman!" [70] Enough Irish voters heeded the advice of "A NATU-
RALIZED CITIZEN" that McMichael won the election, carrying even
Kensington by almost 200 votes, while the Democrats, as usual, handily
won every other office in that town.[71]

Finally, the success of Catholic sectarian politics and the Bishop's
partial victory on the school issue account for the overnight mushroom-
ing of the American Republican Party, a political movement to exclude
immigrants from the suffrage and to defend the use of the King James
Bible in schools. American Republican clubs had been operating in nearby
Spring Garden since the end of the 1830s, and for more than a decade
itinerant ministers, spellbound by the Romish menace, had been peddling
the *Awful Disclosures of Maria Monk* about the county. They had little
to show for their pains, though one had been arrested on charges of selling
pornography in the guise of anti-Catholic literature. The school controversy, however, had united 94 leading clergymen of the city in a common
pledge to strengthen Protestant education and "awaken the attention of
the community to the dangers which . . . threaten these United States
from the assaults of Romanism." [72] The American Tract Society took up

[69] Devyr, American Section, 35–38.

[70] *PPL*, Oct. 7, 1843. For the American Republicans' accusations of conspiracy between Bishop Kenrick and Whigs on the Board of Controllers, see Lee, 17–21;
Billington, 214, n.49.

[71] *PPL*, Oct. 12, 1843. Charges of collusion in this election between McMichael and
the Catholics were commonplace at the time of the riots. See the *Address of the
American Republicans* (Cadwalader Collection, folder May 22–June 29, 1844, Historical Society of Pennsylvania, hereinafter cited as CC); George Cadwalader to
J. R. Ingersoll, May 24, 1844 (CC); Grand Jury Report, *PPL*, June 17, 1844.

[72] Lee, 31–32; Billington, 182–84. The quotation is from Billington, 183.

the battle cry and launched a national crusade to save the nation from the "spiritual despotism" of Rome.[73] The whole Protestant edifice of churches, Bible societies, temperance societies, and missionary agencies was thus interposed against Catholic electoral maneuvers in the name of "non-sectarian politics" at the very moment when those maneuvers were enjoying some success. Lewis Levin stepped over from the temperance movement to take command of the American Republican Party and led it with such skill that within one year it was in full control of the political life of the county.

The meteoric rise of the American Republican movement cannot be understood as a capitalist conspiracy to divide and crush the workers, even though it was portrayed in precisely this way by George Lippard's contemporary novel *The Nazarene*, and it did enable the master weavers to destroy the union of their journeymen. To be sure, it enjoyed widespread but ordinarily tacit sympathy from the old Quaker elite of Philadelphia. Many of them shared the sentiment which Sidney G. Fisher confided to his diary:

> This movement of the "native" party is decidedly conservative, because by excluding foreigners so much democracy is excluded, so much of the rabble, so much ignorance & brutality from political power. The natural ally of this party are the Whigs. Their object harmonizes with the instincts & secret wishes & opinions of the Whigs.[74]

Nevertheless, the American Republicans themselves were decidedly not upper class in leadership or following. Levin surrounded himself with out-of-office Whig politicians who opposed their party's 1843 deal with the Catholics and Democrats of the Incorruptible camp. To their ranks he added an imposing array of minor publishers, attorneys, ministers of the gospel and a few master craftsmen as the leading cadres of his party. Among them were an ex-colonel, C. J. Jack, who sought to prove during the riots that a big city can have its village idiot, and Charles Naylor, a Southwark lawyer and former Whig Congressman from the northern suburbs, whom Fisher described as "partially deranged." [75] Thomas Grover, the wharf builder, and Lemuel Paynter, whom Grover had helped put in Congress a decade earlier as spokesman of Southwark's artisans, were well known but hardly upper class. Only William B. Reed,

---

[73] Clifford S. Griffin, "Religious Benevolence as Social Control, 1815–1860," *Mississippi Valley Historical Review*, XLIV (Dec., 1957), 423–44.

[74] Fisher, 177. On the anti-Catholic attitudes of the upper classes, see P. Kenny, "The Anti-Catholic Riots in Philadelphia in 1844," *American Catholic Historical Researches*, XIII (1896), 50–64; Joseph Ripka's testimony, *Journal of the Senate of Pennsylvania* (1838), II, 357–58.

[75] On Jack, see his letter to *Native American* (hereinafter cited as *NA*), Aug. 2, 1844. On Naylor see U.S. Congress, 81st Cong., 2d sess., House Doc. 607, *Biographical Directory of the American Congress* (Washington, 1950), 1379; Fisher, 172.

of all the prominent nativists, had personal ties to the First Families, being a nephew of John Sergeant. But Reed's involvement in bribery scandals connected with the Bank of the United States had not only cost him a Congressional seat; it also left him in disgrace with his fellow gentlemen.[76]

The following these men gathered can be identified from the lists of nativists injured or arrested in the riots and from the rolls of ward club officers printed in their newspaper *Native American*. This enumeration provides almost as many occupations as it does names of individuals, but the trades which appear more than once give a clue to the nature of the rest. They are victualler, butcher, cordwainer, merchant and ship carpenter. All these occupations were not only dominated by native Americans, but were also the traditional trades and crafts of an American seaport.

In Kensington itself, the candidates nominated by the American Republicans for the February elections following the riots (1845) included a tax collector, a carpenter, a blacksmith, a tailor, a carter and a cabinet-maker. In the two wards where the party ran strongest, its candidates were an alderman and former combmaker, two ship carpenters, a chair maker, a brass worker and a victualler.[77] The tightly-knit community of Kensington fishermen not only supplied a candidate for that election, but marched as a body in the American Republicans' grand parade of July 4, 1844. . . .[78]

It appears, then, that Protestantism was a vital force in the ideology of these workingmen. Through its influence they could be attached to the middle-class leadership of a political party whose negative reference group was the Catholic immigrant, provided those leaders draped the movement with the most cherished symbols of artisan culture. Lewis Levin played to the values, the hopes and the anxieties of his audience of artisans with unerring aim. His paper, the *Native American*, displayed Longfellow's *Village Blacksmith* and with equal emphasis acclaimed the continuing "march of improvement." [79] The evils of the times were attributed to the behavior of the corrupt politician, who had allied himself with foreign-born voters, alien to America's egalitarian traditions and subject in their voting behavior to the discipline of the Roman Catholic church. The American Republicans promised to reintroduce into politics the sense of personal honor once exemplified by the Revolutionary Founding Fathers, to win the "entire separation of sectarianism from Politics"

[76] *D.A.B.*, VIII, 461–62; McClure, I, 89–91; Fisher, 125.

[77] The names of activists are taken from Grand Jury of the County of Philadelphia Minute Book, Sept. 2–Oct. 23, 1844; list of American Republican casualties in *NA*, May 7, 1844; article on May 6 rally, *ibid.*; North Ward officers, *ibid.*; Fifth Ward Southwark officers, *NA*, April 23, 1844; Kensington candidates, *NA*, Feb. 22, 1845. The best source for occupations was McElroy's *Philadelphia Directory* for 1843 and 1844.

[78] The candidate was Charles Bakeoven. *NA*, Feb. 22, 1845. On the parade, see Lee, 155.

[79] See editorial and article on Kensington industry, *NA*, Sept. 16, 1844. Longfellow's poem appeared in *NA*, July 30, 1844.

and to secure both objectives through "AN OPEN BIBLE and a PURE BALLOT BOX!"...[80]

Although the economic impact of industrialization was felt in quite different ways and involved remarkably different rates of change for factory operatives, outworkers and the many varieties of craftsmen, all these groups shared common interests enough to allow them to act as a class in support of trade union efforts and such political demands as the legal ten hour day. This unity had been the driving force behind the urban radicalism of the 1830s. Quite different was the impact of the ideology of modernization by which a new sense of social order and discipline was imposed on the industrializing community. Because major elements of this ideology were transmitted through the political demands of evangelical Protestantism, above all liquor licensing and the moral content of public education, the responses of workingmen to modernization varied with their own religious beliefs. No political conflicts of the age touched the daily lives of the people more intimately than these issues. By their very nature, evangelical demands fragmented the working class as a political force in ante-bellum Philadelphia and thereby created for historians the illusion of a society lacking in class conflict.

[80] *NA*, Sept. 16, 1844. The argument that immigration depressed American wages was a late-comer to American Republican editorializing. See *NA*, Nov. 29, 1844.

That Long-Tail'd Blue

CONSTANCE ROURKE

Entertainment is a part of daily life for people in every culture. Its range is wide—from formal entertainment staged for the few to self-structured entertainment, such as banjo-picking or reading, for the many. But whatever its form, entertainment fulfills a vital need for emotional release, for symbolic breaking of conventions, and for diversion from the burdens of rules and responsibilities, pain and sorrow. Since the Second World War, entertainment has become a far more important part of daily life in America, because leisure time has increased, and affluence has been sufficiently widespread to subsidize a large number of professional entertainers for our pleasure. But even in the nineteenth century, when most people worked a twelve-hour day, when the population was far more dispersed, and when electronic mass communication was unknown, entertainment was an important part of life.

In addition to serving psychic and emotional needs, entertainment performs a second function, as a carrier of ideas and attitudes. The popular entertainer is a powerful figure, reflecting and feeding the fears and fantasies of his or her audience. "The subtlest and most pervasive of all influences," wrote Walter Lippmann, "are those which create and maintain the repertory of stereotypes. We are told about the world before we see it. We imagine most things before we experience them." It is this function of entertainment—the role of reflecting and shaping popular opinion—that demands our attention in any consideration of nineteenth-century history.

That Negro minstrelsy became the most important form of mass entertainment in nineteenth-century America is a fact of special poignancy. It demonstrates not only how closely related were the tragic and the comic in the public mind, but how closely entwined were the lives of white and black Americans. As Constance Rourke emphasizes, it was the black American who became the dominant character in American humor, though white entertainers, impersonating blacks, dominated the minstrelsies that toured every city, town, and village from the 1830s to the First World War.

The appeal of the minstrelsy lay not only in the music, rhythm, and catchy phraseology of black folksongs, which white entertainers collected and imitated, but in the racist stereotypes these white minstrels concocted for the entertainment of largely white audiences. The Negro as buffoon constituted the core of the minstrel's appeal to mass audiences in nineteenth-century America. This was as true in the North or West as in the South. The popularity of the minstrelsy, which carried it to the remotest corners of America both before and after the Civil War, can be explained by the fact that it gave white Americans precisely what they wished to see—an impersonation of the black American as a delightfully ignorant, unthreatening, happy-go-lucky servant. The long persistence of this distorted image, evidenced by the continuation of the minstrelsy's enormous popularity well into the twentieth century, reinforces the conclusion that behind the laughter of white audiences at the sight of the grinning, watermelon-eating Negro lurked the fear of the hostile, revengeful, and autonomous American black.

The stereotype perpetuated by the nineteenth-century minstrelsy died hard in America. The descendants of the minstrelsy Sambo were the blackface acts of the vaudeville stage in the first third of the twentieth century, some of the movies and stage appearances of Al Jolson and Eddie Cantor, and a whole genre of movie and radio characters from Stepin Fetchit to Amos 'n' Andy. These characters, while serving the public need for entertainment, simultaneously played their part in shaping the nation's race relations, as did the dancing Jim Crow a century before.

Toward the end of the eighteenth century a genial foreign traveler told of some New York merchants who reached their counting-house by nine in the morning, donned aprons, and rolled hogsheads of rum and molasses around their wharves and were as dirty as their own porters, and could easily be mistaken for them. All day long they heaved, and hallooed, turning at intervals to scribble at their desks. At four they went home, dressed, had dinner, and were at the play at seven; after the play, which they vastly enjoyed, they went to supper, where they sang and roared and smoked and drank until dawn. At nine in the morning their lusty program began again. This sketch remained fresh and pertinent for at least two generations. But it was only a sketch. The outline was not filled in or given variations.

Soon after the Revolution certain other characters were thus briefly drawn—struck off like so many new coins in a visionary moment. The southern planter became a tall strolling figure with a fine presence, in a wide hat. In the *Knickerbocker History* and in *Rip Van Winkle* Irving created a comic mythology as though comic myth-making were a native habit, formed early; and these writings show the habitual playing off of one regional type against another. But his Dutch people were of the past, joining only at a distance with the current portrayal of native characters. A few later Dutchmen with long pipes became foils for Yankee wit. They apparently faded before it. Except for Rip the Dutch character was lost to the general view; and other native types were only transiently considered. A little Frenchman in dimity trousers exclaimed over the rest-

"That Long-Tail'd Blue." From *American Humor: A Study of the National Character* by Constance Rourke, copyright 1931 by Harcourt, Brace, Jovanovich, Inc.; copyright 1959 by Alice D. Fore. Reprinted by permission of the publishers.

lessness of the Yankee in a few early burlesques and reminiscences, and then vanished. The transplanted Irishman was dimly though continuously drawn for thirty or forty years; he was in fact the most frequently attempted of all these figures. He was pictured in Brackenridge's early satire on the backwoods character, *Modern Chivalry*, and appeared in stories like that of *Banagher's Bassoon* on the Yankee stage: Banagher had come from Bangor. The Irish print was clear in airs and jigs and reels and in the language. A horn of hard liquor was known in the West as a little of "the creature" or of "the element." But the Irish character fused readily, it seems, with others, and was often impossible to trace. Within this early period the transplanted Irishman failed to emerge as an insistent figure.

Among this shadowy group there was one powerful exception, one type destined to capture the popular fancy: the Negro. "The blacks," said a traveler in 1795, "are the great humorists of the nation. . . . Climate, music, kind treatment act upon them like electricity." Negroes were remembered fiddling before a play at a Maryland tavern or in their cabins strumming banjos made of flat gourds strung with horsehair. Soon they had the tambo, bones, quills, fife, and triangle. A traveler on the Savannah River heard a mellow distant sound along the surface of the water that came nearer and nearer until it seemed to rise from under the very bow of his boat, when a primitive *bateau* slid from the shadows along the shore, carrying a tall old ebony Negro who stood erect "like some boatman of the Niger," playing on a long, straight wooden tube. Negro rowing songs rose like barbaric chants on the watery highways of the West. Plantation owners on the Mississippi had crews of black oarsmen who sang as they rowed and improvised good-natured verses to match the occasions of the day. A few African creole melodies drifted down through the century. A western poet declared that "among the earliest original verses of the West were sundry African melodies celebrating the coon hunt and the vicissitudes of river navigation." The Negro was to be seen everywhere in the South and in the new Southwest, on small farms and great plantations, on roads and levees. He was often an all but equal member of many a pioneering expedition. He became, in short, a dominant figure in spite of his condition, and commanded a definite portraiture.

In the early 1820's, at almost the precise moment when the backwoodsman appeared in legend with his "Hunters of Kentucky," the southern plantation Negro was drawn on the stage in Cincinnati by young Edwin Forrest. Made up for the part, Forrest strolled through the streets, where an old Negro woman mistook him for a Negro whom she knew; he persuaded her to join him in an impromptu scene that evening. This little sketch seemed unimportant, but Forrest had studied the Negro character; he inaugurated a tradition for faithful drawing. Other impersonations, now lost to view, no doubt followed, like tentative portraits; and punctually in the early '30's, when both the Yankee and the backwoodsman leapt to full stature on the stage, the Negro was also pictured in firm, enduring outlines.

The artist of course was Jim Crow Rice—who was white—the place any one of a number of cities along the route of western travel from Pittsburgh to Cincinnati or Lexington. Rice had heard an old crippled Negro hostler singing in a stableyard as he rubbed down the horses, and had seen him dancing an odd limping dance as he worked—"rockin' de heel." Rice studied the dance and learned the song, with its refrain—

> Wheel about, turn about,
>   Do jis so,
> An' ebery time I wheel about
>   I jump Jim Crow.

These he used in a backwoods play, *The Rifle,* and the small interlude met with such instant success that he enlarged it to an afterpiece, weaving other Negro melodies and dances around the single impersonation. Presently he emerged—still in blackface—in the red and white striped trousers and long blue coat of the Yankee. The coat became the subject of one of his most popular songs, "That Long-tail'd Blue," a ballad telling of the trials besetting the wearer of that garment. A later version was happy-go-lucky, as if the Negro were assured of his own nationalistic position.

This black-faced Yankee had in fact a confident breadth of impersonation. The buttons on his coat and vest were made of five- and ten-dollar gold pieces which he liberally tore off and flung to his audiences. For a time he was accompanied by a tiny comic *Doppelgänger,* small Joe Jefferson in red, white, and blue, who was tumbled out of a valise and danced the odd limping dance opposite him, joining in the plaintive melody. Soon Rice was drawing other Negro portraits, of a Negro dandy of the river towns, a Negro flatboatman, and a plantation Negro. Collecting cornfield dances and plantation melodies, he created a massed musical effect with a few others in blackface in his "O Hush" and "Bone Squash," which he called Ethiopian opera.

The vogue of this new entertainment was enormous. Rice enjoyed a popularity in the '30's and '40's which was said to be unmatched by that of any other American comedian of his time. He carried his impersonations to London, where he drew an extraordinary personal following. After these beginnings, in 1842, Negro minstrelsy was born. Four men gathered in a New York hotel, a rendezvous for show people. The leader was Dan Emmett, a backwoodsman of Irish descent who looked like a Yankee deacon. The other three were Yankees, and one of them had been an actor of Yankee parts. They played the fiddle, the banjo, the tambo, and bones. Emmett said afterward that they were all end-men and all interlocutors; and they all wore "that long-tail'd blue." Massed singing quickly became the core of minstrelsy, and in its wake came larger numbers in the choral dancing of the walkaround.

Blackface minstrelsy has long been considered a travesty in which the Negro was only a comic medium. To the primitive comic sense, to be black is to be funny, and many minstrels made the most of the simple circumstance. This exploitation was deeply resented by the anti-slavery leaders of an early day, and in the end they went far toward creating the idea that the Negro lacked humor. After the Civil War it would still have been possible to reveal the many-sided Negro of the old plantations, but minstrelsy with its air of irreverence seems to have blocked the way. Because minstrels had sported with the Negro and had even sentimentalized his lot in a few songs, because of his tragic fate and a wish to prove that he possessed moral worth, dignity, and capacity, his friends collected and discussed and displayed only his religious pieces, the spirituals which have seemed his special creation. But Negro humor was always abundant, and from it early minstrelsy drew as from a primal source, keeping the tradition for direct and ample portraiture. Burlesque appeared, but burlesque was natural to the Negro.

Many minstrels had lived in the South and West and knew the Negro at first hand. One of them saw an old peddler of watermelons with a donkey cart in a Georgia town, followed him about until he had mastered his lingo, cries, snatches of song, as well as his odd manner. The portrayals, so freshly caught, were whole and rich. Emotion welled up in the small acts and through the olios in spite of crude stage contrivances. Forrest, who had long since become a tragic actor, declared that he knew no finer piece of tragic acting than the broadly comic impersonation of Dan Bryant as the hungry Negro in *Old Times Rocks*.

The songs and to a large extent the dances show Negro origins, though they were often claimed by white composers. Dan Emmett declared that he wrote "Ole Dan Tucker" as a boy of fifteen or sixteen, but this song of the older minstrelsy had a curious history for an independent piece of musical composition. The air resembles Negro airs; the chorus with its shouting dance refrain breaks away from the verses in the habitual manner of Negro choruses. And Emmett offered more than one version of the words in which appear those brief and cryptic bird and animal fables that have proved to be a consistent Negro creation—

> Jaybird in de martin's nest,
> To sabe his soul he got no rest.
> Ole Tucker in de foxes' den,
> Out come de young ones nine or ten.
>
> High-hole in de holler tree,
> He poke his bill in for to see,
> De lizard cotch 'im by de snout,
> He call for Tucker to pull 'im out.

In another version of the song, a touch of woe is mingled in an odd colloquy—

> Sheep an' hog a walkin' in de pasture,
> Sheep says, "Hog, can't you go no faster?"
> Hush! Hush! honey, hear de wolf a howlin',
> Ah, ah, de Lawd, de bulldog growlin'.

Most of these fables contained a simple allegory: the crow was a comic symbol for the Negro himself, though he might at times take the form of a sheep or a hog, while the master or the overseer or the patrol—the "patter-roller"—was the bulldog or sometimes the bullfrog. The jaybird habitually took a sinister part, descending into hell on Fridays; and other birds and animals were freely drawn in symbolical relations. In "Clar de Kitchen," one of Rice's most popular dance-songs, a fragmentary bird and animal fable appears with triumph for the Negro submerged and disguised.

> A jaybird sot on a hickory limb,
> He winked at me and I winked at him,
> I picked up a stone and I hit his shin,
> Says he, you better not do that agin.
>
> A bullfrog dressed in soger's close
> Went in de field to shoot some crows,
> De crows smell powder an' fly away,
> De bullfrog mighty mad dat day.

In all these fables touches of satire were present, directed toward the white man, or toward the Negro himself when he figured as the lumbering hog or sheep, or gave himself wit as a fox. Self-parody appeared in such dances with bird calls as "Turkey in de Straw," which Emmett claimed, but which surely went back to a common dance of the Negro.

Rice and Emmett can only have borrowed the fables, probably with their tunes. Apparently neither had a gift for imitation of the Negro mode of story-telling, for they mixed such stanzas with others of their own composition, or at least plainly not of Negro origin. Emmett offered at least two versions of "Ole Dan Tucker." The song and the character in fact underwent those possessive and affectionate changes and additions which mean that many hands have been at work upon them; the melody showed variations; and the character which they celebrated was likewise variable. Dan Tucker was pictured as a vagabond Negro who was laughed at and scorned by his own kind but who constantly bobbed up among them with outrageous small adventures. Since he consorted with the two sagest creatures in the animal world of the Negro, the fox and the jay-bird, he was endowed with a comical magic; yet for all this he was an outcast, looming large as he combed his hair with a wagon-wheel, shrinking small and growing ridiculous as he washed his face in a frying-pan, and at last through the transformations of many years changing from black to white. Stories appeared about him as though he were a living figure; joke-books were named for him; one of them was ascribed to that "young Daniel" who is introduced casually in a stanza of one of the many versions of the song. No doubt tales and many other verses of the song appeared in improvisations and have been lost. Dan Tucker was a legendary figure, as long-lived as Crockett.

Emmett belonged to a family that had been among the early pioneers from Virginia; in later years his father's house in Ohio had become a station for the underground railroad. In the middle 1820's he was stationed as a fifer in Kentucky and later at a barracks on the Mississippi below St. Louis. He had traveled through the West with a small circus company; and these companies usually included at least one Negro dancer. For a time he played with Rice, who from the first had turned to the Negro for the direct portrait. Thus through his impressionable years Emmett had been brought into close contact with the Negro; indeed he declared that he had always confined himself to "the habits and crude ideas of the slaves of the South," even though in the next breath he insisted that the songs were of his own composition. Negro melodies and fables had possessed his mind. Plantation cries echoed in his walkarounds and choruses. Some of his songs were close to the spirituals, which are the acknowledged creation of the Negro. The opening stanza of his first version of "Dixie" contains a touch of the characteristic biblical picturing—

> Dis worl' was made in jes six days
> An' finished up in various ways—
> Look away! look away! look away! Dixie land!

> Dey den made Dixie trim and nice
> But Adam called it Paradise—
> Look away! look away! look away! Dixie land!

Here the verbal phrasing is unlike that of the Negro, whose habitual approach is swift and elliptical. Controversy has in fact gathered around the entire question of the composition of "Dixie," and Emmett has been denied even the smaller glory of transcription or adaptation. Whatever the circumstance, the traces of Negro origin remain in the biblical touch—never to be found in songs of lighter mood elsewhere in this time—in the cries of the chorus, and in the melody, which sounds like a fiddler's tune.

Similar traces appear elsewhere in the minstrel songs ascribed to Emmett, sometimes only in the words, sometimes in musical phrasing. He often used the Jordan theme recurrent in the spirituals. In his "Jordan Is a Hard Road to Trabbel" a fragment of the story of David and Goliath is joined with topical references to make a comic song. In his "Here We Are," or "Cross Ober Jordan," the river symbolizes another river of freedom, the Ohio—

> I'll sail de worl' clar roun' and roun'
> All by de railroad underground.
> We'll cross ober Jordan, we'll land on tudder shore,
> Den make room in de flatboat for one darkey more.

Here too was a vestige of the great western mode of travel belonging to an earlier day, in the mention of that great ark, the flatboat. And at least one spiritual, "Michael, Row That Boat Ashore," was clearly a boat song. The rhythm and the remembrance of travel along the western rivers ran through many of the minstrel songs.

The spirituals were a source for Foster as well. He haunted Negro camp-meetings for rhythms and melodies; and his songs were immediately appropriated by the minstrels. Krehbiel has shown that "The Camptown Races" sounds like "Lord, Remember Me" with a quickened beat; and while he suggested that the Negro borrowed the "Races" for the spiritual, it seems equally probable that Foster was the borrower, since he used Negro airs and phrasing elsewhere. Many spirituals lend themselves to such transformations. Brought to a rapid stress, "Somebody's Knocking at My Door" could easily become a dance tune; and as it happens, a favorite minstrel song of this period was called "Somebody's Knockin' at Yo' Do'." The music bore no relation to that of the spiritual; only the salient phrase was repeated; but the whole body of this many-sided music is full of such phrases, turned ingeniously and restlessly, as by the Negro himself, to different effects.

The climax of the minstrel performance, the walkaround, with its competitive dancing in the mazes of a circle, was clearly patterned on Negro dances in the compounds of the great plantations, which in turn went back to the communal dancing of the African. The ancestry was hardly remote. Many who heard the minstrels in the Gulf States or along the lower Mississippi must have remembered those great holidays in New Orleans early in the century when hundreds of Negroes followed through the streets a king chosen for his youth, strength, and blackness. License ran high, and the celebrations ended in saturnalia of barbaric, contortionistic dancing. Often the walkarounds of minstrelsy were composed only of bold pantomime and matched dancing, accompanied by strident cries and the simplest binding of words, the words gaining their color from slave life—

> Darkies hear dat banjo ring,
>   Yoe! Ha! Yoe!
> Listen to de fiddle sing,
>   Yoe! Ha! Yoe!
> Dee dah doo dah dum
>   Aha! Aha!
> Oh, massa sabe me, do!
>   Aha! Aha!
> See dat nigger over dar,
>   Yoe! Ha! Yoe!
> He's got de longest hair,
>   Yoe! Ha! Yoe!

Plantation cries, wailing cries, stirring shouts with a tonic beat, ran through all early minstrelsy. Many of the choruses took up similar resounding notes with even greater breadth. The choruses with their open vowels and slurred consonants and rushing syncopated measures proved the reliance of minstrelsy upon Negro airs and chants even when the musical or verbal phrasing moved to another idiom.

Negro minstrelsy had arisen from the Southwest and from Negro life there; it showed many traces of regional origins. "Sugar in de gourd" and "honey in de horn" were heard in minstrel songs as well as in south-western talk. The backwoodsman and the Negro danced the same jigs and reels; the breakdown was an invention which each might have claimed. In the 1850's, a generation or more after the boatman had ceased to be a figure on the western rivers, rowing songs and boatman's songs and boatman's dances became a dominant pattern through minstrelsy; and they borrowed the fancy touch with which the flatboatman had often adorned songs about himself. Sometimes the songs were adorned with corals and dolphins and fireflies. Most of them kept the rolling choruses with a touch of nonsense.

> De spring ob de year am come at last,
> Winter time am gwan an' past—
> Four and twenty boatmen, all in a flock,
> Settin' by de seaside peckin' on a rock.
> Dance de boatmen, dance!
> O dance de boatmen, dance! dance!
> Dance all night till broad daylight,
> An' go home wid de girls in de mornin'!
> Hi! Ho! de boatmen row,
> Floatin' down de ribber on de Ohio.
> Hi! Ho! de boatmen row,
> Floatin' down de ribber on de Ohio.

Whether or not the tall tale was characteristic of the Negro or whether he took a touch of the art from the backwoodsman may never be known, since in an uncharted history the early improvisations have been lost; but magnification appeared in the early phases of minstrelsy with unmistakable stress. Dan Tucker combed his hair with a wagon-wheel. An animal song which belongs to the '40's and probably earlier celebrates a fabulous little black bull—

> He shake his tail, he jar de ribber,
> Hoosen Johnny, Hoosen Johnny,
> He shake his tail, he jar de ribber,
> Long time ago.

The encore verses of one of Rice's most popular songs, "Sich a Gittin' Upstairs," told of a "bone squash" captain who was cut in two in a fight, joined himself together with glue, finished his enemy, and lay down to sleep, only to find on awakening—the day was hot—that the glue had melted and that a thief had run away with his thighs—

> Dis being de case he saw no fun,
> An' having no legs he couldn't run,
> So he shied a stone at de old tief' head
> An' though seven miles off he killed him dead.
>
> A ball one day knocked off his head,
> De people all thought he was quite dead,
> But he picked up his head and ran away,
> And nebber was heard of since dat day.

Western myth-making was woven deep in early minstrelsy, so deep that it can hardly be counted an alien strain.

Another coloring was given by Irish reels, jigs, and lilts; the Negro seemed to pick up the Irish musical idiom with facility, and the composers often adopted fragments of the pleasing tunes. One of Emmett's Jordan songs moves to an Irish lilt; yet it contains biblical pictures in the fashion of the spirituals. Themes of English contradances occasionally broke through the Negro breakdowns and reels. No doubt the minstrel often bridged gaps in his knowledge of Negro music and lore by inventions of his own; the interjected pattern is often evident. Occasionally a fluent strain appears that seems drawn from popular songs of the day, in the mode of "The Old Oaken Bucket," with words that follow the inspiration of Tom Moore.

But the persistent stress was primitive; it was often sorrowful; the effect was exotic and strange, with the swaying figures and black faces of the minstrels lighted by guttering gas flames or candlelight on small country stages, or even in the larger theaters. And within this large and diverse pattern lay a fresh context of comedy. This was plain in the intricate and grotesque dancing, as the blackface minstrels "walked jaw-bone" or accomplished the deep complications of the "dubble trubble" or the "grapevine twist." Even in one of the spirituals "four-and-twenty blackbirds" cropped up with an air of satire as "four-and-twenty elders," and the minstrel songs were filled with such sidelong touches. The whole intention of the bird and animal fables was that of a delicate and shrouded satire. And a far bolder comic quality appeared which had hardly developed elsewhere in the American comic display—that of nonsense.

In an early "Yankee Doodle"—in "Corn Cobs Twist Your Hair"— the flavor of nonsense was unmistakable, but this seemed to spring from a brief extraordinary exhilaration, and almost no trace of the same feeling is to be found in other Yankee talk and stories. Strangely enough, with all his wild excess the backwoodsman never overflowed into pure nonsense. Perhaps the Negro did not invent the nonsensical narratives which appeared in his dialect, but the touch is akin to that in many of the Negro fables in song. Certainly nonsense in minstrelsy shows a sharp distinction from other humor of the day. The minstrel mode went off to a bold and careless tangent.

> Kentuck one night a party meet
> Who say dey goin' to have a treat,
> Dey come from Old Town, short and tall,
> To have a dance at de nigger ball.
> An' sich a gittin' upstairs,
> An' a playin' on de fiddle,
> Sich a gittin' upstairs I nebber did see,
> Sich a gittin' upstairs, an' a playin' on de fiddle,
> Sich a gittin' upstairs I nebber did see.
>
> Mister Brown he come in his mackintosh,
> His head all frizzed like a punkin squash.
> He smoked cigars, the best Havan,
> An' a watch as large as a warmin'-pan,
> An' sich a gittin' upstairs,
> An' a playin' on de fiddle,
> Sich a gittin' upstairs I nebber did see. . . .
>
> Miss Rose come in her mistress' close,
> But how she got dem nobody knows,
> And long before de ball did meet
> She was dancing Taglioni at de corner ob de street,
> An' sich a gittin' upstairs,
> An' a playin' on de fiddle,
> Sich a gittin' upstairs I nebber did see. . . .
>
> A little old man was ridin' by,
> His horse was tryin' to kick a fly.
> He lifted his leg towards de south
> An' sent it bang in his own mouth.
> An' sich a gittin' upstairs,
> An' a playin' on de fiddle,
> Sich a gittin' upstairs I nebber did see. . . .

The fling at the end was characteristic, and the song with its sibilant chorus all but pictured the gathering, hustling, dancing crowd in celebration. The satirical touch about Taglioni was possible for the Negro of the river towns.

Triumph was in his humor, but not triumph over circumstance. Rather this was an unreasonable headlong triumph launching into the realm of the preposterous. The triumphant note ran through the careless phrasing of most of the minstrel songs and was plain in the swift pulsations of the rhythms. Yet defeat was also clear—that abysmal defeat which seemed the destiny of the Negro. Slavery was often imaged in brief phrases or in simple situations. Fragments of humble and cryptic work songs appeared—

> Sheep shell oats, ole Tucker shell de corn.

Lines from forbidden devil songs were echoed—

> O I'se sorry I sold myself to the debbil.

Defeat could be heard in the occasional minor key and in the smothered satire. Hitherto the note of triumph had been unmistakable and unremitting among American comic characters. The sudden extreme of nonsense was new, and the tragic undertone was new.

Primitive elements were roughly patterned in minstrelsy. Its songs, its dances, its patter, were soon set within a ritual which grew more and more fixed, like some rude ceremonial. Endmen and interlocutors spun out their talk with an air of improvisation, but this free talk and song occupied an inalienable place in the procedure. In the dancing a strong individualism appeared, and the single dancer might step out of the whole pattern; the jig dancer might perform his feats on a peck measure, and dancers might be matched against each other with high careerings which belonged to each one alone: but these excursions were caught within the broad effect. Beneath them all ran the deep insurgence of Negro choruses that flowed into minstrelsy for many years, even after its ritual grew stereotyped and other elements were added; and the choral dancing of the walkaround made a resonant primitive groundwork.

Within this ritualistic design certain Negro characters were permanently limned, little limping Jim Crow with his plaintive song the first among them, and Zip Coon, that "very learned skoler," rougher, simpler, and more humble, next in the early order. The third figure, old Dan Tucker, was perhaps the most enduring of all in spite of his many transformations; he was always the outcast—

> Git outen de way, git outen de way,
> Git outen de way, ole Dan Tucker,
> You'se too late to come to your supper.

All three of these characters were outcasts even beyond the obvious fate of the slave.

Following these or surrounding them were others of smaller appeal or lesser stature. They all revealed the Negro character: yet they showed that greater outline and more abstract drawing which reveals the world of legend. Magic was mixed with small events in these portrayals; and even real places took on the large and legendary air, as in the nostalgic lines of "Dixie." The biblical allusions heightened the air of legend.

These legends flowed into familiar patterns, these mythical characters slipped into familiar guises. Though the symbolical "long-tail'd blue" was seldom seen after the first few years of minstrelsy, its nationalistic promise was kept. The Negro in minstrelsy took a turn at playing oracle. Little Jim Crow talked comically on political affairs between dances and songs. Later Rice impersonated a bootblack with a bent toward philosophy: the axioms have been lost, but the drawing was said to be lifelike, and the figure occupied a considerable place in the popular fancy of the day. Zip Coon sang a crazy-quilt song with bits of animal fable edging toward politics.

> O ole Zip Coon he is a larned skoler,
> Sings possum up a gum tree an' coony in a holler,
> Possum up a gum tree, coony on a stump,
> Possum up a gum tree, coony on a stump,
> Possum up a gum tree, coony on a stump,
> Den over dubble trubble, Zip Coon will jump.
> O Zip a duden duden duden, zip a duden day.
> O Zip a duden duden duden, duden duden day.
> O Zip a duden duden duden, duden duden day
> Zip a duden duden duden, zip a duden day.
>
> O it's old Suky blue-skin, she is in lub wid me,
> I went de udder arternoon to take a cup ob tea;
> What do you tink now, Suky hab for supper,
> Why chicken foot an' possum heel, widout any butter.
> O Zip a duden duden, duden, zip a duden day. . . .
>
> Did you ever see the wild goose, sailing on de ocean,
> O de wild goose motion is a bery pretty notion;
> Ebry time de wild goose beckons to de swaller,
> You hear him google google google google goller.
> O Zip a duden duden duden, zip a duden day. . . .

Wandering lazily through the many further stanzas were satirical references to Jackson and the bank and Davy Crockett. Zip Coon was to become President of the United States and Crockett was to be Vice President.

Here was that legendary assumption of wisdom which had appeared persistently among American comic characters. This assumption had striking aspects, for the rise of the Negro minstrel coincided with a marked change in his place within the nation. Little Jim Crow appeared at almost the precise moment when *The Liberator* was founded; and minstrelsy spread over the land and grew in popularity as the struggle for emancipation gained in power through the '40's and '50's. The Negro minstrel joined with the Yankee and the backwoodsman to make a comic trio, appearing in the same era, with the same timely intensity. The era of course was the turbulent era of the Jacksonian democracy, that stormy time when the whole mixed population of the United States seemed to pour into the streets of Washington, and when many basic elements in the national character seemed to come to the surface. The Negro minstrel was deeply grounded in reality, even though the impersonators were white, even though the figure was a myth.

The three figures loomed large, not because they represented any considerable numbers in the population, but because something in the nature of each induced an irresistible response. Each had been a wanderer over the land, the Negro a forced and unwilling wanderer. Each in a fashion of his own had broken bonds, the Yankee in the initial revolt against the parent civilization, the backwoodsman in revolt against all civilization, the Negro in a revolt which was cryptic and submerged but which none the less made a perceptible outline. As figures they embodied a deep-lying mood of disseverance, carrying the popular fancy further and further from any fixed or traditional heritage. Their comedy, their irreverent wisdom, their sudden changes and adroit adaptations, provided emblems for a pioneer people who required resilience as a prime trait. Comic triumph appeared in them all; the sense of triumph seemed a necessary mood in the new country. Laughter produced the illusion of leveling obstacles in a world which was full of unaccustomed obstacles. Laughter created ease, and even more, a sense of unity, among a people who were not yet a nation and who were seldom joined in stable communities. These mythical figures partook of the primitive; and for a people whose life was still unformed, a searching out of primitive concepts was an inevitable and stirring pursuit, uncovering common purposes and directions.

But even in life the Negro was not wholly primitive; his satire was often conscious; and the everyday comedy of the Yankee and the backwoodsman almost invariably wore the air of contrivance. Occasionally in practical jokes their humor seemed only gross and physical; yet at best even these contained a deliberate fantasy. As the three figures were projected in stories or on the stage the effect of consciousness was greatly heightened. With all their rude poetry it was about a mind that these myths centered, a conscious, indeed an acutely self-conscious, mind. Masquerade was salient in them all. Minstrelsy was of course white masquerade; and the double use of the mask seemed to create a profound satisfaction for American audiences, as if the sheer accomplished artifice aroused an instinctive response among them. The mask might be worn as an inheritance or for amusement or as a front against the world in any of these impersonations, concealing a childish and unformed countenance: but it was part of a highly conscious self-projection.

Emotion seldom crept through this assumed disguise; none at all was shown by the Yankee characters or those who belonged to the backwoods, though the backwoodsman could indulge in a characteristic mock melancholy. In minstrelsy emotion was near the surface, surging obscurely through the choruses and walkarounds, but this was always communal, never individual. In all the array of popular comedy, which pressed close to circumstance and approximated many of the outer aspects of a common life, individual emotion was sponged out. Anger, love, hatred, remorse, were absent; fear alone was revealed, but only in a dis-

tant and fragmentary fashion, only to be cast away with laughter. If it
created unities, the resilience of the comic spirit seemed a destructive
agent, so blank were the spaces where emotion might have appeared.

Simple ties existed between this trio and the animal world. The
Yankee looked there for swift, familiar comparisons in order to identify
a human being, often satirically. The backwoodsman pictured himself
as a savage and cunning beast and turned to the wilderness mainly for
destruction. At the same time he evoked it. The Negro saw beasts and
birds as emblems of himself and of others; his mood was that of companionship; and he kept to the gentle realm of the cotton-field, the meadow,
the pasture, or the fringe of forest. In some sense wild creatures were
seen in an alliance with man in all these glimpses; yet the unchanging
stress was upon the human character, as if an absorption in character were
primary.

Many minor evidences are at hand to show that the comic trio
tended to merge into a single generic figure. The early "long-tail'd blue"
was a lasting symbol. In stories and on the stage each took on qualities
and even appearances of the others; they fell into many of the same rôles.
A hundred years after the emergence of little Jim Crow, tall talk was to
appear in *Ole King David and the Philistine Boys*.

" 'What dat, ole King Saul?' say Little David.

" 'Dat's old Goliar,' say old King Saul.

" 'Who he?' say David.

" 'De he-coon er de Philistines,' say King Saul.

" 'What do he want?' say David.

" 'Trouble,' say ole King Saul.

" 'Well, you de king, ain't you?' say Little David. 'Can't you ease his
worries 'long dat line?'

" 'Who, me?' say Saul. 'I'm a married man. Cou'se I ain't skeered of
him, but still and at de same time I got a wife and a family dependin' on
me for s'port. So I don't see no reason how come I should git out and git
hurted by no gi'nt.'

" 'He's a gi'nt?' say Little David.

" 'Twenty foot tall,' say King Saul.

" 'What else is he?' say David.

" 'Jest wait to he gits out in de clearin' and starts makin' his say-so,'
say King Saul.

"So 'bout dat time ole Goliar stepped out in de clearin' and commenced makin' his say-so.

" 'I'm a cross betwixt a wild cat and de yaller ianders,' he say. 'I'm
sired by Trouble and dammed by Sudden Death. I drinks nothin' but
stump watter and a rattlesnake bit me and died. I breathes out forked lightnin' and I spits out thunder. When I laughs de skies pop open, and when I
groans hit rolls up like a ball er yarn. I kills my friends and I makes ham-
burgers outer my enemies. Tornadoes and harrycanes follow me round
like pet dogs, and lines and tigers is my playmates. I'm bad. I'm mean.
I'm vicious, and jest natchally can't he'p it. When I gits sick hit takes
nothin' less'n a Hebrew man's meat to cyore me. And I feel a buck auger

comin' on. So look out! I'm reekin' wid meanness and I'm huntin' trouble.' "

The rhapsodic boasting of the backwoods had traveled down the century. But each of the trio remained distinct. None left a deeper print than the Negro in minstrelsy, even though his shadowy figure was the slowest to emerge, and though the minstrel never assumed the many distinct parts taken by the Yankee and the backwoodsman. The appeal of minstrelsy was insistent and enduring; minstrel companies multiplied quickly and spread all over the country; the minstrel songs were quickly appropriated by the nation. "The Ethiopian melodies well deserve to be called, as they are in fact, the national airs of America," wrote Bayard Taylor in 1849. "They follow the American race in all its migrations, colonizations, and conquests." Taylor was writing from California, where minstrelsy was heard almost as soon as the first gold-seeker set foot there, and where it grew as an accompaniment for that wild adventure. A minstrel song, Foster's "Oh, Susannah!" became a rallying-cry for the new empire, a song of meeting and parting turned to nonsense, a fiddler's tune with a Negro beat and a touch of smothered pathos in the melody. Fragments of familiar reels and breakdowns, of boatmen's dances and boatmen's songs, were often caught within the minstrel pattern: much of the pioneer experience was embedded there. No doubt the appeal of minstrelsy came from these draughts upon a common reminiscence, stirring some essential wish or remembrance.

Minstrelsy kept its Negro backgrounds until after the Civil War: then, if the Negro was set free, in a fashion his white impersonators were also liberated. Along with later blackface acting came a strong infusion of Irish melodies and an Irish brogue. German songs were sometimes sung on the minstrel stage; and much later the Jew occasionally emerged in blackface. Again in fantasy the American types seemed to be joining in a single semblance. But Negro music and Negro nonsense still prevailed; through years the old pattern was kept. The young American Narcissus had looked at himself in the narrow rocky pools of New England and by the waters of the Mississippi; he also gazed long at a darker image.

The Heart That Dared Not
Let in the Sun

O. E. RÖLVAAG

America has always been a nation of immigrants. This was especially true in the nineteenth century, when some 20 million people entered the country to pursue the American dream. In the 1820s and 1830s immigrants arrived at a rate of about 65,000 per year. But in the next two decades, when the population of the country grew from 17 to 31 million, the rate of immigration tripled. About 4.4 million immigrants left their homelands between 1840 and 1860 for a new start in the United States. American society was permanently transformed by this inundation of diverse peoples, just as each of the immigrants was transformed by the experience of starting life over in a new land.

Millions of these immigrants were peasant farmers who were fleeing crop failures or persistent poverty in northwestern Europe. America, with its vast resources of open land, seemed the answer to their despair. Even now, in the historical imagination, the romance and glamour of the pioneer experience persists. But the daily life of the immigrant was far from romantic. It has been calculated that one of every three immigrants before the Civil War died within three years of arrival in America—from the hardship of steerage passage across the ocean, from exposure to new diseases for which they had no immunities, from economic hardship after arrival, or from debilitating psychological disorientation. Instant success was very seldom achieved; in fact success at any point in life was rare for the nineteenth-century immigrant. Usually it was the sons and daughters who reaped the rewards of their parents' decision to move to America.

Giants in the Earth, the novel by the Norwegian immigrant O. E. Rölvaag, tells the story of Per Hansa, his wife Beret, and their children, Ole, Store-Hans, And-Ongen, and Peder Victorious. The scene is the Dakotas and the time is in the late 1860s and early 1870s. But the immigrants could be German, Swedish, Irish, Bohemian, or Russian. The scene could be Minnesota, Iowa, Kansas, Missouri, or anywhere else in the trans-Mississippi West. And the time could be almost any decade of the nineteenth century. For in writing about Per Hansa and his family, Rölvaag was attempting to write about the realities of daily life for all who struggled for survival on the Great Plains. The grim reality of pioneer life on the prairie is the major concern of his story. Per Hansa, the father, is a frontier hero of sorts—dauntless to the end, when he is found frozen to death in drifting snow. But his wife Beret personifies the psychological ravages the Great Plains environment inflicted on European immigrants in America. For her the reality of life in North Dakota is interminable winters, painful memories of her Norwegian village and her parents whom she left behind, fears of the wilderness, and deep depression and suicidal urges that sweep over her as she struggles to find her place in the new land. For her the immigrant experience is a sustained tragedy.

The collective result of the vast human migration to America in the nineteenth century was the peopling of the nation, the transformation of the Great Plains into the nation's granary, the "subduing of the frontier," and the conquest of the entire continent, from east to west, at the expense of its original inhabitants. But the thousands of individual experiences that made up the collective result are rarely recorded by historians. They must be sought in novels such as Rölvaag's **Giants in the Earth,** Hamlin Garland's **A Son of the Middle Border** and **A Daughter of the Middle Border,** and Willa Cather's **My Antonia.** In these portraits of everyday frontier life the student will find vivid examples of many crucial issues in the social history of the westward-moving frontier.

It was well enough that winter had come at last, thought Per Hansa; he really needed to lay off and rest awhile. After a good square meal of ducks or fresh fish, he would light his pipe and stretch himself, saying:

"Ha!—now we're really as well off here, my Beret-girl, as anybody could ever wish to be!" . . . He did not always expect an answer, and seldom got one. Then he would throw himself on the bed and take a good after-dinner nap, often sleeping continuously on into the night. . . . Life seemed very pleasant now!

In this fashion he spent quite a number of days; the bad weather still held out. Per Hansa continued to do full justice to the fare. When he had eaten his fill he would point out again to Beret how well off they were, and go to his couch to sleep the sleep of the righteous. It was almost uncanny—he could never seem to get sleep enough! He slept both day and night; and still he felt the need of more rest. . . . Now and then he would go to the door to look out at the weather, and glance across toward the neighbours. No . . . nothing to do outside—the weather was too beastly! He would come in again, and stretch himself, and yawn. . . .

The days wore on.

Yes, they wore on. . . . One exactly like the other. . . . Per Hansa couldn't grasp the strange contradiction that had begun to impress him; he knew that the days were actually growing shorter—were being shorn more closely by every passing night; but—weren't they growing longer?

Indeed they were—no question about it! They finally grew so long that he was at a dead loss to find something to do with which to end

"The Heart That Dared Not Let in the Sun." From *Giants in the Earth* by O. E. Rölvaag, pp. 203–15, 223–39. Copyright, 1927, by Harper & Row, Publishers, Inc.; renewed, 1955, by Jennie Marie Berdahl Rölvaag. Reprinted by permission of the publisher.

them. He assured himself that all this leisure was very fine; that he needed to ease up a bit; during the fall he hadn't spared himself; now it felt like a blessing to sit around and play the gentleman. Times would be strenuous enough for him once more, when spring came with fair weather and his great estate needed to be planted; he would just lay off and rest for a while yet! . . .

The days only grew longer and longer.

In the end, this enforced idleness began to gall him. The landscape showed a monotonous sameness . . . never the slightest change. . . . Grey sky—damp, icy cold. . . . Snow fell . . . snow flew. . . . He could only guess now where the huts of Hans Olsa lay. There wasn't a thing to do outdoors; plenty of wood lay chopped and ready for use; it took but a little while to do the chores. . . . Beyond this, everything took care of itself outside.

Per Hansa sat by the table, or lay down on the bed when he got tired of sitting up; tried to sleep as long as possible; woke up with a start; turned over and tried to sleep again; rose and sat by the table once more, when he grew weary of lying down.

The days wore on, and yet got nowhere. . . . Time had simply come to a standstill! He had never seen the like; this was worse than the deadest lay-up in Lofoten!

The boys were almost as badly off; they too sat restless and idle; and because they had nothing at all to occupy their minds they often came to blows, so that the father had to interfere. . . . But he was never very rough with them; poor boys, what else could they find for amusement? . . . The mother always reminded him of their books. . . . Yes, of course—certainly they must learn to read, the father said; no heathen were going to grow up in his house! He tried to be stern with them over this matter; but then . . . after all, boys were boys, he remembered!

At length he realized that this sort of life could not go on. He didn't give a hang for the weather—put on his coat and bade the boys do the same; then they went out and attacked the woodpile. They sawed and they chopped; they lugged in wood and piled it up; first they stacked up as much chopped wood as they could stow in the odd corners of the house; then they built a curious little fort of chopped wood out in the yard—very neatly and craftily constructed—and piled it full, too; this work cheered them up and kept their minds occupied, though the weather was bitterly cold and inclement. They toiled at it from early morning until late at night, and hardly took time off to eat their dinner; the boys began to get sick of the job and complained of being tired. The woodpile lasted exactly four days; when they had chopped up the last stick there was nothing left for them to do outside.

Then they sat idle again.

The bad spell of weather held out interminably. A cold, piercing wind from the northeast blew the livelong day, and moaned about the corners at night. . . . Snow flew . . . more snow fell.

No sun. . . . No sky. . . . The air was a grey, ashen mist which breathed a deathly chill; it hung around and above them thick and frozen. . . . In the course of time there was a full moon at night, somewhere be-

hind the veil. Then the mist grew luminous and alive—strange to behold.
. . . Night after night the ghostly spectacle would return.

Per Hansa would gaze at it and think: Now the trolls are surely
abroad! . . .

One evening Tönseten and Kjersti came over. They sat and talked
until it grew very late. One could readily see that Syvert was out of
sorts about something; he puffed at his pipe in glum, ill humor, glared
at Per Hansa's walls, and didn't have much to say. When he did speak
his voice was unnecessarily loud.

Kjersti and Beret sat together on the bed; they seemed to be finding
a good deal to chat about.

Kjersti was in an unusually neighbourly mood; she had come over
to ask if . . . well, if she couldn't do something for Beret? She had some
woollen yarn at home in her chest, very soft and very fine. Would Beret
be offended if she knitted a pair of socks for the little newcomer they
were all awaiting? . . . It was fine yarn, the very finest! Beret must just
try to imagine how lonesome she was, sitting at home all alone with that
useless husband of hers—and no little newcomer to wait for! . . . She
had plenty of yarn; she could easily make the socks long enough to serve
as leggings, too. The work would really bring joy to her—and to Syvert,
too, poor fellow, to whom no little newcomer would ever arrive!
. . . Ah, well! . . . God pity us, Syvert wasn't so bad, after all—
far be it from her to complain! . . . At that, Kjersti happened to think
of a story she had heard, about a couple who couldn't seem to get a child
though they wanted one very badly. Here the story was, since they
happened to be talking about such matters. . . . This wife had so little
sense that she sought the aid of a witch woman, who gave her both *devil's
drink* and *beaver-geld;* she rubbed herself with the stuff and drank some
of it, too, but no change came; that is, not until one summer when a shoal
of herring come into the fjord and with it a fleet of strange fishermen.
. . . Alas! desire makes a hot fire, once it has been kindled! But what do
you suppose?—her husband became just as fond of that child as if he
had been the father of it! . . . Wasn't that a queer thing? . . . But when
the boy was a year old and was on the point of being christened—well, on
that very Sunday it happened, as they were sailing across the fjord, that
the boat capsized and the Lord took both mother and child, right there
and then! He had taken away what he had refused to give in honour, and
more besides. . . . There was something mysterious about such things,
didn't Beret think so? And wasn't it strange that the father should have
been so fond of *that* child? . . . Kjersti had known them both very well.

Beret listened attentively to this tale, putting in a word here and
there.

Over at the table, the men had pricked up their ears as the story
began; they heard it all. Per Hansa looked at Syvert and laughed; Syvert,
in turn, glared at the wall and said, angrily:

"I should think you'd be able to find something American to talk
about! . . . We're through now with all that troll business over in Norway!" . . . He got up and started to go. . . .

But Per Hansa wouldn't listen to their leaving just yet; since they had braved the weather to make a call they might as well sit awhile longer. . . . "You'll have the wind astern, Syvert, going home! . . . Come on, sit down and behave yourself!"

On another afternoon all of Hans Olsa's household came over. They stayed till dark; then they began to say that perhaps they'd better be going now—but they made no move to leave. . . . Sörine had brought a gift for Beret. There had been a few bits of cloth lying around the house, for which she could find no use; it had been rather lonesome these days and she had needed something to do, so she had made a little article for this newcomer whom everyone was waiting for! . . . At that, Sörine drew out from her ample bosom a child's cap, of red, white, and blue stripes, with long silk ribbons, all sewed with the greatest care. It was a beautiful cap; all had to see it; there were many warm words of praise. Beret received it in silence; her eyes were wet as she took the cap and laid it carefully in the big chest. . . .

To-night it was Beret who refused to let the visitors leave. She absolutely insisted. Such quantities of food lay outside around the house—far more than they would ever need—that they might as well stay for supper and help to eat it! . . . This proposal overjoyed Per Hansa. It was the plain truth, as Beret said, they had more than they needed—and there was plenty left in the Sioux River, for that matter; to-night they were going to celebrate with fresh fish for supper! . . . He went outside and brought in a generous supply of the frozen fish, which he scaled and cut up; he was in the finest of spirits—it seemed just like the good old days in Lofoten.

. . . That evening was a happy interlude for them all.

. . . No, the days would not pass! . . . Why, here it was, only the middle of November! It seemed to Per Hansa, as he sat by the table puffing his pipe and following Beret around with his eyes, that many winters must have gone by already.

He found himself watching Beret very often; during the last two weeks he had discovered many things about her which he had never noticed before. Just trifles, they were, but so many of them—one thing after another. Sitting here now with nothing else to occupy his mind, he began slowly and carefully to piece together what he had observed; the result pleased him less and less as he went on adding. He tried to wave the truth aside—to deny the plain facts; he even succeeded for a while—in the beginning. . . . Goodness! nothing but trifles—things that were always likely to happen under such circumstances! . . . Oh no! There was no danger that Beret couldn't stand her watch; things would right themselves when the time came; for it was only the law of nature, which man must obey. . . . Of course she couldn't help dreading it, poor thing! . . . Did her face seem a good deal more wasted this time—or was he mistaken? She didn't look well at all. . . . No. . . . Then why didn't she eat more? Good Heavens! she wasn't trying to save on the food? Here

was everything—quantities of it: meat aplenty, and any amount of flour!
. . . She should help herself, this Beret-girl of his, or he would make her
dance to another tune!

One day at table he burst out with it, telling her that she mustn't
act the stranger in her own house! He made his voice sound gruff and
commanding: Now she must sit up and eat like a grown woman. . . .
"Here, help yourself!" . . . He took a big piece of fish from the platter
and put it on her plate; but she merely picked at it, and left the most of
it lying there.

"It is hard when you have to force every mouthful down," she complained.

"But look here, you've got to eat, both for yourself and— Of course
you must eat!"

"Oh, well," she said, wearily, as she got up and left the table. . . .
"It doesn't matter much about the food." . . .

Lately he had also begun to notice that she lay awake the greater
part of the night; he always dropped off to sleep before she did; yet she
would be wide awake in the morning when he first stirred, although he
was by habit an early riser. And if by chance he woke up in the night,
he would be almost certain to find her lying awake beside him. . . . One
night she had called him; she had been sitting up in bed, and must have
been crying—her voice sounded like it. And she had only wanted him to
get up and see what ailed Store-Hans; he had been moaning in his sleep
all night, she said. Per Hansa had risen to look after the boy, and had
found nothing the matter, as he had expected. . . . That night he had
been seriously frightened. When he had come back to lie down she had
started crying so despairingly; he hadn't been able to make any sense of
the few words he got out of her. . . . From that time on, he had been
scared to show her any tenderness; he had noticed that when he did so,
the tears were sure to come. And that, certainly, was not good for her!

As he sat through the long, long day observing his wife, he grew
more and more worried about Beret, poor thing. Every day there were
new trifles to be noticed.

She, who had always been so neat and could make whatever clothes
she put on look becoming, was now going about shabby and unkempt;
she didn't even bother to wash herself. He realized that he had noticed
it subconsciously for a long time. . . . But now he seldom saw her even
wash her face. And her hair, her beautiful hair which he admired so
greatly and loved to fondle when she was in good spirits, now hung
down in frowsy coils. . . . Wasn't it two days since she had touched
her hair? Well—*that* he didn't dare to mention! . . . How could he ever
speak of cleanliness at all to his Beret—his Beret who was always so prim
and often nagged him for being slovenly and careless about his own appearance? . . . Not that she wasn't pretty enough, just as she was, his
Beret-girl; this Per Hansa told himself many times. But one day as he
sat looking at her, he suddenly got up, went over to the window, and
stood there gazing out; and then he said:

"I really think you ought to go and fix up your hair, Beret-girl. . . .
I kind of feel that we're going to have company to-day."

She gave him a quick glance, blushed deeply, rose, and left the room. He heard her go into the stable, where she stayed a long time; he couldn't imagine what she was doing in there at that hour of the day. Her actions made him feel worried and uncertain. When she came in again he did not dare to look at her. . . . Then she began to tidy herself; she took some water and washed, loosened up her braids and combed her hair, and afterward coiled it very prettily. She gave herself plenty of time, and took careful pains. . . . At last he *had* to look at her; his whole self was in the gaze that he fixed upon her; he would have liked to say something kind and loving to her now. But she did not glance at him, and so he dared not speak. . . . In a little while he found an excuse to go out; passing close to her, he said in a tender, admiring voice:

"Now we've got a fine-looking lady!"

All the rest of that day he felt happier than he had been for a long while. . . . Of course his Beret-girl would be all right. . . . Indeed, she *was* all right, as far as that went! . . .

But . . . other days followed. Per Hansa remained idle and had nothing to do but look at his wife. He looked and looked, until he had to face the hard fact that something was wrong.

. . . Had she ever been so brooding and taciturn when she was with child before? He could talk to the boys about the future until they would be completely carried away by his visions; but whenever he tried to draw her into the conversation he failed completely—failed, no matter which tack he took nor how hard he tried. He understood it clearly: it wasn't because she did not want to respond—she *couldn't!* . . . The pain of it surged through him like a wave. God in Heaven, had she grown so weak and helpless! . . . She wasn't even able to take nourishment. . . . There Beret sat in the room with them, within four paces—yet she was far, far away. He spoke to her now, to her alone, but could not make her come out of the enchanted ring that lay about her. . . . When he discovered this, it hurt him so that he could have shrieked. . . .

. . . Another queer thing, she was always losing the commonest objects—completely losing them, though they were right at hand. He had seen it happen several times without taking much notice; but by and by it began to occur so frequently that he was forced to pay attention. She would put a thing down, merely turn around, and then go about searching for it in vain; and the thing would lie exactly where she had placed it, all the time. . . . This happened again and again; sometimes it struck them all as very funny. . . . "It looks as if your eyes were in your way, Mother!" Store-Hans once exclaimed, laughing so heartily that the others had to join in; but Per Hansa soon noticed that she was hurt when they made fun of her.

One day she was looking for the scissors. She had been sitting by the stove, mending a garment; had risen to put on more fuel; and when she sat down again had been unable to find her scissors, which she held all the while in her hand. She searched diligently, and asked the others to help her. Suddenly Ole discovered the scissors in his mother's hand; he ran up to her and jerked them away; the boy was roaring with laughter. . . . Then she burst into violent tears, laid her work aside, threw herself down on the bed, and buried her face in the pillow. All three menfolk felt painfully embarrassed.

And sometimes she had moments of unusual tenderness toward them all—particularly toward Per Hansa. Her concern would grow touchingly childlike; it was as if she could not do enough for him and the children. But it was a tenderness so delicate that he dared not respond to it. Nevertheless, he felt very happy when these moods came; they gave him renewed courage.

. . . Of course she would be all right again as soon as it was over! . . . And now the event could not be far away! . . .

Winter was ever tightening its grip. The drifting snow flew wildly under a low sky, and stirred up the whole universe into a whirling mass; it swept the plain like the giant broom of a witch, churning up a flurry so thick that people could scarcely open their eyes.

As soon as the weather cleared icy gusts drove through every chink and cranny, leaving white frost behind; people's breaths hung frozen in the air the moment it was out of the mouth; if one touched iron, a piece of skin would be torn away.

At intervals a day of bright sunshine came. Then the whole vast plain glittered with the flashing brilliance of diamonds; the glare was so strong that it burnt the sight; the eyes saw blackness where there was nothing but shining white. . . .

. . . Evenings . . . magic, still evenings, surpassing in beauty the most fantastic dreams of childhood! . . . Out to the westward—so surprisingly near—a blazing countenance sank to rest on a white couch . . . set it afire . . . kindled a radiance . . . a golden flame that flowed in many streams from horizon to horizon; the light played on the hundreds and thousands and millions of diamonds, and turned them into glittering points of yellow and red, green and blue fire.

. . . Such evenings were dangerous for all life. To the strong they brought reckless laughter—for who had ever seen such moon-nights? . . . To the weak they brought tears, hopeless tears. This was not life, but eternity itself. . . .

Per Hansa sat in his hut, ate, drank, puffed at his pipe, and followed his wife with his eyes in vague alarm; for the life of him he didn't know what to do. Where could he betake himself? It wouldn't do for him to go from house to house, when things were in such a bad way at home. . . . No, here he was condemned to sit! . . . His temper was growing steadily worse; he found it more and more difficult to keep his hands off things.

He would be seized by a sudden, almost irresistible desire to take Beret, his own blessed Beret, hold her on his knee like a naughty child—just *make* her sit there—and reason with her . . . talk some sense into her!

For this wasn't altogether fair play on her part! Of course it was hard for her these days; but after all, the time would soon come to an end; and *that* was something real to struggle with—something to glory

in! Besides, she had her wonted round of duties to perform. . . . But he!
. . . Here he was forced to sit in idleness, and just let his eyes wan-
der! . . .

. . . And it wasn't right for him to feel this way, either; but the
endless waiting had at last got on his nerves. . . . Strange, how long it
took! Hadn't the time ought to be drawing near pretty soon? . . . During
these days he often thought about the matter of a name. He immediately
decided that if it turned out to be a girl, she should be named *Beret;* that
part of it was settled. But suppose she bore him a boy? In that case he
wasn't so certain. Two boy's names were running in his mind, but—well,
time would tell. . . . If she would only hurry up and bring forth the
child, he would guarantee to find a suitable name for it!

He began to feel weak and miserable as he dragged himself about
the house. . . . Then, one day, came a fascinating thought: if he could
only make a short trip east to the Sioux River, to visit the Trönders! This
spell of cold weather was nothing to mind; it was a long way, to be sure,
but he felt that he could easily manage it. Hadn't he sailed a cockleshell of
an eight-oared boat all the way from Helgeland to West Lofoten in the
dark of winter? This would be mere child's play compared to that
journey. . . . What great sport it would be to fish with a net through the
ice! From the Trönders, who were old settlers in this region, he could
get a lot more valuable information; it was really remarkable, what they
had told him last time, about the fur trade with the Indians north at
Flandreau. . . . Whenever the thought of this journey came to him he
could hardly push it aside.

. . . Useless even to dream of such a thing! Here was poor Beret,
pottering helplessly about—he must think only of her.

And Per Hansa tried his best to think of her to some effect. He had
noticed that she minded the cold; she never complained, but he was well
aware of it; from now on he tended the fire himself and kept the stove
red hot most of the day. In spite of that he couldn't get the house properly
warm when the cold was at its worst; the earthen floor was always cold
and Beret's feet seemed particularly sensitive.

One day Per Hansa got an idea which gave him much diversion.
While they had been busy chopping the wood he had selected a few of
the largest and straightest-grained sticks, trimmed them out square and
stood them behind the stove to dry; he had promised himself that he
would make something out of them during the winter. Now he chose
the best piece he could pick out; he had decided to make a pair of clogs
for Beret; he knew by experience that such shoes were very warm while
they were new. For a long while he couldn't think of any material to use
for the vamps; then he resolutely cut off a corner of the old sheepskin
robe which they used on their bed; he sheared the wool snug, and made
the vamps of that. . . . He did a neat, attractive job and felt rather proud
when the job was finished.

He brought the clogs to Beret and put them on her feet.

It was plain to be seen that she was touched by the gift; but then
she said something that he wished she had left unspoken:

"You might have thought of this before, it seems to me. Here I have

gone with cold feet all winter." . . . The words were uttered quietly;
she meant no reproach by them, but merely said what came into her
mind.

He turned away and went out of the house; outside the door he
paused, and stood for a long time gazing off into the evening. . . . Somewhere out there life was still happy. . . . There was no solitude. . . .
Didn't it seem to call to him?

. . . Per Hansa felt that now he needed to cry. . . .

The days wore on . . . sunny days . . . bleak, gloomy days, with
cold that congealed all life.

There was one who heeded not the light of the day, whether it
might be grey or golden. Beret stared at the earthen floor of the hut and
saw only night round about her.

Yes . . . she faced only darkness. She tried hard, but she could not
let in the sun.

Ever since she had come out here a grim conviction had been taking
stronger and stronger hold on her.

This was her retribution!

Now had fallen the punishment which the Lord God had meted out
to her; at last His visitation had found her out and she must drink the
cup of His wrath. Far away she had fled, from the rising of the sun to
the going down thereof . . . so it had seemed to her . . . but the arm
of His might had reached farther still. No, she could not escape—this
was her retribution!

The stillness out here had given her full opportunity for reflection;
all the fall she had done nothing but brood and remember. . . . Alas! she
had much to remember!

She had accepted the hand of Per Hansa because she must—although
no law had compelled her; she and he were the only people who had
willed it thus. She had been gotten with child by him out of wedlock;
nevertheless, no one had compelled her to marry him—neither father, nor
mother, nor anyone in authority. It had been wholly her own doing. Her
parents, in fact, had set themselves against the marriage with all their
might, even after the child, Ole, had come.

. . . It had mattered nothing at all what they had said, nor what
anyone else had said; for her there had been no other person in the world
but Per Hansa! Whenever she had been with him she had forgotten the
admonitions and prayers of her father and mother. . . . He had been
life itself to her; without him there had been nothing. . . . Therefore
she had given herself to him, although she had known it was a sin—had
continued to give herself freely, in a spirit of abandoned joy.

Now she found plenty of time to remember how her parents had
begged and threatened her to break with him; she recalled all that they
had said, turning it over in her mind and examining it minutely. . . .
Per Hansa was a shiftless fellow, they had told her; he drank; he fought;
he was wild and reckless; he got himself tangled up in all sorts of brawls;
no honourable woman could be happy with such a man. He probably

had affairs with other women, too, whenever he had a chance. . . . All the other accusations she knew to be true; but not the last—no, not the last! She alone among women held his heart. The certainty of this fact had been the very sweetness of life to her. . . . What did she care for the rest of it! All was as nothing compared with this great certainty. . . . Ah, no—she knew it well enough: for him she was the only princess!

But now she understood clearly all that her parents had done to end it between them, and all the sacrifices they had been willing to make; she had not realized it at the time. . . . Oh, those kind-hearted parents on whom she had turned her back in order that she might cleave to him: how they must have suffered! The life which she and he had begotten in common guilt they had offered to take as their own, give it their name and their inheritance, and bring it up as their very child. They had freely offered to use their hard-earned savings to send her away from the scene of her shame . . . *so* precious had she been to them! But she had only said no, and no, and *no*, to all their offers of sacrifice and love! . . . Had there ever been a transgression so grievous as hers!

. . . Yet how could she ever have broken with him? Where Per Hansa was, there dwelt high summer and there it bloomed for her. How can a human forsake his very life? . . . Whenever she heard of one of his desperately reckless cruises through rough and stormy seas, on which he had played with the lives of his comrades as well as his own, her cheeks would glow and her heart would flame. This was the man her heart had chosen—this was he, and he alone! a voice would sing within her. Or when she sat among the heather on the mountain side in the fair summer night, and he came to her and laid his head in her lap—the tousled head that only she could lull to sleep—then she felt that now she was crossing the very threshold of paradise! . . . Though she had had a thousand lives, she would have thrown them all away for one such moment—and would have been glad of the bargain! . . .

. . . Yes, she remembered all that had happened in those days; it was so still out here . . . so easy to remember!

No one had ever told her, but she knew full well who it was that had persuaded Hans Olsa to leave the land and the ancient farm that had been in his family for generations, and go to America. There had been only one other person in the world whom Per Hansa loved, and that was Hans Olsa. She had been jealous of Hans Olsa because of this; it had seemed to her that he took something that rightfully belonged to her. She had even felt the same way toward Sörine, who was kindness itself; on this account she had not been able to hold her friendship as fully as she needed to, either in Norway or here. . . .

. . . But when Per Hansa had come home from Lofoten that spring and announced in his reckless, masterful way, that he was off for America: would Beret come now, or wait until later? . . . Well, there hadn't been a "no" in her mouth then! There she had sat, with three children in a nice little home which, after the manner of simple folk, they had managed to build. . . . But she had risen up, taken the children with her, and left it all as if nothing mattered but him!

. . . How her mother had wept at that time! . . . How her father had grieved when they had left! Time after time he had come begging to Per Hansa, offering him all that he had—boat and fishing outfit, house and farm—if only he would settle down in Norway and not take their daughter from them forever. . . . But Per Hansa had laughed it all aside! There had been a power in his unflinching determination which had sent hot waves through her. She must have led a double life at that time; she had been sad with her parents but had rejoiced with Per Hansa. He had raged like a storm through those days, wild and reckless—and sometimes ruthless, too. . . . No!—he had cried—they would just make that little trip across the ocean! America—that's the country where a poor devil can get ahead! Besides, it was only a little way; if they didn't like it, they could drift back on the first fair western breeze! . . . So they had sold off everything that they had won with so much toil, had left it all like a pair of worn-out shoes—parents, home, fatherland, and people. . . . And she had done it gladly, even rejoicingly! . . . Was there ever a sin like hers?

. . . Then she had arrived in America. The country did not at all come up to her expectations; here, too, she saw enough of poverty and grinding toil. What did it avail, that the rich soil lay in endless stretches? More than ever did she realize that "man liveth not by bread alone!" . . . Even the bread was none too plentiful at times. . . .

Beyond a doubt, it was Destiny that had brought her thither. . . . Destiny, the inexorable law of life, which the Lord God from eternity had laid down for every human being, according to the path He knew would be taken. . . . Now punishment stood here awaiting her—the punishment for having broken God's commandment of filial obedience. . . . Throughout the fall she had been reckoning up her score, and it came out exactly thus: Destiny had so arranged everything that the punishment should strike her all the more inevitably. Destiny had cast her into the arms of Per Hansa—and she did not regret it! Destiny had held up America as an enticing will-o'-the-wisp—and they had followed! . . .

But no sooner had they reached America than the west-fever had smitten the old settlements like a plague. Such a thing had never happened before in the history of mankind; people were intoxicated by bewildering visions; they spoke dazedly, as though under the force of a spell. . . . "Go west! . . . Go west, folks! . . . The farther west, the better the land!" . . . Men beheld in feverish dreams the endless plains, teeming with fruitfulness, glowing, out there where day sank into night —a Beulah Land of corn and wine! . . . She had never dreamed that the good Lord would let such folly loose among men. Were it only the young people who had been caught by the plague, she would not have wondered; but the old had been taken even worse. . . . "Now we're bound west!" said the young. . . . "Wait a minute—we're going along with you!" cried the old, and followed after. . . . Human beings gathered together, in small companies and large—took whatever was movable along, and left the old homestead without as much as a sigh! Ever westward led the course, to where the sun glowed in matchless glory as it sank at night; people drifted about in a sort of delirium, like sea birds in mating time; then they flew toward the sunset, in small flocks and large —always toward Sunset Land. . . . Now she saw it clearly: here on the trackless plains, the thousand-year-old hunger of the poor after human happiness had been unloosed!

Into this feverish atmosphere they had come. Could Destiny have spun his web more cunningly? She remembered well how the eyes of Per Hansa had immediately begun to gleam and glow! . . . And the strange thing about this spell had been that he had become so very kind under it. How playfully affectionate he had grown toward her during the last winter and spring! It had been even more deliciously sweet to give herself to him then, than back in those days when she had first won him. Was it not worth all the care and sorrow in the world to taste such bliss, she had often asked herself—but had been unable to answer. But—then it had happened: this spring she had been gotten with child again. . . . Let no one tell her that this was not Destiny!

She had urged against this last journey; she had argued that they must tarry where they were until she had borne the child. One year more or less would make no difference, considering all the land there was in the west. . . . Hans Olsa, however, had been ready to start; and so there had been no use in trying to hold back Per Hansa. All her misgiving he had turned to sport and laughter, or playful love; he had embraced her, danced around with her, and become so roguish that she had been forced to laugh with him. . . . "Come here, *Litagod*—now we're gone!" . . . She well recalled how lovely this endearing term had sounded in her ears, the first night he had used it. . . .

But this was clear to her beyond a doubt: Per Hansa was without blame in what had happened—all the blame was hers. . . . He had never been so tender toward her as in the days since they had come out here; she could not have thought it possible for one human being to have such strong desire for another as he held. . . . Who could match him—who dared follow where he led? She remembered all that he had wrought since they had set out on their journey last spring, and felt that no one else could do it after him. He was like the north wind that sweeps the cloud banks from the heavens! . . . At these thoughts, something unspeakably soft and loving came into Beret's eyes. . . . No, not like the north wind: like the gentle breeze of a summer's night—that's how he was! . . . And this too, was only retribution! She had bound herself inseparably to this man; now she was but a hindrance to him, like chains around his feet; him, whom she loved unto madness, she burdened and impeded . . . she was only in his way!

. . . But that he could not understand it—that he could not fathom the source of her trouble; that seemed wholly incomprehensible to her. Didn't he realize that she could never be like him? . . . No one in all the world was like him! How could she be? . . .

Beret struggled with many thoughts these days.
. . . Wasn't it remarkable how ingeniously Destiny had arranged it

all? For ten long years he had cast her about like a chip on the current, and then had finally washed her ashore here. *Here*, far off in the great stillness, where there was nothing to hide behind—here the punishment would fall! . . . Could a better place have been found in which to lay her low?

. . . Life was drawing to a close. One fact stood before her constantly: she would never rise again from the bed in which she was soon to lie down. . . . This was the end.

. . . Often, now, she found herself thinking of the churchyard at home. . . . It would have been so pleasant to lie down there. . . . The churchyard was enclosed by a massive stone wall, broad and heavy; one couldn't imagine anything more reliable than that wall. She had sat on it often in the years when she was still her father's little girl. . . . In the midst of the churchyard lay the church, securely protecting everything round about. No fear had ever dwelt in that place; she could well remember how the boys used to jump over the graves; it had been great fun, too—at times she had joined the game. . . . Within that wall many of her dear ones slumbered: two brothers whom she had never seen, and a little sister that she remembered quite clearly, though she had died long, long ago; her grandparents, on both her father's and her mother's side, also rested here, and one of her great-grandfathers. She knew where all these graves lay. Her whole family, generation after generation, rested there—many more than she had any knowledge of. . . . Around the churchyard stood a row of venerable trees, looking silently down on the peace and the stillness within. . . . They gave such good shelter, those old trees!

. . . She could not imagine where he would bury her out here. . . . *Now*, in the dead of winter—the ground frozen hard! . . . How would he go about it? . . . If he would only dig deep down . . . the wolves gave such unearthly howls at night! No matter what he thought of it, she would have to speak to him about the grave. . . . Well, no need to mention it just now.

One day when Beret had to go out she stayed longer than usual. Before she finally came back to the house she went to the spot where the woodpile had stood, visited the curious little fort which they had built of chopped wood, and then entered the stable. . . . It worried her to know where he would find material for a coffin. She had looked everywhere outside, but had discovered only a few bits of plank and the box in which he had mixed the lime. . . . Hadn't she better remind him of this at once? Then perhaps he could go to the Trönders, east on the Sioux River, and get some lumber from them. . . . Never mind, she wouldn't do anything about it for a few days yet.

. . . If he could only spare her the big chest! . . . Beret fell to looking at it, and grew easier in her mind. . . . That chest had belonged to her great-grandfather, but it must have been in the family long before his day; on it she could make out only the words "*Anno* 16—" . . . the rest was completely worn away. Along the edges and running twice around the middle were heavy iron bands. . . . Beret would go about looking at the chest—would lift the lid and gaze down inside. . . .

Plenty of room in there, if they would only put something under her head and back! She felt as if she could sleep safely in that bed. She would have to talk to Sörine about all these matters. . . . One day Beret began to empty the chest; she got Per Hansa to make a small cupboard out of the mortar box, and put all the things in there; but she took great care not to do this while he was around.

She realized now the great forethought he had shown last summer in building the house and stable under one roof. They undoubtedly had the warmest house in the neighbourhood; and then she enjoyed the company of the animals as she lay awake at night; it felt so cosy and secure to lie there and listen to them. . . . She could easily distinguish each animal by its particular manner of breathing and lying down. The oxen were always the last to finish munching; Rosie was the first to go to sleep; Injun's habits were entirely different from those of the others; he moved softly, almost without noise, as if engaged in some secret business. She never could hear him, except when the howl of a wolf sounded near by; then he would snort and stamp his feet. It was probably the wild blood in him that made him so different! . . . Beret had learned to love the pony.

When she was not listening to the animals she had other things to occupy her mind. . . . As a little girl, she had often been taken into bed by her grandmother. This grandmother had been a kindly woman, sunny and always happy, in spite of her great age; each night before going to sleep she would repeat to herself pious little verses from memory. Beret could not remember them all now; but she managed to patch them together little by little, inserting new lines of her own, and repeating them over and over to herself. This she would do for hours at a time, occasionally sitting up in bed to say the verses aloud:

> "Thy heavy wrath avert
> From me, a wretched sinner;
> Thy blissful mercy grant,
> Father of love eternal!

> "My sins are as many
> As dust in the rays of the sun,
> And as sands on the shore of the sea
> If by Thee requited,
> I must sink benighted.

> "Look with pity,
> Tender Saviour,
> At my wretched state!
> Wounds of sin are burning;
> May Thy hands, in love returning,
> Heal my stinging stripes!

> "Weighed by guilt I weary wander
> In the desert here below;
> When I measure
> My transgressions,
> Breaches of Thy holy law,
> I must ponder
> Oft, and wonder;
> Canst Thou grace on me bestow?
>
> "Gentle Saviour,
> Cast my burden
> Deep into the mercy-sea!
> Blessed Jesus,
> Mild Redeemer,
> Thou Who gav'st Thy life for me!"

The day before Christmas Eve snow fell. It fell all that night and the following forenoon. . . . Still weather, and dry, powdery snow. . . . Murk without, and leaden dusk in the huts. People sat oppressed in the sombre gloom.

. . . Things were in a bad way over at Per Hansa's now; everyone knew it and feared what might befall both Beret and him. . . . No one could help; all that could be done was to bide the time; for soon a change must come!

"Listen, folks," said Tönseten, trying to comfort them as best he could. "Beret can't keep this up forever! I think you had better go over to her again, Kjersti!"

Both neighbour women were now taking turns at staying with her, each one a day at a time. They saw clearly that Per Hansa was more in need of help than Beret; there was no helping her now, while something, at least, could be done for him and the children. Christmas would soon be here, too, and the house ought to be made comfortable and cosy!

They all felt very sorry for Per Hansa. He walked about like a ragged stray dog; his eyes burned with a hunted look. Each day, the children were sent over to Hans Olsa's to stay for a while; if they remained longer than they had been told, he made no protest; at last they formed the habit of staying the whole day. He did not realize that it was bad for Beret to be without them so much; he tried to keep the talk going himself, but she had little to say; she answered in monosyllables and had grown peculiarly quiet and distant. In the shadow of a faint smile which she occasionally gave him there lay a melancholy deeper than the dusk of the Arctic Sea on a rainy, grey fall evening.

About noon of Christmas Eve the air suddenly cleared. An invisible fan was pushed in under the thick, heavy curtain that hung trembling between earth and heaven—made a giant sweep, and revealed the open, blue sky overhead. The sun shone down with powerful beams, and started a slight trickling from the eaves. Toward evening, it built a golden fairy castle for itself out yonder, just beyond Indian Hill.

The children were at Hans Olsa's; And-Ongen wanted to stay outside and watch the sunset. Sofie had told her that to-day was Christmas Eve, and that on every Christmas Jesus came down from heaven. The child asked many questions. . . . Would he come driving? Couldn't they lend him the pony? . . . Sofie hardly thought so—he probably would be driving an angel-pony!

Store-Hans, who was listening to them, thought this very silly and just like girls. He knew better! . . . Toward evening he suddenly wanted to go home, and was almost beside himself when his godfather said that he couldn't: all the children were to stay with Sofie to-night. They had to hold him back by force. . . . This was *Christmas Eve*. . . . He understood very well that something was about to go wrong at home. Why had his mother looked so wan and worn of late, and his father acted so queer that one couldn't talk to him?

That afternoon Beret was in childbed. . . . The grim struggle marked Per Hansa for life; he had fought his way through many a hard fight, but they had all been as nothing compared with this. He had ridden the frail keel of a capsized boat on the Lofoten seas, had seen the huge, combing waves snatch away his comrades one by one, and had rejoiced in the thought that the end would soon come for him also; but things of that sort had been mere child's play. . . . *This* was the uttermost darkness. Here was neither beginning nor end—only an awful void in which he groped alone. . . .

Sörine and Kjersti had both arrived a long time since. When they had come he had put on his coat and gone outside; but he hadn't been able to tear himself many steps away from the house.

Now it was evening; he had wandered into the stable to milk Rosie, forgetting that she had gone dry long ago; he had tended to Injun and the oxen, without knowing what he was about. . . . He listened to Beret wailing in the other room, and his heart shrivelled; thus a weak human being could not continue to suffer, and yet live. . . . And this was his own Beret!

He stood in the door of the stable, completely undone. Just then Kjersti ran out to find him; he must come in at once; Beret was asking for him! . . . Kjersti was gone in a flash. . . . He entered the house, took off his outdoor clothes, and washed his hands. . . .

. . . Beret sat half dressed on the edge of the bed. He looked at her, and thought that he had never seen such terror on any face. . . . God in heaven—this was beyond human endurance!

She was fully rational, and asked the neighbour women to leave the room for a moment, as she had something to say to her husband. She spoke with great composure; they obeyed immediately. When the door closed behind them Beret rose and came over to him, her face distorted. She laid a hand on each of his shoulders, and looked deep into his eyes, then clasped her hands behind his neck and pulled him violently toward her. Putting his arms firmly around her, he lifted her up gently and carried her to the bed; there he laid her down. He started to pull the covers over her. . . . But she held on to him; his solicitous care she heeded not at all.

When he had freed himself, she spoke brokenly, between gasps: . . . "To-night I am leaving you. . . . Yes, I must leave you. . . . I know this is the end! The Lord has found me out because of my sins. . . . It is written, 'To fall into the hands of the living God!' . . . Oh!—it is terrible! . . . I can't see how you will get along when you are left alone . . . though I have only been a burden to you lately. . . . You had better give And-Ongen to Kjersti . . . she wants a child so badly—she is a kind woman. . . . You must take the boys with you—and *go away from here!* . . . How lonesome it will be for me . . . to lie here all alone!"

Tears came to her eyes, but she did not weep; between moans she went on strongly and collectedly:

"But promise me one thing: put me away in the big chest! . . . I have emptied it and made it ready. . . . Promise to lay me away in the big chest, Per Hansa! . . . And you must be sure to dig the grave deep! . . . You haven't heard how terribly the wolves howl at night! . . . Promise to take plenty of time and dig deep down—do you hear!"

His wife's request cut Per Hansa's heart like sharp ice; he threw himself on his knees beside the bed and wiped the cold perspiration from her face with a shaking hand.

. . . "There now, blessed Beret-girl of mine!" . . . His words sounded far off—a note of frenzy in them. . . . "Can't you understand that this will soon be over? . . . To-morrow you'll be as chipper as a lark again!"

Her terror tore her only the worse. Without heeding his words, she spoke with great force out of the clearness of her vision:

"I shall die to-night. . . . Take the big chest! . . . At first I thought of asking you not to go away when spring came . . . and leave me here alone. . . . But that would be a sin! . . . I tell you, you *must go!* . . . Leave as soon as spring comes! Human beings cannot exist here! . . . They grow into beasts. . . ."

The throes were tearing her so violently now that she could say no more. But when she saw him rise she made a great effort and sat up in bed.

. . . "Oh!—don't leave me!—don't go away! . . . Can't you see how sorely I need you? . . . And now I shall die! . . . Love me—oh, do love me once more, Per Hansa!" . . . She leaned her body toward him. . . . "You must go back to Norway. . . . Take the children with you . . . let them grow up there. Ask father and mother to forgive me! . . . Tell father that I am lying in the big chest! . . . Can't you stay with me to-night . . . stay with me and love me? . . . Oh!—*there they come for me!*"

Beret gave a long shriek that rent the night. Then she sobbed violently, praying that they should not take her away from Per Hansa. . . .

Per Hansa leaped to his feet, and found his voice.

"Satan—now you shall leave her alone!" he shouted, flinging the door open and calling loudly to the women outside. Then he vanished into the darkness.

No one thought of seeking rest that night. All the evening, lights shone from the four huts; later they were extinguished in two of them; but in the house of Hans Olsa four men sat on, grieving over the way things were going at Per Hansa's. When they could bear the suspense no longer some one proposed going over to get news.

Tönseten offered to go first. . . . When he came back little sense could be gathered from what he said. He had not been allowed inside; the women were in a frenzy; the house was completely upset; Beret was wailing so loud that it was dreadful to hear. And Per Hansa himself was nowhere to be found. . . . "We must go and look for him, boys! . . . Haven't you got a Bible or something to read from, Hans Olsa? This is an awful thing!"

. . . There they sat, each occupied with his own thoughts—but all their thoughts were of the same trend. If Beret died to-night, it would go hard with Per Hansa—indeed it would. In that case he probably wouldn't stay out here very long. . . . But if he went away, the rest of them might as well pack up and go, too!

Sam ran over to inquire; then Henry; at last it was Hans Olsa's turn. He managed to get a couple of words with his wife, who said that Beret would hardly stand it. No one had seen Per Hansa.

"Can you imagine where the man can be keeping himself?" asked Tönseten, giving voice to the fear that oppressed them all. . . . "May the Lord preserve his wits, even if He chooses to take his wife away!" . . .

Per Hansa walked to and fro outside the hut all night long; when he heard some one coming he would run away into the darkness. He could not speak to a living soul to-night. As soon as the visitor had gone he would approach the hut again, circle around it, stop, and listen. Tears were streaming down his face, though he was not aware of it. . . . Every shriek that pierced the walls of the hut drove him off as if a whip had struck him; but as soon as it had died out, something would draw him back again. At intervals he went to the door and held it ajar. . . . What did Per Hansa care for custom and decency, now that his Beret lay struggling with death! . . . Each time Sörine came to the door; each time she shook her head sadly, and told him there was no change yet; it was doubtful if Beret would be able to pull through; no person could endure this much longer; God have mercy on all of them!

That was all the comfort Sörine could give him. . . . Then he would rush off into the darkness again, to continue his endless pacing; when daylight came they found a hard path tramped into the snow around the hut.

The night was well-nigh spent when the wails in there began to weaken—then died out completely, and did not come again. Per Hansa crept up to the door, laid his ear close to it, and listened. . . . So now the end had come! His breath seemed to leave him in a great sob. The whole prairie began to whirl around with him; he staggered forward a few steps and threw himself face downward on the snow.

. . . But then suddenly things didn't seem so bad to him . . . really not so bad. . . . He saw a rope . . . a rope. . . . It was a good, strong rope that would hold any thing. . . . It hung just inside the barn door —and the crossbeam ran just *there!* . . . No trick at all to find these things. Per Hansa felt almost happy at the thought; that piece of rope was good and strong—and the crossbeam ran just *there!*

. . . A door opened somewhere; a gleam of light flashed across the snow, and vanished. Some one came out of the hut quietly—then stopped, as if searching.

"Per Hansa!" a low voice called. . . . "Per Hansa, where are you?" . . . He rose and staggered toward Kjersti like a drunken man.

"You must come in at once!" she whispered, and hurried in before him.

The light was dim in there; nevertheless it blinded him so strongly that he could not see a thing. He stood a moment leaning against the door until his eyes had grown accustomed to it. . . . A snug, cosy warmth enveloped him; it carried with it an odd, pleasant odour. The light, the warmth, and the pleasant smell overcame him like sweet sleep that holds a person who has been roused, but who does not care to awaken just yet.

"How is it?" he heard a man's voice ask. Then he came back to his senses. . . . Was that he himself speaking? . . .

"You'll have to ask Sörine," Kjersti answered.

Sörine was tending something on the bed; not until now did he discover her—and wake up completely. . . . What was this? . . . the expression on her face? Wasn't it beaming with motherly goodness and kindliness?

"Yes, here's your little fellow! I have done all I know how. Come and look at him. . . . It's the greatest miracle I ever saw, Per Hansa, that you didn't lose your wife to-night, and the child too! . . . I pray the Lord *I* never have to suffer so!"

"Is there any hope?" was all Per Hansa could gasp—and then he clenched his teeth.

"It looks so, now—but you had better christen him at once. . . . We had to handle him roughly, let me tell you."

"*Christen him?*" Per Hansa repeated, unable to comprehend the words.

"Why, yes, of course. I wouldn't wait, if he were mine."

Per Hansa heard no more—for now Beret turned her head and a wave of such warm joy welled up in him that all the ice melted. He found himself crying softly, sobbing like a child. . . . He approached the bed on tiptoe, bent over it, and gazed down into the weary, pale face. It lay there so white and still; her hair, braided in two thick plaits, flowed over the pillow. All the dread, all the tormenting fear that had so long disfigured her features, had vanished completely. . . . She turned her head a little, barely opened her eyes, and said, wearily:

"Oh, leave me in peace, Per Hansa. . . . Now I was sleeping so well."

. . . The eyelids immediately closed.

Suggestions for Further Reading

With industrialization and the growth of cities in the early nineteenth-century, the life of the urban worker changed dramatically. The dynamics of this change can be approached through several important articles: E. P. Thompson, "Time, Work-Discipline, and Industrial Capitalism," *Past and Present*, no. 38 (1967), pp. 56–97; and David Montgomery, "The Working Classes of the Pre-Industrial American City, 1780–1830," *Labor History* 9 (1968):3–22. Also important are Walter Hugins, *Jacksonian Democracy and the Working Class* (Stanford, Cal., 1960); Leonard L. Richards, *"Gentlemen of Property and Standing": Anti-Abolition Mobs in Jacksonian America** (New York, 1971; Norman Ware, *The Industrial Worker, 1840–1860: The Reaction of American Industrial Society to the Advance of the Industrial Revolution* (New York, 1924); and the essays in Stephan Thernstrom and Richard Sennett, eds., *Nineteenth-Century Cities: Essays in the New Urban History** (New Haven, Conn., 1969).

Education, transmitted either through formal institutions or the daily experience of living, was a part of everyone's life. For an excellent conceptual discussion of this, see Bernard Bailyn, *Education in the Forming of American Society** (Chapel Hill, N.C., 1964). On education in the early nineteenth century, two recent books merit close attention: Michael B. Katz, *The Irony of Early School Reform: Educational Innovation in Mid-Nineteenth Century Massachusetts** (Cambridge, Mass., 1968), and Carl F. Kaestle, *The Evolution of an Urban School System, New York City, 1750–1850* (Cambridge, Mass., 1973). Warren Burton's *The District School as It Was* (Boston, 1833) provides a fine contemporary description of the educational process in New England in the pre–Civil War era.

Two rich sources for studying the religious impulse in early nineteenth-century America are Whitney R. Cross, *The Burned-Over District: The Social and Intellectual History of Enthusiastic Religion in Western New York, 1800–1850* (Ithaca, N.Y., 1950), and Bernard A. Weisberger, *They Gathered at the River: The Story of the Great Revivalists and Their Impact upon Religion in America* (Boston, 1958).

The western frontier experience, both for old-stock Americans and immigrants, is well described in Everett Dick, *The Sod-House Frontier, 1854–1890: A Social History of the Northern Plains from the Creation of Kansas and Nebraska to the Admission of the Dakotas* (New York, 1937). Merle Curti, *The Making of an Amer-*

* Available in paperback edition.

*ican Community: A Case Study of Democracy in a Frontier County** (Stanford, Cal., 1959) is also valuable. But the most poignant views of frontier life are those available in novels such as Willa Cather's *My Antonia** (Boston, 1926), and Hamlin Garland's *A Son of the Middle Border** (New York, 1917) and *A Daughter of the Middle Border* (New York, 1921). For the eastern immigrant experience in the nineteenth century, the inquiring student is well advised to begin with Oscar Handlin, *Boston's Immigrants, 1790– 1865: A Study in Acculturation** (Cambridge, Mass., 1941); Robert Ernst, *Immigrant Life in New York City, 1825–1863* (New York, 1949); and Barbara M. Solomon, *Ancestors and Immigrants: A Changing New England Tradition* (Cambridge, Mass., 1956).

Entertainment in the lives of nineteenth-century Americans is explored in David Grimsted, *Melodrama Unveiled: American Theatre and Culture, 1800–1850* (Chicago, 1968). The full implications of minstrelsy to the lives of ordinary people is investigated in Alexander Saxton, "Blackface Minstrelsy and Jacksonian Ideology," *American Quarterly* (forthcoming).

A
B 5
C 6
D 7
E 8
F 9
G 0
H 1
I 2
J 3

DISCHARGED

RESERVE

RESERVE

RESTRICTED RESERVE

RESERVE

RESERVE

DISCHARGED

DISCHARGED

RESERVE

DISCHARGED 1077

DISCHARGED

DISCHARGED

RESTRICTED RESERVE

RESERVE DISCHARGED

RESERVE DISCHARGED

DISCHARGED